Political Paradoxes and Puzzles

by
ARUN BOSE

CLARENDON PRESS · OXFORD
1977

Oxford University Press, Walton Street, Oxford OX2 6PD

OXFORD LONDON GLASGOW
NEW YORK TORONTO MELBOURNE WELLINGTON
CAPE TOWN IBADAN NAIROBI DAR ES SALAAM LUSAKA
KUALA LUMPUR SINGAPORE JAKARTA HONG KONG TOKYO
DELHI BOMBAY CALCUTTA MADRAS KARACHI

© Oxford University Press 1977

British Library Cataloguing in Publication Data

Bose, Arun
    Political paradoxes and puzzles.
    1. Political science
    I. Title
    320   JA 66   77–30110

    ISBN 0–19–827413–0
    ISBN 0–19–827417–3   Pbk

Printed in India by P. K. Ghosh
at Eastend Printers, 3 Dr Suresh Sarkar Road, Calcutta 700 014
and published by R. Dayal, Oxford University Press,
2/11 Ansari Road, Daryaganj, New Delhi 110 002

Political Paradoxes
and Puzzles

Preface

The chief aim of this book is to demonstrate the benefits of a scientific approach to the study of political phenomena, as a guide to political action. Such an approach has been increasingly called into question in recent years. But politics are too hard to be left to be managed, or to be articulated, *entirely* by politicians, however gifted or successful they may be. The problem is similar to the problem posed about the 'logic' of scientific discovery in the natural sciences. Those who discover and expound these 'laws' of science are not necessarily able to articulate the methodology they employ. On the other hand, the intricacies of political processes *are* difficult enough to deserve competent attention from specialized intellectuals equipped with sophisticated tools of analysis which have been successfully employed in other areas of human endeavour.

Belief to the contrary is based on the notions (i) that political processes are *trivial*, at least if they are viewed from the angle of an intellectual as an intellectual (even if they are *not* trivial from the viewpoint of the intellectual as a citizen), and/or (ii) that the right thing to do in politics can always be decided from a few ethical first principles. Notion (i) sanctifies a disdainful, eagle-like, Nietzschean attitude towards politics by intellectuals.[1] Notion (ii) justifies intellectuals making and preaching strong value-judgements, akin to religious dicta, to explain away what is good and what is evil in politics. Notion (i) appeals to the intellectuals' vanity. Notion (ii) tempts the intellectual to cultivate a childlike simplicity in matters political.

Parts I and II of this book contain a series of demonstrations that both notions (i) and (ii) may be wrong and uncalled for. They analyse political themes of lasting interest. Their topicality as studies of the immediate background to momentous current events is only incidental—though this may be of interest to many well-informed and knowledgeable readers. The themes chosen are of lasting interest because they have in common the representation of paradoxes and puzzles which are not easily resolved by plain common sense, or by an attempt at rational interpretation on the basis of conventional

[1] See Friedrich Nietzsche, *Thus Spake Zarathustra*, Ch. 28–30, 63.

political theories (*including* Marxian and anarchist theories, which are no longer unconventional).[2] This is at least the case if we do *not* want to suppress 'awkward' facts, either by a methodological value-judgement (to make analysis easier) or by a political value-judgement, which says: 'my side can do no wrong, even if it makes mistakes'. The paradoxes are also hard to resolve if we want to study political decision-making *ex ante*, before the event, rather than *ex post*, after the event. This is chiefly because once we know what has actually happened, we can always simplify the problem of 'explaining' it away, by simply ignoring what else might have happened, but did not.

To mention just one such case: the unquiet peace in Vietnam is a paradox essentially because here is a case of a *divided* (international) communism securing the expulsion of the armed forces of (to paraphrase Lenin) 'the *strongest* link in the chain of international [capitalist] imperialism'. To ignore this paradox, to say merely that the event is 'historically unique, sui generis' (Chomsky, 1973, pp. 11, 13), is emotionally and morally satisfying to many people. But it is less satisfying from the point of view of its predictive value, i.e. in helping us to understand similar situations, than a verdict based on recognition and resolution of the paradox. (However, as we shall see in Part III of this book, at least as far as major events like revolutions—and perhaps also counter-revolutions—are concerned, though no such event is 'historically unique', it recurs only with innovations, and 'history does not repeat itself, except as a farce'.)

Fortunately, it turns out on investigation that *recognition* of the paradoxes actually *facilitates* rational or scientific explanations, which resolve them. For this purpose, analytical techniques can be used which have not been employed very extensively to analyse the kind of political themes discussed in this book. These techniques mostly belong to the genus of the modern mathematical theory of games, originating in the work of John von Neumann and O. Morgenstern (see von Neumann and Morgenstern, 1944), and the modern theory of collective choice pioneered by Kenneth Arrow (1951, 1963, 1970). It must, however, be stressed that no use is made in this book of the extensive modern literature which attempts inter-

---

[2] But *discarding* mystical 'interpretations' like that of Oswald Spengler who wrote: 'Sympathy, observation, comparison, immediate and inward certainty, intellectual *flair*—these are the means whereby he [i.e. Goethe] was enabled to approach the secrets of the phenomenal world in motion' (Spengler, 1926, 1954, vol. 1, p. 25). Such interpretations have nothing in common with those attempted in this book.

pretations of, and predictions about, voting behaviour as the basis
of analyses of opinion polls or recorded voting behaviour.

The theory of games is used mainly in Chapters 2, 6, 8, and 9 (and
to some extent in Chapters 3 and 5). Invented to handle problems of
economic behaviour, the theory has also been used to deal with
problems of international diplomacy, criminal law, etc. But, so far
as the author is aware, it has hardly been used to interpret modern
revolutions and counter-revolutions, successful or abortive, on which
we concentrate in this book.[3] (This concentration seems to be justified,
because in the 1970s we seem to live in an age of several successful
revolutions, and a few successful counter-revolutions. After a couple
of centuries, the study of the politics of revolution and counter-
revolution has again become respectable, even if the somewhat
obsolescent 'evolutionary', routine politics still hold the attention of
most political theorists.)

But not all the political problems tackled in Parts I and II of
this book can be solved with the help of game theory, or, at any
rate, are in fact solved in this way. Some of them are solved (notably
those discussed in Chapters 3 and 5) with the help of the modern
theory of collective choice, and its technique of proving 'impossibility theorems'. The pre-history of this kind of theory goes back to
the eighteenth-century discussions of problems of voting by French
political theorists. Its modern history began with a negative contribution to a version of modern welfare economics by Kenneth Arrow.

Fragments of taxonomic studies of religions, or more generally
of *Weltanschauungen*, contained notably in the works of Karl Marx,
Bertrand Russell, and Sigmund Freud, are also used implicitly, or
referred to explicitly, in various chapters, especially in Chapters 3
and 4. Joseph Needham's *magnum opus* on Chinese philosophy is
relied upon to solve some knotty problems in Chapters 4 and 7.
Chapter 7 also relies heavily on a critical assimilation or adaptation
of Marx's hypotheses about 'unchanging societies' (linked with
'Oriental despotism' superimposed on the 'Asiatic mode of production') to discuss the specific characteristics of Indian subcontinental societies, ancient, medieval, and modern. In this chapter, an
adapted version of the Italian Marxist Antonio Gramsci's post-Lenin
theory of the state and civil society is also used. A somewhat novel
interpretation of the Gandhian element in Indian subcontinental
politics is attempted in some chapters, especially in Chapter 7.

[3] Some reasons for this are discussed in Ch. 1.

Chapter 10 attempts to analyse together, in terms of geo-politics, the question of self-reliance, the use of the oil weapon by West Asian countries, and the possible implications of India's nuclear capability.

I began to use these tools to interpret certain difficult problems of political economy when I was writing my book *Marxian and Post-Marxian Political Economy: An Introduction* (1975). The general problem I was trying to tackle was the gap in Marxian political economy which gives no precise analyses of processes of 'breakdown' or 'non-breakdown' of capitalism and socialism, both of which are supposed to be covered by the theory and represent important questions of twentieth-century political life. Game-theoretic or choice-theoretic syndromes seemed to complement the incomplete deterministic interpretations of the Marxian theory, so as to supply the missing deterministic solutions (op. cit., Chapters 12, 15). Pursuing the matter further, I soon discovered that a wide range of political phenomena, in which I was deeply involved as an interested onlooker, was amenable to treatment by the game-theoretic approach. I was specially encouraged when I found in Martin Shubik (ed.), *Game Theory and Related Approaches to Social Behaviour* (1964)—a book of readings—references to a fairly extensive literature on explicitly 'political' applications of game theory, including discussions of guerrilla warfare (Shubik, pp. 14–18, 59).

However, I suffered a setback when it dawned on me that game-theoretic models of social or political behaviour had also acquired a bad name amongst certain eminent intellectuals.[4] Moreover, there was the forthright assertion that a *science* of social (political) behaviour was *non*-existent, and perhaps could not be brought into existence (Chomsky, 1969, 1971, pp. 50–1; 1970, 1973, pp. 12–13). When I plunged into this controversy, I found myself reading literature of very high quality, which left me with two conclusions. Firstly, I realized that some 'systems analysts', if not game-theorists, *had* definitely produced for use by U.S. policy-makers pseudo-scientific apologetic recommendations dressed up as products of a science of social behaviour. So if some intellectuals over-reacted by adopting a standpoint which is close to the standpoint of 'intellectual nihilism'[5]

---

[4] See Wilson (1968, 1970), Ch. 10–12; Shubik (1964), Ch. 13 for summary accounts of the controversy on this point. A later, and somewhat fuller statement of the position of Anatol Rapoport—one of the chief participants—is to be found in Rapoport (1968, 1974), pp. 69–77, 411–14.

[5] 'Intellectual nihilism' was a term coined by Freud to refer to the standpoint of those who '. . . start out from science, indeed, but . . . contrive to force it into

which Freud had criticized long ago—for this, there was a great deal of provocation. I was thus alerted to the necessity of first trying to remove the apologetic stigma attached to game-theoretic analyses of political phenomena. This I do in Chapter 1. But, secondly, I became in the process all the more convinced that it would be a loss to exclude game theory from the study of political problems. This was especially so because, working through my own political applications of game theory (in Parts I and II of the present work), I found, not only that each model is interesting in itself, but also that there is *some* evidence that collectively they possess certain common features which lay bare some of the 'grand simplicities' of political processes. These common features are discussed in Part III of the book.

The foregoing should make it clear that this is an *analytical* rather than an *empirical* work. Writing about political events is always a process of interaction between the writer and what he writes about; and what he writes about consists of facts, selected like fish out of a vast ocean, which survive for the record (Carr, 1961, 1973, p. 23). This is as true of the present book as of any other written about political events. Where the facts in question are very much in dispute, at least from the vantage-point of those based in India, like myself, who may not have access to some facts well known elsewhere, care has been taken to check their authenticity, though documentation has not always been possible. Fortunately, most of the events analysed are so recent, and the washing of dirty linen in the world's news media has been so complete, that most of the relevant facts survive in the memory of readers, and in less distorted form than facts about the past stored in private or public archives. However, though the themes chosen for analysis in Parts I and II of this book were chosen, as stated at the beginning of the Preface, because they are of perennial interest, it so happens that all of them—without exception—are 'live' political themes, rather like volcanoes pouring

---

self-abrogation, into suicide; they set it the task of getting itself out of the way by refuting its own claims. One often has the impression . . . that this nihilism is only a temporary attitude which is to be retained until this task has been performed. Once science has been disposed of, the space vacated may be filled by some kind of mysticism or, indeed, by the old religious Weltanschauung' (Freud (1932, 1933, 1973), p. 212). As we shall see later, Noam Chomsky's standpoint, when he denies the validity of *any* possible science of social behaviour, is close to the standpoint of 'intellectual nihilism'. On the other hand, Rapoport explicitly affirms that the applications of game theory to international problems *can* be 'meaningful' given certain conditions which he defines very precisely (and which are, in fact, observed strictly in all the applications attempted in this book) (see Rapoport (1968, 1974), pp. 70–1).

out lava from month to month while the chapters were being written and printed. To have kept the coverage fully 'up to date' would have involved literally endless 'postscripting', and this has not been attempted. Fortunately, most subsequent episodes are likely to be explicable in terms of the frameworks of analysis used, so no drastic rewriting is likely to be required: the reader can fill in his own 'postscripts'.

Since this book is addressed to all those who are curious about the possibilities of a scientific approach to politics, to whichever different specialized disciplines they may belong, no prior knowledge is assumed, either about conventional political theories or about techniques of analysis which are rather more widely used in some disciplines than in others. Familiarity with standard political theories, especially those of Machiavelli, Marx, and Bakunin, and with the rudiments of mathematical game theory and of the modern theory of collective choice, will help the reader to arrive at a critical judgement about the contents of the work. Detailed references have been inserted to help readers who wish to do some follow-up reading, whether from scratch, or in order to make a critical assessment. A Glossary makes clear the sense in which various words are used in the technical discussion, so that the reader is not held up by doubts about the meaning of specialized terms.

For the same reasons, the exposition is verbal throughout, supplemented in a few chapters by the use of such elementary devices as payoff matrices in game theory (which are introduced from scratch), or some restatements in appendices involving mathematical symbols, for the benefit of those readers who prefer to read the argument in this form. The exposition is, strictly speaking, *non*-technical in the sense that the *proofs* of the theorems taken over from the theories of games and collective choice are neither reproduced nor discussed. But the use of analytical techniques borrowed from these theories made a certain formalization of the verbal exposition indispensable, and also, hopefully, helpful to readers who are being introduced to these techniques for the first time. Hence, the format in most cases consists of a set of definitions, assumptions, and deductions, which are also numbered to facilitate ready reference. This has been done to avoid cumbersome circumlocution or repetition in the verbal exposition.

I have referred above to my being deeply involved as an onlooker in a wide range of political events discussed in this book. Actually, my 'involvement' goes back to my boyhood in the late 1920s. Contrary to what today's youth may like to believe, interest in politics in the precocious 1920s began early, at least in India. Over this long period, I was also actively engaged in full-time politics at the national level (1940–51), and in part-time, but fairly intensive, political activity in trade union and journalistic work at the 'grass-roots level' in Calcutta, West Bengal (1951–7). In this period, I also had a close, hard look at the day-to-day functioning of the West Bengal Legislative Assembly. After the first general elections held on the basis of adult franchise, it contained a strong contingent of Communists, who steadily increased their strength by 'exposing parliamentary politics from within'—relying on Lenin's directive in his *Left-Wing Communism—An Infantile Disorder*. My involvement with theorizing about politics also began early, in the late 1930s, both at the formal and informal level. (After a ten-year spell in which I concentrated on political economy, rather than political theory proper, I was somewhat surprised to find, as late as 1970, that Political Scientists in India were still swearing by, or swearing at, Oakeshott or Laski, whose works were standard in the 1930s and 1940s.) So to establish my credentials as the writer of this book on political analysis, I can only say what Niccolo Machiavelli said to Lorenzo de Medici: ' . . . just as men who are sketching the land-scape put themselves down in the plain to study the nature of the mountains . . . and to study the low-lying land they put themselves high on the mountains, so, to comprehend fully the nature of the people, one must be a prince, and to comprehend fully the nature of princes, one must be an ordinary citizen' (Machiavelli, *c.* 1514, 1972, p. 30).

In the pages that follow, acknowledgements are made to the contributions of many writers, with detailed sources given in the References at the end of the book.

I take this opportunity to record my thanks to Prasanta Pattanaik for a general discussion about the use of game-theory models in the analysis of political problems, and also for a detailed discussion of the 'Hobson's choice' model used in Chapter 8. I also record my thanks to the anonymous reader of the Oxford University Press for several helpful comments which I have taken into account while putting the finishing touches to the text. Thanks are also due to my wife, Jaya, for clarifying my ideas on the use of ethical rules of thumb as a guide to political action, and for suggesting an interpretation of Claude Autantlara's film story *L'Auberge rouge* (1950), which I have used in Chapter 13. Finally, I thank A. L. Sikri, Librarian, Kirori Mal College Library, and the library staff, for friendly attention and unfailingly efficient help in making books and periodicals available for consultation.

A. B.

Kirori Mal College, Delhi University
January 1976

Note

For technical reasons, there has been a year's interval between the submission of the manuscript and the completion of the process of printing of this book. Issues peripherally noticed in these pages (especially the unfolding revolutions in Southern Africa) are now in the limelight of world politics. But it is likely that methods similar to those employed in Chapter 2 to analyse the 'Vietnamese paradox' will do better than simpler analytical methods in unravelling possibilities in Southern Africa. (However, the 'side-liners' in the Southern African drama—that is, the U.K., the U.S.A., Cuba, and the U.S.S.R. —may or may not play the decisive role that they played in Vietnam, at least not in the same way as the Soviet and Chinese communist 'side-liners' did in Vietnam.)

Of course, the Vietnamese communist revolution seems to have entered a comparatively quiescent period of consolidation. Though memories are quickly fading, it would be a mistake to conclude that the Vietnamese communist revolution is best explained as a simple case of the triumph of third-world 'nationalism' (which was only incidentally communist) buttressed by appeals to xenophobia. Every successful revolution has a 'nationalistic' feature (like every successful revolution of any kind) and may arm itself with revolutionary xenophobia. But close attention to the facts as they *were* suggests that the complexities of the Vietnamese revolution cannot be adequately explained without taking into account the integration of communist internationalism with communist nationalism, and the *absence* of xenophobia, as is done in Chapter 2.

On the other hand, the crystallization in the past year of Chinese communist ideology in the post-Mao era is as yet in its early stages, though it is meaningfully interpretable within the framework of analysis presented in Chapters 3 and 4. The partial, and vicarious, denigration of the personality and ideology of Mao Tse-Tung (with the personality, and 'thoughts', of Chiang Ching serving as an alibi) has not yet produced anything except a somewhat colourless provisional outcome. Several possibilities are still open as I write. The Mao cult may be duly converted into a Lenin-type cult associated with a deified Communist party, having the original feature that a once-over *outer*-party mass struggle rather than a once-over *inner-*

party Stalinist struggle served as the catalyst. Other possibilities are: (i) a politicized people's army, selectively interpreting Mao's doctrines on the role of the revolutionary army, may play a role comparable to the role the Soviet Red Army might have played in the post-Lenin era, if Trotsky rather than Stalin had won the struggle for the succession; (ii) a framework of pluralist Maoism may emerge, with the right to dissent extended to rival Maoist factions (and also, as a more remote possibility, to partially non-Maoist communist factions such as one led by Teng Hsiao-ping, who was twice disgraced by Mao).

In much the same way, the massive revival of electoral politics in the Indian subcontinent in 1977, in varying degrees in Bangladesh, Pakistan, India, and Sri Lanka, represents a vigorous reassertion of the 'basic Indian syndrome' identified in Chapter 7. (Bhutto's successfully rigged elections in Pakistan may serve as a step towards the establishment of a classic Indian stereotype of an electoral system rather than one which works with a permanent opposition serving as a safety-valve for discontent against the permanent rulers.) In a sense, it *is* a case of 'the more things change, the more they remain the same', with the emergence of a newly formed Janata party in India as the reincarnation of the radical Congress which emerged a decade earlier. However, the paranoid politics of the Indian post-1975 emergency may serve as an experience—direct for the radical Congress, and vicarious for its opponents—which will bring about the conversion, for the first time, of all major segments of Indian politics to the practice of political democracy, regarded as an instrument of, rather than as an impediment to, social and economic change. The pointers are: (i) the commitment in *practice* of the major segment of the Indian communist movement, viz. the Communist Party (Marxist), to the preservation of civil and group liberties (especially of the freedom of the Press and the courts) at all costs and at *all stages* of the revolution (notwithstanding their reaffirmation, during the recent Indian debate on the 42nd amendment of the Indian Constitution, of a firm commitment in *theory* to the concept of the dictatorship of the proletariat); (ii) the disenchantment with neofascist utopias by the right-of-centre political parties, who became its victims rather than its masters after the proclamation of the Indian emergency of June 1975; (iii) the discredit of the institution of an 'extraconstitutional centre of power', which was established by Gandhi in the 1930s, fell into disuse after 1945, was revived by the leader of the Bihar political struggle in 1974–5, and was finally vulgarized and discredited by the leader of the Youth Congress in 1976–7.

A. B.

March 1977

Contents

CHAPTER 1

General Introduction

1.1 Paradoxes and puzzles

PARADOXES and puzzles have occupied a central place in social (political) philosophy for a long time. Bernard Mandeville's 'private vices, public benefit' (Mandeville, ed. Harth, 1970, p. 76) is an early example, going back to 1705. (One of its many modern descendants is Bertrand Russell's insight, first expressed in 1920, that it may be that ' . . . all politics are inspired by a grinning devil, teaching the energetic and quick-witted to torture submissive populations for the profit of pocket or power or theory'; Russell, 1968, 1969, p. 145.) Close attention to the mechanism of political decision-making also produced the important 'paradox of voting' attributed to the Marquis de Condorcet in 1785 (Arrow, 1951, 1963, 1970, p. 93).

In economics, among social scientists, we have had well-known paradoxes identified by the physiocrats, Adam Smith, David Ricardo, and Lord Keynes. The physiocratic paradox is that a sovereign should fulfil himself (or herself) by 'doing nothing' (see references to apocryphal anecdotes in Robbins, 1953, pp. 34–5; Heimann, 1956, p. 52). The Adam Smith paradox says that pursuit of self-interest, and *not* altruism, promotes the public interest (quoted in Roll, 1950, p. 148). Ricardo grappled with the paradox—which also engaged Marx's attention—that the greater the capital accumulation, the lower would be the profit rate, and the lesser the capacity for further accumulation (Ricardo, Sraffa (ed.), 1951, Ch. vi, p. 123). The Keynesian paradox is the well-known 'paradox of thrift', i.e. in less than full employment equilibrium attempts to save more would *reduce* savings.

Economists have been somewhat unlucky with many of their paradoxes. Thus no sovereign or government has ever really succeeded, or could ever succeed, in 'doing nothing', i.e. in relying on unalloyed *laissez-faire*—so the physiocratic paradox has never been tested. Adam Smith's paradox is untenable, for reasons discussed in Parts II and III of this book. Ricardo's paradox, about capital accumulation reducing the power to accumulate, is also found to be untenable on strictly logical grounds (see Samuelson, 1957, pp.892–5;

1960, p. 720; Bose, 1975, Ch. 7). On the other hand, the political theorists' paradoxes have continued to hold the attention of a minority of specialists interested in the workings of political processes over the past century. Thus Condorcet's 'paradox of voting'—which points to the fact that the method of majority decisions leads to inconsistencies—has been discussed extensively (for summary accounts see Arrow, 1951, 1963, 1970, Ch. 8, pp. 93–6; Sen, 1970, Ch. 3, pp. 38–9).

It must be admitted, however, that what might be called 'standard' or 'mainstream' political science has paid scant attention to the paradoxes of political processes and events. This is partly because Thomas Hobbes, who tried to found a unified political science based on the notion that the maximization of power is the universal motive (Hobbes, 1651, 1974, Ch. 11, p. 161), made political scientists over-confident about the capacity of this political science to eliminate the paradoxes of politics. However, in real life, the paradoxical features of political processes have been crying out for attention, and engaging the attention of those analysts who want to revive the 'mathematical method' in analysing political problems—which Hobbes pioneered[1] —but who use it, not to assume away paradoxes, but to solve them.

In this book we first try to unravel selected paradoxes or puzzles in global or Indian subcontinental politics. According to its dictionary meaning, a puzzle is a problem designed for testing ingenuity, and a paradox is a condition with seemingly contradictory qualities or phases (see Webster's *Seventh New Collegiate Dictionary*, Indian edn., 2nd reprint, 1969). Some of the problems analysed are 'weak paradoxes' in the sense that they refer to motivated actions producing simply *unintended* outcomes. Others refer to 'strong paradoxes', which arise when motivated actions produce outcomes which are the *opposite* of those intended.

Whether 'weak' or 'strong', the interesting thing about these paradoxes is that, with the help of modern methods of analysis, a precise interpretation of, and a precise method of solving, the paradox can be worked out in each case. Now, the principal analytical method we use is the method of game-theoretic analysis, against which there are strong objections. So in the rest of this General Introduction we try to make an inventory of these objections, and try to convince the

---

[1] Hobbes tried to develop a political science modelled on geometry and physics (see Macpherson, 1968).

reader that game-theoretic analyses of political problems are still worth having.

1.2 Game theory and politics

For the purpose of the present work, the following general statements about the theory of games are appropriate. *First*, the theory supplies a framework or 'a language and a method for describing the fine structure of interlinked decision processes' (Shubik, 1964, p. 18). *Second*, the theory investigates the 'implications of assumptions concerning the goals and behaviour of players, given a description of the game' (ibid., p. 18). (It might be emphasized, as will be clear from a glance at the models used in later chapters, that each game model can 'predict' a sharply contrasting outcome, depending on precise differences in the initial assumptions (about the environment or about preferences of each player) inserted as 'data'.) *Third*, *all* the models used in this book, and apparently many other models of complex games found in the literature (ibid., p. 18), include assumptions based on a blend of normative and 'positive' considerations about the external ('material') environment beyond the control of *all* the players, about the preference-patterns and rational or 'irrational' behaviour by each player, etc. *Fourth*, game theory supplies a scientific method for tackling problems which cannot, *sui generis*, be tackled as simple maximizing problems, and which we would like to see tackled as problems partially under human control and not as pure games of chance tackled by classical probability theory.

The advantages of using game theory in analysing political problems are so great that it would be nice if one could start writing them out on a clean slate, and let the results speak for themselves. Unfortunately, the slate is *not* clean. It must first be wiped clean by discussing various objections to game-theoretic analyses of social (political) behaviour. So this section is devoted to discussing some *initial* objections, and then indicating some of the advantages of using game models to analyse the problems considered in Parts I and II of this book. (An *ultimate* objection, which is not only against mathematical game theory, but against *any* scientific approach to analysing political phenomena, is best discussed in Part III, where some tentative conclusions are drawn, by which time the reader has had a chance to decide for himself what game theory can do.)

These initial objections, and the comments on them, are given below.

1. It is unlikely that a theory which is so abstract that it is modelled on poker, and which can tackle such diverse problems as problems faced by prisoners under heavy sentence for crimes, low savings rates in undeveloped economies, the pollution problem in advanced economies, the Vietnam war, etc., really achieves what it claims to achieve.

Comments: (i) The diversity of problems it can tackle should not make the theory of games suspect, any more than a similar diversity of problems to the solution of which arithmetic (or any human language) makes a contribution makes arithmetic (or all human languages) suspect. (ii) In fact, game theory does *not* supply an 'Open Sesame' formula for solving all problems in politics or economics. (Thus, while the political conditions of capitalist breakdown in some modern contexts probably cannot be analysed except with the aid of game theory (see Bose, 1975, Ch. 12), economic transitions from a capitalist economy to a socialist economy are best analysed *without* the aid of game theory (ibid., Ch. 13).)

2. The word 'game' in the name given to the theory makes light of grim and serious matters in politics or economics, which involve life and death, the well-being or starvation of millions.

Comment: There is so much force in this semantic objection that a prominent game-theorist wholly agrees (Shubik, 1964, p. 9). However, no precise substitute has been suggested, because it is hard to find one (apart from the problem that the name is now standardized).

3. Political game-theoretic analyses are sometimes condemned because they are identified with 'war games' which have been particularly discredited as they were played before the German 'Barbarossa' operation against Russia, and the Japanese attack on Pearl Harbor in 1941 (Wohlstetter, 1964, in Shubik, 1964, p. 219; Wilson, 1968, 1970, Ch. 1–9, 11–12). 'War games', which seem to have been played since about 3000 B.C. (e.g. the Chinese war game Wei-Hai) (ibid., p. 13), seem to be *trebly* discredited. Firstly, they are invariably linked with real wars, which are generally unpopular nowadays. Secondly, they seem frequently to have been played by changing the 'rules' (or assumptions) arbitrarily, in the middle of the 'war game', to predetermine the desired outcome. This is rather like cheating at cards, and offends those with a scientific (or ethical) temperament. Thirdly, the best-known 'war games' have been associated with major *defeats* suffered in war, by the Germans in Russia, the Japanese in the Pacific, the Americans in Vietnam (ibid., espe-

cially Ch. 12; also *The Pentagon Papers*, Sheehan, 1971). This conclusively offends the pragmatists.

Comments: A 'war game' merely represents an attempt to conduct experiments to *rehearse* wars. *Modernized* war gaming *has* involved the use of the sophisticated methods of operations research, systems analysis, and, to a limited extent, modern game theory (see Wohlstetter, 1964, in Shubik, 1964, pp. 217–21, and Wilson, op. cit., Ch.10, for somewhat conflicting reports of the actual extent to which game theory has, in fact, been used in war games). On the other hand, the mathematical theory of games has also been used by vocal critics of the *misuse* of game theory for war-mongering purposes (e.g. by Anatol Rapoport and Kenneth Boulding; see Wilson, op. cit., Ch. 10). In addition, it has been employed in the theoretical literature to assess the best possible tactics available to guerrillas and police (*without* being loaded in favour of either) in skirmishes (Shubik, 1964, pp. 14–19). An interim verdict on a difficult subject, to be more fully discussed in Part III, could read as follows. Like many scientific theories, not excluding the scientific versions of the Marxian theory of revolution, game theory is probably strictly 'neutral'. It can be used or misused to promote good causes (e.g. revolutions), as well as bad causes (e.g. counter-revolutions), or even to facilitate a bad outcome (e.g. a counter-revolution) while trying to promote a good one (e.g. a revolution).

4. Political game-theorizing is supposed to suffer from a built-in tendency towards distorting the facts to suit preconceptions. In particular, there is a tendency to (i) convert, arbitrarily, n-person problems into 2-person ones, (ii) assume strictly 'rational' error-free behaviour by all 'players', (iii) ignore or underplay common interests and concentrate on a conflict of interests (Wohlstetter, 1964, pp. 209–25).

Comments: *Re* (i): 2-person game problems (like 2-variable simultaneous equations) are simpler to handle than n-person problems (or n-variable equations), but that is all. N-person games (like n-variable equations) are solvable, like 2-person games (or 2-variable equations). Moreover, in many situations conversion of an n-person game into a 2-person one is valid and necessary, when the problem collapses into a partial conflict–co-operation relation between two groups of persons, each with an internal coincidence of interests. *Re* (ii): this is certainly not the case. *Firstly*, game theory is useful in solving many (economic or) political problems precisely because there is the paradox that the best outcome is 'irrational' in the sense that it differs from the *preferred* best outcome. *Secondly*, the possibility of error by a party to a problem can always be taken care of by assigning numerical values to the probability of action on the basis of preference-patterns, of expected behaviour, of likely outcomes, etc. (The models of this book, which abstract from the possibility of error, could easily be made more complex by bringing in the error-factor.) On the other hand, if it is argued that in political affairs 'errors' matter more than anything else, this probably simply reduces to a problem of definition of the term 'error'. *Re* (iii): this may *in fact* have been the case (Wilson, 1968, 1970, Ch. 10; Wohlstetter's rebuttal is not entirely convincing (1964, pp. 209–25)). But there is no *necessity* for it to be so. In pure theory, only with the 2-person zero-sum game is absolute conflict assumed; in most other game-theoretic models the situation is one of a blend of conflict and co-operation (absolute co-operation, with no conflict at all, is a degenerate one-person case in game theory (Shubik, 1964, p. 18; Wohlstetter, op. cit., pp. 214–16)).

5. Game-theoretic models in politics are amoral, or, better, immoral, because by stressing conflict against co-operation they actually *generate* and *perpetuate* conflict, where negotiations, compromise, and co-operation are called for.

Comment: This line of thinking probably originated with Bertrand Russell in his study *Power* (1938, 1946, p. 34) which has the doctrine 'power . . . [must] be tamed, and brought into the service of the whole human race, white and yellow and black, fascist and communist and democrat; for science has made it inevitable that all must live and all must die'. *If* this is so, it follows *logically* that *all* political problems (both international and domestic or internal) reduce to one-person problems, which, as we have just seen in the preceding paragraph, are *degenerate* cases in game theory, that is to say, cases which do *not* need game-theoretic treatment. However, even if the earth-destroying scientific nuclear power does look like freezing the late-twentieth-century international (interstate) *status quo*, there is no similar development of science which could freeze the internal or domestic *status quo* within each state. Indeed, those who agree with Russell that nuclear power has made wars obsolete, argue that (internal) revolutions are becoming the key tactic (Arendt, 1963, 1973, pp. 16–17). As for game theory encouraging conflict and discouraging negotiations, two out of the three main game-theoretic models used in this book (in Chapters 2 and 8) do nothing of the kind.

The foregoing suggests that some of the criticisms of game-theoretic analyses of political problems strike home, while others do not. But every effort has been made in this book to keep clear of the defects recognized above.

1.3 Reading this book

In reading this book, the reader can start with any chapter in Parts I or II, according to taste (each part is more or less self-contained, as are most individual chapters in each part). But Part III is better read after reading at least one of the earlier parts, and the chapters of Part III should preferably be read as a group, starting with Chapter 11.

Glossary of Terms

To avoid unnecessary circumlocution, it seems desirable to fix the meaning of certain terms which have several standard uses in the literature. In the present study this is done as the terms are used. However, the meaning of the more important, or more frequently used, groups of terms are given here, for ready reference. We begin with a general term, and go on to political and game-theoretic terms. The terms are *not* introduced in alphabetical order, because they are too few in number to make this necessary, and also because some of them can only be defined in terms of others which must be defined (and be read) before them.

General

Rationalization is used in the chapters of Part III in a sense which is common in mathematical usage: to clear an explanation of irrational (or mystical) entities. The use of the term in another, more commonly used sense, viz. to explain *away* by plausible, but spurious reasoning, is generally avoided (except perhaps in one place) to eliminate possible confusion.

Political

Super-power is possessed by a state which has the nuclear capability to destroy most man-made assets on the earth's land mass.

Global political problems refer to problems in which super-powers are involved.

Regional power is possessed by a state which dominates regions which are by-passed by the main currents of super-power (global) politics.

Regional political problems refer to problems of regional power.

The *social 'status quo'* refers to the totality of arrangements of a socio-economic political system e.g. capitalism or socialism.

The *institutional 'status quo'* refers to a *particular type* of a socio-economic political system, e.g. state capitalism (or a particular sub-type of state capitalism) or Soviet-type or Chinese type socialism or communism[1] (or a sub-type of each of these).

The *constitutional 'status quo'* refers to the state-structure, to change or preserve which is one of the functions of *both* 'evolutionary' (i.e. non-revolutionary) *and* revolutionary politics.

The *interstate (territorial) 'status quo'* refers to the territorial demarcation between states. It is disturbed when new states or autonomous regions within a state are established, or state boundaries are changed, or old states disappear. The rationale of all four types of disturbance is a common one. All four types have been politically significant, especially in the modern world.

---

[1] The two words are used interchangeably in different chapters to refer not only to political doctrines, but also to social systems based on (i) social ownership of the principal means of production, which are (ii) ruled by communist parties. To eliminate confusion, *non*-Marxian 'socialism' is explicitly referred to as social democracy or its sub-types, e.g. Fabianism.

A *revolutionary process* implies 'novelty, beginning, violence' (Arendt, 1963, 1973, p. 47). It may change any politically significant subset, or the full set of the social, institutional, constitutional, and the interstate *status quo*'s. *Revolutionary politics* is concerned with the promotion of a revolutionary process.

A *semi-revolutionary process* implies a *milder* version of the revolutionary process. It has so far not been known to involve a change in the social *status quo*.

Revolutionaries are those who are involved in making revolution.

Counter-revolutionary processes counter incipient, successful, or abortive revolutionary processes.

Counter-revolutionaries are those who seek to counter revolutionaries at home or abroad, whether or not these are engaged in abortive or successful revolutions.

Radical politics is distinguished from both revolutionary and counter-revolutionary politics—or from 'evolutionary' politics—in so far as it is concerned with the aspiration to change, or attempts to change, elements of the institutional *status quo*, but *not* the social *status quo*, in a capitalist or a socialist society, so as to outmanoeuvre revolutionary, counter-revolutionary, or 'evolutionary' politicians.

A *radical institutional model or prototype* refers to a programme to promote radical politics.

A *voting system* is inherent in *any* collective decision-making, since, at least in the modern context, with which we are mainly concerned in this book, opinions must diverge. Absolute ('totalitarian') despotism by one individual over others who tender absolute (unconditional and unquestioning) obedience is an impossibility, though repressed voting may take the form of different postures of genuflection.

An *implicit voting system*, operating through a 'black market in votes', exists when voting is illegal (whether the voting is clandestine or in public, 'secret' or open)—as in the higher echelons of a military apparatus which converts itself into a military-political junta, or in a communist party apparatus based on 'democratic centralism'.[2]

An *electoral system* is an *explicit voting system* (e.g. state-level or party-level voting in a one-party or one multi-party bloc set-up in a communist or fascist society) which is purely 'conspicuous' or demonstrative, and reflects *not at all* the cross-currents of opinion involved in actual collective political decision-making. Thus an electoral system is *not* a parliamentary system, though the latter also involves elections.

A *parliamentary system* is an *explicit voting system* in which opposing parties or groups cast conflicting votes, in camera or in public, whether or not some or all opposition groups function (or are allowed to function) as 'safety valves'. (An opposition group functions as a 'safety valve' when it never challenges the institutional *status quo*, or perhaps does not even challenge the political *status quo*, or when its opposition is limited to challenging some of the other *status quo*'s referred to above.) A political group may begin life as a 'safety valve' and convert itself into a semi-revolutionary or, under certain circumstances, into a revolutionary group, or the process may be the other way round. However, in the process, it may have to 'shed its skin' like a snake, or at least to change its

[2] The term is discussed in Ch. 3–4.

name. *Implicit* voting involving conflicting votes by groups is *implicit* (or black) parliamentarism (Gramsci, 1971, pp. 255–6). An explicit parliamentary system usually also has as an adjunct a *parliamentary black market* in votes, whose characteristic feature is that legal votes are bought and sold for direct or indirect money payment in an illegal (black) market in votes.

The meanings of some of the terms presented above are already in use, explicitly or by implication, in the works of well-known writers, though they have not attracted as much attention as they deserve. Of these, Antonio Gramsci and Hannah Arendt have already been mentioned. Others are: Karl Marx (see Marx and Engels, 1950, pp. 62–5, for his use of the terms revolution and counter-revolution); Noam Chomsky (1969, 1971, p. 23, for his use of the term 'counter-revolution'); Herbert Marcuse (1968, for a sharp distinction between revolutions which initiate qualitative (social) change and those that do not); Duncan Black (1948, 1969, for his general conception of the essential similarity between economic market-pricing systems and political voting systems). In general, Kumar (1971) may be consulted for classified extracts from seminal writings on revolution which show that the sense in which various political terms are used in this book is not always novel.

Game theory

A *semi-autonomous decision-making unit* in interdependent collective decision-making (or *game*) is referred to as a *player*, an *individual*, a *group*, a *class*, a *political party*, a political subculture, or conglomerate, a *state* (or group of states), a *country*.

A *strategy* in political action is a general plan of action on what to do in every contingency.

The *outcome* of a game in politics is the *end-result* or *prospect* of the game which will depend on (i) events in the environment which are beyond the control of *any* player, and (ii) the strategies employed by each player.

The *payoffs* from strategies adopted by players are the *values* attached to the outcomes or prospects of each strategy adopted by the players. In the game-theory models used in this book the payoffs are generally in terms of qualitative results, e.g. total or partial victory or defeat in war. But in Chapter 6 the payoffs are expressed, as is more often the case in the general literature on game theory, in quantitative values.

In writing out these definitions of game-theory terms, I have leaned heavily on those given by Martin Shubik in his Introduction to *Game Theory and Related Approaches to Social Behaviour*, pp. 12–14.

PART I

Global and Regional Political Problems

GLOBAL political problems, as defined in the Glossary of Terms above, are problems connected with the main currents of super-power politics. Super-power, it is said there, is possessed by a state which has the nuclear capability to destroy most man-made assets on the earth's land mass.

Thus global politics refer, as it were, to events on the high road of world politics. By contrast, regional politics refer to events off the high road of world politics.

Part I of this book is devoted to analyses of global political problems, which emerge both as *interstate* and *intrastate* problems involving super-powers. Some of them are 'paradoxes'. others are 'puzzles', as we have defined these words in Chapter 1.

There will hardly be any dispute that Chapter 2: 'The Vietnamese paradox', Chapter 3: 'Personality cults', and Chapter 6: 'The balance of global super-power: some results' qualify as examples of such interstate or intrastate problems.

But Chapter 5: 'Capitalist-socialist co-existence' also qualifies, because the problem is worth discussing both as an interstate and an intra-(socialist) state problem.

Chapter 4: 'Chinese communist ideology' deserves detailed discussion in Part I for at least three distinct reasons. First, because the actual super-powers, the U.S.A. and the U.S.S.R., are keenly interested in it. Second, it has a worldwide impact as a powerful ideology today (partly because it has appropriated to itself much of what should have been copyrighted as the impact of Vietnamese communist ideology). Third, though China is not at present a super-power in terms of the definition employed in this book, it is generally thought to be the third *potential* super-power, and may become an actual super-power by the end of the twentieth century (aided especially by a newly developed oil-power which may match that of the U.S.S.R. and the U.S.A.).

CHAPTER 2

The Vietnamese Paradox

2.1 Introduction

WHAT puzzles most people about the Vietnamese revolutionary war is that the 'wrong side'—'wrong' from the factual (in terms of material resources), if not the moral, point of view—won. If it is considered a 'unique historical event', there is, strictly speaking, nothing to discuss. Unique events do not require, indeed, they defy, analysis. Nothing can be *learnt* from them, though one may admire or express one's astonishment at the event. But if an event is *not* 'historically unique', analysis, dissection, discussion is interesting and worth while, both from a scientific and a moral viewpoint. This point is further discussed in Chapter 11.3.

It might seem that the puzzle of the Vietnamese war can be solved by interpreting it as a modern version of the David and Goliath legend. In this legend, Saul and the Israelites won with the help of David, whose 'secret weapon' was pebbles in a sling, with which he slew Goliath of the Philistines in single combat, after which the Philistines took to flight. To many modern observers, the Vietnamese 'secret weapon' was their specific use of guerrilla warfare (perfected by Vo Nguyen Giap), which in the end prevailed against modern American methods of massive, mechanized warfare. Some may pay serious attention also to a claim reportedly made by Chou En-lai to American visitors during the phase of China's 'ping-pong diplomacy' in 1970 that the revolutionary side had made use of the Western imperialists' 'secret weapon' against China during the Opium Wars in reverse, by smuggling drugs into S. Vietnam. Any complete account of the Vietnam war must include these elements.

However, Giap's 'secret weapon' was less disputably and dramatically the chief 'cause' of the French débâcle in Indo-China, symbolized by the surrender at Dien Bien Phu, than of the U.S. military pull-out from Vietnam.[1] Nor did mutinies and surrenders by drug-

---

[1] On the other hand, as we shall see in Chapter 9, even a sincere and determined bid to imitate Vietnamese guerrilla warfare failed to produce a David and Goliath type outcome in West Bengal (India) in the late 1960s.

3

addicted U.S. and South Vietnamese soldiers dramatically end the U.S. military adventure in Vietnam.

Of course, any instructive analytical model (or syndrome) of a complex political event must *simplify*, concentrating on the essentials and deliberately disregarding the non-essentials. But an interpretation of the Vietnamese war with the help of the David and Goliath syndrome 'fits the facts' of the French misadventure in 1953 *better* than the misadventure of the Americans in 1973. It seems to be a *relevant simplification* of the Franco-Vietnamese war, but doubtfully so of the American–Vietnamese war.[2]

We might conceivably do better by adopting as the relevant simplified statement about the American–Vietnamese war, the paradox already stated in the Preface:

S.1: 'A *divided* (international) communism secured the expulsion of the armed forces of the "strongest link in the chain of international [capitalist] imperialism".'

To bring out the details of the paradox a little more clearly, we might rephrase the above statement as:

S.2: 'A *divided* (international) communism got the better of a *less divided, more powerful* (international) capitalist imperialism, both in the battle-field and in the conference-room.'

Furthermore, to capture an element of paradox which is not explicit even in S.2, we can supplement it with the statement:

S.3: 'The Vietnamese revolutionaries *tamed* their *allies* (friends) in order to get the better of their *enemies*.'

The next two sections are devoted to a discussion of the factual content of statements S.2–3, and of the precise nature of the paradox involved.

2.2 The facts of the paradox

In this section, we dissect statements S.2 and S.3, and discuss the factual evidence in support of each part (not necessarily in the order in which they occur).

'*A divided (international) communism . . .*' as one of the two sides in the Vietnam (–America) war is an assessment essential to the resolution of the Vietnamese paradox attempted in this chapter.

---

[2] For the facts of the Vietnamese war, here, as elsewhere in this book, the author has relied on Neil Sheehan, 1971, *The Pentagon Papers*, Chomsky (1969, 1971; 1970, 1973; (1973), Arendt (1969, 1972); the anonymously written (1970), *History of the Vietnam Workers' Party*; Vo Nguyen Giap (1970, 1971); and daily newspaper reports in the Indian (English and Bengali) Press.

Below, we first argue that the international communist schism (focused on Sino-Soviet ideological antagonism) is *irrevocable* and serious. We then discuss reasons for thinking that material support from the Soviet Union and People's China was an *essential* factor in the war, so that one of the two sides in the war *was*, indeed, a divided international communism.

It should be noted, first of all, that it was precisely in the phase of the war just preceding the American military pull-out that the international communist schism hardened into what looked like being an *irrevocable* split. Talk of an 'irrevocable split' may sound like an *ex cathedra* statement.[3] But it is strongly suggested by plausible factual support for hypotheses about (i) the fundamentally religious nature of contemporary communism, (ii) its affinities with monotheistic, proselytizing religions, in contrast to polytheistic religions,[4] and (iii) the well-known irrevocability of ideological splits in monotheistic in contrast to polytheistic religions.

As regards (i), the religious element in modern Marxian communism has been vividly symbolized (and made almost self-evident) by the mummification of Lenin's mortal remains in 1924, for which no *non*-religious rationalization is available. (On the other hand, parallels in Buddhism, Christianity, and Islam abound.) Recognition of this fairly obvious truth has been resisted, often tacitly, for at least three identifiable reasons. *First*, conversion of a revolutionary ideology into a religion is considered *unnatural*. This, of course, is against the run of the evidence, as Alexis de Tocqueville's recently popularized remarks on the uninhibited revolutionary religion of France in 1789 remind us (Tocqueville, 1856, reprinted in Kumar (ed.), 1971, pp. 113–15, in Pizzorno (ed.), 1971, pp. 23–6). Actually, there is hardly any evidence that *any* 'earth-shaking' social upheaval has ever been put through (whether as a revolution or a counter-revolution) without movements of a religious nature. Ex-communist writings of the 'God that failed' variety simply ignore this evidence, but are also *inconsistent*, because they themselves exude much religious fervour. *Second*, there is the genuine problem of reconciling the logical-scientific and fideistic aspects of Marxian communist ideology. However, Antonio Gramsci's insight that logic cannot be

[3] Like Mao Tse-tung's assertion that Sino-Russian ideological differences were irreconcilable and would last 9,000 years (Snow, 1971, 1972, p. 149).

[4] The reference is to a religion with many gods, as was the Greek religion at the time of Plato, Socrates, Aristotle, and is the Hindu religion, which also absorbed alternative philosophical systems.

decisive in carrying (ideological-philosophical) conviction except when there is already an intellectual crisis, that *in general* 'not reason but faith' is the decisive element supplies the beginning of an answer (Gramsci, 1930s, 1971, pp. 338–9). (Gramsci was quite categorical that international communism was still going through its 'populist' phase, in which it relied more on faith than on reason to 'educate the popular masses whose culture was medieval' (op. cit., pp. 392, 395–6).) *Third*, the belief that a 'materialistic' approach (which is a hallmark of Marxian ideology) is irreconcilably opposed to a religious approach, has also obfuscated the issue. But here, too, we can profit by Gramsci's forthright reminder that 'popular religion [in which category he explicitly includes popular superstitions—witchcraft, spirits, etc.—and *popular* Catholicism] is crassly *materialistic*' (op. cit., p. 396). Thus materialism is by no means *ipso facto* non-religious, or anti-religious; nor is Marxian materialistic communism.

We turn now to (ii), i.e. evidence of the affinities of the religious element in modern Marxian ideology with monotheistic, intolerant, proselytizing religions, in contrast to polytheistic or pantheistic, rather more tolerant religions. Early textual evidence is found in Marx's journalistic dispatches on India, where with monotheistic fervour he castigates the Hindus' 'brutalizing worship of nature, exhibiting its degradation in the fact that man, the sovereign of nature, fell down on his knees in adoration of Hanuman, the monkey, and Sabbala, the cow' (Marx, 1853, reprinted in Marx and Engels, *The First Indian War of Independence 1857–1859*, Second Impression, no date, Moscow, pp. 20–1). In strict logic, an atheistic believer in the materialistic interpretation of history of the Marxian variety has no good reason to side with monotheistic as against polytheistic or pantheistic religions, *qua* religions.[5] Moreover, implicit in the above passage in the early Marx is the notion of man as 'sovereign of nature' which the later Marx roundly denounced as a 'bourgeois idea'' (Marx, 1875, in Marx and Engels, 1949, p. 17).

As regards (iii)—the irrevocability of major schisms in monotheistic religions—it is well known that such major schisms as have occurred in monotheistic religions (e.g. Christianity and Islam) have proved irrevocable. (The failure of briefly advertised recent attempts

---

[5] Of course, it is perfectly possible for a Marxist to recognize the superior status in the ladder of progress of a socio-economic formation (e.g. capitalism) corresponding to a specific monotheistic religion (e.g. Lutheran Christianity) compared to another (e.g. feudalism) corresponding to another monotheistic (e.g. Catholic Christianity) or pantheistic (perhaps Tibetan Buddhist) religion.

at ending the schism which separated the English Protestant churches from the Catholic Church is the latest piece of evidence.) On the other hand, in polytheistic or pantheistic religions (e.g. Hinduism) schisms are followed by reconciliations and the absorption of pro- liferating sects[6] (as also, of course, the legalization of such obnoxious practices as untouchability, the predecessor of the colour-bar sanc- tioned by monotheistic religions). The greater tolerance and altruism of a polytheistic religious tradition, compared to a self-centred monotheistic one, but also its sophistical condonation of the practice of untouchability, is gently but firmly brought out in *Lalon Fakir*, a post-liberation, pre-1975 film from Bangladesh.

More vividly than the potential irrevocability of the international Sino-Soviet communist schism was its immediate *intensity* demon- strated by Sino-Soviet border tension. (Actually, this is also an *independent* factor which makes the Sino-Soviet communist schism potentially irrevocable. For the Sino-Soviet border conflict is the outgrowth of an *internationalist* communist ideological conflict. Such conflicts *cannot* be solved by transfer of territory or of population, as national conflicts between communist states, or even border con- flicts involving nationalist capitalist states, have been solved in Europe.)

The divided condition of international communism was also under- scored during the closing stages of the Vietnam–America war by an unprecedented, ongoing phenomenon, which will be discussed in other chapters of this book. The reference is to *competitive* moves by both the Chinese People's Republic and the Soviet Union for *détente* with America, the leader of international (capitalist) imperial- ism. There were certainly interlinkages between the trilateral negotia- tions between the U.S.A. on one side and (revolutionary) Vietnam, China, and the Soviet Union on the other, though only speculative accounts have been published.[7] But there can be little doubt that the trilateral pattern of negotiations favoured the U.S.A. as against revolutionary Vietnam.[8]

[6] K. M. Sen (1961, 1967), pp. 84–5.

[7] Noam Chomsky, after a close study of reports in the American Press, dis- counts widely publicized reports of Russian–Chinese pressure on the Vietnamese communists to sign the Paris Agreements of 1973 (Chomsky, 1973, p. 165).

[8] An example is the scare, emanating from American semi-governmental sources, about an imminent Soviet 'preventive' attack on China's nuclear instal- lations, which may have been chiefly responsible for the Chinese decision to build underground cities. On the other hand, Chou En-lai's self-hypnotizing xenophobic conviction that a *joint* U.S.–Soviet–Indian–Japanese attack on China was on the cards, at a time when there were *no* signs of *any* action by these powers.

Finally, it is necessary to consider in what precise way the international communist schism affected the revolutionary side in the war. There is, of course, *no* evidence of any publicized internal split among the Vietnamese communists, in North or South, along the lines of the anti-Liu Shao-chi or anti-Lin Piao upheavals in China. Nor is there, retrospectively, much value to be attached to Western Press speculation that there was a pro-Soviet faction eager to settle for a Korean-type semi-permanent standstill along the 1954 North–South demilitarized zone, at loggerheads with a pro-Chinese faction which was anxious to evacuate the revolutionary forces to south China, to carry on a protracted guerrilla war from there.

However, all this does *not* mean that the Vietnamese communists were essentially revolutionary *nationalists*, who fought more or less *alone* as the Yugoslav communists led by Tito are said to have, as is is often claimed by their friends and foes (see references in Chomsky, 1969, 1971, p. 42; 1970, 1973, pp. 10–12; 1973, p. 15). Supplies of rice from China (Vietnam became a heavy importer after 1965 (Chomsky, 1973, p. 165)), and of arms from the Soviet Union, played an absolutely decisive role in Vietnamese resistance (ibid., p. 165). (Because of the food deficit, and because American troops in direct occupation controlled American arms, the Chinese communist model of relying on peasants for food, and the enemy's (i.e. the Japanese puppets' and war-lords' and Kuomintang's) arsenal for arms, proved unworkable.) For *this* reason, if for no other, *international* communism, divided though it was, must be reckoned as the revolutionary side in the Vietnam–America war.

'... *a less divided, but more powerful (international) capitalist imperialism* ...' as the other end of the see-saw in the Vietnam–America war is a statement which requires shorter discussion. There is hard evidence, of course, that the U.S.A. was bled, though not bled white, in terms of economic and military resources, by the Vietnam war, which was like a running sore. But there is not the slightest basis for thinking that at any stage in the war the economic and military potential of the U.S.A. was less than a match for the Soviet–Chinese resources available to the other side. This statement

---

against China, may have been the cause. Of course, one cannot be sure that the Soviet Union never thought of such a preventive strike against China (though retrospectively this seems unlikely). If the Soviet Union *was* thinking of it at any stage, Nixon's veiled threat that the U.S.A. would take China's side in the event of a Soviet strike (to be discussed also in Chapter 6 below) may have put a stop to it.

is strongly supported by the fact that the economic crisis in the U.S.A. (and elsewhere in the capitalist world economy) was paralleled by economic crises in the Chinese and Soviet economies. However, though more *powerful*, it is well known that as the war wore on, American society became morally nihilistic,[9] sorely divided internally, and increasingly isolated internationally. Did this ever lead to an eclipse of *effective* American power by the power wielded by the other side? The answer is a categorical No. As noted above, international communism was *also* divided. Apart from the balance of potential power always being in favour of the Americans, the ideological-political, mainly De Gaulle-engineered splits on the international-capitalist side never reached the dimensions of the Sino-Soviet split, or the split *within* China during the cultural revolution. (Moreover, there is a close parallel between the *politics* of the Chinese cultural revolution (which climaxed during the crucial stages of the Vietnam–America war) and the politics of the anti-war movement in the U.S.A. The mass political upheaval in China subsided after the ouster of Liu and Lin served as safety-valves. In much the same way, the ouster of Johnson, and more recently of Agnew, as well as of Nixon have served as safety-valves which have made the politics of *mass* dissent temporarily obsolete in America.)

' . . . *got the better of* . . . ' is that part of statement S.2 above which is perhaps likely to be hotly disputed. And yet the essential facts are pretty clear. There was little hope, of course, that the *substance* of the January 1973 Paris Agreement which preceded the American military pull-out would coincide with its *letter and spirit*, which called for the *unification* of the *whole* of Vietnam through the mechanism of a multi-party electoral system (maybe even a parliamentary system, in which *opposing* political parties *contest* elections). The *Realpolitik* of the agreement was obviously an initial *partition within a partition* (i.e. a partition of *South* Vietnam), which was, however, *at the expense* of the *counter-revolution*, and a direct *gain* for the *revolution*. True, it did *not obliterate* outright the counter-revolution in South Vietnam. Nor has *any* 'classical' communist revolution. The Chinese revolution has not yet obliterated its counter-revolutionary antipodes at Taiwan. The Cuban revolution has yet to obliterate the American counter-revolutionary (naval) base at Guantanamo on Cuban soil.

---

[9] As powerfully foreshadowed in the Elizabeth Taylor–Richard Burton film, produced by Ernest Lehman, of Edward Albee's *Who's Afraid of Virginia Woolf?* (Albee, 1962, 1967).

Even the Soviet revolution did not 'obliterate' Finland as an 'active' counter-revolutionary base ('active' in 1918, 1940, 1941) until the architect of the Finnish counter-revolution, Mannerheim, finally resigned as president in 1946, and the Soviet Union felt sufficiently reassured to abandon its Porkkala base in Finnish soil, close to the Finnish capital. All in all, the Paris accord was a clear gain for the revolution (as it has turned out in 1975, a decisive one) in Vietnam. It was by no means a 'Korean-type' settlement, to which international communism (including Communist China and the Soviet Union) was a party, after the Korean war in the 1950s. (The Korean semi-permanent standstill along the lines of the 1953 armistice involved *no* territorial gain for the Korean revolution, which was mainly a 'revolution from above' in contrast to the 'revolution from below' in South Vietnam. It actually involved, instead, *some* loss of territory by northward adjustment of the armistice lines.)

'... *both in the battle-field and in the conference-room*': This, the last part of statement S.2, is factually the least disputable, but ideologically the least edifying to most analysts of the Vietnamese revolution. Revolutionaries and pro-revolutionaries will object to the elevation of the conference-room to the same pedestal as the battle-field, to the bracketing-together of violence with negotiating skills. So also will those, fewer in the present decade than in the 1960s, who are still committed to non-violence in politics (including among them those who, like the Gandhians in India in 1942, have a precise preference for non-violence over violence, but for violence over non-violent inaction or passivity). All three groups of political activists have a clear-cut preference *either* for violence, or for non-violence, but will sanction either, *provided* one or the other *predominates* as the *main form* of political struggle. In *no* case will they attach *equal* importance to *both*, as is done in statement S.2, and *was* the case in the Vietnam–America war. (This is easily established, whether we use as bench-marks to judge the qualitative importance of violence (warfare) and negotiations in the war, the actual time spent in combat or the time spent in military lulls, with or without negotiations (ritualistic or serious).) Furthermore, conventional approaches to the problems of violence and negotiations in politics throw little light on certain startlingly novel features of the procedures adopted during the Vietnam–America war.

The unprecedented procedures adopted in the war included: (i) 'insurrecting' (e.g. during the Tet offensive of 1968) or bombing (e.g. during the air attacks on Hanoi in 1972) the enemy to the conference-table, (ii) patterned escalation/de-escalation in the intensity of warfare and negotiations, (iii) saying one thing and meaning another (within mutually agreed credibility limits), or Orwellian 'double-speak' as the *dominant* language for long stretches of the Kissinger–Tho negotiations, (iv) a deliberate going back on one's word, almost as often as standing by one's word, or calculated bad faith used, however, as a device for sorting out issues and *not* for creating a permanent deadlock, (v) mutually recriminatory 'breakdowns', used almost as often as mutually congratulatory 'resumptions' of negotiations, to fix priorities in the long search for terms of a settlement. In other contexts, such methods have prevented or broken up negotiations, prolonged wars and conflicts, or formalized 'negotiated surrender' by the *weaker* party (as by A. Dubeck in Czechoslovakia in August 1968). In this case, they promoted and consummated negotiations, and resulted in withdrawal by the *stronger* party.

S.3 above: 'The Vietnamese revolutionaries *tamed* their allies (friends) in order to get the better of their *enemies*' fits the essential facts of the Vietnam–America war surveyed so far in this section. In the foregoing survey, *both* the divisions of international communism *and* its solidarity with Vietnamese resistance to international capitalist imperialism have been stressed. These two facts, pointing in opposite directions, are not easily reconciled. One way of reconciling them is to hypothesize that in the negotiations in camera between the Vietnamese revolutionaries and the Chinese and Soviet communist leaders, the former successfully *tamed* their friends, who were engaged most of the time in a triangular brinkmanship *vis-à-vis* each other, and also *vis-à-vis* America, and *made them* serve the interests of the Vietnamese revolution on a top-priority basis. Indeed, it will be suggested in later sections of this chapter that the clash of war-making capacities and aims of America and revolutionary Vietnam produced no determinate outcome. On the other hand, the hard core of Soviet–Chinese policy preferences (arising out of their *conflicting* interests, commitments, and aims) did produce an outcome which favoured the Vietnamese revolution. In the absence of a factual record of Vietnamese–Soviet–Chinese negotiations during the Vietnam–America war, we may hypothesize that Vietnamese communist skill in focusing on this hard core of Soviet–Chinese preferences decided the issue.

However, as preliminary to such a resolution of the Vietnamese paradox in these terms, we have to examine now its precise nature.

2.3 The nature of the Vietnamese paradox

As we have seen in the previous section, the facts more or less support the statement of the Vietnamese paradox as set out in statements S.2 and S.3 above, viz. that the weaker side, which was also more divided, won, and that allies had to be tamed in order to subdue the enemy.

In view of this paradoxical feature, the Vietnam–America war cannot, obviously, be interpreted in terms of an analytical model of 'economic determinism', or, more generally, of a model of 'materialistic determinism', which explains the outcome as the result of the balance of strictly economic or material resources. (If the American side—stronger, and also less divided—had won, such an analytical model would have been quite suitable.) On the other hand, as noted in section 2.1, the paradox is *not* more apparent than real, it *cannot* be easily explained in terms of a David and Goliath syndrome. It is tempting, therefore, to think that the use of game-theoretic models might solve our problem. Unfortunately, in investigating this, we start with an initial disappointment.

It seems, at first sight, that the problem is analysable as a 'battle of wills' type of game-theoretic problem. A simple problem of this type is the 'battle of the sexes' problem (Luce and Raiffa, 1957, Ch. 5, sect. 5.3, pp. 90–2). A husband prefers to go to a prize fight, the wife prefers to go to a ballet, but both prefer to spend the evening together, rather than go to the preferred evening's entertainment. There are two 'equilibrium outcomes' possible, i.e. neither can move away from either 'equilibrium outcome' without worsening his or her pay-off (which is the valuation placed on the prospect of a game). If the husband can convince the wife that he will go to the prize fight at any cost, both watch the fight; if the wife is more determined and insists on going to the ballet, they both see the ballet. Thus the essence of the 'battle of the sexes' problem is that both must be *together*, which was by no means the essential feature of the Vietnam–America war (or the unquiet peace). (Of course, there are elements of 'togetherness' in its *secondary* features, as noted in sect. 2.2: the Paris Agreement of 1973 did *not* obliterate outright America's outpost in South Vietnam, negotiations *preceded* and formalized the American troops' withdrawal from Vietnam, etc.) Moreover, in the 'battle of the sexes' game, there is *no* assumption that either partner is the 'stronger', whereas such an assumption is at the heart of the Vietnamese paradox as stated above.

An alternative version of the 'battle of wills' type of game is modelled on the real-life American teenagers' game 'Chicken' (Wilson, 1968, 1970, pp. 163–4), which has been used to interpret a confrontation between two nuclear powers. In this game, *either* power giving way (i.e. acknowledging defeat *without a fight*) is an 'equilibrium outcome', because neither can be *sure* that the other is not determined to destroy it by a first strike rather than acknowledge defeat. So a nuclear war is averted. But *both* powers waste resources in nuclear brinkmanship, which could have been 'rationally' avoided, by adopting policies of nuclear disarmament and 'accommodation'. This model does not apply, either, to the problem we want to analyse. It does not apply *exactly*, because, although both sides had the nuclear capability at least to destroy Vietnam (if not each other),[10] at least in the post-Dulles (i.e. post-1954) epoch, each side also *knew* that the other side would *not* use its nuclear power in the Vietnam–America war.[11] Thus the environmental assumption as regards nuclear power which is relevant in the present case is the *opposite* to the one made in the Chicken-type game about a nuclear confrontation. Nor does the Chicken-type game model apply *generally* to the Vietnam–America war because in this 'game' there was active, gruesome war, not just the animated suspension of a confrontation, because in this war *both* sides were *not* evenly matched (one side was definitely the stronger), *both* sides did *not* give in, only *one* side did, etc.

Making an about-turn, we could construct an analytical 'decision-making' model of the Vietnam–America war, in which the 'battle of wills' aspect is almost irrelevant. The model probably qualifies as a game-theoretic model. Firstly, it has the basic general structure of a game-theoretic model about political conflicts, viz. a set of assumptions about the (physical) 'environment' and the preferences (or aims) of the 'players', which are mutually consistent, and which determine a definite 'outcome' (Shubik, 1964, pp. 73–4). Secondly, in so far as

[10] This is definitely true of America and the Soviet Union. It was almost certainly true of People's China in the phase preceding the American military pull-out.

[11] Mao Tse-tung was quoted by Jawaharlal Nehru as having said that he did not mind losing a few millions in a nuclear war, since several million Chinese would survive (Russell, 1969, 1970, p. 210). On the other hand, People's China has declared that it will never be the first to make a nuclear attack.

the problem is not formulated as a simple maximizing problem, it resembles a game-theoretic problem. Thirdly, it resembles, to some extent, a game-theoretic 'assurance problem' model, which has been used in the literature to discuss situations where a man will make a donation, or save, or (in a socialist society) agree to an institutional change, if others will, but not if others do not (Sen, 1967, pp. 114–15; 1969, pp. 3–6; Bose, 1975, Ch. 14, sect. 14.4, pp. 253–7). (It is not, however, a straightforward assurance-problem model, which is essentially a variant of the 'battle of the sexes' model (Sen, 1969, pp. 3–4).) Fourthly, the outcome is paradoxical, as is the case with many game-theoretic solutions, i.e. the 'stronger' side loses, the allies are 'tamed' to get the better of the enemy, not those involved as 'front-liners' but those on the side-lines determine the outcome.

This analytical model of the Vietnam–America war is presented in the next section and discussed in later sections of this chapter.

2.4 The solution of the Vietnamese paradox

Definitions

D.M.Z. is the demilitarized buffer zone between North and South Vietnam, established by the Geneva Accord of the 1950s.

N.L.F. is the National Liberation Front of South Vietnam, led by Vietnamese communist revolutionaries.

P.R.G. is the Provisional Revolutionary Government of South Vietnam, established by the N.L.F.

Revolutionary Vietnam refers to the communist revolutionary forces of North and South Vietnam.

'Front-liners' are the Americans and their South Vietnamese allies on one side, and revolutionary Vietnam on the other, who were *directly* involved in the fighting in South Vietnam.

'Side-liners' refer to the Soviet Union and People's China who were involved indirectly, from the side-lines, in the fighting, by giving food, arms, and political support to revolutionary Vietnam.

Total victory is an outcome (of the war) which would imply the *obliteration* of the South Vietnamese outpost of international (imperialist) capitalism.

Partial victory is the outcome which would imply the partial liberation of South Vietnam from capitalist rule, by a revolutionary partition of South Vietnam which could be a decisive step towards total victory.

Partial defeat is the outcome which would imply a 'Korean-type' solution, i.e. a semi-permanent partition of Vietnam into a socialist North Vietnam, and a capitalist South Vietnam, along the D.M.Z.

Total defeat is an outcome which would imply *either* (i) the destruction of Vietnam in a nuclear clash, *or* (ii) a counter-revolutionary (American–South Vietnamese) occupation of the whole of Vietnam (without the possible evacuation of the Vietnamese revotionary communist cadre to south China, for protracted guerrilla warfare in Vietnam conducted from there).

Note. Obviously, the meaning given to the words 'victory' and 'defeat' in the above list is biased in favour of revolutionary Vietnam. A pro-American (or counter-revolutionary) bias could just as well be introduced by replacing elsewhere in this section the word 'victory' by the word 'defeat' (and vice versa) wherever it occurs. The results would be the same, completely unaffected by the change in bias. However, while the nature of the bias introduced is immaterial, a biased terminology helps by eliminating unnecessary circumlocution in exposition.

The environment

E.1 Outright total victory as a *substitute* for partial victory is *excluded*. (The reasons are (i) The U.S.A., the most powerful counter-revolutionary (imperialist) power, was actively involved 'in place', as a front-liner in the Vietnam–America war. This was *not* the case in the other classical communist revolutions, i.e. the Soviet, the Chinese, and the Cuban.[12] (ii) There was no sign of a 'disorientation' of the chief counter-revolutionary power (America), no evidence of its failure to grasp the socialist content of the extension of the Vietnamese revolution to South Vietnam. (There *was* such a disorientation *vis-à-vis* Cuba (Guevara, 1961, in Gerassi (ed.), 1969, 1972, pp. 198–9; Castro (Fidel) quoted by Tikhonov, 1974, p. 68); earlier *vis-à-vis* China, at least until the death of Roosevelt (acknowledged by Mao Tse-tung, 1945, 1956, pp. 328–9), and perhaps later (Schram, 1966, pp. 236–7); still earlier *vis-à-vis* Russia, on the

---

[12] The American air-lift of millions of K.M.T. troops to challenge the Communist seizure of Japanese-held territory after Japan's defeat (Hu Chiao-mu, 1951, p. 68), and *before* the climax of the Chinese revolution, or wars of intervention against Russia and Cuba *after* their revolutions, represent *indirect, limited* involvement.

eve of the communist revolution, symbolized by the Imperial
German Government's grant of safe conduct to the sealed train
in which Lenin returned from exile in Switzerland to take part
in the Bolshevik revolution in Russia.)

E.2 Partial victory is *possible*, but is contingent on *joint* Soviet–
Chinese backing, with food, arms, and political support (in war
and negotiations). (Such Soviet–Chinese active support was
made *possible* by (i) China's contiguity with North Vietnam,
(ii) Soviet contiguity with China, and (iii) an *alternative* Soviet
sea-link with North Vietnam through the rapid expansion of
Soviet shipping, protected by a strengthened Soviet navy.)

E.3 Partial defeat is *unavoidable*, without *joint* Soviet–Chinese
backing (as specified in E.2). (The reasons have already been
stated in sect. 2.2 above: (i) Vietnam's food deficit after 1965,
which could only be made up from China or through China,
(ii) revolutionary Vietnam could *not* depend on the enemy's
arsenal for arms because they were under direct American
control.)

E.4 Total defeat is *ruled out*, by the balance of nuclear power, and
its implications recognized by the three involved nuclear powers
(as stated in sect. 2.3 above), as well as by the U.S. government's
political inability to challenge the 1954 Geneva Accord *in
toto*.

War aims and preferences

American–South Vietnamese:

1. Isolate and crush P.R.G.
2. Failing 1, isolate and crush revolutionary Vietnam, subvert
   semi-revolutionary Laos and Cambodia (Sihanouk and
   Burchett, 1973).
3. Failing 1 and 2, negotiate with revolutionary Vietnam for
   cease-fire and American military pull-out. (Buttress this by
   strictly parallel[13] *détente* negotiations with *both* People's
   China and the Soviet Union.)

Revolutionary Vietnamese:

1. Fight for a step-by-step revolutionary unification of North
   and South Vietnam at all costs and by all means.

---

[13] In the *double* sense that (i) Vietnamese issues would be kept out of American–
Chinese or American–Soviet negotiations, but (ii) both the Chinese and the
Soviets would be kept guessing about each other's intentions *vis-à-vis* America,
and America's intentions towards them.

2. Fight with the backing of *either* China *or* the Soviet Union if necessary, and with the backing of *both* if possible.[14]

Soviet–Chinese:

1. Each (Soviet or China) would like to help revolutionary Vietnam when the other (China or Soviet) does not, and (in view of environmental assumption E.2) put the entire blame on the other (China or Soviet) for the partial defeat.

2. But if the other side (China or Soviet) helps revolutionary Vietnam, each (Soviet or China) would like to help it also to win a partial victory, and share the responsibility and the kudos for the partial victory.

3. A total or partial victory in the Vietnam–America war is preferred, as a gain for international (even though divided) communism, to a total or partial defeat, regarded as a loss for international communism.

Outcome

Of the *four* possible outcomes, the extreme ones, viz. total victory and total defeat, are ruled out by environmental assumptions E.1, E.4.

The choice between the *two* intermediate outcomes, viz. partial victory and partial defeat, is left *undetermined* by the war aims and preferences of the American–South Vietnamese and revolutionary Vietnamese 'front-liners'.

However, the Soviet–Chinese war aim 1 determines a unique outcome, viz. partial victory, since neither can be sure that the other will *not* help revolutionary Vietnam alone, and put the *entire* blame on the other for the partial defeat.

Moreover, Soviet–Chinese preference 3 makes the 'equilibrium outcome' also the *preferred* outcome.

Thus we have the paradox mentioned more than once earlier, viz. (i) not the 'front-liners' but the 'side-liners' determine the outcome, which is also the preferred outcome (since the American–

---

[14] Involving (i) non-alignment, or (ii) multiple alignment, or (iii) selective alignment with one against the other, *vis-à-vis* the two international communist blocs. Examples of (i) are the refusal to take sides in the Sino-Soviet ideological or border disputes. Examples of (iii) are: siding with Bangladesh during its freedom struggle against Pakistan, aligned with India and the Soviet Union against a Chinese caveat, backed by the U.S. Seventh Fleet; no change in its attitude of support for Kashmiri self-determination (demanded by Pakistan, China, and the U.S.A.), after this was converted into an international (though not an internal Indian) non-issue, first by India, and then by the Soviet Union.

South Vietnamese preferences allow it, and the others prefer it), (ii) it is precisely the mutual distrust (and conflict) between the Soviets and the Chinese which makes it possible for the revolutionary Vietnamese to tame these allies and utilize their material and political support to get the better of the American–South Vietnamese enemy.

The role played by mutual distrust in determining a definite outcome makes the present model resemble a prisoners' dilemma (Luce and Raiffa, 1957, pp. 94–7), variants of which have been used to discuss the problem of pollution (Samuelson, 1973, pp. 503–5) and of capitalist breakdown (Bose, 1975, Ch. 12, pp. 199–213). However, the resemblance to a game-theoretic 'assurance-problem' model, already referred to in the previous section, is stronger. The reason is that in our Vietnam–America war model, the 'equilibrium outcome' is also the preferred outcome, that there is no need for an *enforcement* of the preferred outcome. (*This*, it has been emphasized in the literature (Sen, 1969, p. 7), is one of the crucial differences between the prisoners' dilemma and the 'assurance-problem' models in game theory.)

The analytical exercise of this section represents 'experimental gaming' in which the environment and the observed outcome are data, and the analysis pin-points the motivation which makes the entire analysis self-consistent (Shubik, 1964, in Shubik (ed.), 1964, p. 73). A similar model could have been used *before* the conclusion of the Vietnam–America war, to investigate what variation in the motivation could have produced another 'equilibrium outcome', viz. partial defeat (given the environment which rules out total victory or total defeat). (Alternatively, we could discuss what precise *change* in the environment and/or the motivation could 'predict' a resumption of the Vietnam–America war.) Such alternative exercises would represent 'operational gaming' (Shubik, op. cit., p. 73). Thus game-theoretic analyses used to investigate political events are *not* vacuous exercises, telling us simply that whatever happened did happen.

2.5 Alternative assumptions and outcomes: their ethical evaluation

The aspects of the solution of the Vietnamese paradox presented in the previous section which make it resemble both the 'assurance problem' and 'prisoners' dilemma' game-theoretic models, make the Soviet–Chinese line of action qualify as revolutionary action which is neither strictly 'selfish' nor strictly 'selfless', but is hard-headed (if somewhat schizophrenic) 'unselfish' action.[15]

If, however, Soviet–Chinese war aim 1 is amended to delete the second part, so that it reads:

1a. Each (Soviet or China) would like to help revolutionary Vietnam when the other (China or Soviet) does not,

and Soviet–Chinese war aim 2 is also deleted, their war aims 1a and 3 are consistent, and, given environmental assumption E.2, the outcome would be *partial defeat*. Such action would qualify as strictly 'selfish' action by Soviet or Chinese communism. The 'Vietnamese paradox' model would then *coincide* with the original prisoners' dilemma game-theoretic model. (If we disregard the perverse political gains arising from each communist side putting the blame on the other for the partial defeat, and count only the economic cost of wasted aid which produces the partial defeat, 'selfish' action would also be a case of *hypocritical* 'self-sacrificing' action.)

On the other hand, unalloyed altruistic (or truly *'selfless'*) action, on the basis of Tolstoyan ethics, would be represented by *unconditional* and *unlimited* aid to revolutionary Vietnam. On the basis of strict Tolstoy–Russell ethics, this could have involved peace marches and negotiated peace-making for a 'Korean-type' solution (i.e. a partial defeat). On the basis of the pragmatic Gandhian variant of 'selfless' ethics, it could conceivably have involved armed (non-nuclear) intervention by a 'selfless' communist power (the Soviet or China) against the American intervention in South Vietnam.[16] Action on the basis of a possible third variant of 'selfless' ethics could have involved (i) a nuclear strike by the Soviet Union at the U.S.A., (ii) a Chinese nuclear strike at Saigon in South Vietnam, or (iii) evacuation of Vietnamese revolutionary communist cadre to south China bases for conducting a protracted guerrilla war against American imperialism from there. (This third variant of 'selfless' revolutionary action could be supported on Maoist-Marxist political principles,[17] though there is no evidence that Mao Tse-tung or any

[15] For a discussion of these different kinds of action, see Bose (1975, Ch. 12, pp. 208–12), and Ch. 13 of this book. A similar classification of lines of action by Anatol Rapoport is discussed by Andrew Wilson (1968, 1970, pp. 165–6).

[16] Britain's wars against Germany were supported on Gandhian political principles. So also was Indian armed intervention against Pakistani volunteers who invaded Kashmir in 1947–8.

[17] Like the Soviets, the Chinese communists adhered in practice to 'unselfish' action *vis-à-vis* the Vietnam–America war. But Mao Tse-tung alone has explicitly and consistently repudiated nuclear pacifism, and he is the supreme theorist (and

Maoist ever proposed such a line of action. Nor, for that matter, is there any evidence that anyone proposed the Gandhian type of armed intervention by the Soviet Union or China in Vietnam.)

Curiously, *all* these variants of 'selfless' action would have produced outcomes worse than the outcome of 'unselfish' action, viz. partial victory. As already indicated, a Tolstoy–Russell line of 'selfless' action would have produced a partial defeat. 'Selfless' action on Gandhian principles, given the environmental assumption E.1 and the Soviet–Chinese war aim 1, would have produced at best a partial victory, but at worst (with a revision of the American policy of the non-use of the strategic nuclear weapon noted in sect. 2.3) a total defeat. 'Selfless' action of Maoist-Marxist principles would also have produced, temporarily, or permanently, a total defeat.

A similar evaluation on ethical principles of alternative lines of revolutionary communist action will be found in Chapter 9, where again 'unselfish' action does better than 'selfish' or 'selfless' action in predicting outcomes which achieve communist revolutionary aims. The matter is discussed further in the concluding Chapter 13.

2.6 Retrospect in 1975

In this chapter, as also in the Appendix attached to it, no reference has been made to two major developments subsequent to the American military pull-out from South Vietnam. The first is the post-Watergate political crisis[18] in the U.S.A., which had not, till the end of 1975, actually produced a constitutional crisis, though it had altered the balance of power between (i) the executive, (ii) the intelligence agencies (the Central Intelligence Agency, and, to a lesser extent, the Federal Bureau of Investigation), (iii) the judiciary, and (iv) the legislature (against (i) and (ii), and in favour of (iii) and (iv)).[19] The second is the series of events in 1975 in the Indo-China region which included: (i) 'total victory' in Vietnam (as the term is defined in sect. 2.4 above), (ii) the counterparts of Vietnamese 'total victory' in Cambodia and Laos as well (i.e. the extinction of the U.S. presence

---

practitioner) of protracted guerrilla warfare. So the third variant of 'selfless' action in Vietnam *could* have been justified on Maoist–Marxist principles.

[18] Which was touched off by public exposure of Richard Nixon's 'dirty tricks' employed against the Democratic Party's headquarters at Watergate, during the presidential elections which gave Nixon a landslide victory.

[19] Curiously, the U.S. military bureaucracy (the 'Pentagon') is more or less unaffected by this shifting power balance. On the other hand, the power of the Press has increased effectively, against (i) and (ii), but is somewhat muzzled by (iii).

—both military-technical and aid-giving technical-economic—as well as of its Cambodian and Laotian power-holding or power-sharing allies, from Cambodia and Laos), (iii) the 'peaceful' transition from a monarchy to a republic in Laos, to a communist-ruled 'constitutional monarchy' and then to a republic in Cambodia, and the implementation of a final decision in favour of the unification of the political state structure of North and South Vietnam on the basis of nationwide general elections.

These events were certainly casting their shadows before the American military pull-out and 'partial victory' in South Vietnam. But there are strong reasons to believe that it is the American military pull-out *without* a synchronized political withdrawal which cut the Gordian knot of the Vietnamese tangle and resolved the paradox. What achieved this was the recognition at a decisive moment in the war by the Vietnamese communist revolutionaries of the *impossibility* of an *outright* 'total victory' (as specified in E.1 in sect. 2.4), and total concentration on the objective of 'partial victory' (as defined in sect. 2.4 above). Indeed, the attempt at an *ex post* rationalization of the resolution of the Vietnamese paradox, with the benefit of hindsight, by taking credit for developments which matured only in 1975 or 1976, is not likely to be very successful. Both the post-Watergate developments in American domestic politics and the Indo-Chinese developments in 1975 and 1976 are adequately interpreted as chain-reactions detonated by the Vietnamese 'partial victory' earlier. If the Vietnamese revolutionaries had held out for a 'total victory' instead, not only is it likely that the Vietnam–American war would have been prolonged, with neither a 'partial' nor a 'total' victory again in sight, but that a stalemate, with the initiative in U.S. hands, would have continued at least in Laos (if not in Cambodia).[20] Moreover, with the Indo-China wars prolonged, the post-Watergate political crisis

[20] The definite crystallization of a Chinese communist policy of promoting a Sino-American *détente* directed against a Soviet–American *détente*, after the Helsinki European Conference, and during the Kissinger–Ford visits to China in 1975, might well have stalemated the Indo-China wars, if they had not ended earlier. For it has definitely muted Chinese criticism of the U.S. Indian Ocean base at Diego Garcia (which Vietnam has strongly opposed). It has also made Chinese spokesmen proclaim in the debate on the Angolan civil war at the United Nations in December 1975 what amounts to a policy of preferring *no* anti-imperialist revolution to a Soviet-aided revolution. (Of course, the Soviet Union had also adopted such a policy *vis-à-vis* the anti-American liberation war in Cambodia, though it corrected the mistake later.) On the other hand, however, the Fretilin-led liberation movement in Timor received the joint support of the Soviet, Chinese, and Indo-Chinese communists against an Indonesian invasion in December 1975. So Chinese policy in Angola may be only a regional ex-

in the U.S.A. might have been defused, with the focus on Vietnamese, rather than on Nixonian 'intransigence'.[21]

Appendix to Chapter 2:

The U.S.–Vietnam war game
—a mathematical restatement

In a game-theory model of the U.S.–Vietnam war, the problem can be split up and represented by two 2-person games, the first involving the 'front-liners', defined to refer to the U.S.–South Vietnam combination as player 1 and revolutionary Vietnam (defined to refer to North Vietnam and the Provisional Revolutionary Government of South Vietnam) as player 2. (All other definitions and assumptions are as stated in the text of Chapter 2 above.)

We write pay-off to each player as P^k, where $k = 1,2$ is a function of strategies i for player 1, and j for player 2 in each game.

1. In the *first* game, involving only the front-liners, each player has a choice between 0 ('partial defeat') and 1 ('partial victory') (see definitions on pages 24–5).

Thus

$$P^k = F^k(i,j) \quad \text{for } k = 1,2$$
$$i = 0,1$$
$$j = 0,1$$

The preference-orderings of the two sets of pay-offs by players 1 and 2 (as stated in pages 26–7 of Chapter 2) are:

$$F^1(1,0) \angle F^1(0,1)$$
$$F^2(0,1) \angle F^2(1,0)$$

---

periment rather than an expression of a settled global policy like Chinese policy *vis-à-vis* Bangladesh. The war memoirs of Dung Van Tien, published in May 1976, are reported to have made it clear that the decision to join final battle to liberate South Vietnam was taken only after the U.S. Congress made a drastic cut in military aid and compelled South Vietnam to fight a 'poor man's war'. But this U.S. decision was the outcome of the Vietnamese 'partial victory' embodied in the Paris agreement.

[21] A strong pointer was the unanimous support for President Ford's brinkmanship over the Cambodian capture of the U.S. ship *Mayaguez* in the U.S. Congress in May 1975.

It is easy to see that this produces a deadlock, or a stalemated war, given the environmental and other assumptions.

2. The outlook improves if we now concentrate on the game played by the 'side-liners', i.e. the U.S.S.R. and China.

In this second game, we refer to the U.S.S.R. as player 1, and to China as player 2, i refers to the U.S.S.R.'s strategy and j refers to China's strategy. In each case, the choice is between 0 (*not* aid revolutionary Vietnam) and 1 (aid revolutionary Vietnam).

The preference-orderings in this game are:

$$F^1(0,0) \angle F^1(0,1) \angle F^1(1,0) \angle F^1(1,1)$$
$$F^2(0,0) \angle F^2(1,0) \angle F^2(0,1) \angle F^2(1,1)$$

Here, as in the original prisoners' dilemma game, uncertainty as to what 'the other fellow will do' and mutual distrust play a major role. But, as in an assurance-problem game, the 'equilibrium outcome'—(1,1) for each—is also the preferred outcome, preferred to the other 'equilibrium outcome', viz. (0,0) for each, and therefore needs no enforcement (because of preference 3 in the Soviet–Chinese war aims) (see text of Chapter 2).

The unique outcome of the second game also breaks the deadlock in the first one, and determines the unique outcome, viz. 'partial victory'.

It should be noted that in these two linked games, or two sub-games of the U.S.–Vietnam war, the paradoxical element is *not* what it is either in the original prisoners' dilemma or in the assurance-problem game. The uniquely given equilibrium outcome is *not* suboptimal as in the prisoners' dilemma, *nor* (taking the two sub-games together) is it optimal in terms of the preferences of both. In this case, one side 'wins' and the other 'loses'; within the restrictions imposed by the environment (i.e. total victory being excluded, at least immediately) the winner takes all. As already stated, the paradoxical elements are that it is the 'side-liners' and not the 'front-liners' who determine the outcome, and it is precisely mutual distrust between the Soviet and the Chinese which make it possible for the revolutionary Vietnamese to tame *both* and get the better of the formidable U. S.–South Vietnamese adversary.

CHAPTER 3
Personality Cults

3.1 Introduction

The communist (in official Soviet terminology, socialist) personality cult[1] has been widely condemned in its Joseph Stalin incarnation, since 1956, though it was widely admired for more than twenty years earlier. The cult of Mao Tse-tung, both the man and his thought (or ideology), also in the making since 1936, officially launched in 1947, is still mainly admired. Condemned or admired (by communists, or non-communists or anti-communists), the cults about these two personalities represent the communist personality cult in its most highly developed forms. Moreover, these two cults have had (and continue to have) a worldwide impact: these two personalities truly bestride the continents, like the submerged Colossus of Rhodes, to which Shakespeare's Cassius likened Julius Caesar. There have also been lesser communist personality cults, *either* less heroic *or* less colossal in impact, e.g. the Yugoslav cult of Josip Broz Tito, or the North Korean cult of Kim Il Sung. On the other hand, it is doubtful if one can speak of a communist personality cult of Ho Chi Minh (see Lacouture, 1967, 1969, Ch. 11).

A phenomenon which has had a worldwide impact for over half a century, and shows no signs of fading, is one which ought to have a theory to explain it. However, both criticism and admiration have been predominantly emotive in nature, and the accidental, or 'irrational', nature of the phenomenon has been over-emphasized. Consequently, few systematic and convincing attempts have been made to work out a theory of the communist personality cult, which would identify its hypothetical social function and which could be discussed logically, after taking into account such relevant facts as are available for general consumption. Of course, as is to be expected, a very large number of experts have worked on several specific insights (the best integrated study I have come across is that by Robert Jay Lifton (1968, 1970), which also contains a useful

[1] The word 'cult' is used here in the sense of a system of religious beliefs, worship, and ritual, which is how Mao Tse-tung explicitly defines it (see Snow, 1971, 1972, pp. 67, 144–5).

summary of various points on which other writers have worked (ibid., pp. 19–20, 147–9)). However, none of these ventures seems to capture the essentials of the phenomenon, or to supply interpretations which I find satisfactory.

So in this chapter a fresh attempt is made to work out a hypothesis about the communist personality cult. We start with a retrospective, synoptic view of the facts about the phenomenon which are available for general consumption (and which have closely engaged the attention of the present writer continuously since the early 1930s) (sect. 3.2). An attempt is then made to construct a definition of the communist personality cult, which lists the main observed features of the phenomenon (sect. 3.3). In the next section (3.4), several inadequate explanations, mostly in terms of a discussion of analogues, are discussed. An interpretation in terms of the modern theory of individual and collective choice is then presented in sect. 3.5. This is followed by an *alternative* interpretation in terms of the modern mathematical theory of games (sect. 3.6). In sect. 3.7 possible *substitutes* for communist personality cults in communist societies[2] are considered.

3.2 A retrospective outline

Since the death of Karl Marx there has been a tendency to refer to founders and creative contributors to Marxian communist doctrine, and successful leaders of Marxian communist practice, in superlative, eulogistic, grandiloquent terms, which, if taken seriously, can be accepted or rejected by fiat, but not tested as true or false by available evidence. This has grown with the demonstrated political successes of the communist movement. At a certain point, the tendency crystallized as a tendency to create communist personality cults.

The nearest Frederick Engels came to launching a cult of Karl Marx[3] was to say at Marx's graveside in 1883 that Marx was 'the greatest living thinker who has ceased to think' (Marx and Engels, 1949, p. 153). (Five years earlier, Engels had merely described Marx as 'the man who was the first to give Socialism . . . a scientific foundation' (ibid., p. 143).)

[2] In this chapter, as elsewhere in the book, in general the confusing official communist practice of referring to communist revolutions or societies or personality cults as socialist revolutions, societies, and personality cults will be avoided.

[3] Marx did *not* launch a cult of his own personality or of Marxism, though he was intolerant, cantankerous, self-confident, like many medieval or modern scholars and revolutionary political leaders.

Vladimir Ilyich Lenin came closer to launching a cult of Marxism when he asserted seriously the unprovable propositions: (i) 'The Marxian doctrine is omnipotent because it is true' (1913) (Lenin, 1947, p. 70); (ii) in the period 1872–1904 'the Marxian doctrine gained a *complete* victory' in the labour movement (1913) (ibid., p. 77). (Earlier, in 1908, he had made a more moderate claim in realistic recognition of the challenge of Marxian 'revisionism', viz. that 'By the 'nineties this victory [i.e. of Marxian doctrine] was *in the main* completed' (ibid., p. 220)[4].) The Marxian communist cult that did, unquestionably, originate with Lenin is the cult of the Communist party, the 'revolutionary party of a new type' formally worked out in his 'What is to be done' (1902), of which more will be said in sect. 3.7, below.

Though Lenin himself did not do this in his lifetime, a personality cult of Lenin *was*, however, symbolically launched when after his death Lenin's body was embalmed and put on eternal display in the Red Square at Moscow (to which reference has been made in Chapter 2 of this book). This was soon followed by the widespread (perhaps universal) practice in the Bolshevik party of treating Lenin's every word as quotable scripture, beyond criticism, in settling all inner-party disputes. The logical next step was the launching of a cult of Leninism (or Leninist ideology) by Joseph Stalin, first positively in his *Foundations of Leninism* (1924), and then negatively (directed against his opponents among Bolsheviks) in his *Problems of Leninism* (1926).

The cult of Lenin and Leninism sponsored by Stalin led, logically, to a successor cult of Stalin, in the context, especially, of events as cataclysmic as those of 1924–51, and on the basis of the slogan 'Stalin is the Lenin of today'. Thus, unlike the cult of Lenin, the cult of Stalin was launched during Stalin's lifetime, probably first inside the Communist party's Central Committee sometime in the 1920s by Sergei Kirov (whose assassination in 1934 sparked off the Soviet purges and spy trials). The build-up of Stalin's image to cult proportions outside the Soviet Union was the work of such publicists as Emil Ludwig, the writer of biographical fiction, Bernard Shaw, the playwright, John Gunther, the journalist-reporter. Among the few writers who sympathized with Stalinist Communism of the 1930s, but opposed the makings of a communist personality cult, was the Bengali poet, Rabindranath Tagore, who made his position

---

[4] Italics mine.

clear in his letters from Russia, written in 1930 (Tagore, Bengali Calendar 1368, pp. 726–30).

The Stalin cult reached its *first crescendo* in 1937–8. Its highlights were: Nikolai Bukharin's confession of his failure as a communist revolutionary, and his eulogy of Stalin as 'the hope of the world . . . a creator' (in the trial in which he was convicted of treason and executed), and the 18th Congress of the Communist Party of the Soviet Union, in which Stalin lamented, somewhat prematurely as events were to show, that 'there were no enemies left to fight' in the Soviet Communist party and society. The Stalin cult reached its *second crescendo* with the publication and circulation of the *History of the Communist Party of the Soviet Union (Bolsheviks)*[5] in 1940, during the period of the Soviet-German Non-aggression Pact, which preceded the German Nazi invasion of the Soviet Union in June 1941.

The third, and *final crescendo* of the cult of Stalin came during the celebration of his seventieth birthday, and the 19th Congress of the Communist Party of the Soviet Union, a little before his death. This was the period of the Soviet victory against the German Nazi invaders, of communist revolutions (mostly with the aid of armed non-intervention by the Soviet armies) in eastern and central Europe, the Soviet victory in the brief war against Japan, followed by the successful communist war of liberation in China, etc.[6]

Unlike the Lenin cult, which *emerged* after Lenin's death, the Stalin cult did not *survive* the death of Stalin. At first, the cult seemed to fall into disuse. Then there was the violent denigration of Stalin, or the 'de-Stalinization'. Finally, symbolized by the removal of his embalmed remains from the Lenin mausoleum, Stalin survived as a deflated historical personality in the Soviet Union, though as a somewhat more inflated personality in China.[7] (The strict non-publication of Stalin's works in the Soviet Union, which dates back to 'de-Stalinization', means, however, that Stalin joins the exiled Trotsky, the executed Kamenev, Zinoviev, Bukharin, Radek, Preobrazhensky, etc. as only a half-person, or half-a-non-person. These

[5] The authorship was at first attributed to a commission of the Central Committee of the Soviet Communist party, and later to Joseph Stalin.

[6] This period also saw the only irrevocable setbacks suffered by the Stalin cult in Stalin's lifetime, viz. successful defiance by Josip Tito's counter-cult, and indirect competition from a Mao Tse-tung cult.

[7] In the September 1970 Lushan Plenum of the Chinese C.P., Lin Piao's directive that ninety-nine per cent of the classics to be studied should consist of Mao's works was countermanded, and Stalin's works were included among the classics (Schram, 1974, pp. 298, 352). But earlier Mao explicitly said of Stalin that 'he opposed our revolution, and our seizure of power' (ibid., p. 214).

are persons who are mentioned in Soviet literature, but strictly one-sidedly, i.e. only negatively in the case of Stalin's opponents, or on a low key, partly negatively and partly positively, as far as Stalin himself is concerned. But in no case is any mention made of what they had to say in their own defence.)

The most highly developed communist personality cult known so far is the cult of *both* Mao Tse-tung's person *and* of his thought (ideology). Like the Stalin cult, it has emerged in the lifetime of the person involved. It differs from the Stalin cult in at least *three* respects, viz. (i) it was *not* built only by using as a scaffolding the Lenin or the Stalin cult as was definitely the case with the Stalin cult. (There are, however, many strong hints that Maoist doctrines are *not* self-sufficient.)[8] (ii) Unlike the Stalin cult, which was an outgrowth of a Leninist cult about the near-divinity of the Communist party, the cult of Mao Tse-tung has never been fully integrated with a cult of the Chinese Communist party;[9] (iii) unlike the Stalin cult, which relied heavily on terror by the punitive organs of the communist state against suspected opponents within the party, exercised behind the backs of the party and the people (and endorsed *post factum*), the Mao Tse-tung cult has relied on inciting the masses to acts of terror in the streets, as well as inside homes[10] to remould suspected heretics, with a preference for mental (psychological) terror over physical torture and liquidation[11] inside the police station.

[8] This comes out in the fact that, like Stalin who quoted Leninist scripture meticulously to begin with, Mao Tse-tung also quoted Marx, Lenin, or Stalin (especially Stalin, in his 'New Democracy', which, however, Stalin never approved of).

[9] This came across most clearly when Mao declared to the party leaders during the cultural revolution that 'The pretext of "inside and outside [the party] being different" shows a fear of the revolution' (Ch'en, 1971, p. 24). A few months later, Mao drove the point home by announcing to the party leaders that he was personally 'responsible for the havoc' raised by the cultural revolution (ibid., pp. 42–3).

[10] Strongly symbolized by the inquisitorial methods used against members of Liu Shao-chi's family, and then by some converts among them against Liu Shao-chi in his home.

[11] Mao Tse-tung, unlike Stalin, does not seem to have liquidated his chief opponents or potential rivals. He has repeatedly disgraced and rehabilitated Li Li-san, one of his chief leftist opponents (see Li Li-san's speech at the 18th Congress of the Chinese Communist party, 1956, pp. 248–58). Teng Hsiao-ping was personally responsible for the nearest the Chinese Communist party has ever come (at the 8th Congress) to deflating the Mao Tse-tung cult (for details, see later in the text of this section). He was personally attacked by Mao Tse-tung during the cultural revolution (Ch'en, op. cit., p. 40) and disgraced. But he was rehabilitated after the downfall of Lin Piao and was again a deputy premier in 1974. Mao seems to have allowed one of his old opponents (never rehabilitated)

Dedicated hero-worship of Mao Tse-tung, which was the immediate prelude to the emergence of the Mao Tse-tung cult, most probably began with the eulogistic pen-portrait in Edgar Snow's *Red Star Over China* (1937). (Neither Liu Shao-chi's authoritative *How to be a Good Communist* (1939, 1951) (denounced during the Chinese cultural revolution), nor his *On Inner-Party Struggle* (1941), nor publications of the Communist International of the period, make any eulogistic references to Mao Tse-tung.)

The cult proper, officially called Mao Tse-tung Thought, seems to have been launched formally inside the Chinese Communist party around 1943 (it is very much there in Liu Shao-chi's article, 'Liquidate the Menshevist Ideology within the Party', 1943). It was launched for foreign consumption in an interview granted by Liu Shao-chi to the American journalist Anna Louise Strong in 1946, and published in *Amerasia* in 1947. The cult of Mao Tse-tung Thought was endorsed as the official creed of the Chinese Communist party in an amendment to the Party Constitution introduced by Liu Shao-chi at the 7th Congress of the party in 1947 (Liu Shao-chi, 1950, 1951, pp. 16, 28–35, 143). (The preamble on the general programme to the Party Constitution categorically declares Mao Tse-tung Thought to be the sole source of the Marxist-Leninist theory which guides the party (Liu Shao-chi, op. cit., p. 143). This was reaffirmed in Lin Piao's foreword to the second edition of *Quotations from Chairman Mao Tse-tung* (1966, 1967), or the so-called 'Red Book' of the Red Guards of the cultural revolution, written when Lin Piao was still the designated successor to Mao Tse-tung, as Liu Shao-chi had been earlier.) Identified at first as 'Chinese Marxism' (Liu Shao-chi, *On the Party*, pp. 29–30), it was claimed in 1951 to be the 'classic' version of Marxism-Leninism appropriate for all colonial and semi-colonial societies, Leninism being the 'classic' Marxist theory of revolution in imperialist countries (Lu Ting-yi, 1951, pp. 18–19). The Mao Tse-tung cult, like the Stalin cult, is very much a cult both of the *person*, and of his *thought* (or ideology). (Denials (e.g. Robinson, 1969, p. 29) are based on a mis-reading of facts about *both* the Stalin *and* the Mao cults. Admirers of the

---

to escape to the Soviet Union during the cultural revolution, viz. Wang Ming, and may have allowed Lin Piao to do the same. On the other hand, Mao certainly treated Liu Shao-chi to prolonged agony as a living whipping-boy or Guy Fawkes effigy when he was still nominally the President of the Chinese state (Robinson, 1969, p. 65). He has certainly driven a disgraced party leader, Kao Kang, to suicide.

theoretical quality of Mao's best 'thoughts' will also find some of Stalin's early writings admirable. On the other hand, there is no evidence that 'the main emphasis [with the Mao cult] is not upon the mortal man but on the immortal scriptures' (Robinson, op. cit.) The Mao Tse-tung who publicized his swimming of the Yangtse, who personally initiates the cultural revolution, who clinches the *détente* with Nixon, or reconstructs an axis with Bhutto, is no less active *in person* in promoting his cult than Stalin was.)

The Mao Tse-tung cult suffered one serious setback after the 20th Congress of the Communist Party of the Soviet Union in 1956, which denigrated Stalin and discredited the communist personality cult in the international communist movement for a time. Under its impact, at the 8th Congress of the Chinese Communist Party in 1956, (i) Teng Hsiao-ping, proposing a revision of the 1947 Party Constitution, claimed 'our Party abhors the deification of the individual', and (ii) in the preamble to the Party Constitution, the reference to the Thought of Mao Tse-tung was *deleted*, and the declaration was incorporated that 'No political party or person can be free from shortcomings and mistakes in work' (*8th National Congress of the Communist Party of China*, 1956, pp. 137, 143, 200–1).[12]

However, the setback was short-lived, and the revived Mao Tse-tung cult has experienced several crescendos. The first was during the 'Great Leap Forward' drive in the economy (1960–1), which survived the correction of its exaggerated expectations (sponsored by Mao) by the Chinese Communist party. The second was during the cultural revolution (1966–7). The third was reached in the post-cultural revolution period of the alleged (abortive) challenge to the Mao Tse-tung cult offered by a Lin Piao cult in the making. (It is doubtful whether the Mao Tse-tung cult has been either strengthened or shaken much in the oblique tussle with a weak cult of the dead Chou En-lai in the spring of 1976, which led to Teng Hsiao-ping being disgraced for the second time since the cultural revolution.) A fourth crescendo may be in the making since 1974 in the context of an ongoing anti-Confucian ideological struggle, in which some commentators see the beginnings of an *ideological* revolution, one which is more all-embracing than the earlier cultural revolution in re-moulding the Marxian 'superstructure' of Chinese communist society.

[12] This was slightly balanced by Liu Shao-chi's claim that 'our Party, under the leadership of the Central Committee headed by Comrade Mao Tse-tung, has not made any mistake in its line' (op. cit., vol. 1, p. 98).

The foregoing narrative is a forceful reminder that we are face to face with a bizarre phenomenon which recalls others such as Caesarism, Napoleonism or Bonapartism, fascist leader-cults, cults about charismatic religious leaders, paranoiac Roman, Moghul, or Russian emperors (or Chinese empresses), etc.

3.3 The *differentia specifica* of communist personality cults

Indeed, there are such strong resemblances between the modern communist personality cults and the kindred phenomena just mentioned, that it is easy to start discussing them, but to lose one's bearings, and end up by discussing something else.

To avert this, and to keep as firm a grip as possible over the problem under discussion, we need a precise definition of the communist personality cult. To work out a complete definition is difficult. But the *differentia specifica* of modern communist personality cults, which distinguish them from kindred phenomena, may be identified in terms of the attributes listed below. (The next section is devoted to assessment of kindred phenomena in terms of these attributes.)

S.1. The cult originates in a communist personality's recognized (acclaimed) political success in promoting an irreversible, or at least as yet non-reversed, 'revolutionary process' which has a worldwide impact. (A 'revolutionary process' is a term used in this study, as explained in the Glossary, to refer to a process which involves a change in any subset, or the full set of the (i) social, (ii) institutional, (iii) constitutional, and (iv) interstate *status quo*. A change, in (i), refers to a change in the socio-economic system, e.g. from capitalism to socialism, in (ii) refers to a change from one particular type of socio-economic system (e.g. of capitalism or socialism) to another, in (iii) to a change in the state-structure, (iv) to a change in the territorial demarcation between states. Stalin promoted (ii) and (iv), and to some extent (iii) and (i) (in the central and east European people's democracies). Mao Tse-tung has vigorously promoted changes in all four types of the *status quo* in China.)

S.2. The cult is based on its scriptures penned by the communist helmsman or coryphaeus[13] which expound doctrinal first principles on the basis of which all questions about politics, and in general all questions about human life, can, in principle, be answered. This is

[13] The term 'great helmsman' has been used to refer to Mao (Liu Shao-chi, 1956, p. 105) and 'coryphaeus' to refer to Stalin.

certainly true of the Mao Tse-tung cult, for which the 'Red Book' of quotations from Mao Tse-tung contains these first principles.[14] It was also true of the Stalin cult, at least after the publication of the *History of the Communist Party of the Soviet Union* (*Bolsheviks*). For Lenin, neither Marx's writings, nor his own, incorporated, more or less self-sufficiently, all or most such 'first principles'. German philosophy, English political economy, and French socialism were the 'sources and component parts of Marxism' (Lenin, 1947, pp. 70–5). However, he seems to have regarded Marx's writings if not as stating complete first principles by themselves, then as the *sole channel* through which communists may learn the first principles from which everything can be understood. This prepared the ground for the later *codification* of relevant Marxism by Stalin and Mao. Thus, while the reading of Marx and Lenin was never discouraged by Stalin, and the reading of Marx, Lenin, and Stalin was never discouraged by Mao, under the Stalin cult's influence the stress was on reading Stalin, and under the Mao Tse-tung cult the stress has been on reading Mao. On the other hand, encouragement (or opportunity) of reading the three 'sources' of Marxism, i.e. German philosophy, English political economy, and French socialist theory *in the original*, has been far less strong than the encouragement to read *about them* in the Marxist classics or in the commentaries by Marxists.

S.3. The cult is based on the conviction that the personality at the centre of the cult is *infallible*, like the other 'great teachers', i.e. Marx, Engels, and Lenin (and, in the case of the Stalin cult, also Stalin). Hence, the corpus of doctrines of the cult includes a method for rationalizing every belief, thought, and action inspired by the cult as being ultimately correct, and infallibly so. (Criticism (i.e. expression of doubt about the scriptures) and self-criticism (i.e. admission of mistakes by upholders or opponents of the cult) are allowed. But this is because (i) 'the truth is on our side, and the basic masses, the workers and peasants, are on our side' (Lin Piao, (ed.), *Quotations from Chairman Mao Tse-tung*, 1966, 1967, p. 220). In other words, the function of criticism is only to prove other doctrines, and persons other than the cult's personality, wrong. (ii) Sceptics, including 'reactionaries', should be allowed to 'bloom and contend', so that they can be exposed and hostile ideology eradicated (Mao Tse-tung, quotations in Ch'en, 1971, pp. 33–4, 49, 51–4);[15]

---

[14] See, however, n. 7 of this chapter.
[15] This is a specifically Chinese communist (Maoist) doctrine, unknown to Stalinist theory and practice.

(iii) self-criticism is the normal method of functioning of the cult's supreme personality because of (a) an eternal flux in the forces of life—'theory is grey, but green is the golden tree of life' (Goethe) —and (b) the primacy of matter over mind (even an infallible one) are articles of faith in Marxian ideology. However, it is also an article of faith in the cult's Marxian ideology that the supreme personality *infallibly* corrects himself. So, the outcome of criticism and self-criticism can never, by definition, endanger the cult's survival.)

S.4. The cult's founder engages in eternal strife against rival ideologies, to keep everlasting green and growing the tree of the cult's ideology. The contention is first against anti-cult, or non-cult, Marxists, who are called 'revisionists', because they revise pre-cult Marxian doctrine in directions *contrary* to the cult's own revision. They are either liquidated (as most of Stalin's Marxist opponents were), or driven to suicide (as Kao Kang was, by Mao Tse-tung (Schram, 1966, pp. 284–5)), or expelled (and exiled, like Leon Trotsky was by Stalin), or converted (as Bukharin was, briefly, during Stalin's struggle against the Old Bolsheviks, or as Li Li-san was, after fifteen years in a political wilderness (*8th National Congress of the Communist Party of China*, 1956a, pp. 253–8)). This first 'revisionist' group is usually eliminated after the Communist party and society officially endorses the communist personality cult, so that 'there is no one left to fight'. The struggle is then entirely against the false devotees of the cult, called (by the Chinese) 'neo-revisionists', who pay lip-service to the cult, but oppose its juggernaut progress in practice (as Mao accused Teng Hsiao-ping of doing during the cultural revolution),[16] or are chosen to serve as highly placed 'whipping-boys' (as Liu Shao-chi seems to have been, during the cultural revolution), or who plot secretly to destroy one personality cult and replace it by another (as Lin Piao is alleged to have done on the eve of the Sino-American *détente*).

Curiously, at no stage have the founders of communist personality cults contended directly (and seriously) with pre-Marxian, or modern anti-Marxist or non-Marxist ideologies. Just as the ideology of the cult is supposed to embody all that is best in man's heritage by definition, revisionist or neo-revisionist ideology is supposed, also by definition, to embody all that is worst in that heritage. So 'alien'

---

[16] Mao said Teng was 'deaf', had 'for six years . . . made no general report of work to me', and was 'lazy' (Ch'en, 1971, p. 40).

pre-Marxian, anti-Marxian, and non-Marxian ideologies have been fought at second hand, by proxy, so to speak. (This seems to be true even of the only apparent exception, viz. the campaigns against Confucius and Confucian ideology in China, on which more will be said in the next chapter.)

S.5. The cult's personality being mortal, its ideology's immortality must be ensured at all costs. Stalin hoped, but failed, to achieve this by making a 'democratic-centralist'[17] Communist party, dedicated to the Stalin cult, its institutionalized custodian. Mao evidently hopes to do better, by institutionalizing periodic renovatory assaults by the masses, who use the methods of direct democracy (in violation of the rules of democratic centralism) but act in the name of Mao Tse-tung Thought, on the democratic-centralist Communist party, itself dedicated to the cult of Mao Tse-tung.

S.1–5 capture most of the observed common attributes of the most important communist personality cults, as well as the special attributes of the cult of Mao Tse-tung. These attributes are also mutually complementary, and support one another. Thus S.1, which traces the origin of the cults in recognized personal successes in non-reversed revolutionary processes, is essential to propose the claim to infallibility (S.2). On the other hand, this claim can hardly be identified (or tested) unless it is constantly *contrasted* with others' fallibility (hence S.3). Finally, devotion to the cult can hardly be cultivated unless the durability (immortality) of its ideology makes up for the mortality of its personality.

3.4 Analogies and inadequate explanations

Not all the attributes of communist personality cults mentioned in the previous section are found in the kindred phenomena with which they are often confused.

The least illuminating is the analogue of the fascist leader-cult. The best-known fascist leader-cults, the Italian and the German, do not have attribute S.1, because the institutional changes (in capitalism) they introduced have all been reversed. Moreover, the fascist cults collapsed at the first touch of adversity. (By contrast, the Stalin cult survived the major reverses of Hitler's surprise attack and open defiance by the Yugoslav communists. The Mao cult survived the challenge during the 'hundred flowers' campaign (see reference in Liu Shao-Chi (1956), p. 64, and also Schram (1974), pp. 216, 330,

---

[17] This will be discussed further in sect. 3.5.

337), during the 'Great Leap Forward' in the economy, during the early stages of the cultural revolution.) The second attribute (S.2) is also missing in the fascist leader-cults. Fascist ideologies may have been derived from the romantic philosophical tradition of Nietzsche, Fichte, Rousseau, or Heidegger, but the doctrines of the fascist leaders were never systematized, as Stalin's and Mao's have been, to form the basis for the continuation of the cults after the death of their leaders.[18]

The analogy with the hero-worship of the 'nationalist' leaders of Asia in the twentieth century is closer. However, of these, the least like a communist personality cult is the legend of Kemal Ataturk, who probably did not expound a special ideology of his own, but was invested with one by Stalin and Mao, rather than by Kemal himself (Mao, 1940, in Mao Tse-tung, 1954, vol. 3, pp. 125, 251). (The same probably holds for the alleged Nasser cult of more recent times, which has been discarded by Sadat.) Sun Yat-sen's 'Three People's Principles', viz. 'alliance with Russia, co-operation with the communists and assistance to the peasants and workers' (Mao Tse-tung in 1940, see ibid., p. 135), sanctified by Mao, are practical, rather than profound, ideological principles such as might have been inscribed in the scriptural texts of an ideological cult which survived him.[19]

The cult of Gandhi bears a stronger resemblance to communist personality cults. It reveals all five attributes S.1–5 to some extent. Indeed, parallels may even be drawn between Mao's methods during the Chinese cultural revolution and the Gandhi-directed boycott of schools and colleges in India in the 1920s, his proposals for a re-volution in methods of education, his exercise of dictatorial powers over Congress party policy during crucial periods as an 'outsider', sometimes when he was not even formally a member of the Congress organization, etc. However, Gandhi's highly original, but not too successful, post-Tolstoyan ideology was not well integrated with his almost equally original,[20] but decidedly more successful Real-

---

[18] Only Oswald Spengler's *Decline of the West* qualifies as systematized 'ideology' of German (though not Italian) fascism. But it does not put the main focus on a fascist leader-cult (see Spengler, 1926, 1954, vol. 1, Ch. 1).

[19] But note that Mao is said to have referred to Sun as 'a genius', along with Marx, Engels, Lenin, and Stalin, as recently as in 1971, in accounts which were not authorized for publication till the end of 1975 (Schram, 1974, p. 294).

[20] 'almost equally original', because Gandhian Realpolitik may have been an extension to Indian politics of the highly original methods of Realpolitik worked out by a master of Realpolitik in Bengal, Chitta Ranjan Das, who died in 1924.

politik (based on the ultimate principles: non-violence is better than violence, but violence is better than passivity in politics). Hence, this analogy, too, does not take us very far in our attempt to find a rational explanation for communist personality cults.

Nehru articulated his 'ideological principles'—on the basis of which, unlike Gandhi, he *acted* more successfully than did Gandhi on *his*—even less clearly than Gandhi. He acted, methodically and successfully, to implement an amalgam of Gandhian and British Fabian 'ideological principles',[21] in his advocacy of 'non-alignment' in world politics, and in his institutional-economic strategy of the 'socialistic pattern' in India, which he accurately defined as a type of 'mixed economy', with the accent on a growing public sector, i.e. as a version of state capitalism. However, at least as important as these was Nehru's contribution to the Realpolitik of establishing a self-perpetuating 'political dynasty', which has solved several 'succession problems' of the Congress party leadership in India which arose after the 'abdication' of Gandhi in favour of Nehru in 1946,[22] the assassination of Gandhi in 1948, after Nehru's death, etc. The modalities of Nehru's solution of such problems had nothing to do with any 'ideological principles' expounded by him, nor with any 'personality cult' comparable to the communist personality cult[23] (which is why it cannot help us in finding a rationale for the communist personality cult). But it was a solution to a problem of a general nature, which engaged the attention of Hobbes (1651, 1974, Ch. 19), and which has emerged as a major political problem in modern times in communist societies (as we shall see in the next chapter) and on the Indian subcontinent (in an acute form in Bangladesh, where it has become a wider problem involving both a civil and military political élite). It may possibly also re-emerge as a major problem in western societies. Straws in the wind are: the unusual solutions to modern succession problems in France and Germany (with the rise and fall of Charles de Gaulle in France and the ouster of Willy Brandt in West Germany) and in the U.S.A. after the assassination of President Kennedy and the ouster of President Nixon.

The analogy with Caesarism or Bonapartism is rather more promising. What Shakespeare's Cassius or Brutus says of Julius Caesar

[21] The reference is to the pro-Soviet communist, pro-Stalinist late Fabianism of Sidney and Beatrice Webb, and of Bernard Shaw.
[22] i.e. when Gandhi declared Nehru to be his 'political heir'.
[23] On this see Tibor Mende (1958), pp. 34–8.

sounds remarkably like what Trotsky has said of Stalin, or a Liu Shao-chi (or a Lin Piao) might have said of Mao. Napoleon's remark 'one must first plunge into a big battle, and then see what happens', quoted by Lenin to justify his own 'gamble' with a socialist revolution in conditions in Russia which were 'unripe' for such a revolution, is very much like Mao's 'I ignited the cultural revolution' speech in October 1966 (Ch'en, 1971, pp. 42–5). One can even invoke literary licence to imagine that Caligula's madness was a feint for communistic reforms as was the alleged communistic paranoia of Stalin's last days (Albert Camus's play of 1944 (Camus, 1965, pp. 12–18) bears this interpretation, although it was probably written about Hitler). But all this is rather laboured, and helps us little in our search for a rational explanation of modern communist personality cults. Caesarism and Bonapartism represent, at best, cults of military-political leadership. They do *not* represent cults about political personalities who also founded ideologies,[24] who laid claims to infallibility and ideological immortality, as modern communist personality cults do.

Analogies with phenomena in the long history of doctrinal disputes in the Christian churches also yield some (imperfect) insights. Bertrand Russell thought that the essence of the Stalin cult was that Stalin, the holder of supreme power in the Soviet state, was able to make modern Russians obey him, rather than dialectical materialism (Russell, 1946, 1962, p. 16, n.2). He suggested that this was traceable to the Byzantine *denial* of the Socratic-Arian Christian dictum that 'we should obey God rather than Man' (ibid., p. 16). On the other hand, he interpreted the Lutheran Protestant revolt as a revival of the Socratic-Arian Christian doctrine (ibid., p. 19). Mao's revolt against communist orthodoxy can easily be traced to the Socratic-Arian Christian dictum, paraphrased as 'we must obey the Thought of Mao Tse-tung rather than the Communist party which rules in his name'. However, Russell clearly underestimates the role of Stalin's ideological, as distinct from his administrative, activity. Mao's dictum, too, is that we should obey *both* God (Mao Tse-tung Thought) and Man (Mao Tse-tung). The difference between Stalin and Mao, and their respective cults, as suggested earlier, is a matter of specific, albeit important, detail, viz. on whether strict democratic

[24] though Napoleon did leave behind him the classic principles of bourgeois law, which he helped draw up as the *Code Napoléon*. It was Carl von Clausewitz who very nearly established a Napoleonic 'ideology' which unified the theories of politics and war (Rapoport, 1968, 1974, p. 21).

centralism in the party, or violation of democratic centralism, *provided* it is done in the name of Mao Tse-tung Thought (or, more generally, 'dialectical materialism'), is to be relied upon to make the cult immortal.[25] *Unlike* the Mao Tse-tung cult, a Dubcek cult *might* conceivably have emerged in Czechoslovakia in 1968, which broke the self-imposed limits of the Stalin and Mao cults, and declared, as Russell evidently advocated, that 'we must obey God [dialectical materialism] rather than Man [the Communist party]'. But it did not. Even the authoritative Soviet indictment of Dubcek's policies did not accuse him, or anybody else in the Czechoslovak Communist party, of building up a Dubcek cult with such a set purpose (see Pravda Editorial, Defence of Socialism—supreme internationalist duty, Tass, 22 Aug. 1968 (Engl. trans.)).

Thus the analogies considered in this section remind us that modern communist personality cults are *not* to be dismissed as rare freaks of nature. They may be with us for a long time,[26] as some of the kindred phenomena have been in the past. However, these parallels are too inexact as analogues to explain communist personality cults. (There is the additional difficulty that most of these kindred phenomena have been described rather than explained, in terms of some social function—if any—that they have fulfilled.)

So we seem to have reached a tantalizing dead end: the phenomenon (communist personality cult) *is* serious, but analogies *do not* explain it! However, the problem might be solved if we could construct down-to-earth hypotheses about the possible function of personality cults in communist societies. To these we now turn.

3.5 A choice-theoretic explanation

To examine a possible rational explanation of the communist personality cult with the help of the modern theory of collective choice, we must start with a digression on problems of economic planning.

There are two more or less universal, and apparently indelible, features of communist economic planning:

[25] At one time, until the 9th Congress of the Chinese Communist party in April 1969, it looked as if Mao Tse-tung's Red Guards and Red Rebels would actually be encouraged to *destroy* the edifice of the Chinese Communist party. Such an outcome was visualized in the Bengali poet Rabindranath Tagore's play of 1911, *Achalayatan,* in which the personality about whom there was a cult incited his red-capped peasants to raze the establishment built in his name to the ground. But the dénouement so far is only that the party hierarchy has been reshuffled.

[26] Mao expects his own cult to last a few centuries (Schram, 1966, p. 329).

S.6 'Politics is in command' over the planning process, i.e. political processes working *outside* the economic market structure set plan targets.

S.7 The method of 'democratic centralism' is used in drawing up plans.

These are the observed features of communist planning, whatever importance one attaches to unverifiable reports about (i) marginal adjustments brought about by such factors as transactions in the black market (or the so-called 'parallel economy') which exists in communist countries (with the possible exception of China and Cuba), and (ii) administrative (executive) interference with the planning process by holders of power in the party and the state (e.g. Khrushchev) or by personalities who have founded a cult (e.g. Stalin's 'fulfil the five year plan in four years' drives or Mao's 'Great Leap Forward' drive).

S.6 is discussed in more detail, with reference to the technical literature on communist planning, elsewhere (for a discussion, with a summary of references to the literature, see Bose, 1975, Ch. 14). Suffice to note here that in communist countries plan-*formulation* is invariably[27] the outcome of a political voting process working 'outside the market' (though the market is *also* a kind of voting system which operates as a check). But plan-*implementation* is based on the utilization of market forces. The arguments in favour of such strictly 'political' planning, involving a *splitting-up* of the planning process into two parts, are not entirely clear. It may be that an *integrated* planning process, in which the planning centre sends down 'quota' directives, and the enterprises send up 'price' information, can do better than all alternatives.[28]

Now, in the literature on the modern (mathematical) theory of collective choice (originating in the work of Kenneth Arrow (1951, 1963, 1970)), there has been an extensive discussion of an 'impossibility theorem' which is applicable to 'political' planning, including the 'democratic-centralist' type of political planning which we are discussing here.

Briefly, the theorem proves that the mutual compatibility of the following four political-economic conditions is impossible:

[27] except, perhaps, in Yugoslavia during a short (since terminated) experiment in full 'market planning' in a communist political set-up.

[28] provided, at least, that the problems of 'parallel economy' transactions and 'counter-planning' by enterprises against the planning-centre through a game of bluff are solved independently of the planning process adopted.

S.8. The condition of 'unrestricted domain' (i.e. the existence of a complete social ordering, or the ordering of alternative social states, in the minds of individuals).

S.9. The so-called 'weak Pareto principle' (which says that if everyone prefers x to y, then society must also prefer x to y).

S.10. The so-called 'independence of irrelevant alternatives' (which says that social choice between x and y is unaffected by (i) individual ranking of any other alternative, and also (ii) the intensity of preference for x and y (Sen, 1970, Ch. 7, pp. 89–91)).

S.11. The condition of (personal) *non*-dictatorship.

In particular, it has been pointed out that in a 'multi-stage voting system' (which refers to an essential feature of communistic 'democratic centralism', as contrasted to single-stage 'direct democracy') there is either a violation of condition S.11 (non-dictatorship) or of condition S.8 (unrestricted domain) (Pattanaik, 1971, Ch. 3, pp. 59–61).

In other words, since conditions S.9–11 can reasonably be assumed to hold always, this formal result can be interpreted in the present context to state:

S.12. With political, democratic-centralist, communist planning, there must either be (i) (personal) dictatorship or (ii) restricted domain (i.e. it will exclude some logically possible configurations of individual preferences).

Now S.12 (i), i.e. democratic-centralist political planning based on personal dictatorship, implies *abolition* of individual choice (except on the part of the dictator), or *effective* rationing of all goods and resources, as *attempted* under Soviet 'War Communism' (1919–21) or with a similar experiment in China during the 'Great Leap Forward' drive in the early 1960s. Both attempts were more or less abandoned as failures. In terms of S.12, the failures could be attributed to the *absence* of a communist personality cult during Soviet 'War Communism', and the *ineffectiveness* of the communist personality (Mao Tse-tung) cult during the 'Great Leap Forward'.[29] Thus S.12 (i) seems to supply a rationale for a communist personality cult in the context of democratic-centralist political planning in a communist society, though it does this only *negatively*.

[29] Mao's remarks to Edgar Snow in 1970, that a personality cult was needed in China earlier, but is not needed any more, seem to confirm this (Snow, 1971, 1972, pp. 67, 144). For an unauthorized account of Mao's successful defence of his cult in the 'self-criticism' after the 'Great Leap Forward', see his speech at the Lushan conference in July 1959 (Schram, 1974, pp. 131–46).

On the other hand, S.12 (ii), viz. democratic-centralist political planning with restricted domain, does seem to supply, directly and *positively*, a rationale for the communist personality cult.

By establishing various 'value-restricted' patterns of individual preferences, a communist personality cult may make it possible for democratic-centralist socialist planning to work. It may do so in various ways: (i) it may establish more or less homogeneous (i.e. *identical*) preference patterns among individuals, or at least give 'single-peaked' preference patterns (which is equivalent to a condition in which any one in any triple of possible alternatives is accepted as 'not worst' by all voters (Sen, 1969, p. 205)), (ii) it may make individuals adopt extremist positions around any one issue of planning (which is equivalent to a 'single-caved' preference pattern (Inada, 1964). ((ii) may have been achieved by Stalin during the First and Second Five Year Plans. According to some studies, (i) may be Mao's achievement in the aftermath of the cultural revolution (Wheelwright and McFarlane, 1970, 1973, p. 20).)

In fact, of course, communist personality cults have sometimes been reduced to 'personal' political planning in which 'democratic centralism' becomes a meaningless ritual. The rationale of this is suggested by a particular 'escape route' from the impossibility result which has been formally discussed in the literature. If we (i) do not insist that *all* concerned must be consulted when making a plan, and (ii) assume that there is a 'planner' who acts on the basis of his 'impersonal' or 'ethical' preferences, then the impossibility result can be avoided. (The planner's 'ethical preferences' are said to be determined when he considers that there is an equal chance of his being in the shoes of those for whom he plans (Sen, 1969, pp. 210–13; Pattanaik, 1971, pp. 151–66; Harsanyi, 1955).) Assumption (i) is justified on the reasonable ground that it is *unavoidable*, since any political plan must decide investment patterns, whose results affect the unborn, who cannot possibly be 'consulted' (Sen, 1961; 1969, p. 212, n.1). Assumption (ii) directly *prescribes* a communist personality cult, albeit of a personality who is completely, benevolently 'ethical'. (There may be doubts about this: doubts as to whether Stalin did put himself in the shoes of the collective farmers during the Soviet First Five Year Plan, or whether Mao did this in the aftermath of the cultural revolution.) But if assumption (ii) holds, it requires, strictly, a *single* supreme planner. For if there is more than one 'planner', each acting 'impersonally' and 'ethically', there is a problem of non-uniqueness in the outcome of political plan-making, which must be avoided (Pattanaik, 1971, p. 166, interpreting Sen, 1969, pp. 212–13).

3.6 A game-theoretic explanation

Drastic changes in the institutional *status quo* are an observed feature of communist societies. Thus in the Soviet Union there have been such changes during War Communism, the new economic policy, the pre-World War II Five Year Plans, during the Khrushchev reforms, the more recent 'economic reforms' in industry and agriculture, etc. There have also been several drastic changes in the institutional *status quo* in China. Whether some of these changes are regarded as mistakes or not, none of them have been completely undone (by a *return* to the *status quo ante*). Moreover, Marxian doctrine, albeit somewhat nebulously, ordains changes in the institutional *status quo* as society advances from the 'lower stage' to the 'higher stage' of communism (see Marx's 'Critique of the Gotha Programme', or Lenin's 'The State and Revolution').

It is also an observed feature that all decisions for such institutional change in communist societies have been, formally as well as in substance, *unanimous* decisions, first by the Communist party's central committee and the communist central government, then by the entire Communist party (through a 'democratic-centralist' procedure, which includes such phenomena as (i) dissidents at various levels conceding defeat, (ii) engaging in abject, Tolstoyan 'self-criticism', which is sometimes directed by one ex-dissident against another, (iii) 'unanimous' denunciations of those who try to prevent unanimous decisions being taken, and finally (iv) a popular vote, at soviets, or people's congresses, or 'on the streets', or, more rarely, at national elections).

All this can be rationalized by a game-theoretic 'assurance-problem' model (which we have already met in Chapter 2) of institutional mutation of a communist society which is facilitated by a communist personality cult.

We start with the following *assumptions about the environment*:

S.13. There is 'full socialism', i.e. revolutionary socialization of all the means of production has been achieved.

S.14. Decisions about institutional reforms in the communist society must be taken *unanimously* by all members of the community.

To these we add assumptions about individual preferences:

S.15. Each individual will reveal his preference (i.e. 'vote' for) institutional reform if others will do so. He will vote against it, if he thinks others will vote against.

S.16. However, each individual will prefer all voting for a proposed institutional reform, to all voting against it.

Assumptions S.15–16 together define the problem as an 'assurance problem'. A third feature of the individual's preference pattern in such a setting, viz. that each individual regards some voting for, others voting against, the proposed reform as a second-best outcome, is ruled out by environmental assumptions S.13–14. Assumption S.16 in the individual's preference-ordering may be regarded as reflecting a belief in institutional change in a communist society as a sign of progress towards 'full communism'. Assumptions S.15–16 are mutually compatible, and ensure that all voting unanimously for a proposed institutional reform of the communist society will be regarded as the best outcome. However, the best outcome will materialize *only if* each has the assurance that all others will vote for change.

This is where the communist personality cult comes in. It supplies the needed assurance, and allows the best outcome to materialize. It also ensures a *unique* best-outcome solution of the problem. (Formally, the unique best-outcome solution is sure only in a strictly two-person version of the assurance-problem game (Sen, 1969, pp. 13–15). But a communist personality cult converts the many-person problem into a two-possible outcomes game, by making it impossible for anyone to visualize any outcome other than all voting *for* the reform proposed by the cult's personality, or all voting against. Assumptions S.15–16 then ensure a unique best-outcome solution.)

3.7. Alternatives to communist personality cults

One of the communist personality cults, the Stalin cult, has fallen into disuse (though there is no sign of such a thing happening to the Mao Tse-tung cult). Such a possibility does not seem to have been visualized during Stalin's lifetime, at least not by Stalin (or Mao).[30] But it is a fact, at least in the Soviet Union and eastern Europe (no communist country has revived the Stalin cult, though many have

[30] Judging by the studied deflation of the Stalin cult by Stalin's appointed successors, Malenkov, Molotov, Beria, and Khrushchev, *they* apparently did, at least Khrushchev said so, in his 'secret' speech on the Stalin cult at the 20th Party Congress of the C.P.S.U.

criticized the denigration of the cult by the Soviet Communist party). This fact of life has caused Mao Tse-tung to formulate a doctrine of the possibility of peaceful, counter-revolutionary 'change of colour' by a Communist party and society.[31] It has also made him experiment with new methods to make the Mao cult immortal.

The conclusions Mao Tse-tung seems to have drawn from the fading-out of the Stalin cult will be discussed in the next chapter.

Here we concentrate on the phenomenon that a communist society has survived in the Soviet Union, despite the elimination of the Stalin cult. (For our purposes, a communist society is one in which the principal means of production are publicly owned.) A complete theory of the communist personality cult must take this into account.

The *first* function of a personality cult in a communist society is that it makes the political democratic-centralist planning system work.

Now, some ideas put forward in the analytical literature on the Arrow-type 'impossibility theorems' can be suitably interpreted to see how a political democratic-centralist planning system can work *in the absence* of a communist personality cult, viz.:

(i) A communist élite[32] may make plans arbitrarily, in the name of 'society', which is set up 'as an abstraction vis-à-vis the individual', though the early Marx rejected this method (Marx, 1844, 1961, p. 105).

(ii) Plan-making may be possible without the personality cult, because 'value-restricted' individual preferences may crystallize, to eliminate the 'impossibility' result. Such 'value-restricted' preferences may emerge independently of the personality cult because of (a) the euphoria of a proletarian internationalist patriotism (on which more will be said in later chapters of Part I of this book), (b) the prevalence of a tendency to think in extremist terms on issues involved in making plans, (c) a watered-down 'limited leadership' by party leaders, which achieves the desired purpose (this is the case if there is universal agreement with the opinion of the leader about the relative position of any *one* alternative in every triple of alternatives (Sen, 1969, p. 206)).

(iii) If the condition of 'independence of irrelevant alternatives'

---

[31] But at least up to March 1969 Mao Tse-tung thought 'The broad masses and the majority of the party members and cadres in the Soviet Union are good and revolutionary' (Ch'en, 1971, p. 158).

[32] a self-selecting meritocracy formed on the basis of pragmatic notions about what constitutes communist merit.

can be disregarded, multi-stage 'rank-order voting' makes it possible to work out political democratic-centralist plans. (In rank-order voting, alternatives in each voter's preference-ordering are ranked according to marks given in descending order, and the alternative scoring top marks in the ballot wins (Sen, 1970, p. 39). It has been suggested in the post-Arrow literature on the impossibility result that the importance of the condition of independence of irrelevant alternatives has been over-emphasized, because a fetish has been made of the alleged impossibility of interpersonal utility comparisons.[33] If we grant that *partial* interpersonal comparisons of utility are always possible, multi-stage rank-order voting may eliminate the impossibility result with respect to democratic-centralist political planning.

There remains, however, the *second* function of the personality cult in communist society, its role as an instrument of institutional change (discussed in sect. 3.6).

A preliminary point to note is that a particular cult may not fulfil this function very well *indefinitely*. From being an instrument of institutional change, the cult may become an instrument of institutional inertia or conservatism. Failing powers of the personality of the cult, physiologically, intellectually, or ethically and morally—which he may not be willing to, or be able to, or be allowed by his devotees to, recognize—may be responsible. (This may have been the case with the Stalin cult, though evidence is inconclusive.[34]) Judging by half-a-century's observation, and/or by the Marxian hypothesis about communist societies, the institutional mutation of such societies seems inevitable. If so, a communist society must destroy a personality cult which has become a conservative force.

However, once a communist personality cult has created a 'crisis of conservatism', and has been discarded, it is unlikely that a substitute communist personality cult will easily replace it. (Despite praise of Leonid Brezhnev's 'leading role', or earlier of Nikita Khrushchev's, neither a Brezhnev nor a Khrushchev cult has crystallized.)

A cult of the infallible Communist party, which represents the infallibility of the revolutionary people (or at any rate, of the majority

[33] Sen (1973, 1974), Ch. 1. Roughly, the argument is that to compare my satisfaction with yours is impossible, because I am not you. But this overstates the difficulty, for my satisfaction may be partially comparable with yours.

[34] Stalin's alleged paranoia does not seem to have been noticed during wartime summit meetings—or was it because Stalin, or his observers, were suffering from perfect schizophrenia?

of the people who can do no wrong), might do better as a cult to supply the element of 'assurance' needed to facilitate decisions on institutional change. Whoever is in charge of the party apparatus, rather like Protestant monarchs of Europe who claimed the title 'defender of the faith', might then invoke the cult of the infallible party to secure such decisions.

The price of trying to do without *all* 'cults'—of personality, or party, or people—in a communist society, to establish 'the rule of reason', may be institutional inertia or conservatism. The communist society is then converted into a club which debates, but does not decide. On the other hand, a moral or ethical 'revolution' may abolish the individuals' preference-patterns indicated by S.15–16 in sect. 3.6 (i.e. the preference-pattern which creates an 'assurance problem' in the matter of institutional change in a communist society). In that case, disregarding the condition of 'independence of irrelevant alternatives' (for reasons stated earlier in this section), multi-stage rank-order voting may ensure decisions in favour of institutional change. Such decisions will be based on debates about the merits of alternative proposals, will also reflect irreducible 'value judgments' of individuals (e.g. about the future which no one can forecast with certainty), but will *not* be the outcome of a communist 'cult' of personality or party, or an infallible people.

CHAPTER 4

Chinese Communist Ideology

4.1 Introduction

CHINESE communist ideology has a number of traits which distinguishes it from Marx's, or Lenin's, or Stalin's versions of Marxian ideology.

But there are several traits of Chinese communist ideology which are not distinctive at all, but are often thought to be such by critics, admirers, or believers. Some of the critics maintain that Chinese communist (identified as Maoist) ideology has some traits which prove that it is not Marxian or communist at all. Some admirers argue that Maoism is closer to a modern socialist anarchism than to Leninism or Stalinism. Some believers also identify distinguishing traits which are not, in fact, to be found in *any* version of Marxism, including Maoist Marxism.

In this chapter we first discuss false notions about the originality of Chinese communist ideology. We then discuss those traits which do seem to be distinctive, which constitute original contributions to Marxian ideology, and their implications.

4.2 Unoriginal traits

There are some traits of Chinese communist (Maoist)[1] ideology which seem to be *falsely* regarded as original and distinctive, distinguishing it from other versions of Marxian ideology.[2] These traits can be said to be reflected in Maoist propositions which can be roughly classified as referring to (i) problems of power, revolution, and war, (ii) the specific characteristics of the Chinese revolution, and (iii) problems of world politics and world revolution. They are discussed below, along with comments. (As elsewhere in this book, every effort has been made to check words and events referred to from supporting as well as critical comments. The aim is to ensure

---

[1] For reasons which are well known, and have been indicated to some extent in the previous chapter, in this chapter Chinese communist ideology will be *identified* with Maoist ideology.

[2] As was indicated in the previous chapter, in this book *all* interpretations of Marxian ideology by those who claim to be Marxists are regarded as versions of Marxian ideology.

that no misrepresentation occurs, though Mao can often be quoted
for, and counter-quoted against, many principles in dispute between
communists, and among communists and their critics.)

(i) *Power, revolution, war*

Power: (a) 'Political power grows out of the barrel of a gun' (Mao,
1954a, p. 272), (b) 'Whoever has an army has power, for war settles
everything' (ibid., p. 271), (c) 'the army is the chief component of
state power' (Lin Piao (ed.), *Quotations from Mao Tse-tung*, p. 53).

In general, (b) and (c) are fully in line with the Marxian theory of
the state (sketched by Marx in his writings on the Paris Commune)
as systematized by Lenin in his 'State and Revolution', and practised
by him in the period from February to November 1917.[3] Only
Antonio Gramsci's theory of the state and revolution is a Marxian
theory which can be distinguished to some extent from the Marxian
orthodoxy as represented by (b) and (c). Gramsci distinguished between the role of the struggle for communist hegemony over 'civil
society' (or 'the ensemble of organisms commonly called "private" ')
and communist seizure of state power (or 'political society'). In
Tsarist Russia, he thought, the latter was more important; in the
West, the former (Gramsci, 1971, pp. 12, 238). Admittedly, there is
no trace of this Gramscian doctrine in Mao, but neither is there
any in Lenin or Stalin (although Stalin, through his spokesman
Zhadanov, wanted writers to function as the 'engineers of the human
soul', and Mao has always stressed the role of the cultural revolution,
specially since he wrote his 'New Democracy'). Also, (b) by no means
upholds any 'militarization' of the communist revolution, for in the
same text it is asserted that 'Our principle is that the Party commands
the gun, and the gun will never be allowed to command the Party'
(Mao, vol. 2, 1954, p. 272). This dictum, that 'the Party commands
the gun . . . ', very strictly supplemented by the dictum 'the gun will
never be allowed to command the Party' (italics mine), puts Mao
squarely on the side of Leninist orthodoxy, as categorically asserted
in Lenin's 'Partisan Warfare' (1906) (Lenin, 1947, sect. iii, p. 170).
Indeed, the *only* Marxian departure from this dictum has been articulated on the basis of the experience of the Cuban revolution. Thus
we have Fidel Castro's dictum: 'Who will make the revolution in

---

[3] But Lenin did stress 'politics is the reason, and war is only the tool, not the
other way round. Consequently, it remains only to subordinate the military point
of view to the political' (quoted in Rapoport, 1968, 1974, p. 37). Mao's 'the
Party commands the gun' is a progeny of this Leninist dictum.

Latin America? Who? The people, the revolutionaries, with or without a party' (Debray, 1967, 1968, p. 96), and the way the dictum emerged from practical experience has been described in Che Guevara's *Reminiscences of the Cuban Revolutionary War* (pp. 195–7). However, as is emphasized in Debray's interpretation of the doctrine (op. cit., pp. 94–8) on the specific question of the role of the communist party, this is a departure from *both* Leninist and Maoist doctrine and practice, and from the theory and practice of the Vietnamese revolution. Finally, the Maoist dicta (a), (b), (c) quite ruthlessly rule out the notion that Maoism encourages or sanctions 'a complex interaction of Communist party cadres and the gradually evolving peasants' associations, a relation which seems to stray far from the Leninist model of organisation' (Chomsky, 1967, 1971, p. 113). (Nor, unless one reads into microscopic studies by eye-witnesses what one already believes, is there much evidence that the 'submission of party cadres to popular control' in the Maoist model has been qualitatively more than in the Leninist model, as believed by some (e.g. Chomsky, 1967, 1971, pp. 65, 113–14).) However, as already suggested in the previous chapter and as will be discussed further below in the present chapter, there is *submission* of *both* the party cadres *and* the popular masses (as also the guerrillas or the army) to the communist personality cult in the Maoist model.

Revolution and revolutionary struggle: (a) Marx, Engels, Lenin, Stalin, and Mao have all *without exception* experimented with alternative concepts of modern communist revolutions, viz. bourgeois-democratic revolutions under bourgeois leadership, democratic bourgeois revolutions under proletarian leadership, bourgeois-democratic revolutions under *joint* bourgeois-proletarian leadership, proletarian (socialist) revolutions, and concepts of the continuation of the proletarian revolution over a long period *after* the establishment of a proletarian dictatorship, and throughout the 'lower stage of communism'.[4] They have also, all of them, experimented with alternative concepts of slow (when under bourgeois leadership) or rapid (when under proletarian, i.e. communist, leadership) transition from the bourgeois-democratic to a proletarian revolution, in a two-stage process of 'permanent'[5] or 'uninterrupted' revolution. On these

---

[4] See Lenin, 'Economics and Politics in the era of the Dictatorship of the Proletariat', sect. 5 (1947, pp. 450–2).

[5] The term 'permanent revolution', used by Engels, was later used by Leon Trotsky, and opposed by non-Trotskyist Marxists (especially by Stalin and Mao), who contraposed the concept of 'uninterrupted revolution'. The issues of the controversy are now only of academic or historical interest.

matters, there is nothing distinctive in Maoist doctrine, except that, rather late in the day, he developed a theory of bourgeois-democratic revolution under joint bourgeois-proletarian leadership (the theory of 'new democracy'), then a theory of bourgeois-democratic revolution under proletarian (communist) leadership (*his* version of the theory of 'people's democratic revolution'), somewhat overstressing the 'long time needed' to 'complete' the bourgeois-democratic stage *before* passing to the proletarian (socialist) stage of the revolution (Mao, vol. 3, 1954, pp. 95–101, 109–15, 128, 130). In practice, this was quickly superseded by events, and the Chinese revolution, after a brief phase of 'bourgeois-democratic revolution under proletarian (communist) leadership', merged with the general, post-World War II stereotype of proletarian (socialist) revolutions in Europe and Asia (corresponding to a Stalinist concept of 'people's democratic revolution').[6] Thus if, under pressure of events, Mao revised his concepts of revolution many times, and was 'inconsistent', so were Marx and all other originators of Marxian thought.[7]

(b) It is widely believed that an aphorism that 'armed struggle is the main form of revolutionary struggle' is an essential ingredient of Maoism, not to be found in other versions of Marxian doctrine. But as we shall see below, under (ii) in this section, and also in the next section, in Mao's own writings (e.g. Mao, vol. 4, 1956, pp. 193–4; vol. 2, 1954, p. 268) the proposition is *not* put forward as being true in *all* circumstances. The circumstances in which it is claimed to hold are precisely defined, more or less within the framework laid down in Lenin's 'Partisan Warfare' (1906) (1947, pp. 164–75).

(c) Neither does the available evidence support the belief that Mao's strong emphasis on the agrarian-peasant revolution under proletarian (communist) leadership in all 'stages' of the revolution is either 'un-Marxian' or represents an original contribution to Marxian doctrine. Mao himself cited textual support from Stalin's writings for his 'agrarian-peasant' theories (notably, in his 'New Democracy' (vol. 3, 1954, pp. 137–8); actually, the textual support extends back through Lenin's theories to Engels's 'Peasant War in Germany'). Even Mao's doctrines regarding the role of the *rich*

---

[6] defined to refer to proletarian (socialist) revolutions which (i) utilized a non-soviet electoral system, (ii) utilized a multi-party system under communist leadership which included ex-social democrats and peasant parties (and not merely a splinter group of the peasant socialist revolutionaries as in the Russian socialist revolution), and (iii) relied on support from the Soviet Union.

[7] not excluding Trotsky (see Cohn-Bendit, 1968, 1969, IV, 4, pp. 234–45).

peasantry, which favoured 'antagonistic, limited co-operation' with them (Mao, 1954, pp. 87–91; 1954b, pp. 215, 220–1; 1956, pp. 191–2), are compatible, not only with Lenin's theories during the New Economic Policy just before his death, but also with Stalin's arguments in defence of the New Economic Policy against Soviet left-communists.[8] (The only aspect of Maoist agrarian policy for which no direct support can be found in the writings of Lenin or Stalin is the policy of non-elimination of landlords, not only during the period of the anti-Japanese united front, but *also* during the preceding period of the anti-feudal anti-imperialist democratic revolution (Mao, 1954, pp. 87–91; 1954b, pp. 215, 220–1; 1956, pp. 191–2). But there is hardly any evidence that this aspect of Chinese communist policy unduly prolonged the Chinese revolutionary struggle. Moreover, all landlords *were* eliminated, swiftly and ruthlessly, on the morrow of the seizure of power by the Chinese Communist party. So the importance of this 'deviation' from, or 'contribution' to, Marxian doctrine is historically almost nil.)

(d) It has sometimes been argued that Maoist practice in the Chinese revolution, and by implication Maoist theory, denies the role of a general strike, or the mass political strike (advocated by Lenin in the context of the 1905 Russian revolution), as an instrument of modern revolutions under proletarian (communist) leadership.[9] But Lenin's advocacy was conditional, and not absolute, and this was made explicit in his 'Partisan Warfare', sect. 1 (1906) (Lenin, 1947, pp. 165–6). What, precisely, Maoist doctrine has to say on this point will be discussed further later in this chapter.

War: (a) 'Politics is war without bloodshed, while war is politics with bloodshed' (Lin Piao (ed.), *Quotations from Mao Tse-tung*, p. 50). *Comment*: This is merely a restatement of the Clausewitz doctrine, viz. 'war is a continuation of politics by other means', which was fully endorsed by Lenin (see his 'Collapse of the Second International' (1915), sect. ii, where he refers to it as 'the main thesis of dialectics' and speaks of Clausewitz as 'one of the greatest writers on

[8] It is also known that Stalin gave his personal approval to a strategy of an alliance between the proletariat (the communists) and *all* the peasantry to be adopted by Indian communists ('Mighty advance of the national liberation movement in the colonial and dependent countries', For a Lasting Peace, For a People's Democracy, 27.1. 1959, The Draft Programme of the Communist Party of India, For a Lasting Peace, for a People's Democracy, 11.5 1951).

[9] This was the interpretation which made one section of the Indian communist movement oppose a nationwide general strike which another section tried to organize in March 1949 (see 'Struggle for People's Democracy and Socialism', *Communist*, June–July 1949, Bombay).

the history of war, whose ideas were stimulated by Hegel' (1964, *Works*, p. 219).

(b) '. . . war can only be abolished through war, in order to get rid of the gun, it is necessary to take up the gun' (Mao, 1954, p. 179). *Comment*: Except in the context of the Leninist doctrine that 'capitalism means war', this dictum is indistinguishable from the standard doctrine upheld by war-mongers after the defeat of the German Nazis had discredited their doctrine of 'eternal war'. But it makes sense when paraphrased as a Leninist doctrine to say: war can only be abolished through a war which abolishes capitalism (on a global scale). But the restatement of this dictum in 1967 seems to fit in with the newly developed Maoist theory of communist 'social imperialism'. In terms of *this* doctrine, the Maoist dictum on war can only be paraphrased as: war can be abolished (only) through a war which abolishes capitalism *and* (communist) 'social imperialism' on a global scale.

(c) '. . . the East Wind is prevailing over the West Wind[10] and war will not break out . . . [However] if you are afraid of war day in and day out, what will you do if war eventually comes? . . . Both possibilities have to be taken into account' (Lin Piao (ed.), *Quotations from Mao Tse-tung*, p. 56). *Comment*: This is fully in line with the Leninist doctrine which says neither war nor peace is inevitable, but both are possible, as long as there is capitalism (anywhere on earth). (The doctrine needs some paraphrasing, however, in the light of the Maoist theory of communist social imperialism.[11])

(ii) Peculiarities of the Chinese Revolution

(a) 'armed struggle is the main form of struggle and an army composed mainly of peasants is the main form of organisation. . . . every landlord or bourgeois bloc of parties uses the gun to have power . . . without armed struggle the proletariat and the Communist Party could not win any place for themselves or accomplish any revolutionary task' (Mao, 1954a, pp. 268–9, 271–2; 1956, pp. 193–4). *Comment*: These dicta are compatible with the ideas expressed in Lenin's work 'Partisan Warfare' (already referred to above). They are closely related to Stalin's dictum: 'In China, armed revolution is

[10] Explained by Mao to mean: 'the forces of socialism have become overwhelmingly superior to the forces of imperialism' (Lin Piao (ed.), *Quotations from Mao Tse-tung*, p. 68).

[11] The dictum 'the East Wind is prevailing over the West Wind' was put forward by Mao in Moscow in 1957, long before the theory of communist 'social imperialism' as a possible source of war was developed in China in the late 1960s and early 1970s.

fighting the armed counter-revolution. This is one of the peculiarities and one of the advantages of the Chinese Revolution'—to which Mao makes a specific acknowledgement (Mao, 1954a, p. 268).[12] Mao specifies the concrete circumstances in China which make these dicta valid as being: (1) localized agricultural economy (instead of a unified capitalist economy) and the imperialist policy of division and exploitation by marking off spheres of influence (1956, p. 194), (2) the feudal divisions in the country which make it essential for feudal, bourgeois, or proletarian parties which are serious about power to have 'armed forces under their direct command' (1954a, pp. 269, 271–2), (3) the fact that China is 'a loosely knit country which lacks democracy' (1956, p. 193), indicated by the absence of a 'legislative body to make use of, nor the legal right to organise the workers to strike'[13] (1954a, p. 267).

(b) It is widely believed, at least in India, that one of Mao's contributions to Marxian revolutionary theory is to uphold a 'tit for tat' approach, interpreted to mean 'an eye for an eye, a tooth for a tooth' approach towards the enemy.[14] This would imply adoption of a policy of letting the enemy *dictate* the revolutionaries' tactics. A 'tit for tat' slogan *was* put forward by Mao in 1940 and 1941 (vol. 4, 1956, pp. 204–5, 237–8), and also in 1945, on the eve of the final communist capture of power, and was repeated in 1967 in the 'Red Book' (i.e. Lin Piao (ed.), *Quotations from Mao Tse-tung*, p. 10). But the context makes it quite clear that the slogan was no more than a paraphrase of the dictum, already noted above, that the armed revolution must face the armed counter-revolution in China. It cannot be interpreted as a policy of letting the enemy dictate the revolutionaries' strategy and tactics or the form and intensity of revolutionary struggle. For, as we shall discuss in more detail in sect. 5.3 below, one of Mao's original contributions to Marxian and military doctrine is the concept of the 'strategic defensive' and the

[12] It seems the Communist International's recommendations to the Chinese Communist party in 1930 and 1931 coincide more clearly with these standard Maoist dicta (Glunin *et al.*, 1973, pp. 60–1), and there is a dispute as to who got them from whom.

[13] The legal right to strike seems to have been taken away after the 1922–3 railway strikes and the general strikes in Shanghai and Honkong in 1925 (Mao, 1954, pp. 19, 299).

[14] This interpretation of Mao's 'tit for tat' slogan was put forward by the Andhra communist leadership during the Telengana armed struggle against the fanatical Razakars in Hyderabad before its merger with India in 1949–50. It also influenced the Indian Marxist-Leninist communists (Maoists) in the late 1960s and early 1970s.

concept of (guerrilla) tactics based on the watchwords: 'The enemy advances, we retreat; the enemy halts, we harass; the enemy tires, we attack; the enemy retreats, we pursue' (Mao, 1954, p. 138). It is easy to see that these are the direct *opposite* of a principle of 'an eye for an eye, a tooth for a tooth', of letting the enemy's policy, strategy, and tactics *dictate* the revolutionaries' policy, strategy, and tactics, which would represent a kind of 'subservience to spontaneity' first castigated (in a different context) in Lenin's 'What is to be done?' (Ch. ii, sect. A) (Lenin, 1936, 1946, pp. 52–6).[15]

(c) The Chinese communist (Maoist) theory and practice of the revolutionary united front is based on classically Leninist principles of (i) 'striking together, marching separately', (ii) 'watching your [revolutionary] ally as if he were an enemy', (iii) ensuring the leading role of the proletarian (communist) party, put forward in Lenin's 'Two Tactics of Social Democracy' (Lenin, 1936, 1946, p. 100) (for references to Mao's works on his united front policy, see Mao, 1954a, pp. 262–6). However, Maoist doctrine on the united front also contains the integrated formulation of the three principles of (i) self-defence or justifiability (' . . . never attack unless attacked; if attacked . . . certainly counter-attack'), (ii) victory or expediency ('we do not fight unless we are sure of victory'), and (iii) truce or restraint ('After we have repulsed an attack . . . and before they launch a new one, we should stop at the appropriate moment and bring the fight to a close . . . we should on our own initiative seek unity . . . and, upon their consent, conclude a peace agreement with them. We must on no account fight on daily and hourly without stopping, nor become dizzy with success . . .' (Mao, vol. 3, 1954, p. 199)). These represent an extension of Leninist principles, successfully practised from 1940 to date. (There is no essential originality about another aspect of Mao's united front policy which has attracted attention, but is of very slight importance. Mao Tse-tung has *almost* consistently treated non-communist allies (even if they were puppets) more gently than dissidents among communists.[16] But in

[15] In December 1975 Teng Hsiao-ping, talking to President Ford, formulated the slogan of 'tit for tat struggle' in the context of a world people's struggle against a new world war originating in Soviet–U.S. 'contention' for world domination. But the specific slogans for the Chinese people were 'dig tunnels deep, store grain everywhere and never seek hegemony'—which fit in with our interpretation (*Frontier*, Calcutta, 20 Dec. 1975, p. 1).

[16] Thus bourgeois members of the Democratic League, formed in the last days of pre-communist China, and allied to the Chinese C.P., have never been the targets in recent inner-party struggles against 'capitalist roaders'. This is evidently because they have not shown the slightest signs of any *independent* political

the same way Stalin, as far as is known, treated 'non-Party Bolsheviks' (allied with the Communist party in the Soviet elections based on the 1936 Soviet Constitution) better than dissidents within the party.)

(d) Maoist doctrine fully endorses the leading role of the industrial working class in the revolution to end imperialism, feudalism, and capitalism, and to continue the proletarian revolution to attain 'the higher stage of communism' (Mao, 1954, p. 19). Of course, Lenin, both in theory (e.g. in 'The Dictatorship of the Proletariat' and the 'Renegade Kautsky') and in practice (in the decrees he drafted for the Soviet Government), upheld the disfranchisement of the land-lords and the bourgeoisie for a generation, and the temporary estab-lishment of a 'master class'[17] of workers. Maoist theory is not definite on this point. Maoist texts referring to the period of the anti-Japanese united front say freedom of speech and the right to elect and be elected are guaranteed to members of the landlord and bourgeois classes who are not (habitually) 'capitulationist' and anti-communist (see Mao, 1954b, pp. 201, 212). Eye-witness accounts of recent developments are contradictory. There is a testimony which says there is no class discrimination. The case is cited of an objection by the son of a poor peasant to landlords' children being allowed to join the Red Guards being withdrawn after self-criticism (Robinson, 1969, p. 15). But there are other eye-witness accounts which testify that a more thoroughgoing class discrimination than is implicit in the class disfranchisement proposed by Lenin is in operation, accom-plished by levelling educational opportunities. Thus it seems the rule is enforced that an engineer's son must work as a farm labourer, only his grandson will be allowed to go to the university, provided he shows the necessary aptitude.[18] This is a consistent application of Frantz Fanon's 'The last shall be first and the first last' principle (Fanon, 1961, 1973, p. 28, which Mao formulated earlier, in 1927[19]), though it does not seem to have been implemented in practice in the Algerian revolution which gave birth to Fanon's slogan.

---

initiative, after some of them were criticized by Mao for criticizing the Chinese C.P. during the 'hundred flowers campaign' in the late 1950s (see Schram, 1974, pp. 315, 330, 337, and his 'notes' on pp. 122, 216). However, the members of the Democratic League were in the forefront of Chinese Press criticism of India in the early 1960s over the Indo-Tibetan border, which later coincided with Chinese communist criticism.

[17] The phrase is Bertrand Russell's (1946, 1962, p. 755).

[18] J. Kalapurackal, 'What's good about Peking', *Times of India* (Delhi), 7 Apr. 1974.

[19] See Mao's 'Investigation into the Peasant Movement in Hunan' (1927) (vol. 1, 1954, p. 28).

(iii) World politics and world revolution

(a) Communist China's recent moves for a *simultaneous rapprochement* with both its national enemies, American imperialism (also branded by Mao 'the enemy of the people of the world' (Lin Piao (ed.), *Quotations from Mao Tse-tung*, p. 66)) and Japanese imperialism, and with all the world's capitalist imperialist powers are strictly in line with a similar policy of simultaneous co-existence with all capitalist powers adopted by Lenin in his last years. (Communist China's earlier policy of seeking co-existence with one set of imperialist or capitalist powers against another, dominant since the beginning of the Japanese invasion of China and the American boycott of Communist China, American military protection for the base of the Chinese counter-revolution in Taiwan, armed intervention in Korea etc., was also in line with Lenin's early policies of a separate peace with imperialist Germany, support for revolutionary China, Turkey etc.) It fits in also, of course, with Communist China's post-Leninist theory of Soviet social imperialism, about which more will be said later in this chapter and in Chapter 7.

(b) Experiments with Lenin's co-existential principle of mutual 'non-interference' between communist and capitalist states in each other's internal affairs by communist countries have involved (i) strict non-export of revolution in the sense that there has never been active armed intervention by a communist country in the internal domestic politics of another (capitalist) country to promote a communist revolution, (ii) passive non-interference to the advantage of counter-revolutionary anti-colonial capitalist regimes suppressing abortive or otherwise unsuccessful communist revolutions, (iii) active non-interference (or anti-fascist or anti-imperialist interference) in favour of successful communist revolutions, (iv) partial 'export of revolution' in the sense of export of arms or volunteers to revolutionaries fighting die-hard colonial regimes or to states resisting aggressors armed by capitalist imperialists,[20] (v) support to 'revolution from above' as well as to 'revolution from below' in foreign (non-communist) countries.

Both the Soviet and Chinese communists have adhered to the framework specified by items (i)–(v) above in interpreting the Leninist co-existential principle of mutual non-interference.

[20] Leninist-Stalinist 'non-interference' has never implied stoppage of the export of the 'ideology of communist revolution', barring special exceptions, by Lenin in the case of Kemalist Turkey in the 1920s, and by Stalin in the case of Nazi Germany after the Soviet–German Non-Aggression Pact of 1939.

Thus, as regards (i), Soviet communists have strictly adhered to it. (Armed non-intervention in favour of communism by Soviet occupation forces in eastern Europe after fascist aggression against the Soviet Union through these countries was defeated, and is not a violation of (i).) Communist China has not only stuck to this policy, but has not even had an opportunity to imitate in East Asia Soviet armed non-intervention in Eastern Europe.[21] As regards (ii), both the Soviet and Chinese communists adopted this policy *vis-à-vis* the communist-led resistance to the Indian army's entry into Telengana in the former Hyderabad State in 1949–50, during communist insurrections in Burma and Malaya since 1948, and during the abortive communist insurrections in Sri Lanka in 1971.[22] Policies similar to type (iii) have been adopted by both in North Korea and Vietnam (though these cases could also be covered by a type (iv) policy, which has mainly been employed by both Soviet and Chinese communists in Black Africa and the Arab States). Type (v) policy has also been adopted by both, though the distinction between successful revolutions 'from above' and 'from below' has become blurred in modern revolutions. Thus the Soviet communists opposed the Cambodian 'revolution from above' headed by the monarch Sihanouk until he proved successful, and then corrected the mistake. On the other hand, the Chinese communists opposed a 'revolution from below' in Bangladesh, a policy which they corrected, though five years after Bangladesh was established as a state. Both have sometimes justified their support to governments in the Indian subcontinent (the Soviet communists to the Indian government and the Chinese communists to Ayub Khan) on the understanding that they were promoting 'revolutions from above'. (The Chinese communists did this rather more explicitly *vis-à-vis* the Sukarno regime in Indonesia which was backed by pro-Chinese Indonesian communists. The Soviet communists have done this explicitly *vis-à-vis* the Congress government in India, at least after Brezhnev's visit to India in 1974.)

[21] In 1966, when the cultural revolution in China was beginning, Chou En-lai did threaten to do so *if* China was attacked for helping victims of U.S. aggression 'in Asia, Africa or elsewhere' (Han Suyin, 1967, 1973, pp. 229–30). But the U.S.A. prudently avoided any *fresh* attack, although she protected the counter-revolutionary regime in Taiwan. So nothing came of it.

[22] Both the Soviet and Chinese communists adopted an essentially type (ii) policy *vis-à-vis* the abortive Maoist communist uprising in West Bengal in 1970–1. The Soviets never supported it, and the Chinese abandoned the movement when it failed (see *Economic and Political Weekly*, Bombay, 4 Nov. 1972, pp. 2223–4).

(c) There has been a widespread belief, at least in India, that it is a fundamental objective of Chinese communist policy, but not of Soviet communist policy, to subvert, by all means short of outright interference (ruled out in types of policy (i)–(iv)), political systems in ex-colonial countries which are based on the parliamentary system.[23] *In fact*, the Chinese communists recognized the stability of the Indian state based on a fully fledged parliamentary system with adult franchise *before* the Soviet communists did.[24] Of course, Communist China's cultivation of close friendship with Pakistan began when Pakistan still had a restricted parliamentary system based on restricted franchise, inherited from the last phase of British colonial rule, and was developed under an electoral system[25] called 'basic democracy' which was an extension of a military dictatorship. But it has suffered no setback with the establishment of a fully fledged parliamentary system (based on adult franchise) in Pakistan under Zulfikar Ali Bhutto.[26] Indeed, *vis-à-vis* the entire Indian subcontinent, including Sri Lanka, with the partial exception of Burma, and a complete exception only in Nepal, there is no sign of any special Chinese communist antipathy towards parliamentary political systems.

(d) The belief that Soviet economic relations with the Third World countries prove that Soviet policy is a 'social imperialist' policy, while Chinese communist policy is not, also seems to be without basis. This belief seems to be based on *three* crucial contrasts, generally emphasized by Chinese communist spokesmen, viz. (i) the Soviet Union charges interest, insists on repayment of loans extended to these countries; China gives interest-free loans or gifts, (ii) the Soviet Union supplies goods at world market prices, and/or buys cheap and sells dear from these countries; China sells at subsidized prices, (iii) the Soviet Union sells arms to these countries at high prices; China gives arms free. For reasons which will be discussed in Chapter 7 it is doubtful whether, on the Chinese definition of a communist 'social imperialist' policy, Chinese communist policy itself is not social imperialist.

[23] defined in the Glossary above as 'an explicit voting system in which opposing political parties or groups cast conflicting votes'.
[24] in 1954, two years before the Soviet Union.
[25] defined in the Glossary as 'an explicit voting system which is purely "conspicuous" or demonstrative'.
[26] which is likely to crystallize as a complete imitation of the Indian parliamentary system, except that non-Muslims will be constitutionally debarred from holding certain offices.

4.3 Traits which *are* distinctive and original

In this section an attempt is made to identify and make an inventory of the truly distinctive and original traits of Chinese communist ideology. In the next section there is an exploratory discussion of such questions as: how far they represent something more than original contributions to a Marxian *theology*, how far they are likely to survive as theology or as contributions to a scientific philosophy or political theory.

Theory and practice: (i) social practice is 'scientific' or 'artistic' practice, as much as productive or political practice, (ii) direct personal practical experience is important, but a part of practical experience (i.e. about the past, about foreign countries) must *necessarily* be indirect, (iii) theories, plans, programmes must continually, for ever, be tested and re-tested in practice, to eliminate mistakes and discard obsolete theories, plans, programmes (Mao Tse-tung, 'On Practice', 1937, in Mao, 1954, pp. 282–97), (iv) 'under certain conditions', in the contradictions between theory and practice, theory plays the decisive role (Mao Tse-tung, 'On Contradiction', 1937, in Mao, 1954a, p. 41).

Contradictions:[27] (a) Their *nature*: (i) non-antagonistic contradictions may become antagonistic contradictions, and vice versa (Mao Tse-tung, 'On Contradiction', in Mao, 1954a, pp. 50–1), (ii) the initial inferiority of the 'revolutionary' (growing) element in a contradiction will be followed by a temporary balance of opposing forces, and finally by the superiority of the revolutionary forces (ibid., pp. 37–40), (iii) external contradictions influence internal contradictions and operate through them (though the internal contradictions arise 'from an inner necessity' independently of the external contradictions) (ibid., pp. 15–17), (iv) the main (principal) contradiction at one stage may turn into a secondary (non-principal) contradiction in another, and vice versa (ibid., pp. 35–7), (v) contradictions are universal and absolute, and can never be all solved and eliminated, even by the most perfect panacea. But each particular contradiction can, and must, be solved, leading on to fresh contradictions (ibid., pp. 18–19, 21). (b) *Solving contradictions*: (i) as a contradiction changes in form (e.g. from non-antagonistic to antagonistic), or the main contradiction becomes a secondary contradiction, or the rising

[27] The Marxian theory of contradictions refers to the contradictory, mutually exclusive, opposite tendencies in all processes of nature (including mind and society). Here we are concerned with social contradictions.

revolutionary forces become dominant in a social contradiction, the form of struggle must also change (ibid., pp. 18–21, 23, 35), (ii) in general, persuasion is the main form of struggle to deal with non-antagonistic (or secondary) contradictions, and coercion is the form of struggle to deal with antagonistic contradictions (ibid., pp. 50–1), (iii) in each situation, the main contradiction must be identified and solved by methods which do not aggravate the minor contradictions and complicate and postpone the solution of the main contradiction (ibid., pp. 37, 51), (iv) the solution of the principal contradiction in any situation establishes another set of principal and non-principal contradictions to be solved (ibid., pp. 36–7, and see also Mao, 1966, in Ch'en, 1971, p. 115).

In the foregoing, no reference has been made to Mao's further development of his theory of contradictions in his 'Talk on Questions of Philosophy' (1964), viz. 'The most basic thing is the unity of opposites. The transformation of quality and quantity into one another is the unity of the opposites quality and quantity. There is no such thing as the negation of the negation. Affirmation, negation, affirmation, negation . . . in the development of things, every link in the chain of events is both affirmation and negation' (Schram, 1974, p. 226). Unauthorized for publication, at least up to the end of 1975, it contains one statement which is hard to understand, i.e. that quality and quantity represent the 'unity of opposites'. Another statement is straight out of Lenin, who also said 'In brief, dialectics can be defined as the doctrine of the unity of opposites' (*Works*, vol. 38, p. 223), and is therefore not original. But Mao's assertion that 'there is no such thing as the negation of the negation . . . ' is highly original, and will be discussed in the next section.

Protracted revolution: This is the theory which underlies Mao Tse-tung's well-known theory of protracted war ('On Protracted War', in Mao, 1954a, pp. 157–243; ibid., pp. 116–56; 1954, pp. 175–253; 1956, pp. 171–218). Purely *semantically*, the term could refer to *either* (i) a revolution in which there is (a) *permanent war* (or 'politics with bloodshed') over a long period and (b) a *continuity* of revolutionary political power which is *never destroyed* in the ebb and flow of the struggle, *or* (ii) a revolution in which there is (a) *alternation* of bloody and bloodless politics and (b) there is *discontinuity* of political power, which is won, lost, regained, and finally consolidated. (Roughly, the Chinese revolution corresponds to (i), and the Russian revolution corresponds to (ii).) But *historically*, the term seems to have been coined by Mao, and has been used only in sense (ii). We shall stick to this usage.[28] Apart from (i) (a)–(b), this Chinese communist theory of protracted revolution or war contains the additional, highly original features (c) the concept of the strategic defensive, (d) the concept of guerrilla tactics (with stress on the establishment of guerrilla bases[29]), (e) an *inverse* correlation between the declining importance of the industrial general strike and urban insurrections, and the growing importance of rural-based peasant war (with *no place* for urban guerrilla struggle at *any* stage, and urban strikes and insurrections playing *no role* at the *climax* of the revolutionary struggle). (Features (ii) (c)–(e) have already been referred to in the previous section, and will be discussed further in the next.)

The united front: As already stated in sect. 4.2 above, the specific Chinese communist contributions to the Marxian theory of the revolutionary united front are the principles of (i) self-defence or justifiability, (ii) victory or expediency, (iii) truce or restraint. To these must be added the Chinese communist *rejection* of the interpretation of the Marxian theory of the revolutionary united front as a doctrine of communist acceptance of the hegemony of the 'lesser evil' among the non-communist contenders for power, when the communists are themselves not in power, or in a position to contend for power. Such an interpretation of the theory *has* been given elsewhere several times since 1935, with no advance towards the making of a communist-led revolution. (However, there are some signs that Chinese communist ideology does permit the doctrine of *endorsing* or approving of the 'lesser evil' in a *foreign* country, e.g. in Pakistan, or India. This is, of course, a standard interpretation of the Leninist doctrine of 'peaceful co-existence' of capitalist and socialist states in international diplomacy, to which almost all ruling communist parties generally adhere. The rationale is that, unlike the case with *domestic* politics, 'realistic' support to the 'lesser evil' in a foreign country does no harm to the communist regime which is entrenched in power domestically. Indeed, the policy can be continued until a friendly communist regime assumes power in each country.)

Consecration of the Chinese path of revolution: The consecration

---

[28] In the next section, and again in Part II, Ch. 9, a reference will be made to a third sense in which the term 'protracted revolution' can be used which has features of both senses (i) and (ii).

[29] and on mobile as against positional warfare.

of the 'road of Mao Tse-tung' as the path for other ex-colonial countries, including India, to follow, began with a key-note speech by Liu Shao-chi in November 1949 ('For a Lasting Peace, For a People's Democracy', 30 Dec. 1949). Lu Ting-yi was more categorical when he declared in 1951 that 'the classic type of revolution in the colonial and semi-colonial countries is the Chinese revolution'[30] and that 'the victory in China of Marxism-Leninism and of Mao Tse-tung's theory of the Chinese revolution will help the people of the Asian countries to free themselves from the influence of bourgeois democracy of the old type, to resolutely take the path of the new democratic revolution of the people . . . ' (1951, pp. 17–19). After an interlude in the 1950s, in which very little was heard of the consecrated Chinese path for all Asian or all ex-colonial countries, came Lin Piao's declaration in September 1965 of a Maoist strategy of world revolution, with the accent on rural revolutionary base areas and the countryside which would encircle the cities and ultimately take them (see summary in Han Suyin, 1967, 1973, p. 156). This is an *original* narcissistic trait in Chinese communist ideology, because, contrary to prevailing impressions, other successful communist revolutionaries have stressed the *non*-imitability of their revolutions,[31] while the Chinese communists *alone* stress the imitability of theirs, and make this an article of faith.

The 'narcissistic trait' in Chinese communist ideology just mentioned is not, of course, the only form 'revolutionary' narcissism may take. It is sometimes given a very different meaning, with an implication for policy which is the polar *opposite* of the one just indicated. Thus, if revolutionary communist narcissism in China were combined with a doctrine of the Chinese as the 'chosen communist revolutionary nation'—by analogy with the notion of the

[30] He added that the classic type of revolution in the imperialist countries is the (Russian) October Revolution (Lu Ting-yi, 1951, p. 19). Strangely enough, this is *not* the view of Lenin or Stalin (or, for that matter, any orthodox communist party in the imperialist countries, at least after the publication of Lenin's 'Left-wing Communism—An Infantile Disorder' in 1920).

[31] Lenin thought that in 1917–18 the 'objective conditions' of a proletarian socialist revolution were 'ripe' in Germany, but the 'subjective conditions' were 'ripe' in Russia, and by no means idealized the Russian revolution as an imitable prototype. In fact, his 'Left-wing Communism—An Infantile Disorder' seems to have been interpreted by orthodox western communists as a manifesto for *not* trying to imitate the Russian revolution. Stalin's post-World War II prototype of 'people's democratic revolutions' obviously differed from the Russian Soviet revolution. Even Che Guevara, who came closest to recommending the Cuban revolution as the Latin-American prototype, did *not* rule out the role of the parliamentary political system (Guevara, 1969, 1972, p. 206), which would mark a departure from the Cuban prototype.

Israelites as God's chosen race—one could deduce that Chinese communists would *not* proclaim the imitability of their revolution, but insist on the *impossibility* of 'true' communist revolutions anywhere outside China. Applying the Freudian theory of narcissism as the *opposite* of the 'aggressive instinct' (Freud, 1932, 1973, pp. 135–6), one could then predict that the Chinese communists would then be interested in 'de-stabilizing' all regimes which could imperil their unique revolution, and supporting, as a 'lesser evil', all regimes which do not do so. One objection to such a hypothesis about Chinese communist ideology is that there is not the slightest evidence that Chinese communists *do* believe that the Chinese are the *only* people capable of making a 'true' communist revolution. The nearest one can get to such evidence is the 'impressions' of some foreign diplomats or statesmen who have met the Chinese communist leaders, and the negative evidence that Mao Tse-tung himself is not on record as upholding the narcissistic consecration of the 'Chinese path' of communist revolutions to all nations which is to be found in the writings of Liu Shao-chi or Lin Piao referred to above. When direct evidence confirming a hypothesis is lacking, one must fall back on the indirect evidence in policy moves which confirm the policy predictions flowing from the hypothesis. It must be admitted that Chinese communist policy towards India, Pakistan, and Bangladesh (which will be discussed further in Part II) *can* be well explained in terms of this alternative hypothesis about the form of Chinese communist narcissism. But Chinese communist support for the Cambodian communist revolution of 1975, at least, contradicts the hypothesis, though the failure of every other Maoist-inspired communist revolution so far might strengthen it.

On the interstate 'status quo': The Chinese communist doctrine on this point has hardly been articulated theoretically in Maoist scriptures, or party documents. But, judging by the unfolding of Chinese communist foreign policy, with active personal participation by Mao Tse-tung in recent years, it may turn out to be among the most far-reaching Maoist contributions to Marxian ideology. The contribution consists of two basic propositions, viz. (i) all former semi-colonies which have been victims of capitalist-imperialist territorial incursions should have their pre-imperialist borders restored (whether this is done at the expense of non-communist states (like India) or communist states (like the U.S.S.R.)), and (ii) no ex-colonial or post-colonial state should be allowed to disintegrate (proposition

(ii) has been seen in action particularly in the case of the disintegration of post-British, neo-colonial Pakistan, and the emergence of Bangladesh[32]). Both these propositions are original Maoist contributions to Marxian doctrine. Thus the Soviet Union has followed, on the question of borders, the policy of advocating border changes in favour of communist states in Europe, wherever they relate to recovery by communist states of territory lost to capitalist or fascist imperialism and recovered in the war against fascism. (The difference between the Soviet Union and China on the question of borders is roughly that the Soviet Union favours undoing fascist territorial acquisitions, while China favours undoing *all* territorial acquisitions by capitalist imperialism (fascist or pre-fascist).) On the question of disintegration of post-colonial states, the Chinese have been original in resolutely opposing disintegration, while the Soviet Union has somewhat reluctantly agreed to recognize it, once its anti-imperialist, revolutionary potential is revealed, albeit only incipiently, even if there is no communist leadership of the process of disintegration.[33]

Change of colour of a communist (socialist) society into a capitalist one: Every version of Marxian doctrine contains a theory of the counter-revolutionary restoration of capitalism. The systematic destruction of the 'material basis' of capitalism embodied in capitalist property and production relations, the restoration of social (production) discipline on the basis of socialist production relations, plus the dictatorship of the proletariat exercised through the Communist party—these are supposed to prevent a counter-revolutionary capitalist restoration. The distinctive feature of the Maoist version of the doctrine, perfected in the 1960s, is the *belief* that the Communist party itself may become the *chief* instrument of capitalist restoration, so that the apparatus of the socialist social structure, of the proletarian dictatorship may remain intact, but be powerless to prevent a capitalist restoration. This may happen, according to

[32] At the height of the Bangladesh crisis, *before* the final stage of the liberation war jointly fought by the Indian army and the Bengali guerrillas against the threat of imminent American intervention through the Seventh Fleet, there were unconfirmed reports in the Indian Press that a 'highly placed' Chinese spokesman (Chou En-lai?) had suggested to Han Suyin that the Chinese would underwrite the non-disintegration of the Indian state, if India underwrote Bangladesh's re-integration into Pakistan.

[33] Thus the Soviet submarines shadowed the American Seventh Fleet in the Bay of Bengal, when the fleet was sent there with the declared aim of trying to help the Pakistani forces in the final stages of the Bangladesh liberation struggle. On the other hand, the Chinese anti-guerrilla experts are said to have tried to help the Pakistani forces.

Maoist doctrine, if the Communist party cadres are 'corrupted' (ideologically and morally), and themselves initiate an 'inevitable change of colour' of the communist (socialist) society[34] (Lin Piao (ed.), *Quotations from Mao Tse-tung*, pp. 33–5).

The theory of social (i.e. socialist) imperialism: This theory is an outgrowth of the theory of 'change of colour' of a communist society. Though not yet sanctified by a dictum of Mao's authorized for publication, it is a persistently recurring theme in Chinese communist foreign policy declarations, especially after the *rapprochement* with the U.S.A. in 1973. It started, in the pre-*rapprochement* period, as no more than a revival of Leninist accusations against the European social democrats in the 1920s, with the difference that the target was the Soviet Communist party, which was accused of serving American imperialism in implementing its neo-colonialist policies. It was argued, for instance, that Soviet economic aid to India was an indirect method of helping American capitalist imperialism to extract 'super-profits' from a neo-colonial India. In the post-*rapprochement* period, the argument seems to be rather different. As already mentioned in sect. 4.2 above, the argument now is that Soviet social(-ist) imperialism is extracting 'super-profits' for itself, rather than as a broker for American capitalist imperialism, by such methods as making loans at interest instead of making gifts or interest-free loans (especially with respect to arms deliveries), buying cheap and selling dear, charging prices for goods sold and paying prices for goods bought from the less developed capitalist countries (like India) which are unfavourable compared to prices charged and paid to advanced imperialist capitalist countries.[35] Crystallizing in this form, the Chinese communist theory of 'social imperialism' is highly original, and has long-term implications which will be discussed in the next section.

Moral versus material incentives in a socialist (communist) society: The Maoist doctrine that 'material incentives', especially if they are individualistic (but even if they are 'collectively shared'), are incompatible with *both* the lower *and* the higher stages of communism is another highly original contribution to Marxism. The alternative

[34] Whether the 'change of colour' is expected to be peaceful or not is not made clear, though it is said a peaceful 'change of colour' is possible (Han Suyin, 1967, 1973, p. 177).
[35] Charges that the Soviet communist leaders are behaving more and more like the 'new Tsars' with their refusal to cede territory to Communist China (or even to Japan) may ultimately be integrated into the theory of Soviet 'socialist imperialism'.

is to rely on 'moral incentives', on *selfless* motivation, through psychological remaking of the 'soul of man' through a religious-type movement carried out with the thoroughness of modern science (Han Suyin, 1967, 1973, pp. 176–7). (Some difficulties with this approach will be discussed in the next section, and again in Part III.)

The communist personality cult of Mao Tse-tung and his 'thought': The original traits of the Chinese communist personality cult of Mao Tse-tung has already been discussed at length in the previous chapter. They are (i) while Stalin tried to use a Lenin cult as scaffolding, Mao Tse-tung developed the Mao cult independently, though he tried seriously to come to terms with the Stalin cult,[36] (ii) the cult of Mao has never been fully integrated with the cult of the Communist party, and permits the violation of democratic centralism, which is the basis of the cult of the party, *provided* that this is done in the name of Mao Tse-tung or his 'thought', (iii) in the Mao cult, there is a preference for public terror by the masses over secret terror by the police, for mental (psychological) torture over physical torture, (iv) unlike the Stalin cult, which did *not* take into account the risks arising from the mortality of Stalin,[37] in the Mao cult the emphasis is on the immortal 'thought', as well the mortal personality, with specially designed checks to protect the vulnerable cult after the death of its personality.

This list of original traits of Chinese communist ideology probably represents the main original contributions of Chinese communism to Marxian ideology. The next, concluding section of the chapter is devoted to a tentative assessment.

4.4 A tentative assessment

The most important contribution of Chinese communism to general philosophy seems to be a clarification of the 'instrumentalist' element in Marxian philosophy.

It has been well known for some time that Marx *pioneered* in introducing, but did not much develop, the instrumentalist approach in philosophy (Russell, 1946, 1962, p. 750). He did this by insisting that there is a constant (dialectical) interaction between subject and

[36] He even eulogized Stalin's *History of the Communist Party of the Soviet Union* in 1941 as 'the best synthesis and summary of the World Communist movement of the past hundred years' (Mao, 1956, p. 19)—i.e. as the best Marxist scripture since the *Communist Manifesto*.

[37] Stalin seems to have taken it for granted that no one would dare to demolish his cult. At least, discounting his daughter Svetlana's memoirs, there is no firm evidence to the contrary.

object, the knower and what he knows, that 'In practice man must prove the truth' (Marx's second thesis on Feuerbach, Marx and Engels, vol. 2, 1949, p. 365). But this seminal idea was somewhat submerged in Marx's general philosophical writings, because of his preoccupation with the traditional idealist-materialist, metaphysical-dialectical syndromes which were dominant in general philosophy at the time.

With his explicit inclusion of 'scientific' (and 'artistic') practice as a form of social practice, on the same footing as political practice (the 'class struggle'), his insistence that 'theory rather than practice may play a *decisive* role in certain situations', his stand that theory and practice must repeatedly, and for ever, interact and *test* each other (all noted in the previous section)—with these, Mao cultivates, develops, and elaborates the instrumentalist element in Marxian philosophy.[38] (Or course, Antonio Gramsci had already done this *before* Mao—more systematically in some respects, and less systematically in others.[39])

Mao's contribution to the cultivation of the instrumentalist element in Marxian philosophy may or may not have something to do with the impact of the lecture tour by the American instrumentalist philosopher John Dewey in China in 1919.[40] But there is no doubt that the maelstrom of the Chinese revolution in the 1920s and 1930s was the main genetic source. The original Maoist theory of a 'protracted revolution' is a classic example of a theory being handled as an instrument, a weapon,[41] whose results or effects 'prove' it to be true, after all alternative theories have been repeatedly 'tested' in practice, and have been proved 'untrue'. At the same time, there is the Maoist doctrine that contradictions are universal, but that in each situation (moment) there are contradictions which are (and must be) solved, in order to pass on to other contradictions also to

[38] Mao's reported contraposition of 'affirmation, negation, affirmation, negation . . .' to the 'negation of negation' which is repudiated (referred to in the previous section) sums up Maoist-Marxian instrumentalism. For, with Marx and Engels, the 'negation of negation' operates through the 'annihilation of *material* agencies' (Engels, 1894, 1947, p. 197), but Mao's substitute principle operates through the affirmation of non-material ideas (or theory), which discover the material agencies of change.

[39] See *The Modern Prince* in Gramsci, 1971, pp. 123–202, for Marxian instrumentalism developed in a very different context.

[40] See Schram (1966), pp. 52–3; also criticism of Dewey in 1920 by Russell's anarchist-communist students in Peking (Russell, 1968, 1969, pp. 187–8).

[41] 'Marxism-Leninism bears the same relation to the Chinese revolution as the arrow to the target' (Mao, 1956, pp. 18, 36).

be solved, in an endless chain.[42] This doctrine had its intricate political applications in the theory and practice of the anti-Japanese united front based on the principles of 'self-defence' or 'justifiability', 'victory' or 'expediency', and 'truce' or 'restraint', which were discussed in the previous section. This particular contribution emphasizes the limits which Maoism-Marxism imposes on what Russell has referred to as an exaggeration of man's (and the earth's) cosmic importance in space and time, which is an element in pure instrumentalist philosophical systems.[43] In modern anarchism, which is decidedly Rousseauian, as modern pure instrumentalist philosophies in some sense are,[44] no such limits are recognized in the clarion calls for 'war to the finish... [for] the root and branch destruction of the bourgeois social order' (Bakunin, 1953, 1964, p. 373).[45]

According to Russell, the Achilles heel of pure (non-Marxian) instrumentalism is its neglect of evidence, which Marxian philosophy does *not* neglect (Russell, 1946, 1962, p. 749). However, since neither 'being' nor 'becoming', nor the causes or effects of events can ever be completely known, we have to make do with simplified 'models' of causes and effects, i.e. we have to abstract from some of them in *practice*. In doing this, there is always the danger of over-emphasizing *either* 'causes' *or* 'effects' in scientific hypotheses or political plans, programmes, etc. Some of the Maoist dicta surveyed in the previous section seem to testify to the existence of these opposite dangers.

An example is the *consecration of the Chinese path of revolution for all Asian or all ex-colonial countries*. This generally means a mandatory recommendation of the Chinese pattern of 'protracted revolution', with the accent on armed rural struggle. However, as we noted in sect. 4.2 above, Mao's advocacy of 'protracted revolutionary war' in Chinese conditions was based on the existence of the precisely identifiable 'objective' conditions: (1) localized agricultural economy and *rival* imperialist spheres of influence, (2) feudal divisions which make it essential for all political parties contending for power to maintain private armies, (3) absence of democracy, illustrated by the

[42] See Mao, 1966, in Ch'en, 1971, p. 115.
[43] Russell (1946, 1962), p. 753. Russell's ideas on this point are, however, somewhat obsolete in the context of the recent 'grand tour of the planets' by terrestrial spacecraft, and the modern historian's view that there is a constant interaction between the present and the past in historiography (Carr, 1961, 1973, p. 23).
[44] Russell (1946, 1962), pp. 481, 660, 781–2.
[45] See also Mikhail Bakunin and S. G. Nechayev, *The Revolutionary Catechism*, 1869 (Kumar, 1971, pp. 115–20).

absence of legislative bodies and of the legal right to strike. Now, as will be noted in Part II, Chapters 8–12 below, there have been several serious, but unsuccessful attempts at armed struggle in other Asian countries, including India, conducted with the conviction that the 'objective conditions' (1)–(3) noted above exist in these countries. All of them have been unsuccessful in initiating a 'protracted revolution' in which there is (i) permanent war, and (ii) continuity of revolutionary power which is never destroyed, in the ebb and flow of a protracted struggle. A *pure* 'instrumentalist' (at least as his position is interpreted by Russell) would *not* think of investigating whether assumptions (1)–(3) hold, or can be replaced by others.[46] He will either (a) hope that the 'next attempt at armed struggle' would still prove that the consecrated Chinese path is valid for India, or (b) call off the whole enterprise, i.e. the Indian revolution. A *Marxian* instrumentalist will not, of course, opt for (b).[47] Nor will he opt for (a), because this is strictly Utopian and not scientific.[48] Instead, he will (c) reinvestigate the basic assumptions about the 'objective conditions', and, if necessary, find substitutes for (1)–(3), and (d) investigate how far the armed insurrections in India in practice differed from strict Maoist precepts (e.g. that urban guerrilla struggle should be avoided, that in the rural guerrilla struggle for political power excessive terrorism, as well as 'economism', should be avoided, that united front principles of (i) self-defence, (ii) expediency, and (iii) restraint should be implemented, etc.). The outcome of such a Marxian-instrumentalist reassessment may or may not produce an *alternative* theory of protracted revolution, which (i) *differs* from the Chinese version in *not* relying on armed struggle as the main form of struggle, in *not* ruling out electoral activity by communist revolutionaries for the capture and retention of partial (legislative and executive) political power, but (ii) *agrees* with the Chinese version in postulating a protracted revolutionary struggle (in the sense that there is *continuity* of partial political power through the ebb and flow of the revolutionary struggle), in applying the Chinese concept of the 'strategic defensive', etc.[49] However, as we shall see in the

[46] because a pure instrumentalist judges *solely* by the 'effects' of a belief (or a programme) and *not* by its 'causes' (Russell, 1946, 1962, p. 780).

[47] because to a Marxist the inevitability of a communist revolution everywhere is *both* an analytical prediction *and* a value judgement.

[48] since, with a scientific approach, one must provisionally accept the verdict of experiments, and cannot go on hoping for ever that the next experiment will prove a hypothesis correct.

[49] See Part II, Ch. 9 below, where this is discussed.

chapters of Part II, *all* Maoist critiques (there are several) of aborted and suppressed armed uprising in India seem to adhere to the strict injunction of the 'pure' instrumentalists that we must judge by effects, and not by causes. (None of them questions the existence in India of 'objective' Chinese-type pre-revolutionary conditions which are *assumed* to exist, though of course none of them reaches the *bourgeois*-instrumentalist conclusion that the (Indian) revolution should be called off.)

Of course, Maoist politics does not always reflect a pure instrumentalist disregard of 'causes', or past facts, in favour of future 'effects' in judging policies and programmes. As we have seen in sect. 4.2, Maoist doctrines on the interstate *status quo* contain two basic propositions: (i) the frontiers of countries which were victims of territorial encroachments by nineteenth-century capitalist imperialism should be restored, and (ii) no ex-colonial state should be allowed to distintegrate. Now, (i) is clearly *anti*-instrumentalist, in disregarding 'effects' (e.g. on future revolutions) altogether, and judging *only* by 'causes' or past facts.[50] But this is hardly Marxian, for a Marxian approach must take into account both interacting causes and effects. (This perhaps explains why the Chinese communist stand has been modified *in practice* on instrumentalist considerations, leading to border agreements with Burma, Pakistan, etc.[51]) Proposition (ii), on the other hand, can be justified most easily on the bourgeois-instrumentalist (conservative) ground that whatever preserves the stability of a pre-existing bourgeois state is justifiable, even if the disintegration of one bourgeois state leads to the creation of two bourgeois states (as happened after the disintegration of

[50] Only former *semi*-colonies (like China) can produce pre-imperialist maps to support their anti-imperialist territorial claims; ex-colonies (like India) cannot. So (i) favours semi-colonies against colonies. The rationale of this is not clear, since colonies suffered more than semi-colonies from imperialist aggression, having been obliterated. Proposition (i) could, however, be upheld by the principle 'what is mine is mine, and what is yours is mine too'—which Mao denounced as uncommunist (vol. 4, 1956, p. 38)—or by making sacrosanct a formula which settles all land disputes on the basis of titles on paper (which reflects landlords' or peasants' ideology).

[51] Even in the China–India border dispute, China at one stage offered (through Sri Lanka) to exchange some of its map-based territorial claims in the eastern segment for territory in the western segment (Ladakh), which it needed then for an easy road-link between China and Tibet. A possible territorial dispute between Communist China and a re-united Communist Vietnam over the South China Sea islands of the Paracels and Spratlys, of which there are some indications since 1975, may also be settled or remain unsettled, depending on how much China insists on punishing Vietnam for *not* breaking with the Soviet Union.

Pakistan[52]). (Whether proposition (ii) is justifiable on the basis of Marxian-instrumentalist logic is doubtful.[53])

The difficulties with the Maoist thesis of the 'change of colour' of a *communist society* are somewhat different. The thesis refers to the danger that the ruling Communist party itself may become the chief instrument serving the 'privileged bourgeois stratum' within a communist country and 'foreign imperialism and reaction' to restore capitalism (Lin Piao (ed.), *Quotations from Mao Tse-tung*, pp. 237–8). The symptoms of the process of such a communist 'change of colour', according to extended interpretations, seem to be: (i) the corruption of communist cadres by the use of 'material incentives' (especially of the individualistic type) in place of 'moral incentives' (or the 'selfless' collectivist type) to promote economic development at the 'lower stage' of communism, (ii) the transition to 'de-centralized' 'market socialism', in which (a) there is market-determined (instead of planned, centralized) price-fixing, and (b) the 'profitability criterion' is used.[54]

---

[52] This was, of course, the basis of the Kissinger–Nixon U.S. Government stand at the time of the Bangladesh war against the creation of Bangladesh, and recognition after Bangladesh became a *fait accompli* (as another bourgeois state).

[53] Of course, in Marxian ideology, modern states represent a hangover from the capitalist (or pre-capitalist) past, to be ultimately eliminated by the international communist revolution. But this doctrine gives no rule as to whether communist revolutions should proceed bottled up within the existing or emerging national states, or promote their disintegration, or any general rule for doing either. In the Pakistan–Bangladesh conflict, the Maoist veto on the disintegration of ex-colonial states has produced some grotesque results. It is reported that on the eve of the Bangladesh war Mao tried, personally, to dissuade Abdul Hamid Bhasani from struggling against the Pakistani military dictatorship headed by Ayub Khan (Ali, 1970, pp. 140–1). Earlier, after the 1965 Indo-Pakistan war over re-infiltration into Kashmir by Pakistani guerrillas, Chen Yi, then China's foreign minister, is reported to have said that Ayub Khan's 'basic democracies' controlled by landlord interests had something in common with Chinese people's communes (ibid., p. 134). In ex-colonial Angola in December 1975 the official stand of the Chinese communist government has crystallized as one which would oppose the disintegration of Angola at all costs, even at the cost of rule by the Organization of African Unity, which was also supported by the U.S.A., and the accommodation of American-aided Angolan troops (if not the South Africa-aided ones) (see report of speech at U.N. General Assembly by the Chinese representative, Lai Ya-li, *Frontier*, Calcutta, 20 Dec. 1975, p. 4).

[54] For a popular exposition see Han Suyin (1967, 1973), pp. 176–7. However, there is some doubt about (ii) (a). According to some economists, rigid (bureaucratic) centralized pricing, and *not* de-centralized price-fixing by free markets, is the defect of the Soviet-type economy. (Under the recently introduced 'economic reforms' in the Soviet economy, prices continue to be fixed centrally. This was also the case with the Dubcek–Sik reforms in Czechoslovakia for most 'strategic' commodities.) Indeed, it is sometimes said that 'flexible price-fixing by the market, according to forces of demand and supply' is actually one of the *virtues* of the Chinese communist economy (Robinson, 1974, pp. 269, 320).

(i) and (ii) are said to be phases in the process of 'change of colour'—which may be short or long[55]—and which, if unchecked by Maoist ideological resistance, will eventually lead to capitalist restoration, in the sense of restoration of private property in the means of production and exploitation of a class of wage-earners by a class of capitalist owners who are engaged in exploiting the property-less wage-earners on the basis of private enterprise.[56]

An analytical problem of this schema is that it seems to be based, ultimately, on the notion that there is an obvious 'self-contradiction' in the idea that the cultivation of 'individualistic, materialistic, consumer' motivation in the lower stage of communism can prepare the way to a regime of 'selfless moral' incentives in the higher stage. But Marxian theory, including its Maoist version, definitely admits similar paradoxical 'self-contradictions' as basic tenets, e.g. the consolidation of the dictatorship of the proletariat in order to prepare for its liquidation, and the abolition of all state systems, to develop the Communist party in order to prepare for abolishing the party and all party systems, to wage revolutionary war in order to abolish war forever (Mao, 'On Contradiction', in Mao, 1954a, p. 45). This particular analytical difficulty can, however, be ignored as an esoteric problem of Marxian theology, on which we have nothing as yet to go by except *a priori* reasoning.[57]

However, there are deeper problems involved: (i) there is an analytical proof, using a game-theoretic framework, that if *all* citizens of a communist society want to become capitalists, i.e. exploit wage-workers, the break-down of communism and the restoration of capitalism is impossible[58] (Bose, 1975, Ch. 15, pp. 272–7), (ii) there are some doubts about the sharp, black-and-white contrasts that are

[55] lasting 'only several years or a decade, or several decades at the most' (*Quotations from Mao Tse-tung*, 1967, p. 34).

[56] The process is said to have started in Yugoslavia in 1951, spread to the Soviet Union under Nikita Khrushchev, where it continues in the post-Khrushchev era. It is said to have been reflected in the Dubcek-Sik reforms in Czechoslovakia, though China has denounced the 'restoration of socialism' there by the Soviet Union and its other East European communist allies (Han Suyin, 1967, 1973, pp. 89, 176–7).

[57] since we do not yet know of a war which has 'ended all wars', or of a proletarian dictatorship which has been replaced by a state-less society, or of a Communist party rule which has been succeeded by a party-less society.

[58] This is the result of the existence of an 'isolation paradox' similar to one which has been formulated in the discussion among economists of the problem of low savings in less developed countries. In this context, capitalist restoration is only possible if some citizens of the communist society *prefer* being exploited as wage-workers in a capitalist society to remaining citizens of a communist society.

often drawn[59] between (a) 'material' incentives in Soviet-type communist economies and 'moral' incentives at work in Communist China, and (b) 'selfish' motivation in Soviet-type economies and 'selfless' motivation in Communist China. A problem of 'élitist' communism, defined as the exploitation of a privileged status by a section of a communist society, may arise as much from unequal political or social (or 'ideological') influence (e.g. in China) as from an unequal distribution of personal incomes (e.g. in the Soviet Union). On the other hand, there are ways of reducing 'élitism' arising from 'material incentives' (in which some producers who 'receive more human labour [embodied in consumption goods] than they supply, while others receive less human labour than they supply'[60]), without switching from individualistic 'material incentives' to collectivist 'moral incentives' (Bose, 1975, Ch. 14, pp. 269–71). By the use of such methods, a communist society may be debarred from a 'change of colour' into a capitalist society, though it may not succeed in abolishing the hard core of communist 'élitism' for which in Marxian doctrine there is no place in the 'higher stage' of communism.

Associated with the Maoist 'change of colour' thesis, is not only the thesis just assessed—that 'moral incentives' should be preferred —but also the theory of 'social (communist) imperialism'. As we have seen in the previous section, this theory, at the stage of incubation reached around mid-1975,[61] seems to refer to two phenomena which can clearly be distinguished from one another, viz. (i) communist revisionists in control of ruling Communist parties in communist countries playing the same role as the European social-democratic 'revisionists' did in the service of capitalist imperialism in the 1920s, or (ii) communist 'élites' in otherwise orthodox communist societies playing the role of 'independent' social-imperialists, who exploit less developed capitalist (or communist) countries mainly in their own interests (and not for the benefit of 'foreign' (capitalist) imperialism).

One initial difficulty with version (ii) of the Maoist theory of social imperialism is that in practice Maoist policies of China seem to have such social-imperialistic aspects no less than Soviet communist policies. In this version of the theory, communist social imperialism implies manipulation of interstate trade or aid, so as to

[59] Sen (1973, 1974), pp. 95–100.   [60] von Weiszacker (1973), sect. xi.
[61] At the end of December 1975 there was a further extension of the theory to cover alleged 'Soviet communist colonialism' in Angola. Disregarded here, this will be discussed in Chapter 6 below.

impede the progress to self-reliance (and ultimately to the 'abundance, in the 'higher stage' of communism) of less developed capitalist or communist countries. Now, the main instance of Soviet communist conduct along these lines was the abrupt termination of Soviet technological aid to Communist China after the schism in international communism.[62] But, then, Communist China is charged with having done something similar to Cuba, when, in 1965, she abruptly cut down by half her rice exports to Cuba, with a matching cut in her sugar imports from Cuba.[63] Moreover, on the general question of manipulating export-import prices and agreements to secure favourable terms of international exchange, it seems it is the Chinese communists, and *not* the Soviet communists, who are adepts at it, and 'never miss an opportunity for a good bargain'.[64] As regards terms of aid, as distinct from trade, the contrast that the Chinese communists make between their 'disinterested' interest-free loans to less developed countries and Soviet loans at positive interest to them is not really fundamental. *Both* types of loans may (or may not) impede progress in these countries towards self-reliance,[65] which is a commonly accepted objective of a non-imperialistic programme of aid to less developed countries. Foreign loans (whether interest-free or not) may impede progress towards self-reliance if in the period of net resource outflow that must follow a period of net resource inflow the annual repayment obligation (inclusive or exclusive of interest) exceeds the annual surplus available for domestic investment (Bose, 1975, Ch. 10, pp. 167–71, Ch. 11, pp. 181–5). (On the other hand, a general policy of foreign aid involving only outright *gifts*, which could avoid the problem, is *not* in keeping with the

[62] The Soviet justification of this action is that it was retaliation against Chinese communist propaganda among Soviet experts in China directed against the Soviet Communist party and government. This is not convincing, since Soviet communist experts *are* constantly exposed to such propaganda in other non-communist countries, though not generally by the ruling party in those countries. Romania is a communist country where Soviet experts were exposed to propaganda against official Soviet policies during the crisis in Czechoslovakia in the mid-1960s.

[63] This complaint was made by Fidel Castro in a speech in Havana on 14 March 1966 (quoted in *Indian Left Review*, Delhi, Mar.–Apr. 1972, p. 108).

[64] Robinson (1974), p. 314. There are some estimates which suggest that the Russians imported American wheat on better terms than the Chinese imported American wheat in 1973. If true, this would prove that the Russians are now better than the Chinese at making good bargains with the Americans (to which the Chinese can hardly object, since the American suppliers are 'capitalist-imperialists').

[65] Self-reliance is defined as a situation where a country does without foreign loans at subsidized rates.

principle of 'to each according to his work, from each according to his powers' which Marxism prescribes for the 'lower stage' of communism, and which appeals to common sense, judging by the misuse of gifts by less developed capitalist countries (Bose, 1975, Ch. 11, p. 196-8).[66])

Thus, to some extent at least, the Maoist charge of 'social imperialism' against the Soviet communist leadership is a case of the pot calling the kettle black.[67] But in so far as this is so, Maoist polemics against Soviet communist 'social imperialism' has produced more than a dirty term of inter-communist abuse. It supplies a theoretical concept to the corpus of Marxian doctrine on the subject of inter-state communist relations whose importance will probably grow with time.[68]

One more of Mao's original contributions to Marxian theory and practice must now be assessed. This is the Maoist version of the communist personality cult, first invented by Joseph Stalin, on which something has already been said in the previous chapter.

As indicated in sect. 4.3 above, the original features of the Maoist version of the cult are (i) reliance on open mass terrorization of enemies and suspected renegades by refined methods of psychological torture, (ii) *non*-reliance on a complementary cult of the infallible Communist party, (iii) explicit attention to the problem of 'revolutionary successors' (Han Suyin, 1967, 1973, pp. 179–80) to take over when Mao is no longer present as the supreme interpreter of Maoist 'thought' or ideology.

How far (i) and (ii) will ensure (iii) is hard to say. (i) may produce a hostile reaction, delayed till after Mao's death, as Stalin's secret terror did (and unlike the anti-Stalin movement, it may be an active *mass* movement). However, (ii) may ensure what Stalin (with his

[66] It is doubtful whether free Chinese arms to Sihanouk of Cambodia (Sihanouk and Burchett, 1973, p. 207) or to the Arab countries has produced qualitatively better results (for communism) than priced Soviet military assistance to North Vietnam.

[67] with the difference, of course, that inegalitarianism with respect to material comforts seems to be definitely less prevalent in Chinese than in Soviet society under communism. But inegalitarianism with respect to political influence may be equal or more in China compared to the Soviet Union, except that those who are 'more equal than others' may be less secure in China.

[68] The problem was anticipated, when the Soviet Union was still the only communist country, in analytical literature on the theory of international trade by Jacob Viner (1944, pp. 450–60). It was also an insight in an otherwise inchoate ersatz 'ideology' of Oswald Spengler, who wrote in 1926 'Hard as the half-developed Socialism of to-day is fighting against expansionism, one day it will become arch-expansionist' (1926, 1954, vol. 1, p. 37).

cult of the Communist party) could *not* ensure, i.e. a mass movement upholding Maoism after Mao, in active opposition to a party apparatus which denigrates or criticizes Mao. But it is one thing for the masses (specially the youth) to march victoriously against the Communist party as true defenders of Maoist ideology when Mao is alive and active as the supreme interpreter and arbiter in disputes, and another to do it when he is no longer alive. So (ii) also has a negative side to it. It deprives the Mao cult of an institutional custodian in the shape of the Communist party apparatus.[69]

In the absence of a cult of the Communist party, the purity of Mao Tse-tung 'thought' in post-Mao China will be in the custody of the 'masses of the Chinese people', deified by Mao ('Our God is none other than the masses of the Chinese people': Lin Piao (ed.), *Quotations from Mao Tse-tung*, pp. 170–1).[70] However, the cult that the Chinese masses 'can do no wrong' may lead to indecision, especially in the matter of introduction of institutional changes in Chinese communist society, which, as we noted in Chapter 3, is one identifiable social function of a communist personality cult in a communist society.

For one thing, there may be interminable doctrinal disputes, with *all* contenders quoting the Maoist scriptures,[71] as was roughly the situation in the Bolshevik party in post-Lenin Russia, with all contenders quoting Lenin against each other, until the emergence of the Stalin cult got rid of the problem.[72] But if each individual Maoist in post-Mao China acts according to his own personal interpretation

[69] similar to the apparatus of the Church acting as the infallible custodian of the purity of the (Catholic) Church of St. Peter, or the 'democratic-centralist' collective leadership of the present-day Soviet Communist party acting as the custodian of the infallible cult of the Communist party.

[70] apparently on the basis of a conception similar to the Christian conception of Jesus Christ as the Son of Man.

[71] This is perfectly possible. Thus one Maoist group may justify struggles of organized workers and peasants against students on the ground that Mao says the 'workers, peasants, soldiers, revolutionary intellectuals and revolutionary cadres', *in that order*, 'form the main force' in the cultural revolution (Ch'en, 1971, p. 118), another may counter-quote Mao's instruction that this is 'all wrong', 'none of those who have repressed student movements has ended well' (ibid., pp. 129–30). Or one group may quote Mao's injunction on the importance of study, another may counter-quote Chou En-lai quoting Mao as saying 'The more you study, the more stupid you become' (ibid., p. 131). Mao seems to recognize the possibility and has no ready solution to the problem (Snow, 1971, 1972, p. 174).

[72] It is said that when a member of an Indian Communist party delegation to Moscow in 1950 tried to uphold his point of view against others by quoting Lenin, Stalin replied that he could always find quotations from Lenin to refute him, but would not, because he was against 'quotational Marxism'.

of the Maoist ideology, he would be acting rather like the Christian Anabaptists, who repudiated all law, claimed to be guided at every moment by the Holy Spirit who cannot be guided by formulas (Russell, 1946, 1962, p. 20), and who have remained small sects though they arrived at a form of communism. (Alternatively, at the opposite extreme, they could recognize Maoism in everything, tolerate all laws, all scriptural interpretations by groups and individuals, all conduct in the name of Mao, in the tradition of the British Quaker do-gooders, or of a polytheistic religion like Hinduism, and cease to be actors in a revolutionary drama.)

On the other hand, one of the possible consequences of unrestrained polemics among Maoists, the emergence of a new personality cult as a 'successor' to that of Mao, is unlikely in China. This is partly because Lin Piao has already been denounced (by Mao) for having tried to do this in Mao's lifetime.[73] The episode has resulted in the enunciation of a Maoist doctrine similar to the Sunni Muslim doctrine of 'Khatme Nabuwwat' (i.e. the finality of Mohammed's prophethood) which still provokes riots and threatened general strikes against heretics in Pakistan.[74] The Maoist version of the doctrine would declare Mao to be the last of the *founders* of Marxian doctrine. (There would still be scope for Mao to appoint by his 'testament' someone as the trusted interpreter of Maoist ideology after his death, rather as the Muslim caliphs were believed to have been appointed. But in the absence of a sanctified apparatus like an Islamic theocracy (or an obedient Communist party) to uphold the interpreters, the interpreters may come to a sad end.[75])

A more serious possible consequence of unrestrained polemics among rival Maoists is the emergence of a synthesis of Maoism and Confucianism or, if the post-Mao revulsion against Maoism is strong, of pure Confucianism, functioning as an instrument for ending indecision and ordering social life in post-Mao China. Awareness of some form of Confucianism as a serious alternative to

[73] Available evidence suggests that Lin Piao did try to do this, though the allegation that he tried to assassinate Mao may or may not be true. (See Schram, 1974, Text 26, pp. 290-9 for an account of Mao's references to Lin Piao's conduct on the eve of his death.)

[74] See report from Lahore in *Times of India*, 11 June 1974, of a riotous political movement against members of the Ahmadiya Muslim sect who do not subscribe to this doctrine. Such a movement preceded the first rule by martial law in Pakistan in 1954.

[75] unless the institution is backed by a belief in reincarnation, as the institution of the Dalai Lama in Tibet has been for centuries.

Maoist-Marxism has been recognized by Maoists for many years.[76] With modern western bourgeois ideology never securing more than a foothold in China, with the possible challenge of Soviet communist 'revisionism' effectively discredited (both as ideology, and as the ideology of a potential 'national enemy'), with a challenge from Buddhism suppressed vicariously by the Sino-Communization of Tibet, the most likely alternative to Maoist-Marxism as the 'ideological superstructure' of post-Mao China is some form of Confucianism. Another feature which makes Confucianism a serious contender is that, like Maoism, it relies on a complete *ethical* system of good and bad motives to run society.[77] Until recently, while the Confucian tradition of 'self-cultivation' of the body and the mind was commended to communist revolutionaries (Liu Shao-chi, 1939, 1951, p. 8; Mao, 1964, in Ch'en, 1971, p. 95), it was strongly criticized for discouraging social (productive) and revolutionary (political) practice (Liu Shao-chi, 1939, 1951, p. 24; Mao, 1939, in vol. 3, 1954, p. 20; Mao, 1964, in Ch'en, 1971, pp. 96-7). A possibly novel feature of the revived campaign against Confucianism in 1974 is the denigration of Confucius as an unscrupulous, unethical political intriguer. Since historically reliable records about the personal life of Confucius do not seem to exist,[78] this attack on the *politics* of Confucius may be explicable as the attack on the last barrier to an immortal cult of Mao Tse-tung.[79]

---

[76] See Liu Shao-chi, *How to be a Good Communist* (1939, 1951), Ch. 1; Mao Tse-tung, 'Orientation of the Youth Movement' (1939), in Mao, vol. 3 (1954), pp. 12–21; Jerome Ch'en, *Mao Papers* (1971), p. 95.

[77] More will be said about this in Part II, Ch. 11–12, and in Part III.

[78] Needham (1962), sect. 9, pp. 3–32, says Confucius was born to a family which claimed descent from the imperial house of Shang (p. 3), that 'opinions differ' as to whether he ever held official (political) positions (p. 4). Needham also reports that according to some Chinese writers Confucius was a 'feudal' and a 'counter-revolutionary', but that according to Kuo Mo-jo (disgraced during the cultural revolution) Confucius sympathized with rebellious officials who had taken up arms against feudal nobles (p. 7). But Mao in 1964 declared that Confucius was a 'shepherd' who later became an official and was cut off from the masses (Ch'en, 1971, p. 95).

[79] Maoists may not like the Confucian warning that it is dangerous to let a prince say whatever he chooses, with no one daring to disagree, because ' . . . if what he says is bad, will he not come near to ruining his country by a single phrase?' (Needham, op. cit., p. 11).

CHAPTER 5

Capitalist-Socialist Co-Existence

5.1 Introduction

By capitalist-socialist co-existence, we shall mean the co-existence of a capitalist and a socialist (i.e. a communist[1]) socio-economic system. In this chapter, we first consider certain questions about global co-existence, and then pass on to questions about co-existence within national territories, e.g. Germany, Korea, China.

5.2 Global co-existence: some questions

The global co-existence of capitalism and socialism has been a fact of life ever since communist hopes of a synchronized world communist revolution, and anti-communist hopes of the restoration of capitalism in Russia, foundered in the 1920s. For a long time, this global co-existence simply meant a state of 'no war, no peace' or hot wars and 'cold wars' between divided or united capitalist and socialist blocs of states. Later, especially in the 1970s, new dimensions were added, viz. 'normalization' of interstate relations, arms-control negotiations, growth of inter-system international trade to significant dimensions, 'competitive *détente* or *rapprochement*' between rival communist and capitalist blocs directed against each other.

These developments in reality have been inadequately mirrored in theory, both communist and non-communist or anti-communist. In communist theory the words 'peaceful co-existence' (used by communists of all hues), 'peaceful competition between the two systems', with the accent on 'economic competition' (used by *some* communists, *sometimes*), have been introduced. But what these words and phrases mean is by no means crystal clear. Anti-communist theory suffered an early setback when, in the 1930s, on the basis of the standard tools of neo-classical (Walrasian) economic analysis, the thesis that 'socialism *cannot* be a rational economic system' (and therefore must inevitably collapse) was disproved.[2] There now remain only fragments of a theory of the inevitability of capitalist restoration based

---

[1] or 'the lower stage of communism', where the principal means of production are collectively owned, but reward is according to work.

[2] See Nove and Nuti (1972), Introduction and Part I, for the essential literature.

on empirical studies of the productivity in capitalist economies, especially in agriculture, which is seen as superior to productivity in socialist economies.[3] A syncretic non-communist theory has also emerged, which falls back on the observed trends of long-term growth of output (and productivity) in *both* the modern capitalist *and* socialist economies towards projecting an *indefinite* co-existence of both capitalism and socialism on a world scale.

Actually, out of all this fuzzy theorizing, four crucial questions can be picked out. These are:

Q.1 Will *socialism* inevitably be undermined, on a global scale, by *economic* competition with capitalism?

Q.2 Will *capitalism* (instead of socialism) be undermined, globally, by *economic* competition with socialism?

Q.3 Will capitalism inevitably be undermined, on a global scale, by *political* (and ethical) competition with socialism?

Q.4 Is the indefinite co-existence of capitalism and socialism on a global scale certain?

Q.1–2 in the above list concern theses based on the philosophy of *economic* determinism. Q.3, on the other hand, concerns a thesis based on a philosophy of *political* determinism. Modern researches in economics and politics have produced results which can be pressed into service to supply interesting answers to all these questions.

To simplify the exposition in the next section, the thesis underlying *Q.1* will be referred to as the '*anti-communist thesis*'. The thesis involved in *Q.2* will be referred to as the '*Soviet communist thesis*', that in *Q.3* as the '*Chinese communist thesis*'. The thesis underlying *Q.4* will be referred to as the 'non-communist' or the 'common-sense' thesis. There will probably be no serious objections to this nomenclature, as far as the 'anti-communist' and 'non-communist' theses are concerned. The designation 'Soviet communist thesis' is more controversial. But it is justified because it is an idea which does occur (though not as a *pure* 'economic determinist' thesis[4]) in Soviet communist literature, and does *not* occur in Chinese communist literature, which harps on the idea underlying Q.3.

---

[3] What we have here are fragments, rather than a whole theory, because there is no theory of capitalism or of socialism which says that the one with superior productivity must prevail, though most theories agree that it is desirable that an economic system should promote *some* growth in productivity.

[4] in so far as the role, albeit a subsidiary one, of political factors is never denied.

5.3 Global co-existence: some answers

The least persuasive is the '*anti-communist thesis*' underlying Q.1, which says that socialism will inevitably be undermined in economic competition with capitalism. In its original form, as set out by Ludwig von Mises,[5] the argument was that without private property in the means of production, and without market transactions, there can be no rational (or determinate) allocation of resources, without which no economic system can function. As already noted, there were theoretical flaws in this argument.[6] The modern argument builds on the observed data, more or less acknowledged now by the Soviet Union, if not yet by China, about the superior productivity of man and machine in advanced capitalist as compared to socialist economies, especially in agriculture, transport, etc. But, as already stated in note 3 above, there is no theory of capitalism or socialism which speaks of the operation, as regards rival socio-economic systems, of some kind of Darwinian law of the survival of the fittest in terms of productivity. To be sure, the Marxian theory says that the emergence and survival of a socio-economic system depends on the capacity of its 'production relations'[7] to promote the growth of social 'productive forces' (which includes growth in productivity as a result of technological progress). But this implies a prediction that socialism can survive as long as it promotes *some* growth in 'productive forces', which may be less than in the rival capitalist system.

The '*Soviet communist thesis*' is seldom expounded in its pure form, proclaiming the inevitability of a breakdown of capitalism brought about by *purely* economic factors. The role of a final *political coup de grâce* to capitalism is always recognized. But the notion persists that in competition with socialism, capitalism would atrophy basically due to its *economic* self-contradictions. The analytical basis of this notion could be the Marxian theory of the long-run tendency for the rate of profit to fall, thus reducing the rate of capital accumulation, which is the *raison d'être* of capitalist production (Marx, 1959, Chs. 13–14). But there are logical flaws in all theories of the tendency for the capitalist rate of profit to fall, Marxian or other (Samuelson,

[5] See Nove and Nuti (1972), Ch. 3: 'Economic Calculation in the Socialist Commonwealth'.
[6] Ibid., Ch. 2: 'The Ministry of Production in the Collectivist State' by E. Barone (1908); Ch. 4: 'On the Economic Theory of Socialism' by O. Lange (1936–7).
[7] of which property relations are the most important.

1957; Robinson, 1967, Ch. 5; Bose, 1975, Ch. 7, pp. 139–40). Of course, using the tools of the modern economic theory of 'production of commodities by means of commodities' (Sraffa, 1960) it is possible to identify problems of 'under-accumulation', of the adaptation of the commodity compositions of output and demand, of the tendency towards a declining average rate of capital accumulation in capitalist economies (Bose, 1975, Ch. 9). But there are remedies for these problems in the form of institutional change within the framework of capitalism, e.g. colonialism, imperialism, neo-imperialism, monopolistic sales promotion (Bose, 1975, Ch. 10).

The tools of modern commodity production theory also help us to specify *exactly* the condition which must obtain if capitalism is to suffer euthanasia in economic competition with socialism. This is that capitalism must specialize in the production *only* of 'luxury products', more generally 'non-basic' products which roughly comprise both 'luxury products' (e.g. motor cars and air-conditioners) and the producer goods (e.g. steel, machines) which are used to produce *only* luxury products, and must import *all* its 'basic products' from the socialist economies.[8] If this is the case, capitalism is completely, and helplessly, *at the mercy* of the socialist economies *economically*. A blockade imposed by the socialist economies on the capitalist economies could destroy capitalism, with the political aspects of the destruction being easily taken care of, at the cost of only temporary unemployment in the socialist economies. However, there is *no reason* to suppose that capitalist economies *would* specialize in the production only of non-basics in this way. On the contrary, it is likely that for a long time to come the socialist economies— China not excepted—will remain dependent on the capitalist economies of North America and Australasia for making up their internal deficits in 'semi-basic' products, especially food-grains.[9] In general, we may conclude from pure analysis (also confirmed by the empirical evidence of the twentieth century) that (i) 'objective economic conditions' are 'ripe' for socialism in almost any country, and (ii) nowhere have capitalist property relations acted as 'fetters', retarding all further growth of output (or further technological progress).

[8] Basic products are those which enter, directly or indirectly, into the production of *all* products in a system (e.g. coal, steel, or electricity in an economy with modernized agriculture) (Sraffa, 1960, pp. 7–8, 51).

[9] Semi-basic products are food-grains, other foodstuffs, and necessary consumer goods, which are combined in variable proportions in the producers' consumer-goods baskets (see Bose, 1975, Ch. 6, p. 113; Ch. 13, p. 219).

In contrast to the 'anti-communist' and the 'Soviet communist' theses, the 'Chinese communist thesis' has the merit of recognizing that 'economic factors' are 'neutral' in the contest between capitalism and socialism. It relies on an *ideological-political revolution* (involving militant dedication, and a 'selfless' communal ethos as the motivation for political action), instead of on economic self-contradictions, to destroy capitalism on a global scale. But this may fail to eradicate capitalism, because the breakdown of a social system (capitalist or socialist) is the product of *interdependent* decisions based on the preferences of *both* revolutionaries *and* counter-revolutionaries. There is a game-theoretic proof, which resembles the solution of the 'prisoners' dilemma' problem in standard game theory, that militant, 'selfless' dedication to the revolutionary cause may abort an anti-capitalist revolution as much as the 'selfishness' of corruptible revolutionaries. (This proof has been published in Bose, 1975, Ch. 12, and is reproduced, with elaboration, in Part II, Ch. 9 of this book.) Briefly, the argument is a two-pronged one. Firstly, 'selfless' dedication may turn out to be a *hypocritical* cover for 'selfish' revolutionary action (by which the 'selfless' revolutionaries gain, individually or as a group, in material benefits or intangible 'political influence', at the expense of other exploited or oppressed classes). Secondly, if revolutionary action *is* genuinely 'selfless', it may be ineffective because it merely complements (and facilitates) 'selfish' action by others. Thus the 'Chinese communist thesis' is no more convincing than the 'Soviet communist' one, which it controverts.

The foregoing does *not* mean, however, that the non-communist 'common-sense' thesis, viz. that an *indefinite* co-existence of capitalism and socialism on a global scale is *certain*, must necessarily be accepted as the best available one. Of course, we must recognize the fact that capitalist and socialist economies specialize in producing and trading in *both* basic *and* non-basic (and semi-basic) products, and are likely to continue to do so. This *does* mean that there is no *economic* 'inevitability' about the breakdown of either capitalism or socialism. But this does *not* mean that an indefinite survival of both capitalism and socialism on a global scale is assured. On the contrary, with the game-theoretic formulation of the problem of 'capitalist breakdown', referred to above, it can be proved that 'unselfish' action by revolutionaries *can* promote a capitalist breakdown (see Bose, 1975, Ch. 12, sect. 3–7; also Part II, Ch. 9 of the present work). (This is reassuring, as several 'breakdowns' of capitalism *have* in fact

8

occurred in the twentieth century, and theory ought to be able to formalize such events without recourse to such a *Deus ex machina* as dislocation caused by war.) A game-theoretic 'socialist break-down' thesis is also available, which makes use of the 'isolation paradox' which has been identified in the literature on optimizing the social rate of savings—but its conditions are more stringent than the conditions of 'capitalist breakdown' (see Bose, 1975, Ch. 15, for an exposition). The stringent condition is this: individuals in a socialist society must want capitalism, *even if* they know that some of them will *not* be capitalists, but be exploited as wage-workers by private capitalists. This is an *essential* condition for the breakdown of socialism and the restoration of capitalism, simply because a capitalist society without capitalist exploiters and exploited wage-workers is an illusion. We conclude, therefore, that the non-communist 'common-sense' thesis is no more convincing than the others considered earlier.

Thus the analytical answer to each of the four questions about global co-existence formulated in the previous section is No. But in the process of arriving at these answers, some issues may have been clarified.

5.4 Intranational co-existence

In the present section we discuss the problem of co-existence in the special context of a number of countries in the modern world which have been partitioned for two decades or more into socialist and capitalist parts, i.e. Germany, Korea, China.

The problem of co-existence in this group of countries has five common features:

(i) The outcome of civil wars (and subsequent cold wars and mutual economic boycott), which have been fought in these countries (with the exception of Germany), has not eliminated either socialism or capitalism.

(ii) The socialist and capitalist parts of these countries have con-solidated themselves on the basis of separate statehood (with sub-global international recognition).

(iii) Neither the socialist nor the capitalist state has been able to subvert the socio-economic system of its rival state internally through 'bloodless politics'.

(iv) In all these countries there have been moves towards *détente*, as the first step towards 'reunification'.

(v) In at least two of these countries (Germany and Korea), the establishment of national *confederations* has been mooted publicly at some time or another, as a possible step in the process of reunification.

Of course, despite these five common features, there were several individual variations. Thus as regards (iv), there was more of a *rapprochement* (if not a *détente*) between the U.S.A. and China[10] than between China and Taiwan.[11] On the other hand, as far as Korea was concerned, the position seemed in a certain sense to be the reverse of this. The dramatic and rather unexpected North–South joint statement of July 1972 on 'the three principles of independence, peaceful reunification and great national unity'[12] seemed to have been all but rescinded in 1973 and 1974. But North Korea alleged that this was due to pressure from the U.S.A. and Japan, which never endorsed the North–South joint statement. But at the end of 1975 North Korea still opposed the separate representation of North and South Korea in the U.N., offered a peace treaty and U.S. military pull-out from South Korea to facilitate reunification.[13]

Regarding (v), a German confederation to enclose the socialist and capitalist parts of Germany was proposed by Walter Ulbricht, on behalf of the German Socialist Unity (communist) party in 1957 (*20 Jahre DDR—20 Jahre deutsche Politik*, 1969, p. 43), and was mentioned in Socialist Unity party documents in 1966 (Ulbricht, 1968, p. 512), and 1967 (*20 Jahre DDR—20 Jahre deutsche Politik*, 1969, p. 520). The details of the proposal mentioned over the years include: (i) an equal number of representatives of the two German states are to meet to draw up details of the proposed confederation, (ii) both Germanys are to be de-nuclearized, and to withdraw from

[10] The U.S.A. and Communist China seem to have discussed in 1972 a plan for U.S. withdrawal of its military protection to Taiwan, in return for a Chinese pledge to adhere to peaceful means to achieve reunification. But there seems to have been no progress towards implementation up to spring 1976.

[11] However, there has been no parallel *rapprochement* or *détente* between Communist China and capitalist Taiwan, even after the death of Chiang Kai-shek.

[12] See *Korean Trade Unions*, No. 138 (1973), p. 3.

[13] South Korea has subsequently suppressed a students' movement for reunification, and come under martial law. The North Koreans claim that this is at U.S.–Japanese instigation. The evidence cited is a military build-up in South Korea under U.S. operational control, the U.S. proposal for the entry of North and South Korea as separate states into the U.N., and a South-Korean–Japanese agreement to exploit the underwater resources of the continental shelf off South Korea (*Korean Trade Unions*, Nos. 137–8, 1973; Letter to the Congress of the U.S.A. from the North Korean People's Assembly, 25 Mar. 1974). In 1975 the U.S. Defence Secretary Arthur Schlesinger threatened nuclear retaliation to a North Korean attack, and the U.S. agreed to recognize North Korea if 'the Soviet Union or China' recognized South Korea.

military alliances, (iii) the sovereignty of neither state is to be surrendered to the confederation, (iv) the confederal assembly is to make *recommendations* (only) regarding trade, currency, transport, workers' rights, etc. in each constituent state (*20 Jahre DDR—20 Jahre deutsche Politik*, 1969, pp. 243, 286, 520). However, the West German and American response has been almost completely negative (see Kissinger, 1960, pp. 135–9, for the American argument).[14]

On the other hand, in recent years East Germany, too, seems to have lost active interest in the confederation. It has been concentrating on (a) 'normalization' of interstate relations on the basis of equality, including mutual recognition, withdrawal from rival military blocs, simultaneous entry into the United Nations as *separate* independent states, with a view to (b) achieving a 'step-by-step rapprochement of the two German states until the time of their unification on the basis of democracy and socialism' (The Constitution of the German Democratic Republic, promulgated on 8 April 1968, Ch. 1, Article 8(2)).[15] This restatement of East German objectives bears the interpretation that the offer of a confederation as a framework of co-existence of capitalism and socialism in Germany has been withdrawn for all practical purposes, and has been replaced by *immediate* 'normalization' and *eventual* 'socialist reunification', without a confederation serving as an intermediate stage in the process. For the present, at any rate, the German capitalist-socialist *détente* fits into a wider pattern of all-European capitalist-socialist *détente*, rather than a German capitalist-socialist co-existence within the framework of a confederation.[16]

The North Korean commitment to a Korean capitalist-socialist confederation, first announced in a speech by Kim Il Sung on 23 June 1973 (*Korean Trade Unions*, No. 137, 1973, pp. 2–7), seems to be stronger. The offer was made about a year after the joint North-South declaration by the two Korean government delegations, referred to above, but had been all but rescinded by the Southern regime. The offer of a confederation made by Kim Il Sung *explicitly* says that the proposal is 'to institute a north-south Confederation,

[14] In Kissinger's view, the confederal proposal is acceptable only if a *new* East German government formed after U.N.-supervised elections is the East German representative at the confederal centre (ibid., Ch. iv, sect. 4, pp. 137–8).

[15] I am indebted to G. Katragadda and Nandlal Gupta, of the All-India Indo-GDR Friendship Association, for making available East German documents, and to Partha Sarathi Gupta for translating some material from German.

[16] This was made explicit at the Helsinki Conference on Security and Co-operation in Europe in August 1975.

leaving the two existing social systems in the north and south as they are for the time being' (ibid., p. 6).[17] The seriousness of the North Korean confederal proposal is underscored by their insistence that (i) ' . . . our country should be prevented from being split into two Koreas permanently as a result of the freezing of the national division, and that the north and south should also work together in the field of external activity' (ibid., p. 6), and (ii) 'north and south should not enter the UN separately . . . if they want to enter the UN before the reunification of the country, they should enter it as a single state under the name of the Confederal Republic of Koryo . . . after the Confederation is set up' (loc. cit.). Thus, unlike the G.D.R., the Democratic People's Republic of Korea wants to forgo inter-national recognition, if necessary, in order to exert pressure on South Korea for accepting a confederation. (This may be because an all-European *détente* is rather more important for East Germany than German reunification. For North Korea, on the other hand, partial reunification on a confederal basis is more urgent than any over-all East Asian *détente*.)

Despite growing antagonism between North and South Korea towards the end of 1975, there are no signs of North Korea veering towards acceptance of a German-type partition in Korea, which would involve acceptance of U.S. troops in South Korea (as U.S. troops are tolerated in West Germany). On the contrary, with the united backing of all the communist powers, North Korea has been demanding the withdrawal of U.S. troops as the first step to reduced tension based on 'nuclear blackmail' by the U.S.A. against North Korea, to be followed by an all-Korean settlement 'without outside interference'. Though there is less stress on a 'confederal' solution —so that theoretically a Vietnam-type solution is not ruled out—the proposal for a confederation has not been revoked. Total opposition to a German-type settlement is indicated by rejection by *both* the U.S.S.R. and China, as well as by revolutionary North and South Vietnam, of U.S. proposals to recognize North Korea, if either the U.S.S.R. or China recognizes South Korea, and then withdraws its veto on the admission of both North and South Vietnam to the United Nations.

[17] Of course, the North Korean confederal offer is coupled with a call for 'joint exploitation of Korea's natural resources' against the interests of foreign capitalist monopolies, and for 'mass participation in patriotic work for national reunification' *against* the South Korean martial law regime. But these are con-sidered to be 'anti-monopoly capitalist', anti-imperialist, and *not* anti-capitalist measures.

However, whether or not confederations become practical politics in Korea (or Germany), it is clear that the framework of confederation could promote capitalist-socialist co-existence within national territories in essentially the same way as global capitalist-socialist co-existence discussed in the preceding section of this chapter. No new questions of principle arise, so the answers to the questions about capitalist-socialist co-existence within German or Korean national territories are the same as the answers to the questions about global capitalist-socialist co-existence.

5.5 China and Taiwan

So far as is known, Communist China has not offered either (i) mutual recognition and 'normalization', or (ii) a 'confederation on the basis of the existing social systems' to capitalist Chinese Taiwan. Successfully rejecting the 'two Chinas' concept,[18] she has secured international recognition of her claim over Taiwan as Chinese national territory. This implies a *unanimous* acceptance (by China, Taiwan, and the international community) of an integration of Taiwan into the unitary, or an adjusted semi-federal[19] political structure of Communist China.

However, as already stated, in return for the gradual withdrawal of U.S. military protection for Taiwan, China seems to have agreed to try out a policy of 'bloodless' integration of Taiwan into China. This has left, as a residue, an internal problem of socialist-capitalist co-existence in Chinese national territory.[20]

At present, the China–Taiwan co-existence problem is a case of two largely 'parallel' economies, one socialist, the other capitalist, whose economic interdependence is only indirectly established, via large-scale foreign trade by both the capitalist and socialist parts with Japan.

The *necessity* for this state of affairs to continue is dictated by (i) the U.S. veto on violent political intergration of Taiwan and China (in the manner of the Tibetan integration), (ii) the Kuomintang's capacity to prevent the communization of Taiwan by 'bloodless politics', and (iii) Communist China's lack of a navy strong enough to force the issue *vis-à-vis* the U.S.A., without increasing the

[18] and an *independent* Taiwan is *not* desired by the Kuomintang (capitalist) Chinese who control Taiwan at present.
[19] which would provide for control by the central government over an 'autonomous' Taiwan.
[20] Of course, colonial Hongkong and Macao also pose such problems.

relative strength of Soviet naval power in the Pacific at the expense of U.S. naval power.

In the circumstances Communist China seems to be concentrating on forcing Japan to choose between expanded trade with her and trade and investment in capitalist Taiwan. Since Taiwan imports many of her 'basic' products from Japan, this strategy, if consistently (and successfully) enforced, *could* make Taiwan's economy 'wither away' over a long period, till it is politically 'ripe' for a 'bloodless' communization.

On the other hand, Communist China may decide (as she seems to have decided with respect to Hongkong and Macao) that the Taiwan capitalists' international trading contacts are assets utilizable for developing China's socialist economy. In that case, she may have an interest in the development of triangular trade between China, Taiwan, and Japan, which will serve socialist China's interests, as has been achieved with expanded triangular trade between China, Hongkong, and the world capitalist market. But in the case of Hongkong, China also makes a virtue of her respect for the lease agreement between China and Britain, which Communist China has inherited. In the case of Taiwan, she can work out a *modus vivendi* for such triangular economic contacts only on the basis of the political-constitutional framework of an autonomous Taiwan, where Communist China tolerates a capitalist 'island' on condition that its foreign trade earnings (if not its production and foreign trade targets) are under socialist China's control. This could extend China's 'internal socialist-capitalist co-existence' over a long period, as long as it is needed by Communist China.[21]

5.6 An asymmetry

The discussion in the previous section suggests the hypothesis of another kind of 'internal', capitalist-socialist co-existence within a national territory. This would be the case of a *socialist* (instead of a capitalist) 'island' embedded (and controlled by) a *capitalist* 'mainland'.

As we shall see in Part II, Ch. 9, the outlines of such a possibility were dimly (*very* dimly) visible in West Bengal in India in the late 1960s. (It was also visible to a lesser extent in the late 1960s in Kerala.)

[21] It may not be needed if (and when) Communist China and the Soviet Union reconstruct their anti-capitalist joint front and challenge the U.S.A. and Japan, economically and politically.

However, there is an *asymmetry* between the China–Taiwan socialist-capitalist co-existence hypothesis (which is still alive in the 1970s, and the India–West Bengal capitalist-socialist co-existence hypothesis (which seems dead in the 1970s). It is *easy* for a politically dominant socialist 'mainland' to regulate its economic relations with a capitalist 'island', in the *socialist* interest. But it is difficult for a politically subordinate socialist 'island', tolerated only for reasons of Realpolitik by the capitalist 'mainland' to regulate *its* economic relations with the capitalist 'mainland' in the *socialist* interest.

This is because a capitalist 'mainland' will, *sui generis*, encourage smuggling and black-marketing, and 'buying cheap and selling dear' by state-capitalist enterprises, in the socialist 'island', specially if the socialist management of the economy is weak and inefficient. But a socialist 'mainland', if it has decided to tolerate a capitalist 'island', will, *sui generis*, in its own interest, encourage efficient *economic* management there, and rely on *political* subversion to obliterate it, when it is no longer required.

CHAPTER 6

The Balance of Global Super-Power:
Some Results

6.1 Introduction

SUPER-POWER has been defined in the Glossary as the nuclear power to destroy most man-made assets on the earth's surface.

In this chapter we analyse a few results of the emergence of a balance of global super-power, enjoyed by the U.S.A. and the U.S.S.R. *vis-à-vis* each other (and the world). (In the next section, there is a reference to a situation that may be created by the emergence of a third global super-power, China.)

6.2 Nuclear peace

For thirty years the world is said to have been on the brink of an all-out, global, third, nuclear war, for 'ideological' reasons, or even by 'accident'. But, in fact, there has been 'nuclear peace', in the sense that, though there have been wars, there has been no nuclear, all-out, general war.

Over this long period, there has been a brief period in which the U.S.A. held the atomic monopoly, and was completely 'invulnerable', while the U.S.S.R. was completely 'vulnerable', because (i) the U.S.A. had the nuclear striking power, and (ii) the U.S.S.R. had no retaliatory capacity. Later, with the development of the missile systems, a situation of 'mutual invulnerability' has been established, in which *both* the U.S.A. *and* the U.S.S.R. can only produce a stalemate by a 'first strike', as well as by a 'second strike' (for a discussion, see Kissinger, 1960, pp. 27–40).

Throughout the period of the U.S.A.'s world atomic monopoly, explanations of the 'nuclear peace' can be given in terms of 'ideological factors', viz. (i) the difficulty involved in an American total about-turn from the anti-fascism of World War II, to anti-communism of a nuclear (third) world war, (ii) the Soviet communist insistence on 'armed non-intervention' in favour of communism strictly *only* within the framework of legitimacy of territorial divisions at the end of the anti-facist war.[1] In the later period, the explanation

[1] which is why the Soviet Union did *not* protect the communist take-over of

can be given in terms of the technological fact of 'mutual invulner-ability'.

However, these explanations do not tell us precisely why a nuclear peace persisted, despite several threats and alerts about all-out nuclear war—the first during the 1958 Suez war, and the last during the 1974 West Asian war. So it is worth investigating the possibility of a general explanation for the period of 'mutual invulnerability' (which seems to have come to stay).

A model, called 'Chicken', employed in game theory, and men-tioned in Chapter 2 of this book, seems to be suitable for the purpose (see Shubik, 1967, pp. 242–3; Wilson, 1968, 1970, pp. 163–4, for references).

Figure 1 represents the pay-off matrix in a 'Chicken' model of a super-power nuclear war game between the U.S.A. and the U.S.S.R., which are more or less evenly matched. The pay-off matrix, as already explained in Chapter 2 above, reproduces the valuations placed on the prospects of the game by each party. The upper half of each of the four (interior) rectangles measures the U.S.A.'s pay-off, and the lower half the U.S.S.R.'s pay-off. Each country's pay-off is measured on some (separate) cardinal scale.[2] Each numerical entry for a pay-off carries a *negative* sign, because it is assumed that *any* strategy with nuclear weapons involves a net cost (at least the allocation of resources for making them, even if they are not *used* in war so as to

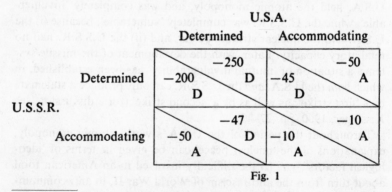

Fig. 1

governments except in territory which it had occupied in terms of agreements between the anti-fascist allies during World War II. It made no move when the French and Italian communists were expelled from the governments of their respective countries.

[2] i.e. the American and Soviet pay-offs with each outcome are not comparable, but American pay-offs with all outcomes, and Soviet pay-offs with all outcomes, *are* comparable among themselves.

invite destructive retaliation). In the given context, each country can adopt one of two *strategies*, viz. to be *determined* to fight it out (or D), or to be *accommodating* (or A). Consequently, there are *four* possible outcomes, represented by the four interior rectangles, viz. (i) *both* are determined, or D,D (north-west rectangle), (ii) the U.S.A. is accommodating, the U.S.S.R. is determined, or A,D (north-east rectangle), (iii) *both* are accommodating, or A,A (south-east rectangle), and (iv) the U.S.A. is determined, the U.S.S.R. is accommodating, or D,A (south-west rectangle).

Given the mutual distrust assumed (ultimately due to capitalist-socialist antagonism), outcome A,A is excluded, even though it is the least costly for both countries. Of the remaining outcomes, D,D or 'bilateral determination' will be rejected, because each country is better off with unilateral determination or unilateral accommodation, i.e. either with A,D or D,A (*proof*: For the U.S.A., $-47 \angle -250$ and $-50 \angle -250$. For the U.S.S.R., $-45 \angle -200$ and $-50 \angle -200$). This ensures that there will be no all-out nuclear war. The reason is that for each country the penalty of bilateral determination is four or five times the cost of (or penalty of) unilateral determination or accommodation. Thus each country has a strong incentive to be unilaterally determined, if possible, but to 'chicken' out, or to give in unilaterally, if necessary. Which country *does*, in fact, give in, is accidental, and also irrelevant. Both A,D and D,A are 'equilibrium outcomes', depending upon who can convince whom that *he* is unilaterally determined to fight it out.

The numerical values for pay-offs in this example have the peculiar feature that for each country the difference between unilateral determination (D) and unilateral accommodation (A) is small. This formalizes the explicit facts of the case during the Cuban (missile launching-pad) crisis in the early 1960s, when the U.S.S.R. gave in but gained its fundamental aim of the survival of Communist Cuba. (On the other hand, the 'loss' the U.S.A. had to bear in spite of its 'determination' in the Cuban crisis is the survival of a communist country in the American continent and some economic loss from the embargo imposed on Cuba.) This model can perhaps also formalize what might have been the behind-the-scenes facts during the Czecho-slovakian crisis in the late 1960s, when it was the U.S.A. which gave in, or during the 1974 West Asian war, when the U.S.S.R. probably gave in to a brusque nuclear alert by the U.S.A. However, it is easy to see that the nearness of the pay-offs for accommodation and determination is *not* necessary in order to have equilibrium outcomes with unilateral determination/accommodation. The cost of accommodation may be doubled, to reach -100 (in the north-east and south-west rectangles), but the equilibrium outcomes would still be the same.

It might seem from Figure 1 that the really 'rational' solution would be for both to minimize their costs by opting for the outcome A,A so that each suffers a cost of maintaining a nuclear stockpile of -10 (in the south-east rectangle). But, as already mentioned, in the context of mutual distrust no strategy will achieve this outcome. To eliminate mutual distrust between capitalist U.S.A. and socialist U.S.S.R., both must agree to the indefinite co-existence of capitalism and socialism, for which, as we have seen in the previous chapter, there is no rationale. Indeed, Figure 1 explains the paradox that while the 'peace camp', which stands for elimination of mutual distrust between capitalism and socialism, has had only a peripheral impact on world politics for thirty years, a 'nuclear peace' has been preserved because the 'rational' self-interest of the nuclear warmongers needed it over this long period. In the absence of unforeseen developments in weapons' technology,[3] or in the technology of biological warfare, there is no reason to suppose that this paradox will not also remain with us in the future.

We thus reach the conclusion:

S.1 Given (a) the nature[4] of the balance of global nuclear super-power, and (b) the problem of antagonistic (or 'competitive') capitalist-socialist co-existence involved in it, super-powers will engage in a build-up of nuclear arms, but maintain a nuclear peace.

This has three implications: First, are we to conclude from S.1 that a strategic arms limitation agreement (SALT) is a mirage? Not necessarily, since strategic superiority in nuclear arms (i) is unlikely to eliminate the state of 'mutual invulnerability', so as to give one

---

[3] Tactical nuclear weapons are apparently similar to strategic nuclear weapons in so far as military exercises have shown that their effect is desolation of the combat zone and decimation of the population. So the pay-off matrix is of the same type as in Figure 1, assuming the war is fought in the territory of both combatants (see Kissinger, 1960, p. 78). On the other hand, dead-pan precision missile systems, *without* invulnerability, may (a) revive non-nuclear weaponry—possibly even make nuclear weapons obsolete, as poison gas became after 1918—and (b) bring back *non*-nuclear *global* wars. But there can be developed mutual invulnerability with the 'balanced terror' of high-precision missile systems. In that case, there will be a non-nuclear, missile-based global peace, very similar to the global nuclear peace of the past thirty years.

[4] i.e. its *technological* nature, in terms of first and second nuclear strike capabilities.

super-power a decisive advantage; (ii) even if it does, a decisive victory in an all-out nuclear war is unlikely to be attainable; (iii) strategic superiority will, in any case, be most probably too short-lived to allow the super-power with temporary 'strategic superiority' to make the 'ideological' political decision to exploit it in war. It follows that, despite mutual distrust, *both* the super-powers have an interest in SALT. (Moreover, the reduced secrecy with respect to the nuclear arms build-up that SALT entails is not an unmixed evil, despite mutual distrust, because nuclear super-power *requires recognition* from the 'enemy' if it is to be fully effective.) (For a discussion of these issues, see Kissinger, 1960, Ch. 6, pp. 210–86.)

Second, it is paradoxical, but true, that it is precisely the vaguely felt 'total destructiveness' of nuclear arms which ensures nuclear peace, given the context of antagonistic co-existence of capitalism and socialism on a global scale. To see this, we cut the problem down to its essentials by *imagining* a state of antagonistic co-existence between a capitalist 'first power', the U.S.A., and its socialist opposite number, the U.S.S.R., both of whom have the power to fight a *non-nuclear world* war. We can now construct a 'prisoners' dilemma' type of game-theory problem, viz. Figure 2, which has a unique equilibrium outcome: war.

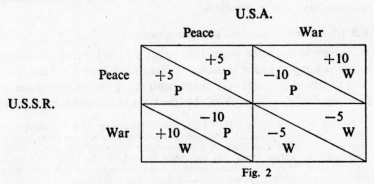

Fig. 2

In this case, unlike the case portrayed in Figure 1, each country acting distrustfully alone, minimizes its potential losses (i.e. maximizes its assured 'gain') by opting for a W,W outcome, that is, by going to war. So the equilibrium outcome is uniquely given by the south-east rectangle. What this case has in *common* with the case in Figure 1 is that the best outcome, P,P (both sides offering and keeping the peace), is ruled out by mutual distrust. But the important *difference* between the two cases is pin-pointed by the fact that here a unilateral pacifist capitulation to avert war (corresponding to unilateral accommodation in the nuclear war case) carries a *bigger* penalty (-10) than a bilateral war (-5).

The third implication of our conclusion is that, although S.1 is framed in terms of a two-super-powers game, it seems to be valid with a three-super-powers game (including China). (In 1960 Henry Kissinger visualized the possibility of China acquiring by 1975 the nuclear capability which the U.S.S.R. had in 1960 (Kissinger, 1960, Ch. vi, sect. 4, C, p. 253).) By 1974 China seems to have had India and parts of the U.S.S.R. within the range of its nuclear war-headed missiles, and was said to be concentrating on bringing Warsaw within range. It was also thought to have been working on plans for making intercontinental missiles capable of reaching Washington.[5] So a world with three global super-powers is a distinct possibility.[6] The reason why the 'Chicken'-game type of analysis extends to a three-super-powers problem is this. Given the nature of nuclear super-power technology, in a three-super-powers world the three will be paired off in three separate duels,[7] each of which will be played as a standard 'Chicken'-type of game. Moreover, any attempt by any one super-power to incite the other two to get involved in a nuclear clash will be pointless.[8]

6.3 Global *non*-domination by super-powers

The world has taken a long time to get used to the idea of nuclear super-power producing a nuclear peace rather than a nuclear war. The theory of it is still very vague, with stress on the emergence of 'multi-polarity' as a result of the break-up of communist and anti-

---

[5] However, towards the end of 1975, there were reports of a 'slow-down' in Communist China's progress in developing capability for a nuclear strike against New York. The expected firing of an intermediate-range ballistic missile across India into the Indian Ocean has also been delayed, maybe because China is concentrating on switching from liquid to solid fuel-based nuclear systems to reduce her vulnerability, or on spy satellites over the U.S.S.R.

[6] The somewhat remote possibility of the emergence of a *fourth* nuclear super-power is disregarded here. Japan does not have the political capacity to qualify, and her economic capacity is in doubt in the context of the oil crisis. India has every reason to stick to her resolve *not* to become a 'nuclear-weapons power'. Even if she is forced to—by a U.S. nuclear base at Diego Garcia, or a Chinese nuclear umbrella for Pakistan—she will not then become a nuclear super-power, as we have defined it, but only a regional nuclear power.

[7] We are assuming, of course, that there will then be a problem of a triangular co-existence of capitalism, and Soviet and Chinese communism.

[8] because the two will not agree to commit suicide for the benefit of the third.

communist (capitalist) international blocs.[9] But in practice the recognition is much more in evidence. The heightening of super-power tension, even the American nuclear alert during the West Asian war, is *not* followed any longer by the revival of scares about a global nuclear war (as happened after the Cuban missile crisis, for example).

However, what has taken the place of the earlier expectations of global nuclear war is the expectation of global joint domination by the two super-powers. This new thesis seems to be no more convincing than the one it has replaced, as can be seen with the help of another 'prisoners' dilemma' type of model portrayed in Figure 3.

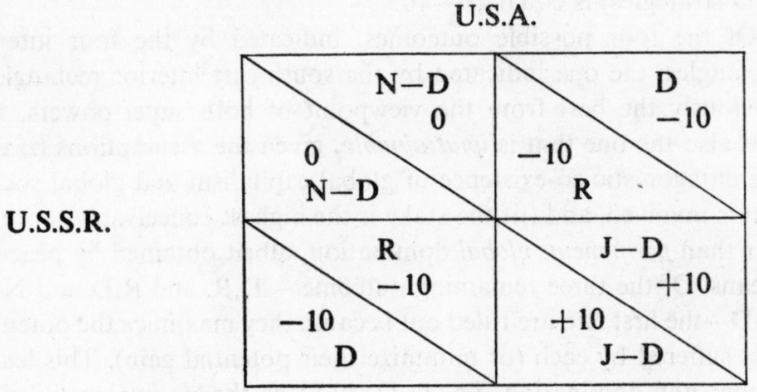

U.S.A.

	N–D 0	D –10
U.S.S.R.	0 N–D	–10 R
	R –10	J–D +10
	–10 D	+10 J–D

Fig. 3

Here, the upper triangles in the interior rectangles indicate the U.S.A.'s strategy and pay-off, and the lower rectangles the U.S.S.R.'s strategy and pay-off. The *north-east* interior rectangle indicates the outcome when the U.S.A. tries for global domination (D), and the U.S.S.R. resists (R). The *south-east* interior rectangle indicates the outcome of joint global domination by the U.S.A. and the U.S.S.R. (J-D for both U.S.A. and U.S.S.R.). The *south-west* interior rectangle indicates the outcome when the U.S.S.R. tries for global domination (D), and the U.S.A. resists (R). The *north-west* interior rectangle indicates the outcome when neither tries for global domination (N-D for both U.S.A. and U.S.S.R.). The numerical assumptions are that the spoils of joint global domination are valued at +10 per super-power share (making a total of +20), the cost of nuclear global destruction per super-power is −10 (making a total cost of global

[9] Actually the only genuine 'multi-polarity' is expressed in a potential three-super-power conflict.

destruction valued at -20), and the spoils of global *non*-domination is 0 for each super-power.

There are four possible strategies that each country can adopt: 1. to try for global domination (D) when the other resists (R), 2. to claim a fifty-fifty share in joint global domination (J-D), 3. to resist (R) when the other tries for global domination (D), and 4. when neither tries for global domination (N-D). Now, given the assumption of a balance of nuclear super-power on a global scale, strategies 1 and 3 imply global destruction, it being assumed (for simplicity) that the cost to each country of bilateral global destruction (D,R or R,D strategies) is equal at -10.

Of the four possible outcomes, indicated by the four interior rectangles, the one indicated by the south-east interior rectangle is obviously the best from the viewpoint of both super-powers. But it is also the one that is *unattainable*, given the assumptions (i) that the antagonistic co-existence of global capitalism and global social-ism is involved, and (ii) the stake is the highest conceivable: nothing less than *permanent*, *global* domination, albeit obtained by peaceful means. Of the three remaining outcomes—D,R and R,D and N-D, N-D—the first two are ruled out because they maximize the potential loss suffered by each (or minimize their potential gain). This leaves global non-domination, i.e. N-D, N-D as the unique equilibrium outcome for both.

Thus we reach a second paradoxical conclusion:

S.2 Given (a) the nature of the balance of global nuclear super-power, and (b) the problem of antagonistic and distrustful capitalist-socialist co-existence involved in it, super-powers will opt for a strategy of global *non*-domination.

6.4 Revolution and counter-revolution

The global non-domination outcome does *not*, of course, imply the freezing of the global *status quo* (including the territorial or the capitalist-socialist social *status quo*, or a *status quo* debarring institu-tional change in capitalist and socialist societies). Still less does it imply a monotonic retreat into isolation—into 'Fortress America' or 'Fortress Soviet Union'—by the two super-powers.

On the contrary, it implies joint toleration *or* legitimization of suc-cessful revolutions, as in Cuba, Bangladesh and Communist South Vietnam (or Portugal), and of successful counter-revolution, as in Chile, of changing patterns of 'multiple alignment' of either super-power with countries like Yugoslavia, India, Romania, Pakistan, the West Asian Arab states, etc.

The reason, as noted in the previous chapter, is that nuclear global super-power by no means abolishes the problem of antagonistic co-existence between capitalism and socialism. Balanced nuclear super-power, by promoting a nuclear peace, and non-global domination by the super-powers also promotes revolutions and counter-revolutions.[10]

Thus we reach our third conclusion about the results of a balance of global super-power, which comes as a corollary of the previous two:

S.3 In an age of balanced nuclear global super-power, and antagonistic capitalist-socialist co-existence, nuclear peace and global non-domination by the super-powers provides scope for revolutions and counter-revolutions.

6.5 Nuclear super-power, communist schism, and communist 'social imperialism'

The three results (S. 1–3) of the balance of nuclear super-power and antagonistic capitalist-socialist co-existence, plus the internal (national) monolithic communist unity for a schismatic strategy seem to be the necessary and sufficient conditions for 'peaceful' international communist schisms, such as have occurred between Yugoslavia and the U.S.S.R., China and the U.S.S.R., Romania and the U.S.S.R., Cuba and China, etc.

One special implication of the international communist schism facilitated by the U.S.A.–U.S.S.R. nuclear super-power balance is the emergence of China as a potential nuclear (global) super-power, which has already been considered in sect. 6.2 above. This would convert the present global problem of capitalist-socialist antagonistic co-existence into a *triangular* problem of antagonistic co-existence of capitalism, Soviet-type socialism, and Chinese-type socialism. At present, when still *not* a nuclear super-power, but only a nuclear regional 'great power', China seems to align herself sometimes *against* the U.S.A., and reluctantly *with* the U.S.S.R., and sometimes *with* the U.S.A., mostly *against* the U.S.S.R. An example

[10] This has already been noted in serious literature on political science in Hannah Arendt's remark that the emphasis in the relationship between war and revolution has shifted more and more to revolution (Arendt, 1963, 1973, p. 17). However, she has arrived at this conclusion by an analysis which is different from the one presented in this book.

of the first is her basic alignment in the Vietnam–America war, discussed in Chapter 2 of this book. Examples of the second are China's participation since the Sino-Indian border war, in a *de facto* military-political bloc with the U.S.A. and Pakistan, and her support of the U.S.–Japan military pact (reported by Kakuei Tanaka, the Japanese Premier, after the normalization of Sino-Japanese relations in 1973). The main motive behind such 'inconsistent' alignments seems to be a desire to redress the nuclear power balance between China and the U.S.A., and China and the U.S.S.R. When China *does* become a nuclear super-power, this motive will disappear, though 'ideological' motives may still produce similar shifting patterns of alignment. For *both* the attainment of nuclear super-power status, on a par with the U.S.A. and U.S.S.R., *and* the ideological reasons discussed in Chapter 2 (sect. 2.1) above, make the schism between Soviet and Chinese communism probably irrevocable.

In a tri-polar super-power world of the future, is communist 'social imperialism' likely to solidify as an important problem? (See Chapter 4, sect. 4.2–4 of this book.)

Of the *three* distinct versions of the theory of communist 'social imperialism' which can be identified, the first two are unconvincing in such a context, on the basis of the results presented earlier in this chapter. These are: (i) a communist 'social imperialism' (either Soviet or Chinese) as an appendage of American capitalist imperialism, akin to social-democratic 'social imperialism' of an earlier age; (ii) a communist 'social imperialism' as a partner, on an equal footing, of American capitalist imperialism in global joint domination. If (ii) is ruled out for reasons stated in sect. 6.3 above, (i) does not arise, as the analysis portrayed by Figure 3 makes clear. (Factually, the large crop of revolutions and counter-revolutions taking place under the shadow of bi-polar nuclear super-power in recent years, some of which are recalled in the previous section, support the analytical conclusion just reached that versions (i) and (ii) of the theory of communist 'social imperialism' need not be taken very seriously.)

Version (iii) of the theory of communist 'social imperialism' is not so easily disposed of. In this version, the focus is on episodes in the development of Communist Russia and Communist China which resemble the well-known phenomena of capitalist colonialism, imperialism, and neo-imperialism.[11] As more evidence (about the

[11] Though often used interchangeably, they could be used to refer to three

past as well as the present) about both capitalist and communist societies is compiled, some striking parallels between the external exploits of capitalist and communist societies may be hard to ignore. Such parallels may be drawn between (i) the English Puritan colonization of Northern Ireland and Chinese communist colonization of Tibet, (ii) the English (Puritan and Victorian) colonization of 'empty spaces' in North America or Australasia, and Russian communist settlements in Soviet Asia and Siberia, (iii) imperialist capitalist exploitation of scarce minerals and mineral oils in Africa and West Asia, and the alleged Soviet communist seizure of non-ferrous metal deposits in Mongolia,[12] or Chinese seizure of Tibetan natural resources, (iv) the retardation of the growth rate of backward capitalist and socialist economies by (a) manipulation of international terms of trade and (b) imposition of repayment obligations on account of foreign economic aid, by *both* capitalist neo-imperialism *and* Soviet[13] or Chinese communist 'neo-imperialism' (see discussion in Bose, 1975, Ch. 9–10, and Ch. 4, sect. 4.4 of this book).

However, it is comparatively easy to find a rationale for these phenomena in terms of analytical models of capitalism, but more difficult to do so in terms of analytical models of (communist) socialism of either the Soviet or Chinese variety.

Capitalist colonialism, imperialism, and neo-imperialism may be interpreted as easy, pre-modern institutional substitutes for the instruments of versatile modern technology (of production, distribution, and exchange) for handling problems of (a) discrepancy between the commodity-compositions of aggregate demand and output, and the connected problems of (b) the 'under-accumulation' of capital, and (c) the tendency for the rate of capitalist accumulation to decline.[14]

Problem (a) continues to plague Soviet and Chinese communism, partly because their average technological level is lower than in advanced capitalist countries, partly because there is strong pressure

---

distinct phenomena (see Bose, 1975, Ch. 10). Roughly, with colonialism, 'empty spaces' (perhaps made empty by near-genocide) are colonized, with imperialism, there is a *net* outflow of resources from the exploited to the exploiting country, with neo-imperialism, there is a *net* inflow of resources, followed by net outflow, from the exploited to the exploiting country.

[12] There is a New China News Agency report of Soviet seizure of copper-molybdenum deposits in Mongolia (*Times of India*, Delhi, 24 June 1974).

[13] Repayment obligations to the U.S.S.R. are now posing a problem for India (*Times of India*, Delhi, 29 June 1974).

[14] See Bose (1975), Ch. 9, for a discussion.

for greater choice in consumption. But problems (b) and (c) do not, unless a *fetish* is made of matching the capitalist rate of accumulation by the communist rate of accumulation, for which there is no ultimate justification in terms of Marxian communist ideology, or of *any* theory of a socialist economy. Moreover, at least in principle, improved supranational techniques of communist joint political-economic planning, better forecasting of shifts in consumer tastes (as attempted currently in the U.S.S.R.), or a puritanical de-emphasis on consumption (as in China) can solve the (a)-type of problem arising in communist societies. Thus there is no *necessity* for communist societies to imitate colonialist, imperialist, or neo-imperialist instruments of policy employed by capitalism.[15]

What has just been said also covers Chinese communist charges of Soviet 'colonization' of Angola made in December 1975. The context is competitive arms deliveries to Angolan guerrillas, before and after the withdrawal of Portuguese imperialist forces, by the U.S.A., the U.S.S.R., and Communist China,[16] and the entry of South African white-racist and Cuban communist armed personnel on opposing sides. The Chinese communists claim that they armed all three factions of guerrilla fighters until the Portuguese withdrawal was announced, and have stopped arms deliveries to all three after an escalation in arms deliveries by the Soviet Union, followed by the U.S. (and South Africa), occurred subsequent to the Portuguese withdrawal. This amounts to a Chinese communist strategy that either Soviet-aided guerrillas should come to terms with U.S.-aided ones, or the communist countries should join hands to leave them in the lurch. (For, as just argued, there is no *necessity* for communist countries to embark on colonization, whether in Siberia, Tibet, or Angola.) If the Chinese recipe is accepted by all communist states, this would result in the paradox that in avoiding a communist 'colonialism', the communist states would ensure the joint rule by the capitalist super-power and the entire bloc of communist countries in whichever ex-colonial country the capitalist super-power might want to enter to combat communist influence. But, as indicated in earlier references in this book to the crisis in Angola, there is no firm evidence that Chinese communist policy in Angola is a settled policy.

[15] In principle, 'non-imperialistic' remedies for (a), (b), and (c) are also available to modern advanced capitalism (see Bose, 1975, Ch. 10).

[16] There seems to be no doubt that the U.S. started the escalation, and that the U.S.S.R. followed.

The pre-Angolan strategy of united communist resistance to the capitalist super-power, which paid off in Indo-China, seemed to be at work in 1975 and 1976 *vis-à-vis* Korea, the Portuguese ex-colony of Timor, and Rhodesia or Zimbabwe.

PART II
Indo–West Asian Regional Problems

As indicated in Chapter 6, the balance of global super-power leaves scope for the rise of regional political power, for revolution, and counter-revolution. Included among the latter, by implication, are both successful and abortive revolutions and counter-revolutions, and the mutations within social systems which abortive revolutions or counter-revolutions might generate.

The chapters of Part II of this book are devoted to analyses of certain unusual events in the Indo-West Asian region, viz. an abortive counter-revolution in East Bengal, an abortive revolution in West Bengal, and the assertion (with some prospects of consolidation) of a regional political power. Each of these events has specific paradoxical features which are considered in detail in Chapters 7–10.

Further, the events discussed in these chapters also point to a general paradox about economics and politics in the Indian subcontinent, which may hold for what in standard parlance is now called South Asia (to include Burma, Sri Lanka, along with the Indian subcontinent proper), or even for the entire West Asian region, and on to most of Africa. Chapter 7 tries to identify this general paradox.

CHAPTER 7

The Specifics of Indo-West Asian Regional Politics

7.1 Introduction

Subcontinental India, or, more generally, South Asia, has lived for a long time with all (or almost all) the classical 'causes' of a modern communist revolution, namely acute poverty, extreme inequality,[1] strong discontent, vehemently (even abrasively) articulated experiments with adapted versions of every known 'model' of communist revolution which has proved successful anywhere in the world.

Thus a 'Russian style' model of an Indian communist revolution was formalized in the illegal Communist party document 'Proletarian Path' in 1940, and was seriously tried out, with variations, in 1949 with a railway general strike (which never came off) as its main lever.[2] Two or three variants of a 'Chinese model' of communist revolution were tried out, in Telengana (formerly Hyderabad state) in 1948-9, and again in Andhra Pradesh and West Bengal in the 1960s[3] (for the West Bengal experiments, see Chapter 9 in this book). Variants of a 'Cuban model' of a 'revolution which becomes communist',[4] have been tried out in Sri Lanka.

Why is it that the region has produced neither a successful communist revolution nor a successful counter-revolution (as has been repeatedly achieved in the Latin American mainland, the latest example being the Chilean counter-revolution)?[5]

[1] assuming that 'poverty' can be separated from 'inequality' as a social problem, which it can be, to some extent.

[2] The 'Proletarian Path' owed its inspiration more to Lenin's perspectives in the unsuccessful Russian revolution of 1905 than to his strategy in the successful revolution of 1917. The 1949 perspectives of an Indian communist revolution were not explicitly traced back to the 'Proletarian Path', but did resemble it in essentials.

[3] All three explicitly acknowledged the Chinese communist revolution as the 'basic model' for a successful Indian communist revolution, but only the West Bengal experiment received the official endorsement by the Chinese Communist party for a while.

[4] by dedicated revolutionaries becoming communist rather than dedicated communists becoming revolutionaries through experience.

[5] As we shall see in Chapter 9, even the successful Bangladesh revolution, which was not a communist revolution, has not quite been reversed and become a successful counter-revolution.

To pose the question in this way is more illuminating than stereo-typed attempts to explain the absence of revolution or counter-revolution such as have occurred elsewhere in terms of (i) the multi-class (and hence indecisive) composition of Indian political parties of the right and the left, or (ii) the 'corrupting influence' of foreign capitalist imperialism, or foreign communist 'social imperial-ism'. For, as we have noted in Part I, or as is implicit in the analysis given there, the entry of the 'revolutionary classes' was a necessary, but not a sufficient, condition of the successes of the Indo-Chinese (or Chinese) communist revolutions. And the expulsion of 'non-revolutionary' classes is certainly not a sufficient condition, though it is partially[6] a necessary condition. So to concentrate on (i) may not throw much light on the specifics of Indian subcontinental politics. To concentrate on (ii) may yield some insights—as we shall see later in this chapter and Chapter 10. But restraint is advisable, if only because South Vietnam, Cambodia, and Laos were saturated with the 'corrupting' influence of the most powerful and resourceful capitalist imperialism. Nor, as we have noted, was the alleged 'cor-rupting influence' of Soviet communist 'social imperialism' missing in North Vietnam. These countries still went through modern com-munist revolutions and anti-communist counter-revolutions such as have not been seen in the Indian subcontinent.

But the question just posed supplies, by itself, only the starting-point of a promising investigation. It tends to predispose answers in terms of a series of 'historical accidents', or of an innate Indian incapacity to make any kind of revolution or counter-revolution (due to an addiction to a cult of political 'non-violence'), or of the inherently 'passive basis of ... [an] unresisting and unchanging [Indian] society'.[7]

We might conceivably do better by asking a somewhat different question. Why is it that modern attempts at revolution and counter-revolution in this region have only produced definite mutations of what is identifiable as a backward state-capitalist society, in which political competition is the dominant form of economic competi-tion? If the question is posed in this way, the focus is immediately on a process by which, as in Lampedusa's The Leopard, 'things are

---

[6] partially, because in the process of these revolutions only sections of the 'non-revolutionary' classes were eliminated, while others (sections or individuals) were 're-educated' and assimilated.

[7] Marx (1853), p. 34. Marx, however, thought that British interference had brought about the 'only social revolution ever heard of in Asia' (1853a, p. 20).

changed so that they will not change'.[8] In other words, revolutionary energies are not absent, but are consumed in promoting changes in the political and territorial *status quo* within a given social *status quo* (for meaning of these terms as used here, see Glossary of Terms).

With the question put in this way, an obvious step towards finding an answer is to identify a 'secular' syndrome which specifies the common specific features of the main historical stages through which the societies of the Indian subcontinent have passed. We can then try to put the focus on a 'modern' version of this secular syndrome, within which the main currents of subcontinental economics and politics operate. If we can do that, we might be able to give a rational interpretation of the 'general paradox' referred to in the introduction to Part II, and also make more acceptable some of the assumptions about the environment made in the analyses of the events surveyed in Chapters 8–10.

The hypothesis just outlined has been much overworked, and is suspect for that reason. Blowing bubbles in the air about an 'Indian genius' or mystique in politics has been a favourite pastime with all brands of Indian nationalists, most Indian socialists, and a small minority of Indian communists. So far, the hypothesis has been based on inchoate notions about Indian *mores* or ideology, and its politics and economics. But it remains a promising hypothesis.

7.2 A 'secular' political-economic syndrome

Using code names for ready reference later, the 'secular' Indian subcontinental syndrome is represented by commitment of all political interest-groups to:

S.1 'Pluralism': This involves the antagonistic co-existence of political-economic conglomerates which split society from top to bottom, cutting across, rather than coinciding with, the horizontal lines of division between classes and strata.

S.2 'Legitimism': Its main expression is the preoccupation with making, interpreting, and revising laws to achieve the objectives of each conglomerate at the expense of others.

S.3 'Statism': This is expressed by the utilization (by manipulation, infiltration, and seizure) of the instruments of state power by each conglomerate to secure sectional (economic and political) gains at the expense of others.

[8] See Lampedusa, 1958, 1974, pp. 28, 36 ff.; for an attempt to interpret the process portrayed by Lampedusa as a bourgeois process in Italy and France, see Debray (1970, 1975), p. 143.

S.4 'Parliamentarism': This implies commitment to either implicit (or 'black') parliamentarism (roughly, political intrigue between conflicting groups to determine political decisions) or both implicit and explicit parliamentarism (i.e. the utilization of what has been defined in the Glossary as a parliamentary voting system).

S.5 'Extra-parliamentarism': This refers to (i) manipulation, infiltration, and seizure of the instruments of the infrastructure of state power (or the 'molecules of civil society' (Gramsci, 1971, Part II, sect. 2, especially pp. 233–8)) and (ii) the systematic use of extra-parliamentary techniques of political action including, notably, (a) law-breaking, and (b) counter-coercion of the majority to counteract coercion by the holders of state power by those who challenge the holders of state power.

As the senses in which the code names attached to features S.1–5 of the 'secular' Indian syndrome are used differ somewhat from the senses conveyed by standard usage, a general discussion may help.

Feature S.1, 'pluralism', implies, of course, that all attempts to create a 'homogeneous society' in India, at any stage of historical development, have failed. (The most determined attempts in the modern period have been made in Pakistan, with consequences which are well known.) But it also implies: (i) No attempt to establish a horizontally stratified society organized on the basis of occupation or distributive privilege, on caste or classical class lines, has succeeded either. (ii) The lines of division between the conglomerates may be ethnic, religious, or (in the modern period) drawn on the basis of political subcultures, cutting across religions, caste, or class divisions.[9] (iii) The antagonistic co-existence *between* conglomerates is reproduced *within* each conglomerate on the basis of legally recognized dissidence, or 'illegal' dissidence which too is recognized subject to a system of penance or penalties. (iv) The birth of each new conglomerate (e.g. religious sect, or, in the modern period, a political subculture) represents an 'ethicalist' challenge to existing conglomerates. But conglomerates survive only if they represent new 'legitimist'[10] trends.

To clarify the meaning of the feature S.2 of the 'secular' Indian syndrome, 'legitimism', it is best to proceed indirectly by first discussing what it does *not* mean. It was noted above in Chapter 4 on

---

[9] usually along diagonal lines drawn from top to bottom, so that castes or classes or interest groups are *not* symmetrically represented in all the conglomerates.   [10] For definitions, see below.

Chinese communist ideology, sect. 4.2 (ii), that one of the specific distinguishing features of pre-Communist China was the absence of a 'legislative body to make use of, (nor) the legal right to organise the workers to strike' (Mao, 1954a, p. 267). On a narrow interpretation, this specific feature refers only to the absence of parliamentary institutions (including among them a semi-independent or elected judiciary, a presidential or ministerial executive, etc.), the so-called 'rule of law', or generally, in Chinese communist parlance, 'bourgeois democracy of the old type' (Lu Ting-yi, 1951, pp. 17–19). But it is possible to have a wider interpretation of this peculiarity of pre-Communist China (which would subsume the 'narrow' interpretation). This can be worked out by asking the question: *what* could take the place of the vacuum left by 'the absence of legislative activity' as far as the essential political problems of the conservation, exercise, or seizure of political power are concerned? Obviously, the substitute could *not* be a 'dictatorship unrestricted by *any* laws', for most dictatorships *are* restricted by *self-made* laws. (This is true of fascist or Soviet-type communist dictatorships, as well as 'parliamentary democracies' in capitalist countries which are regarded as 'bourgeois democratic dictatorships' by Marxists and neo-Marxists. Of course, all of them involve 'implicit' parliamentarism, although only the last involves also 'explicit' parliamentarism.) In other words, the so-called 'rule of law' in capitalist democracies, fascist rule by decrees or edicts or 'concordats', revolutionary communist rule by 'decrees' or on the basis of the framework of 'socialist legality' (emphasized in the Soviet Union and several East European communist countries in recent years) may be regarded as different species belonging to the same genus, which can be given the name 'legitimism'. Each of these various types of 'legitimism' implies 'legislative activity' which, according to Mao Tse-tung, was *absent* in pre-Communist China. What *was* the Chinese substitute for 'legitimism' which seems to be almost universal?

A society which is really free from the domination of some variety of 'legitimism' in our sense does not seem to have been known to exist in the West in fact. It has, however, been strongly present in an anarchist 'moral' tradition which goes back to the Anabaptists, as mentioned in previous chapters, and is also found in the writings of medieval as well as modern writers such as Bakunin, Tolstoy, Gandhi, Chomsky, Marcuse, some of whom will be referred to again in later chapters of this book. Indeed, it is perhaps true that ever since written texts were actually used in all countries outside China, the ultimate instruments for achieving political objectives actually in use have been 'legitimist'. But China seems to have been the exception.[11] There the dominant tradition seems to have been what could be called, by contrast, an 'ethicalist' one, for over two thousand years, during which the opposing Confucian and Taoist systems (*both* 'ethicalist' in contrast to 'legitimist' systems) stamped out and obliterated the influence of the Chinese variety of 'legitimism', viz. the 'Legalists'[12] or Fa Chia, who were dominant briefly in the third and fourth centuries B.C., but permanently discredited 'legitimism' in China by their excesses.[13]

The foregoing preliminaries help us to define precisely the 'legitimist' and 'ethicalist' systems as the alternative ultimate instruments for achieving political ends which are true polar opposites of one another. (It will be apparent to a reader familiar with Joseph Needham's work on Chinese civilization that the definitions given below are based on his interpretation of Chinese social philosophies.)[14]

S.2a 'Legitimism' is represented by a corpus of 'positive laws'[15] (interpretable, capable of being manipulated and revised), binding on those who use it, imposed on those against whom it is used.

[11] This may have something to do with the Chinese hieroglyphic script. If each word is a separate letter, it is preferable to simplify social regulation by issuing a few 'moral precepts' which are easily written down in still fewer hieroglyphics, rather than a large number of interpretable (or even non-interpretable) laws which have to be written down in a still larger number of hieroglyphics.

[12] See Needham, (1961), sect. 5, pp. 95–6; (1962), sect. 9, 10, 12, 18. Confucians were afraid of definite laws because they were afraid people would study and manipulate them (ibid., 1962, sect. 18, p. 522). Taoists wanted rulers to rule without appearing to do so (ibid., 1962, sect. 10, p. 62). (Though Needham has nothing to say on this, it is worth investigating whether French physiocratic *laissez-faire* notions had a Chinese Taoist inspiration.) The Chinese 'Legalists', by contrast, held (i) that the ethical virtues of benevolence, righteousness, and love are not worth having, (ii) that *wicked* officials should be employed, so that people love the statutes 'and not their own relations', (iii) that laws should be self-enforcing and non-interpretable, so that there is no manipulation (ibid., sect. 12, pp. 204–8).

[13] Their excesses are illustrated by an apocryphal story. A drunken prince falls asleep, and is in danger of catching cold. The *crown-keeper* puts a coat over him to keep him warm. The prince *punishes* the *coat-keeper* (for negligence), but puts the *crown-keeper* to *death* (for the greater offence of transgression of duty) (Needham, 1962, sect. 12, p. 207).

[14] However, Needham (1962, sect. 18, pp. 529–30) seems receptive to the suggestion by English juristic historians that India, like China, had a strong 'ethicalist' tradition. As will be apparent below, I am unable to agree with this view.

[15] The term 'positive laws' is used in the sense of Thomas Aquinas's classification of laws (see Needham, 1962, sect. 18, pp. 538–9). Because the Chinese Legalists forbade the interpretation of laws, as noted in n. 11 above, the term 'legitimism' has been used in preference to the term 'legalism' as the polar opposite of 'ethicalism'.

S.2b 'Ethicalism' is represented by a non-interpretable self-enforcing system of ethics which is binding in all possible situations *in place of* 'positive laws' (which refer to *specific* situations), are interpretable, etc.

Using this terminology, we can hypothesize that modern China, both pre-communist and communist, has been under the strong influence of a dominant 'ethicalist' tradition, as opposed to a 'legitimist' one. This was probably true of Sun Yat Sen's Kuomintang, though Chiang Kai-shek's Kuomintang probably tried, and failed, to establish a highly centralized 'legalist' regime.[16] As already noted in Chapters 3 and 4, the Chinese communists, following Mao Tse-tung Thought, seem to rely on a modern 'ethicalist' system, although Confucian ethics proper are often ruthlessly inverted in the process.[17] By contrast, modern Indian politics have been dominated by the overpowering influence of highly developed 'legitimist' traditions. Moreover, there are reasons to believe (see following sections) that this domination of 'legitimist' traditions in India goes back to the period of British rule and beyond. However, there are contrasts between Indian 'legitimism' and other legitimist traditions in politics and economics, e.g. Western 'bourgeois-democratic' or fascist or Russian communist. Unlike them, Indian legitimism has always been 'pluralistic legitimism', in a sense which will become at once clear if we recall the sense in which the word 'pluralism' has been defined in the Indian context earlier in the present chapter.

The attribute of 'pluralistic legitimism' of the Indian syndrome logically *requires* the third attribute, S.3 'statism', to be added to it. *Any* 'legitimist' tradition requires 'statism', defined to mean utilization of the instruments of state power. But only 'pluralistic legitimism' requires 'statism' as defined above, viz. the manipulation, infiltration, and seizure of the instruments of state power by each conglomerate for its own sectional gain at the expense of others, so that each conglomerate (e.g. a medieval religious sect, or a modern political subculture) functions like a 'state among states', on the basis of its

[16] In so far as Chinese 'legalism' can be interpreted as representing an attempt to uphold amoral 'positive' laws against (i) accepted morality, and (ii) the goodwill of the people, to overthrow feudal lords, while at the same time keeping the people weak (ibid., 1962, sect. 12, pp. 206, 213).
[17] Confucian ethics include the injunction: 'do not do to others what you would not wish done to yourself' (1962, sect. 9, p. 7). Since concepts of fair play and even-handed justice are decried as 'liberalism' to be eschewed, modern Maoist ethics of the cultural revolution negates this Confucian injunction by upholding Lu Hsun's admonition: 'Beat the drowning dog' (see report in the *Indian Express*, New Delhi edn., 30 July 1974, p. 4).

own brand of 'legitimism'.[18] These conglomerate 'states' are interdependent and engaged in antagonistic competition with each other.
So they are *not* correctly portrayed, even in a simplified model, as
'disconnected atoms' between which there is 'repulsion and constitutional exclusiveness' (Marx, 1853, pp. 33, 36, has such a model for
pre-British India, which must, however, be modified in the light of
the results of modern research into India's past. Some of these results
are mentioned in the next section). It follows that 'statism', as defined
in this chapter, is incompatible with Hegelian worship of, or Hob-
besian advocacy of, the self-perpetuating omnipotent 'protectorate'[19]
or Leviathan, or with the 'Bonapartist' state of Marxian conception,
which rules as an 'independent' entity, *'against* civil society', when
contending classes, castes, etc. of 'civil society' reach a state of political 'equilibrium'.[20] On the other hand, 'statism' in our sense is also
incompatible with the conditions of, or the ideology and the politics
of, coercion-free atomistic *laissez-faire*. For 'statism' in Indian conditions of 'pluralistic legitimism' necessarily implies *mutually coercive*
co-existence of competing conglomerates. (In fact, as will be noted
in sect. 7.4–5, the ideology and politics of *laissez-faire* utilitarianism
has been a non-starter in Indian politics, even in the modern period.)

Both 'ethicalist' and 'legitimist' political prototypes, whether
'pluralistic' or not, need a political voting system, at least to test
opinion before decisions are taken.[21] (The only possible exceptions
are 'ethicalist'—stratified or homogeneous—systems which function
on the basis of an effective communist personality cult, as visualized
in Chapter 4.)

However, a society based on 'legitimism', 'pluralistic' or not, has
a special need of a *parliamentary* voting system, in which political
decision-making involves a voting procedure in which groups,
factions, parties (or conglomerates or subcultures) cast conflicting
votes.[22] (By contrast, in an 'ethicalist' society political disputes are

[18] and *not* like 'a state within a state', which is the case with hierarchical
legitimism as visualized in an ideal feudal or caste system.

[19] See Hobbes (1651, 1974), Ch. 19, 20, 21, 30.

[20] The classical text for this Marxian conception is *The Eighteenth Brumaire
of Louis Bonaparte* (Marx and Engels, 1950, pp. 302–11). But the conception
reappears in the context of pre-British Indian politics in Marx, 1853, pp. 33, 36.
Indeed, according to Marx's thinking between 1850 and 1853, such a state was
an exception in bourgeois Europe but the rule in pre-British India.

[21] Voting can, of course, be with a ballot, or in conclaves or with guns.

[22] even if this is done by army mutineers, with guns (as in 1975 in Bangladesh
after the assassination of Mujibur Rahman and several other leaders of the
liberation struggle), or by army men voting without guns (as in Portugal in
December 1975).

regarded as 'ominous disturbances in the complex network of causal filaments by which mankind was connected on all sides with Nature' (Needham, 1962, p. 528). Consequently, in such a society political disputes and parliamentary voting procedures for resolving them are anathema.) Of course, a parliamentary voting system may exist in the form of implicit (or black) parliamentarism (Gramsci, 1971, pp. 255–6), as in India before the British conquest, or in Pakistan under military rule, or in Bangladesh under a single-party system introduced in February 1975, or the 'non-party' regime established later in the same year. Alternatively, it may exist in the form of both an explicit and an implicit parliamentary voting system, as in India under British rule from around 1905 to 1947, and in residual India since then.

As regards the fifth and final feature of the secular Indian syndrome, 'extra-parliamentarism', it must be noted that while the theory has been articulated in the West over a long period, the practice has been most highly developed in Indian societies. The theory of manipulation, infiltration, and seizure of the instruments of the infrastructure of state power, in order to seize control over the levers of the superstructure of state power, has been articulated by Antonio Gramsci, as noted at several points earlier in this book. But it has been only partially and perhaps imperfectly tested in practice in Western societies (e.g. in Italy or France).[23] (In an 'ethicalist' society, where there is no room for 'parliamentarism', there is, of course, no room for 'extra-parliamentarism' either, since the latter is meaningless without the former.) On the other hand, in India's 'pluralistic legitimism' and the commitment to 'statism', extra-parliamentarism seems to be a necessity, as will be explained in later sections of this chapter, and also in Chapters 8 and 9.

In the above comments on S.5 the focus has been on one aspect of 'extra-parliamentarism', viz. S.5 (i) which refers to 'manipulation, infiltration . . .' etc. of the infrastructure of state power. But there is the other aspect, S.5 (ii), which refers to the systematic use of extra-parliamentary techniques of 'law-breaking', counter-coercion of the majority by those who challenge the coercion of the holders of state power, etc. The most important of these techniques are *political* civil disobedience (as contrasted to unpolitical civil disobedience which is

[23] The reason may be that in Western Europe there is at best a 'dualism' (e.g. the Catholic–Communist dichotomy in Italy, or a Socialist–Communist dichotomy in France) rather than a 'pluralism' of more than two subcultures which is needed to make a Gramscian strategy operative.

justified on the ground, stated by Thoreau, that the civil disobedient pays the penalty (see Arendt, 1969, 1972, pp. 48–56, for a discussion)), and the political general strike, or, more generally, work-stoppage or *hartal* or *bandh* (the first involves closure of shops, the latter also involves strikes by industrial workers, and office-employees, and students). As will be noted in later sections of this chapter, and again in Chapters 8 and 9, this aspect of 'extra-parliamentarism' too has been practised rather more thoroughly in India than in Western societies. (This may be because only in a society like that in India, with its 'pluralistic legitimism', is 'extra-parliamentarism', in our sense, both feasible and unavoidable in routine politics.)

This concludes the general discussion of the five basic features of the 'secular' Indian syndrome. As already indicated, our primary concern is with the *modern* version of the 'Indian syndrome', which contains all five features in fully developed form. But there is some historical evidence that the various features crystallized as early as the ancient or medieval periods of history, or at least in the period of British conquest and rule. The 'modern' version of the syndrome may be acceptable, even if earlier versions (discussed in sect. 7.3–4) are not. On the other hand, the resilience of the modern Indian syndrome, which serves as a framework of analysis of such diverse developments as are analysed in Chapters 8–10 of this book, may be partly due to its strong historical roots. For this reason, as well as because they may be of some intrinsic interest, the next two sections are devoted to an examination of these historical antecedents.

7.3 Historical origins

The notion of a specific 'Indian' political-economic syndrome, which accounts for the 'unchanging' (in terms of technology, 'social relations of production', political history, etc.) nature of Indian society, is found in the writings of Karl Marx (1853; 1853a; 1867, 1958, Ch. 14, sect. 4, pp. 357–8). (It is worth noting that Marx carefully acknowledged British official and semi-official reports as the sources of his ideas (see, in particular, Marx, 1853a, pp. 18–19; 1867, 1958, p. 358, n. 1 and 2). Thus many of the ingredients of Marx's syndrome for Indian (or, more generally, 'Asiatic') societies were accepted by British observers in his day.)

In its barest outlines, Marx's Indian syndrome consists first of all of the so-called 'Asiatic modes of production' represented by self-sufficient village communities, which were divided into occupational castes, served by state-maintained irrigation works. On this 'basis' was erected the 'superstructure' of 'Oriental despotism', state owner-ship of land, the pantheistic and polytheistic Hindu religion, etc. The entire syndrome, 'basis' and 'superstructure', survives in a state of self-sustained 'equilibrium' resulting from 'a general repulsion and constitutional exclusiveness' between contending religions, tribes, castes in the (political) superstructure of society (Marx, 1853, p. 33).

Now, there is scepticism about both the adequacy and accuracy of Marx's pre-British Indian syndrome, shared by modern Marxian and neo-Marxian historians,[24] though there does not seem to be agreement on an alternative.[25] But the evidence cited in the corpus of literature which has grown up around Marx's syndrome supports the hypothesis that all five features of the 'secular' Indian syndrome presented in the previous section had crystallized by stages in ancient and medieval India, and that *this* syndrome explains the 'changing nature' of Indian society which Marx's own version of the pre-British Indian syndrome tended to ignore. (Moreover, as will be argued in the later sections of this chapter, contrary to Marx's hypothesis, this 'syndrome' of pre-British India was preserved, deve-loped, and modernized in the period of British rule and its after-math.[26]) So we can proceed by working with the *notion* of the 'Indian syndrome' which Marx used, provided we adapt his version of the syndrome in the light of evidence, and use it to interpret 'change which prevents change' in Indian society.

To see how this works out, we should note first of all that feature S.2 of the 'secular' Indian syndrome presented in sect. 2 above, viz. 'legitimism', crystallized in ancient India, just as 'ethicalism' crystal-lized in ancient China, as a dominant feature. Both *dharmashastra*[27]

---

[24] A significant contribution to this 'sceptical' literature was made by the mathematician Damodar Dharmanand Kosambi (1956, especially Ch. 1). Kosambi thought Marx's insights on pre-British India were 'misleading' (op. cit., p. 11) but he attempted a reconstruction guided by the basic tenets of Marx's 'dialectical materialism' as set forth in his preface to *The Critique of Political Economy* (op. cit., pp. 8–12).

[25] Of course, most historians deny the usefulness of any 'syndrome' or model to interpret historical events, in India or elsewhere.

[26] It should be noted, however, that Kosambi, who rejected Marx's syndrome, found it possible to agree with Marx's predictions about the results of British rule (Kosambi, 1956, pp. 12–13, 368–70). He seems to have done this on the basis of a rather forced interpretation of Marx's predictions.

[27] *Dharmashastra* literature corresponds roughly to Western natural law and Chinese *tao*. It specifies a code of righteous conduct for all *varnas* or castes and classes, emanating from *sruti* (i.e. works of revelation) as well as from interpreta-tions of *sruti*. The code was supposedly immutable, being of supernatural origin, but was in fact interpretable (Spengler, 1971, pp. 53–61).

and *arthashastra*[28] literature in ancient India reflect a strongly 'legitimist' tendency, as the term has been defined above. According to one interpretation, there was an 'ethicalist' challenge by the Buddhist emperor Ashoka to replace political sanctions (regarded by Buddhists to some extent as antithetical to ethics[29]) by ethical ones.[30] But, rather like its polar opposite, Chinese 'legalism' (referred to in sect. 7.2 above), the Buddhist 'ethicalist' challenge was discredited by its excessive stress on the ideology of submission to the holders of economic and political power.[31] The same story seems to have been repeated by other 'ethicalist' challenges to 'legitimism' in the medieval period, with the 'secularist' experiments of Akbar (who tried seriously to found a new 'universal' religion), the unsuccessful Islamic theocratic regime of Aurangzib (Sarkar, Ch. 28, 34), as well as of the Sikhs and the 'ethicalist' challenge of Chaitanya (ibid., Ch. 35).

How 'legitimism' rules supreme with both the *dharmashastra* and the *arthashastra* approaches throughout the ancient and medieval (as well as the modern) periods is well brought out in a poem on a Mahabharata theme, *Gandhari'r Abedon*, composed by Rabindranath Tagore at the turn of the century. The Pandavas, practitioners of strict *dharmashastra* rules, are going into exile to pay the penalty for losing in a game of dice to the Kauravas. The monarch, Dhritarashtra, scolds his son Duryadhana of the Kauravas for seizing the kingdom by deceit from the Pandavas, upholders of *dharmashastra*, beloved of the populace. Duryadhana replies that in the religion of politics (*rajadharma*) there is only the ethics of success (victory), for which all means used are justified. But he, too, offers to go into exile rather than vegetate in the Pandavas' *dharmarajya* (i.e. a kingdom ruled strictly on *dharmashastra* principles). Dhritarashtra's royal consort, Gandhari, pleads with him to *either* banish their sons, the Kauravas, for violating the modesty of the Pandavas' womenfolk *or* explicitly suspend *dharmashastra* rules for *all* violators of women's modesty in his kingdom. But the casuist Dhritarashtra declares that he will side with his sinful sons and join them to suffer divine punishment rather than side with the Pandavas who are well pro-

---

[28] *Arthashastra* literature expounds rules of regal conduct, principles and practices of government, as well as regulations relating to wealth, and its production and use. It evolved out of *dharmashastra*, whose rules (specially the rules of its component, *rajaniti*) were subject to change and improvement in response to experience (ibid., pp. 54–61).   [29] Ibid., p. 55, n. 15.
[30] Ibid., pp. 80–1.   [31] Warder, 1974, pp. 171–4.

tected by divine grace! In this allegory, both the Pandavas, upholders of *dharmashastra* principles, and the Kauravas, violators of those principles (acting on Kautalaya's *arthashastra* principles), are preoccupied with laws and rules and their enforcement and interpretation.

This Indian 'legitimism' seems to have been based, from the earliest times, on the willing or unwilling recognition by all concerned of the 'pluralistic' nature of society, in the sense defined in the previous section. Of course, some portions of Kautalaya's *Arthashastra* may be interpreted to imply a prescription to *obliterate* and break up non-dominant conglomerates or subcultures (specifically, tribes or *samghas*). On the other hand, the fundamental aim seems to have been to sow dissension through the use of *agents provocateurs* infiltrating the 'enemy' camp, to 'support the weaker against the stronger',[32] so that the absolute despot may try to dominate, and the tribes try to save themselves from domination (for textual evidence, see Kosambi, 1956, Ch. 7, sect. 7.4, p. 203).

'Pluralistic legitimism' in ancient and medieval India seems to have prescribed 'statism', in the sense defined in S.3 in sect. 7.2 above, i.e. the deliberate use of state power for sectional advancement (at the expense of rival conglomerates or subcultures). The different forms of such sectional gains seem to have been very carefully identified, classified, and 'legitimized' as 'black wealth' (accumulated through bribes, gambling, fraud, etc.), 'white wealth' (obtained from such activities as the 'practice of austerities', teaching, etc.), and 'spotted wealth' (acquired by lending money at interest, tillage, commerce, quid pro quo received for benefits conferred) (Spengler, 1971, pp. 98–9). According to one interpretation of doctrine in Kautalaya's *Arthashastra* 'the state . . . was itself the greatest trader, the supreme monopolist. While it liquidated all tribal customs that had become hindrances to commodity production, it looked upon the private trade with the utmost suspicion. The merchant is, along with the artisan, guild-actor . . . beggar, and sleight-of-hand juggler, listed among the "the thieves that are not called by the name of thief" [*Arthashastra*, 4.1], and treated accordingly . . .' (Kosambi, 1956, Ch. 7, sect. 7.5, pp. 205–8). The state budget could be replenished by all possible means, including (i) sale of titles and insignia, (ii) confiscation of the entire property of goldsmiths, (iii) a

---

[32] It is worth noting that Machiavelli explicitly *rejected* this aim on grounds of expediency. The *agent provocateur*, he argued, may turn against his patron, who may lose both his state and his life (Machiavelli, *c.* 1514, 1970, p. 424).

claim to half the earnings of actors and prostitutes, (iv) dummy 'voluntary' contributions by secret agents to induce others to make genuinely voluntary contributions, (v) spies were to trade with genuine merchants and then cause themselves to be robbed by other colleagues as soon as a certain amount of cash had been collected in the transaction, (vi) quarrels would be fomented between two parties, both suspected to be harbouring ideas dangerous to the state; one would be poisoned by spies, the other accused, [and] the property of both confiscated for the treasury. However, there were to be false accusations 'only against the seditious and the wicked, never against others', robbery, murder could also be special measures when the treasury was in need (ibid., pp. 211–12). In recent Indian historical writings much stress is laid on the evidence of upgrading and downgrading collectively, in terms of economic and political status, of the various closed groups of the four-*varna* system of classical antiquity in India, and of the later caste system, as well as of various Protestant religious sects, of interacting landowning, mercantile (guild) and bureaucratic interest groups in medieval, Moghul, and Mahratha-dominated India.[33]

Regarding the fourth feature of our 'secular' Indian syndrome, 'parliamentarism', attempts to document historical evidence of the existence of *explicit* parliamentarism in medieval India, in the form of contending political *parties*, do not seem to have been very rewarding.[34] However, there is considerable evidence of 'black parliamentarism', in the form of court intrigue, of wars between rebellious groups organized as religious sects and the holders of state power, of the break-up of centralized Indian states in both the ancient and medieval periods as a result of political upheavals.[35] (There is an interpretation of Kautalaya's *Arthashastra* which identifies *paura-janapada* as 'propertied citizens who had a strong following (presumably from tribal splinters), enjoyed a special position with respect to the state, and constituted *public opinion*. The opinion was *not* expressed by *plebiscite or vote*, but ascertained by spies and provocateurs (*Arthashastra*, 1.13)' (Kosambi, 1956, Ch. 7, sect. 7.6, p. 212; italics are mine). Ministers were required to be chosen from among the *janapadas*. Every *janapada* administrative unit had its own

---

[33] See Thapar (1974), Ruben (1974), Habib (1974), Gopal (1974); also Sharma (1965), Ch. ii, v.

[34] See Chandra (1959, 1972), in which no evidence is adduced that political parties, as distinct from factions, existed.

[35] Thapar (1974), Habib (1974).

board or council of ministers. 'The rural janapadas were to be wooed as being stronger than the urban pauras . . . [because] if disconten-ted, they could destroy the . . . ruler' (ibid., pp. 212–13).

The foregoing references to evidence of 'statism' and 'black parliamentarism' in ancient and medieval India also cover cases of 'extra-parliamentarism' of type (i), i.e. manipulation, infiltration, and seizure of the instruments of state power, if not of type (ii), i.e. deliberate 'law-breaking', etc. on a mass scale. But there *were* experi-ments with 'fasts unto death' (a technique used both by revolutionary terrorists and Gandhians in the period of British rule and in the modern period).[36]

7.4 Under British rule

As already indicated at the beginning of the previous section, the 'secular' Indian syndrome was by no means dissolved or destroyed by the British conquest. On the contrary, its five features were developed and modernized in this period.

Thus Indian 'pluralism' was preserved and given an up-to-date basis, especially after the 1857 insurrection. Dramatic evidence of this was the codification of Hindu and Muhammadan law, the intro-duction of 'separate electorates' for Hindus and Muslims in a modern parliamentary political system. These measures (as well as the en-couragement of 'cultural autonomy' for Hindus and Muslims[37]) pro-duced the powerful Muslim and non-Muslim political-economic conglomerates which dominated Indian subcontinental politics through the Muslim League and the Congress party in the decade 1937–47, and which finally partitioned pre-1947 India. In this period the antagonistic co-existence of these dominant conglomerates was accompanied by the crystallization of lesser conglomerates, mainly functioning as pressure groups within one or the other dominant conglomerate, and often changing sides. These were the 'scheduled castes' (developed through a system of 'reserved seats' in parlia-mentary elections), the Sikhs, various linguistic groups (emerging as latent subconglomerates through development of the Press and

[36] See Kosambi, op. cit., Ch. 10, sec. 10.4, p. 348, for a short account of a fast by Brahmins at the gates of the Delhi palace, 'till they were on the point of death', in protest against the *jizya* tax. It ended when the *jizya* rate was reduced, and other Hindus agreed to pay the tax.

[37] not only through the establishment of Government-aided Muslim and Hindu educational institutions, but through the encouragement of separate development of Urdu and Hindi which are 'sublanguages', rather than separate languages or dialects of the same language.

school education in the different Indian languages), and, after 1940–2, a communist political subculture.

Indian 'pluralism', as modernized under British rule, was, of course, distinctly 'legitimist', as in the ancient and medieval periods, though, as in earlier periods, each major conglomerate active at this time originated in 'ethicalist' protests. A good example is the ethicalist challenge in the ideas of Rammohun Roy, whose main lasting impact, however, was in the development of the pluralistic legitimism and statism of dominant Indian nationalism of the Congress party.

Rammohun Roy definitely (i) defined *religion* as a set of *political rules* to define property rights, prevent oppression, etc., (ii) favoured a change in Indians' religion 'at least for the sake of their political advantage', (iii) made the separation of legislative and executive powers (which, he claimed, existed in ancient India but was destroyed by the Rajputs and the Muslim conquerors) a *sine qua non* of genuine political activity, (iv) insisted on the rights of the Press to enlighten an élitist public opinion, (v) wanted trial by jury, (vi) a free market in land, (vii) Benthamite contractual relations between the state and the landlords on the one hand, and the landlords and the *ryots* (cultivators) on the other, (viii) organized the Atmiya Sabha, an élitist political lobby as a counterblast to the rival Dharma Sabha (Mukherjee, 1974, pp. 372–82).

An admirer of the French revolution of 1789, Rammohun Roy also articulated the right of the people to rebel against 'any system, religious, domestic and political, which is inimical to the happiness of society' (ibid., p. 381). (With the benefit of hindsight, this could perhaps be regarded as the first expression in modern Indian politics of the idea of 'law-breaking' as an 'inalienable' political right which has produced several variants of 'extra-parliamentary' political action specified in S.5.) However, Rammohun Roy did rather more than this to prepare the ideological basis of later *satyagraha* or political civil disobedience on 'moral grounds'. He did this by upholding a man's 'moral right' to sell his ancestral property in violation of law and custom, on the ground that the individual must have the right to preserve himself. He insisted, however, that such transactions, based on 'moral right', should also be 'legitimized' by common law, and *not* made punishable offences.[38] His attempt to

[38] Mukherjee, (1974), p. 377. Thus his was a 'legitimist' rather than an 'ethicalist' stand in the sense defined in sect. 7.1 above, since he wanted positive law to uphold moral law in this case. However, Roy also recognized acts which deserved moral condemnation, but not 'legal' prohibition (ibid., p. 376).

introduce modern politics through a new religion did not amount to much.[39] But he pioneered with his advocacy of a free Press, of a separation of the judiciary from the executive, of new educational institutions to 'teach Mathematics, Natural Philosophy, Chemistry, Anatomy and other useful sciences', of institutionalized consultation of Indian élite opinion before legislation be undertaken by the British Parliament for Indian society. These were the starting-points of 'extra-parliamentary' infiltration of the superstructure and the infrastructure of political power by Indians over the entire period of British rule. Rammohun Roy's insistence on the responsibility of the state to enforce contracts, to assure contractual security to both landlords and cultivators represents a modernization of 'statism', of the philosophy of manipulating state power to serve sectional interests, in the sense discussed in the preceding sections of this chapter. (They also represent a repudiation by Roy of a puristic version of *laissez-faire* doctrines in which the state is strictly 'non-interventionist' (except to create and defend the institutions of property-ownership)[40].)

An ingredient missing in Rammohun Roy's blueprint of a modern political-economic Indian syndrome was Realpolitik, reconciling what is rational with what is realistic. This seems to have been achieved more successfully by his orthodox conservative opponents (e.g. of the Dharma Sabha) or by the 'Westernized' conservatives under the influence of the British followers of Auguste Comte.[41]

The tensions, birth-pangs, and frustrations of emerging élitist parliamentary 'open' politics in India at the turn of the century are classically portrayed in Rabindranath Tagore's novel *Ghare Baire*, which is a highly politicized novel on the same theme as Henrik Ibsen's *A Doll's House*. The novel merges a highly charged political

[39] In the sense that what ultimately took shape as the 'new religion' based on his ideas, the Brahmo Samaj, survived only as a minority élite group, though it had a relationship with the development of modern Indian politics parallel, to some extent, to the impact of the Fabian Society on the British Labour movement, or of the Saint-Simonians in French politics.

[40] Of course, Roy was a 'free trader' rather than a protectionist. He also wanted British capitalists in India who would make India their 'home'.

[41] On the influence of Comtist positivism on Bankim Chandra Chatterjee and Jogendra Chandra Ghosh, etc. see Bhattacharya (1974). They, rather than Roy, set the fashion of a schizophrenic 'compartmentalization' of personal values which were scientific (positivistic) on the one hand, and conservative (orthodox) political commitments on the other (Bhattacharya, pp. 351–2). However, Roy was not entirely free from such a tendency in so far as he never fully practised what he preached. For an interesting rationalization of this tendency, see Poddar, 1970, Ch. ii, sect. iv, pp. 67–72.

triangle with an equally highly charged lovers' triangle involving Nikhil, a humanist liberal Hindu landlord (who is worried because his Muslim tenants oppose a nationalist movement for the boycott of foreign goods), Sandwip, a Mephistophelean nationalist demagogue (who wants to coerce traders to stop selling foreign goods), and Nikhil's young wife, Bimala. Sandwip proclaims his intention of treating India as the object of his lust, to be seized by force and deceit. Enchanted, Bimala at first concurs, and is increasingly estranged from her husband. But she is ultimately disenchanted with Sandwip when he cynically uses a young terrorist recruit as cannon-fodder. On the side-lines comes and goes Nikhil's old tutor, Chandra-nath, who wistfully hopes that the Lockean principle of honest labour, rather than lust, will prevail as the main instrument of national regeneration.

So much for aspirations and ideological blueprints. What was the outcome? Something has been said at the beginning of this section about the modernized version of Indian 'pluralism' and 'legitimism' in the period of British rule. But major renovations of the 'secular' Indian syndrome in the period of British rule occurred with respect to the features S.3 'statism', S.4 'parliamentarism', and S.5 'extra-parliamentarism'.

As regards 'statism' in this period, India underwent an essentially *state-capitalist* development, with manipulation of the instruments of state power first in the monopoly-colonialist interests of the British East India Company, later increasingly in the imperialist interests of competitive British trade and industry and banking, and finally by various Indian trader-financier-industrial interests which became increasingly anti-imperialist (Bose, 1965, pp. 491, 503–8). The essential *continuity* of an expanding apparatus of state-capitalist controls serving in succession the different British and Indian capitalist interests seems to have received inadequate attention. In particular, there is often not enough emphasis given to the way in which Indian capitalists, with the backing of the Gandhian movement for the boycott of foreign goods (as well as of the initiators of explicit parliamentary politics in India, the Swaraj party), wrested by degrees major control over the internal Indian market by polit-ically manipulating state-capitalist devices to serve their own interests. The process is indicated as follows: (i) The reduction in the import of finished goods as a proportion of total imports from 84 per cent in 1920–1 to 75 per cent in 1936–7, 61 per cent in 1938, and to 31 per cent in 1944–5 (Government of India, 1946, pp. 11, 47). (ii) From 1933–4 to 1938–9, 79·1 per cent of the total value of Government orders were met by 'Indian' industry.[42] In 1944–5 the share of 'Indian' industry in Government orders was valued at 72 times the value of orders placed abroad (ibid., 1946, p. 79). (iii) The purchase by the Indian railways (which were progressively 'nationalized' in this period to become the nucleus of a Government-owned 'public sector') of Indian steel rails (mainly manufactured by Tata Iron and Steel Co.) as a proportion of steel rails purchased from all sources, rose from 61·17 per cent in 1922–3 to 1924–5 to 99·19 per cent in 1937–8 to 1939–40.[43] (iv) During World War II government purchases as a proportion to total purchases of iron and steel were 66 per cent in 1942, of cement 90 per cent in 1942–3, of woollens 98 per cent in 1943, of tea 44 per cent in 1944, of paper 51 per cent in 1943–4 ('Statistics Relating to the War Effort', 1947, quoted in Bose, 1947, pp. 172–3). (v) In the late 1940s it was estimated that 25 per cent of India's food-grains output was marketed in an 'average year' (Government of India, 1959, pp. 14, 98) and that 25 per cent of the 'marketed surplus' was procured by the Government in 1949 (op. cit., p. 100). (vi) In 1947 approximately 144 million people, out of a population of approximately 335 million, were covered by 'statutory' and 'non-statutory' rationing of food-grains. (vii) By the end of the period of British rule, gross book value of fixed and working capital in the Government-owned 'public sector'—which was under the the partial control of Indian legislators, and managed increasingly by Indian bureaucrats and technocrats, at least since the 1940s—stood at Rs. 1236 crores in 1950–1, as compared to approximately Rs. 1472 crores in the 'private sector' in 1949 (Government of India, pp. 32–3).

This increasing Indian control over the growing apparatus of state capitalism in India was closely associated with increasing Indian control over an expanding modern apparatus of state power established by the British conquest. Indian political-economic conglomerates infiltrated and seized control over one component after

[42] 'Indian' industry in official statistics included, of course, foreign-owned enterprises registered in India. But a more or less continuously increasing proportion of investment in such industries was passing into Indian hands in this period.

[43] Bagchi (1972), Table 9.5, p. 315. Curiously, Bagchi seems to cite these official statistics in an attempt to prove that the Indian railways had a prejudice *in favour of* British steel rails! (Op. cit., pp. 324–5). The figures conclusively prove the opposite. In general, Bagchi's main thesis (in Ch. 2) that a *lack* of Government orders was the main cause of non-industrialization in India under British rule is not well substantiated.

another of this apparatus through the development of *explicit parliamentary politics*. Beginning with the pre-1857 politics of religious reform, already referred to, explicit parliamentary politics went through a number of stages, till they became the vehicle of seizure of undivided political power by the Congress in India and the Muslim League in Pakistan. The main stages were: (i) governmental recognition of the views expressed through self-selected élitist organizations of Indian political opinion like the Indian National Congress and the Muslim League, (ii) the conversion of politicized conspiracy trials into instruments of semi-parliamentary politics, (iii) a similar conversion of partially elected legislatures with limited law-making powers into arenas of political conflict, and of conflict-resolution through negotiations, (iv) the conversion of regional councils of elected 'advisers' attached to provincial governors into regional ministries nominated and controlled by the Congress or the Muslim League, (v) the conversion of the central advisory council nominated by the Viceroy into an 'interim central cabinet' consisting of the nominees of the Congress and the Muslim League with a Congress Prime Minister, on the eve of the formation of the independent states of India and Pakistan. (This development of explicit parliamentarism had its mirror-image in the growth of implicit or 'black' parliamentarism in the form of in-fighting within the Congress and Muslim League parties which often determined major political decisions.)

Growing 'parliamentarism' in the period of British rule was also closely associated with, and somewhat overshadowed by, the development of 'extra-parliamentarism' in *both* the forms specified in S.5 in sect. 7.2. Thus type (i), the 'manipulation, infiltration, and seizure of the instruments of the infrastructure of power', was already being exploited to the full before the dawn of 'parliamentary' politics proper in the 1920s.[44] Rather more striking was the development of type (ii), or an extraordinary variety of techniques of political action belonging to the general category of 'extra-parliamentary' political action. They were almost always combined with, and sometimes

---

[44] in the first major political upheaval in India after 1857, which also scored a limited success, i.e. the agitation for undoing the partition of Bengal. One of the supplementary demands was for greater powers for elected municipal councillors. The Viceroy retaliated by proposing a Calcutta Municipal Act with the number of elected councillors reduced by half. Twenty-eight elected councillors resigned in protest (Mr. Bhupendra Nath Basu's Speech, in Prithwis Chandra Ray (ed.), p. 10). Within a decade elected councillors were in control of the Calcutta Municipality, so that the resignations paid political dividends.

dramatically alternated with, parliamentary political action.[45] To this genre of political action belong such techniques as: (i) Gandhian *satyagraha*, both strictly non-violent (as in the 1920s, when it was called off after a single violent episode at Chauri Chawra in Bihar) and violent (as during the 1942 Quit India movement), both 'mass *satyagraha*' or political civil disobedience, as in the 1930s and in 1942, and 'individual *satyagraha*', as in 1940. (ii) Hunger-strikes in prison (by Gandhi and revolutionary terrorist *détenus* and prisoners) backed by legal (parliamentary and extra-parliamentary) agitation for the release of prisoners. (iii) Summit-level political negotiations to take major political decisions (e.g. the round-table conferences of the 1930s, the Gandhi–Irwin Pact, the political negotiations preceding the Mountbatten Award and (partitioned) political independence). (iv) *Hartals* (or general closure of shops), politicized economic strikes by industrial workers, political strikes by students. (v) No-tax campaigns. Intercommunal and interparty pogroms must also be counted as one of the major techniques of political action, in so far as it was the mainstay of the Muslim League at the climax of its political career in 1946–7. All the above examples of extra-parliamentary methods of political action involve deliberate law-breaking in order to remake laws in favour of the law-breaker. Their common feature is the counter-coercion of the passive majority, to counteract, extract concessions from, and, in the limit, to extinguish the coercive political power of the holders of state power. Some evidence has been unearthed recently that controlled law-breaking by peasants trying to manipulate laws in their favour had started *before* Gandhi launched his peasants' *satyagrahas* in the 1920s. In the 1873 *palo*[46] peasants' rebellion in Pabna district in Bengal, peasants stopped paying rents to landlords, and deposited what they considered to be 'fair rent' in the district and sub-divisional courts. The leadership seems to have been given by Agrarian Leagues organized by them, which were most probably advised by lawyers who espoused the

[45] Thus the Gandhian 'non-co-operation' and boycott of legislatures in the 1920s was complemented by the legislative activity of the Swaraj party. But in the 1930s both the Congress 'non-co-operators' and the Congress 'co-operators' joined hands, under Gandhi's discipline, to capture the legislatures now elected on a widened franchise. There was another spell of 'non-co-operation' in 1940–5, at the end of which the Congress captured practically all the non-Muslim seats in all the legislatures.

[46] *Palo* is a contraption made of bamboo used to catch fish in shallow waters in East Bengal. During the *palo* rebellion, thousands of fishermen and peasants would go into the water with *palos* in their hands to hold their political consultations (Chattopadhyay, 1973, p. 60).

peasants' cause against the landlords.[47] These legalistic methods of action seem to have been combined with 'extra-parliamentary' methods such as attacks on residences and *kutcheries*[48] of landlords, and an attempt to rule by decrees passed by 'peasants' courts'.[49]

7.5 The modern Indian syndrome: 1946–mid-1975

In the first thirty years of political independence on the Indian subcontinent since 1946–7, the five features of the secular Indian syndrome were preserved (some of them were further developed), and provided the general framework of the events analysed in Chapters 8–10 of this book. In this section, we first see in what sense these features were preserved and consolidated, despite attempts (which were ultimately unsuccessful) to obliterate some of them.

Thus 'pluralism' has survived several attempts in this period to promote contradictions between political representatives of classes or groups of classes in place of the antagonistic co-existence between 'pluralistic' conglomerates (as defined in sect. 7.2) as the dominant political relations in the Indian subcontinent. Such attempts have been made on the basis of the rival ideologies of: (i) the 'secular nationalism' (e.g. of the Indian Congress party[50] or of the Krishak Sramik Awami League in Bangladesh in 1975[51]), (ii) the communal nationalism of the People's Party of Pakistan,[52] (iii) semi-revolutionary or revolutionary communism,[53] and (iv) post-communist 'total revolution' (originating in the Bihar political struggle which began in 1974[54]). However, the effect, up to the middle of 1975, was the *consolidation* of the 'pluralistic' feature of Indian subcontinental

[47] Chattopadhyay (1973), pp. 60–1, 63.

[48] Ibid., p. 62 (*kutcheries* are administrative offices of landed estates).

[49] Ibid., p. 60.

[50] There were two such attempts in India after 1947. The first was in 1947–9, when an attempt was made by the ruling Congress party to obliterate the communal nationalism of the (Hindu) Rashtriya Sevak Sangh (R.S.S.) and the Muslim League on the one hand, and semi-revolutionary communism on the other. The second attempt was made by Congress nationalism (before and after it split in 1969) in 1969–73, to obliterate Naxalite revolutionary communism, and the semi-revolutionary Communist party (Marxist) as a 'disloyal' opposition in West Bengal and Kerala. Both attempts were half-hearted and ultimately unsuccessful.

[51] The ultimate outcome of this attempt is not clear at the time of writing.

[52] The communal nationalism of the Pakistan People's party was preceded by the communal nationalism of the Muslim League and of the martial law regimes of Ayub Khan and Yahya Khan (as well as the semi-military 'basic democracy' of Ayub Khan) in Pakistan. The explicit constitutional exclusion of non-Muslims (including, after 1974, the Muslims belonging to the Ahmadiya sect) from key positions in the power structure symbolized the communal nature of the nationalism of these political trends.

[53] See Ch. 9 for details.   [54] See Ch. 9, sect. 9.6.

politics through the splintering of communism as well as communal and secular nationalism, as a result of political in-fighting within each. The end result was the proliferation of conglomerates. Traditional conglomerates, cemented by religious ties or caste solidarity, were converted into powerful instruments of political mobilization, especially after electioneering based on adult franchise came into vogue in 1951. The abolition of separate electorates, on the basis of a communally segregated franchise, did *not* abolish community-based or caste-based political groupings. On the other hand, hardening ideological sectarianism, especially among contending communist groups, produced new political conglomerates, based on a hardened political subculture, which established closed groups, which were almost as closed as those based on politicized communal or caste ties. (It should be noted that there is a striking contrast between the phenomenon in this period, and the more or less *opposite* phenomenon of the attenuation of the 'pluralistic' conglomerates in the period under British rule. In that period subcontinental politics was increasingly dominated by the Congress party, which absorbed all secular nationalist trends, and the Muslim League, which absorbed the most effective communal nationalist trends. Communism barely survived as a third pluralistic trend by holding its in-fighting in check.)

'Legitimism', in the sense defined by S.2 in sect. 7.2 above, has also hardened as a trait in Indian subcontinential politics, despite more or less serious attempts at imposing versions of 'legalism' (as defined in sect. 7.2, nn. 2, 6, 10 above). Such attempts have been made by martial law administrations in Pakistan; by the Congress party's parliamentary majority in India, especially in 1970–5 (by the People's Party of Pakistan's parliamentary majority in Pakistan over the same period). Less serious attempts were made by the Swatantra party (wedded to the ideology of 'rule of law') or by the revolutionary Naxalites (who tried to dispense summary revolutionary justice against 'class enemies'). (It should be noted that both the Swatantra and Naxalite challenges originated as 'ethicalist' challenges to crack and restructure the 'Indian political-economic syndrome'. But they ended up as experiments in 'legalism' represented by the treatment of judicial verdicts as sacrosanct by the Swatantra party, and the attempts to enforce revolutionary 'legalism' by the communist Naxalites in their 'annihilation' campaigns; these will be discussed further in Chapter 9.)

Rather more striking has been the crystallization in the modern period of the remaining three features of the 'secular' Indian syndrome, as defined in sect. 7.2 above.

Feature S.3, 'statism', has been refined and perfected in the modern period. Thus the consolidation of 'state capitalism' in this period is shown by such indicators as: (i) permanent price-support programmes to the advantage of agriculture and small-scale manufacturing, which accounted for a little over 55 per cent of the net domestic product in 1960–1, and 53·6 per cent in 1968–9 (Government of India, Aug. 1970, p. 5);[55] (ii) the rise in the share of the Government-owned 'public sector' (excluding the output of services of the Government Administration) in the net domestic product from 5·1 per cent (1960–1) to 12 per cent (1968–9) (ibid., p. 13); (iii) the growth in employment in the Government sector as a proportion of total employment in the large-scale 'organized sector' from 58 per cent (Mar. 1961) to 62 per cent (Mar. 1972) for all branches together, from 11 per cent (Mar. 1961) to 22 per cent (Mar. 1972) for manufacturing industry, from 19 per cent (Mar. 1961) to 52·9 per cent in mining (Mar. 1973) (ibid., 1973–4, p. 78), from 37 per cent (Mar. 1961) to 55 per cent (Mar. 1972) in trade and commerce (ibid., 1972–3, pp. 126–7). Equally significant has been the fact that over this period almost all political parties, of the right-of-centre, as well as of the dead centre and left-of-centre, have become committed to 'state capitalism' in the economy and to 'statism' (as defined in sect. 7.2) in general. The demise early in 1975 of the Swatantra party, which attacked statism (and especially state capitalism) as an evil after independence was achieved, and was consistently committed to strict *laissez-faire*, symbolizes this development.

A new departure in the politics of statism in this period has been the increasing commitment, first in India, then in Bangladesh, and last of all in (residual) Pakistan, by *all* political parties,[56] to the consolidation of state capitalism through the expansion of the Government-owned sector by means of *nationalization*, as distinct from

[55] It is the permanent feature of price-support and other subsidies to privately owned agriculture and small-scale industry which makes these branches of the Indian economy beneficiaries of a state-capitalist 'spoils system' rather than pre-capitalist semi-feudal sectors of the Indian economy. In the context of such a state-capitalist network for the benefit of agriculture, land reform programmes for the benefit of the peasantry could, under certain conditions, merely strengthen state capitalism, as will be argued later in the chapter.

[56] Only the Swatantra party and the communist Naxalites have been totally opposed to such expansion, the first because they are opposed to state capitalism, the second because they are opposed to 'bureaucratic capitalism'.

state capitalism based on (i) 'licensed' private enterprise,[57] and (ii) establishment of *new* Government-owned enterprises (financed from domestic budgetary resources, and/or through Government-to-Government foreign economic aid). Another new departure in this period in the development of 'statist' politics has been the endemic preoccupation with regional state-making and state-breaking as central issues of politics, culminating in the political crisis which led to the emergence of Bangladesh. (By contrast, under British rule, the redrawing of the administrative boundaries of provinces occupied the centre of the political stage only twice: once at the dawn of modern (nationalist) parliamentary politics in 1905–11, and then again at the very end of British rule in 1947.) A third novel development in statist politics in this period was the seizure of the levers of the superstructure of political power at the regional level by the Indian communists for the first time.[58] This, along with (i) the ouster of the 'organization' faction of the Congress by the 'requisitionist' faction from the central cabinet, which led to a long-term split in the Congress in 1969, (ii) the long-term stability of regional ministries representing regional interests,[59] and (iii) the first experiment in a Congress–Communist coalition ministry at the regional level,[60] has added new dimensions to the politics of 'statism' in India. (There have been close parallels in residual Pakistan and in Bangladesh.)

As regards feature S.4, 'parliamentarism', both explicit and implicit (as defined in the Glossary and in sect. 7.2 above), has been further developed in this period. 'Explicit' parliamentarism has taken hold in this period in Indian subcontinental politics through (i) an early (in India) or late (in Bangladesh and Pakistan) transition from restricted to adult franchise, in conjunction with (ii) the proliferation of a 'statist' spoils system (already noted above), and (iii) the involvement of all shades of nationalism and communism in the Indian subcontinent, except the Naxalite communist revolutionaries, in explicit parliamentary politics. (This involvement is dramatized by the universal clamour by *all* political trends in 1974–5 (in India and

[57] This was the only form of state capitalism in Pakistan until the separation of Bangladesh and the advent of the Pakistan People's Party regime in West Pakistan.

[58] The reference is to the communist ministry in Kerala in the 1950s and the communist-dominated ministries in West Bengal and Kerala in the 1960s.

[59] The reference is to the Dravida Munnetra Kazhagham ministry in Tamilnadu which weathered a serious internal crisis in the early 1970s. The Kashmir ministries headed by Sheikh Abdullah in the 1950s and again in 1975 belong to this category, as do non-Congress ministries in the north-eastern border states.

[60] in Kerala, after the ouster of a ministry dominated by the C.P.(M.).

11

Pakistan) that the parliamentary democratic system was facing a crisis due to fascist or neo-fascist challenges, and that it must be *saved* at all costs.[61])

However, 'implicit' or 'black' parliamentarism has probably struck even deeper roots in this period in the Indian subcontinent. As already noted in the discussion of the role of 'pluralism' in Indian subcontinental politics in this period, organized political in-fighting in every political conglomerate has been cultivated as a fine art, and has also been legitimized as an essential adjunct of explicit parliamentary politics. (This will be further discussed in Chapter 10 below.)

As might be expected, 'extra-parliamentarism', feature S.5 of the Indian syndrome, has also been further refined and universalized in the modern period. The first aspect of 'extra-parliamentarism', which has to do with penetration of the infrastructure of power as a prelude to seizure of the levers of the superstructure of power, has hardened in Indian politics with: (i) the radical Congress breaking new ground by (a) seizing control over trade unions affiliated to other political parties, e.g. the C.P.(M.) in West Bengal, (b) experimenting with youth activist groups recruited from among the urban (or rural) unemployed used as shock-troops against rival trade unions and to control elections to legislatures; (ii) the surviving right-of-centre parties (e.g. the Jana Sangh in north India and the Dravida Munnetra Kazhagham in Tamilnadu) organizing their trade union wings to compete with the trade unions of the Congress and the communist parties.[62] The second aspect of extra-parliamentarism, viz. the use of extra-parliamentary techniques of political action, has also become universal. New departures are: (i) *bandhs* or universal work-stoppages with political objectives (involving workers, students, as well as shop-keepers), (ii) *bandhs* and strikes, not only by parties in opposition, but also by parties which control central or state-level governments, (iii) strikes by Government employees and police personnel which do *not* generate revolutionary political crises (e.g. in Bihar in the 1950s, and in Uttar Pradesh in 1974) as well as those that *do* (e.g. in Bangladesh and in West Pakistan). (The main change that

[61] According to unconfirmed claims made by the leaders of the Bihar political struggle which started in 1974, a Bihar-based Maoist communist faction was participating in the struggle. If so, this would mark, indirectly, the entry of Maoist communists into Indian parliamentary politics.

[62] By 1974–5 the only right-of-centre political parties in India which did *not* have trade union wings were the conservative Congress (Organization) and the newly formed Bharatiya Lok Dal.

occurred was that by 1974 *no* political party which mattered was opposed, in principle, to political strikes by workers or students. But until around 1970 *all* political parties, except the communist parties and other left-of-centre groups allied to them, *were* so opposed. On the other hand, it is by no means the case that strike-breaking or strike-scuttling has become anathema. As will be pointed out in the next section, and also in Chapter 9, the radical Congress perfected the techniques of strike-making and strike-settling and strike-breaking, first in West Bengal, and then used it on an all-India scale.)

7.6 The modern Indian subcontinental syndrome: mid-1975

In the second half of 1975, by a somewhat uncanny coincidence, a series of abrupt changes took place in residual Pakistan, India, Bangladesh, and Sri Lanka, which seemed to make the 'modern Indian syndrome' identified in the previous section obsolete. As in the preceding period, the most violent convulsions shook Bangladesh and residual Pakistan; the shake-up was milder, and better contained, in India and Sri Lanka.

At first sight, it might appear that the 'Indian syndrome' has been cracked beyond repair, with each of its five features negated, or being on the way to negation. But on closer scrutiny doubts arise; these are noted below.

The first feature, 'legitimism', might, on first impression, have given way to its opposite, 'ethicalism', in India and Bangladesh. There has been a change in attitude towards work among industrial workers (especially in the public sector), to tax-payment, evasion of customs regulation among the propertied and professional middle classes, to strikes and street agitation in India, though it is too early to judge whether there has been a traumatic change in the 'moral climate'. But the catalyst was the assertion of the law-making powers of the Congress parliamentary majority (on which more will be said below). Thus 'legitimism', as we have defined it, has been strengthened rather than weakened in India, even though voluntary compliance with laws has been much greater than involuntary submission. In Bangladesh an incipient 'ethicalist' drive, anchored to a return to Islamic fanaticism, signalled by a move towards the proclamation of an 'Islamic republic', has been stalled. Meanwhile, the rigours of martial law, of 'legalism' (as we have defined it) rather than 'legitimism', are the dominant *modus operandi* of politics.

'Pluralism' might seem to have become somewhat attenuated in India, with what might turn out to be the irrelevance of extremist communal organizations in India and Pakistan, in both of which such organizations have been placed under ban. To some extent, the proliferation of political conglomerates, marked in the preceding period, has been arrested in India with attempts to establish a two-party system.[63] On the other hand, pluralism is actually strengthened in India by such developments as: (i) the *rapprochement* between Kashmiri nationalists, Naga insurgents, the Sikkim nationalists, and the radical Congress, (ii) the hibernation rather than extinction of the Communist (Marxist) challengers in West Bengal and Kerala, (iii) the convergence with some persisting friction, especially in West Bengal, in the political activities of the radical Congress and the Communist party of India all over India, (iv) the consolidation of the radical Congress–C.P. political alliance in Kerala. In Sri Lanka pluralism—weakened earlier with the suppression of communist insurgency—has been noticeably strengthened as a result of the Trotskyite communists going into opposition after being deprived of the finance portfolio and the right to manage nationalized sectors of the economy. Bangladesh has swung in this period from the formal *de jure* obliteration of pluralism—with the proclamation of a single-party system—to *de facto* political pluralism manifested in an extreme form, centred in the armed forces.

As regards 'statism', there are less signs of its attenuation than of its persistence and consolidation. Thus in India the state-capitalist apparatus is being consolidated rather than further extended,[64] with the concentration on (i) profit-making by public sector enterprises, (ii) production-oriented trade unionism, (iii) interception of black-money earnings, (iv) the procurement of food-grains on an enlarged scale at support prices, (v) stepped-up distribution of homestead land to the landless, (vi) imposition of a long-delayed ceiling on urban land-holdings, etc. New features are: (i) denial of opportun-

[63] on the basis of the fusion of political parties opposed to the radical Congress–C.P. convergence of policies on the one hand, and the suppression of inner-party dissidence within the radical Congress on the other.

[64] However, extension of the public sector in India has continued through the nationalization of most foreign oil companies' assets and some 'sick' engineering plants in West Bengal. In Sri Lanka there has been a major extension in this period through the nationalization of foreign plantations. A contrary trend in Bangladesh, initiated in the last days of the one-party rule headed by Mujibur Rahman, may not amount to much, since there are not many takers of opportunities for private investment.

ities to parties in opposition, or dissident factions within the ruling radical Congress (or within the Dravida Munnetra Kazhagham in Tamilnadu, or the conservative Congress-led 'janata morcha' in Gujarat), to use some of the levers of state power to secure benefits for their supporters, (ii) greater reliance on a politically screened and disciplined bureaucracy and technocracy (loyal to the ruling party) to operate the state-capitalist apparatus, (iii) reduced reliance on inherently discriminatory instruments for distribution of state-controlled economic opportunities and benefits (like licences and permits[65]) and greater reliance on making them available to members of well-defined classes or categories without discrimination on political grounds, though there is no known method of eliminating region by region political discrimination which is effective.

The fourth feature, 'parliamentarism', of the Indian syndrome may take the form, it will be recalled, of both 'explicit' and 'implicit' (or 'black') parliamentarism. In India there has certainly been a change in the scenario in which 'parliamentarism' operates, which may be far-reaching and permanent. Thus scope for 'explicit' parliamentary politics, employing such devices as (i) link-up between political dissidence within the radical Congress and the opposition parties,[66] (ii) highly personalized political vendetta pursued in parliamentary deliberations, (iii) the use of courts of law as the venue for conducting parliamentary political debates by proxy, has been much reduced. The reduced scope is being formalized and made permanent with further constitutional changes, and changes in parliamentary practices, in the direction of major reliance on functioning with restricted publicity and on the basis of the concept of the 'sovereignty' of parliament.[67] Scope for 'black' parliamentarism has also been somewhat drastically curtailed by (i) 'homogenization' of the formerly 'pluralistic' radical Congress party, which had left some scope for *consistent* political dissidence (based on implicit or explicit programmatic differences), (ii) steps towards the establishment of a politically oriented and disciplined bureaucracy and techno-

[65] Members of the youth front of the radical Congress have been asked after reorganization in December 1975 to desist from distribution of licences and permits.
[66] to secure formal recognition of an extra-parliamentary opposition as an all-purpose bargaining agent with which the Government deals.
[67] The constitutional changes may ensure bilateral political co-operation between the judiciary and the legislature and executive on the basis of a more precise definition of the law-making and law-interpreting powers of all three agencies.

cracy, which is committed to the politics of the ruling party,[68] and of a press which is subordinate to the parliamentary majority. But with all these changes, even if they are made permanent, recognition of political pluralism—for which evidence has been cited earlier—*ipso facto* implies continued scope for *both* explicit *and* implicit parliamentarism, maybe with *new* 'political safety-valves' fitted to the *de jure* and *de facto* political structure. This is essentially because the overthrow by military terrorists in Bangladesh in 1975 of one-party rule (as well as the major part of the civilian political élite), and the subsequent inching towards a restoration of explicit parliamentary politics, show once again that it is easier to eliminate political pluralism and parliamentarism *de jure* than *de facto*.

The fifth feature of the modern Indian syndrome, 'extra-parliamentarism', seems to be the only one which very nearly qualifies for omission in India, at any rate after June 1975. There has been an almost complete absence of any open manifestation of extra-parliamentary activity, such as *satyagraha*,[69] which, by analogy with the past, was expected after June 1975. Other well-known methods of extra-parliamentary action, such as *bandhs* and political strikes, have also been much less in evidence.[70] But the change in the scenario is *de facto*, and may be temporary. *De jure*, the right to strike, to offer *satyagraha* on a strictly non-violent basis, to criticize the Government in the Press, have been explicitly re-endorsed, even though powers of detention without trial have been increased, unusual methods to prevent or break strikes have been adopted,[71] and there have been experiments with censorship, self-censorship, and control by ordinance exercised over the Press. What is conceded only *de jure* in India in the second half of 1975—and not even *de jure* in Pakistan or Bangladesh—may become *de facto* reality again. For the unexpected forms which extra-parliamentary political action has taken in India in the past (e.g. during World War II) or in Bangladesh or Pakistan in 1975—or in Portugal after the overthrow of fascism for that matter—show that endless innovations are possible in

[68] rather than the installation of politically appointed cadres. It is clear that from 1975 on, whoever rules India will be intolerant of a politically independent bureaucracy.

[69] Some *satyagrahas* did take place, and were reported in the Press. There were also cases of '*satyagrahas* in reverse' in which shop-keepers pulled down unauthorized sign-boards more or less on their own initiative.

[70] indicated by a steep decline in man-days lost in strikes, punitive actions by the police, etc.

[71] such as non-payment of wages or termination of employment for participation in prohibited strikes.

devising methods of extra-parliamentary political action, and there is no known method of putting a stop to all of them.

The remarks in the previous section suggest that the 'modern Indian syndrome' discussed in this chapter may continue to serve as a suitable framework for interpretation of political events in the Indian subcontinent in the future.

In any case, the modern Indian syndrome identified here seems helpful for analysing some notable developments in the Indian subcontinent in the 1960s and 1970s, which will be discussed in the next three chapters.

CHAPTER 8
Bangladesh Paradoxes

8.1 Introduction

THE process of emergence of Bangladesh was a revolutionary one, according to the definition of such a process used in this book.[1] It frustrated a Pakistani-Bangali counter-revolution and changed the *interstate status quo* by partitioning Pakistan, and re-partitioning pre-1947 India. Of course, there has been no change in the pre-existing *social status quo*, which existed in the form of a state capitalism dependent on foreign economic aid. But there may have been a permanent change in the *institutional status quo*, i.e. in the institutional form of state capitalism, from a pre-existing 'licence-based' state capitalism of a colony of West Pakistan,[2] to a state capitalism with a large Bangali-managed public sector established by nationalization of the bulk of the industrial assets in existence in 1972 in banking, insurance, heavy industries, and the jute industry.[3]

By using a different definition of revolution, and by taking some liberty with facts and their interpretation, it can be argued that the process of emergence of Bangladesh was actually an Indo-Bangali counter-revolution directed against an incipient communist revolution in East Bengal,[4] or that it was neither a revolution nor a counter-

---

[1] which describes it as a process which changes the full set or any politically significant subset of the social, institutional, constitutional, and interstate *status quo*.

[2] See paper by Auspitz, Marglin, and Papanek in 'Bangladesh Documents', Ministry of External Affairs, New Delhi (n.d.), pp. 5–9; Mukherjee (1973), pp. 408–13; Ahmed (1973), pp. 421–2.

[3] Relaxations in 1974 in favour of a Bangali-owned private sector, and further relaxations in favour of both Bangali and foreign private investment may not, in practice, affect the predominance of the large public sector in industry. Lack of politically secure, high-return investment opportunities and of large reserves of scarce resources like oil may deter private investment. For these reasons, attempts to revive West Pakistani private investment may not be very successful. (There have been unconfirmed reports in December 1975 of a decision to pay compensation for appropriated West Pakistani assets on condition that the money is re-invested in Bangladesh along with additional capital in hard currencies; see *Statesman*, Delhi, 1 Jan. 1976; *Times of India*, Delhi, 1 Jan. 1976.)

[4] See Gough (1973), pp. 23–31, for such an argument based on an over-estimation of the 'radicalization of the masses', and of the resistance in some areas by anti-Indian guerrillas against India-based guerrillas, which is alleged to have been more virulent than the resistance offered by India-based guerrillas to the Pakistani forces.

revolution, but simply an over-dramatized change of government.

The present chapter seeks to make only an indirect contribution to such a debate about the nature of the struggle for Bangladesh, by examining some unprecedented, and otherwise paradoxical, features of the initial phases of the struggle. They seem to be capable of a rational interpretation in terms of a game-theoretic model which can appropriately be called a 'Hobson's choice model'. The interpretation is of interest in itself, whether or not one is familiar with the modern controversies on revolutions and counter-revolutions. But it may also help to clarify some of the issues involved in such controversies.

8.2 The paradoxes

The *unprecedented* features of the struggle for Bangladesh are:

S.1 Totally successful (and totally non-violent) parliamentary action and extra-parliamentary action (including totally non-violent civil disobedience, as well as totally violent armed action) used successively to capture state power from a military plutocracy determined to colonize urban Bangladesh and establish an apartheid-type society on the basis of genocidal attacks on the Bangali population.

S.2 A political leadership (viz. the Awami League) born in the quagmire of Muslim League politics in pre-1947 India (see Chapter 7 for details), which is firmly in the saddle through all three successive phases of the struggle identified in S.1.

S.3 Power which is wrested with the *backing of* India (simultaneously engaged in counter-insurgency operations against Maoist Indian communists),[5] Communist Europe, Communist Vietnam and Communist Cuba, *against* U.S. and Communist Chinese opposition.[6]

Support for propositions S.1–3 in recorded facts is fairly strong.

As regards S.1–2: (i) The military rulers were forced to hold the first ever elections in Pakistan on adult franchise, in which the Bangladesh-based Awami League won 160 out of 162 seats in Bangladesh, and 167 out of a total of 313 seats in the Pakistan national assembly.[7] (ii) For roughly three weeks on the eve of the

---

[5] See the next chapter.

[6] The Bangladesh struggle seems to have secured the (reluctant) support of India, the U.S.S.R., Communist East Europe (except Albania and Romania), Communist Vietnam and Communist Cuba in that order (in time). It is worth noting that the government of the martyred President Allende's Popular Front Coalition did *not* support Bangladesh when the issue came up in the U.N. Security Council. Nor did post-revolutionary Algeria.

[7] Ministry of External Affairs, New Delhi (n.d.), 'Bangladesh Documents',

armed struggle, the entire Government apparatus, as well as the economy, was taken over by stages, with the Awami League first ordering work-stoppages, and then issuing directives for phased resumption of work.[8] (iii) The armed struggle, which broke out with the attempted (and largely successful) massacre of the Bangali police and military[9] during a Pakistani military 'crack-down', and was later continued by India-based guerrilla units, was a totally violent armed struggle, in which no holds were barred. Only the facts as regards (iii) have been disputed (as mentioned in n.3 above in this chapter). But General Niazi, commander of the Pakistani forces in Bangladesh in the second half of the liberation struggle, is reported, in reasonably credible Press reports, to have said (a) Pakistan lost the war because the entire people of Bangladesh turned against them,[10] (b) Bangladesh's anti-Pakistan guerrillas had only a 'nuisance value' in determining the outcome of the war, but because they were everywhere, they wore out the morale of the Pakistani forces in the end.[11] On the other hand, the construction put on some reports of fighting in Bangladesh, referred to in n.3 earlier in this chapter, is *prima facie* implausible. It is hardly credible that when the Pakistani forces' genocidal frenzy[12] had provoked all classes of Bangalis to flee (to India as refugees) or fight in self-defence against them, a guerrilla struggle against the India-based anti-Pakistan guerrillas should eclipse the guerrilla struggle against the Pakistani forces.

What is hard to explain about the events mentioned in S.1–2 is not

---

p. 130. In October 1971, to placate those foreign powers (including the U.S.S.R.) who were asking for a 'political' as opposed to a 'military' solution to the Bangladesh problem, 78 national assembly members from Bangladesh were unseated, 58 were filled up by unopposed returns. But mainly because of a step-up in the armed struggle, the by-elections for the remaining 30 seats were never held (ibid., 'Bangladesh Documents', vol. ii, p. 49).

[8] Ibid., 'Bangladesh Documents', pp. 207–11, 223, 226–30, 247–9. Apart from the industrial working class, ethnically non-Bangali, which responded only partially, (i, p. 211), *all* classes obeyed the Awami League directives during the civil disobedience movement. (However, Bangali port and dock workers obstructed Pakistani troop landings by commiting acts of sabotage.)

[9] There was only one Bengal regiment. However, many Bangali airmen in the Pakistani Air Force were stranded in West Pakistan.

[10] However, General Niazi has later been reported as blaming the defeat on (a) Yahya Khan's wrong timing of the attack on India (he did not wait till the monsoons), and (b) Yahya Khan's order to him (Niazi) to surrender, because otherwise 'the Indian army would destroy Pakistan'.

[11] In a speech at the Calcutta Rotary Club after the Bangladesh war, General Arora, commander of the Indian and Bangladesh forces who captured General Niazi and his troops, said this is what General Niazi told him.

[12] On the record there is little doubt about this, even though a war crimes trial has not been held.

so much that they happened at all,[13] but that they happened in such rapid succession, and under more or less the same leadership.[14] A political leadership which has specialized in parliamentary methods *has* planned to organize a 'non-violent' take-over of the administration through political civil disobedience before,[15] but it has never *succeeded* in doing so. A switch from parliamentary politics to civil disobedience with 'controlled' violence was tried out by Gandhi in 1940–2 in India. But the scale and intensity of violence (on both sides) was less than in Bangladesh, and it ended in disengagement and negotiations.[16] Moreover, it has generally been thought to be *inherently impossible* for a political leadership (psychologically and ideologically) to switch successfully from parliamentary politics and extra-parliamentary civil disobedience to a struggle involving guerrilla warfare.[17]

What is paradoxical about the facts recalled in S.3 is that the Bangladesh struggle should have secured the decisive (but reluctant) support of India and the U.S.S.R., and the active and relentless opposition of Communist China, firmly aligned, for the first time, on the side of the U.S.A. India's reluctance was partly due to a Maoist communist insurgency in West Bengal, already mentioned. It was also because of unsureness about the consequences of risking a war which might involve militarily the U.S.A. as Pakistan's military ally,[18] and Communist China as Pakistan's political patron

---

[13] However, such completely successful political civil disobedience and the establishment of 'parallel government' is unprecedented. An event like the violent revolution which finally expelled the Pakistani rulers from Bangladesh is equally unprecedented in the Indian subcontinent since the British conquest.

[14] Having given himself up to the Pakistani military, Mujibur Rahman did not personally lead the armed phase of the struggle. In this phase, Tajuddin Ahmed's leadership was distinguished. But in a struggle in which there were many sacrifices and few successes until the final one, Mujibur Rahman's facing the gallows fulfilled an important political role.

[15] e.g. the radical elements in the Congress party in India in the 1920 and 1930 civil disobedience, and also in 1942.

[16] Transfer of power came five years later after fresh skirmishes in a final struggle, which was *not* led so much by Gandhi as by Nehru and Patel.

[17] The belief was so strong that there was intense speculation in India that a Yahya Khan–Mujibur Rahman deal was in the offing at any time, with Henry Kissinger (then President Nixon's adviser) acting as intermediary. The story had no basis. (Henry Kissinger visited New Delhi and Islamabad merely on his way to Peking in the first move towards a U.S.–Communist China *rapprochement*. Yahya Khan stoutly denied he ever wanted to deal with Mujibur Rahman.)

[18] The danger was real. Shortly before their surrender, the Indian chief of staff, General Manekshaw, broadcast repeated warnings to the commander of the Pakistani forces in Dacca not to try to escape by speed-boat to be rescued by the U.S. Seventh Fleet. It was not clear whether American commando units would be landed to help the Pakistani forces to make a last stand.

(which had, moreover, started diversionary military action against India in aid of Pakistan during the Indo-Pakistan war of 1965). Indeed, so visible was this reluctance for a year, that for a few months preceding India's military intervention, the Indian Congress Government was under fire from the non-Maoist communist left for *not* intervening militarily in Bangladesh.[19] Soviet reluctance was no less marked, revealed in her insistence on a 'political solution', as opposed to a military one, which has already been mentioned. However, once India was forced into taking military action, she acted decisively. So did the Soviet Union.[20] On the other hand, the U.S.A. apparently failed to act in time,[21] and China did not act all.[22]

Other paradoxes connected with the emergence of Bangladesh are:

S.4 U.S. failure to 'generalize' the Bangladesh war (as it had 'generalized' the Vietnam war into an Indo-China war at about the same time) in order to enforce a settlement within the framework of Pakistan.

S.5 Chinese communist failure to stay strictly neutral in the conflict between Pakistan and Bangladesh, instead of siding with the Pakistani colonialists.

S.6 The U.S.S.R.'s failure to insist on a 1965 (Tashkent Conference) type Indo-Pakistan-Bangladesh settlement. (More generally, the U.S.S.R.'s failure to (i) take the opportunity to preside over, or overtly assist in, a subcontinental settlement, (ii) risk abetting the disintegration of Pakistan (which she had begun, successfully, to wean away from total dependence on the U.S.A. and Communist China), (iii) browbeat India to overrule her objections to a Tashkent-type conference.)

S.7 India's rapid military withdrawal from Bangladesh so soon after her military intervention broke the back of the Pakistani army's resistance (especially when the temptation to distrust the Bangladesh Government's capacity to maintain law and order must have been strong).

---

[19] e.g. the Communist party of India clamoured for action by the Congress Government, expecting it to act; the Communist party of India (Marxist) criticized the Congress Government for *not* acting to end president's rule in West Bengal, restoring a state-level government including the Communists (Marxists) as a step towards military intervention to restore parliamentary democracy in Bangladesh.

[20] when its submarines trailed the U.S. Seventh Fleet off the Bangladesh coast on the eve of the Pakistani surrender.

[21] before Yahya Khan's surrender.

[22] Unlike in 1965 when there was a clash on the Sino-Indian border.

S.8 Pakistan militarily attacking India instead of daring India to attack her.[23]

It is easy, especially with the benefit of hindsight, to explain the entire episode of Bangladesh's emergence as the initial *assertion* (but *not* consolidation) of India as a regional power astride the subcontinent, and its eventual recognition by all. One could float the thesis by recalling that in 1965 Pakistan, with U.S. (and Communist Chinese) backing, made a supreme effort to establish its 'parity' of power with India in the Indian subcontinent. One could then round off the argument by citing (i) Nixon's after-the-event declaration that 'it was inevitable that India should win the war, but not that there should have been a war',[24] (ii) the Chinese characterization of India as a 'sub-super-power', made after India exploded her first nuclear device, and repeated after India's Sikkim protectorate was converted into an 'associate state' in 1974.

However, an explanation in terms of India's emergence as a regional subcontinental power does not explain many details of the Bangladesh war. In particular, it does not explain very convincingly why this first *assertion* of India's status as a regional power[25] did not take the form of her forcing Pakistan, with U.S.–Soviet backing (and possible Chinese acquiescence) to accept the Awami League's pre-liberation six-point programme for converting Pakistan into a *confederation*.[26] In the present chapter, we try instead to trace the pro-

---

[23] Kathleen Gough (Gough and Sharma (eds.), 1973, p. 26) in effect denies S.8 when she writes 'hundreds of thousands of regular Indian troops with Soviet equipment were fighting in East Bengal before the end of November [1971]' (i.e. before Pakistan attacked India in the west). But, on the face of it, it is unlikely that 'hundreds of thousands of Indian troops' were fighting a Pakistani fighting force of 95,000 in Bangladesh either before or after November–December 1971, especially when India had to guard against a Pakistani attack in the west, a possible diversionary attack in the north, and U.S. active involvement through a landing by the Seventh Fleet.

[24] Henry Kissinger's statement, reported in the Indian Press, in which he all but admitted that the U.S. 'tilt towards Pakistan' during the Bangladesh war was a mistake, also said categorically that he recognized India as the major regional power in the Indian subcontinent. This was repeated by Kissinger during his visit to India in 1974 after the change-over from Nixon to Ford in the U.S.A.

[25] In Bangladesh, India only *asserted* herself as a regional power, but withdrew, instead of consolidating that power. In Sikkim in 1974, by contrast, she moved to *consolidate* her power.

[26] Although the Awami League's six points talked of a 'federation' (points 1 and 2), what they proposed was in reality a confederation, with (i) the centre dealing only with defence and foreign affairs (and all other residuary subjects to be dealt with explicitly and exclusively by the federating units) (point 2), (ii) two separate currencies or currency funds for the two 'wings' (point 3), (iii) the right of taxation explicitly denied to the centre, with the centre receiving a fixed share of the tax revenue of the states (point 4), (iv) separate foreign exchange accounts

cess by which the emergence of Bangladesh involved the emergence of India as a subcontinental regional power. As we shall see, in this double process the aims and strategy adopted by Bangladesh (in embryo) decided the outcome.

8.3 A Hobson's choice problem

The Bangladesh paradoxes can be rationalized by arranging the facts in a game-theoretic framework. In this section, we do this by first identifying the main facts of the environment, about the basic aims of the countries directly or indirectly concerned, and the 'strategies' adopted by the main 'players', viz. Bangladesh and Pakistan, whose aims and strategies decided the outcome.

The environment

E.1 Ethnic (racial, linguistic) discontinuity between Bangalis and West Pakistani (or north Indian Muslim) settlers in Bangladesh.

E.2 Geographical contiguity of Bangladesh and India (partly counterbalanced by West Pakistani–Indian geographical contiguity in the west).

E.3 Lack of geographical contiguity of Chinese Tibet and Bangladesh (not at all counterbalanced by the geographical contiguity of Chinese Tibet and West Pakistan).

E.4 The presence of Soviet naval power as an offset to U.S. naval power in the Indian Ocean.[27]

E.5 A stalemated Indo-China war.

E.6 U.S.–Soviet balance of nuclear power.

Aims of the powers

A.1 *U.S.*: Back Pakistan up to the brink of war with India for the piecemeal reconquest of Bangladesh by Pakistan. (The aim was determined by E.5–6.)

A.2 *Chinese*: (i) oppose Bangladesh or bifurcation of Pakistan,[28]

---

for the two constituent units; each unit was free to enter into trade agreements with foreign countries; *only* indigenous products were to move free of duty within (between?) the two wings, (v) a militia or a para-military force to be set up by East Pakistan (points 5 and 6) (Ministry of External Affairs, New Delhi (n.d.), 'Bangladesh Documents', p. 13, n. 1).

[27] The U.S.A. did not then have the Diego Garcia base in the Indian Ocean. One of the arguments for expanding the base put forward in 1974 was to deal with contingencies like the Bangladesh war.

[28] The deeper reasons for this opposition have been discussed in Chapter 5, sect. 5.3 above.

(ii) browbeat, but not attack, India, (iii) utilize U.S.–Pakistan alliances to promote a détente with the U.S.A., directed against the U.S.S.R. (and India).

A.3 *U.S.S.R.*: Support autonomy for Bangladesh within Pakistan if possible (to preserve improved relations with Pakistan), and an Indo-Bangladesh military struggle for an independent Bangladesh if necessary.

A.4 *India*: (i) Support autonomy for Bangladesh within Pakistan if possible, and an independent Bangladesh if necessary, (ii) (a) counter-attack Pakistan only if first attacked by her, (b) if attacked by Pakistan, eliminate completely her forces in Bangladesh,[29] (c) with India's defence secured with the mutual assistance pact with the U.S.S.R., risk U.S. military intervention in Bangladesh.

A.5 *Pakistan*: (i) Avert Bangali élitist control over West Pakistan at all costs, (ii) preserve Pakistani élitist control over Bangladesh at all costs, (iii) lose to India, but never appear to lose to Bangladesh.

A.6 *Bangladesh*: End Pakistani élitist (colonial) control over Bangladesh at all costs.

Now, E.1–6 and aims A.1–4 pretty obviously leave the issue open. To close the gap, and determine an outcome, we have to rely on aims A.5–6. But how A.5–6, i.e. the aims of Pakistan and Bangladesh, determine the outcome, and what the outcome is, depends on the *strategies* adopted by these 'active' players to achieve their respective aims.

We know that cut down to essentials, the strategies adopted by Bangladesh (S_b) as well as by Pakistan (S_p) were:

Strategies

S_b: Bangladesh offers Pakistan a (Hobson's) choice between (in Pakistan's eyes) three evils, viz. concede (i) a confederal Bangladesh, or (ii) an independent Bangladesh, or (iii) accept a Bangali majority rule in a unitary Pakistan.

S_p: Pakistan makes the counter-offer of another (Hobson's) choice between (in Bangladesh's eyes) two evils, viz. give up (i) demand for

[29] By encircling the Pakistani forces in Dacca, forcing them to surrender, and holding them prisoner in India at the request of the Bangladesh Government, India fulfilled this aim. The criticism that India should have 'destroyed' the Pakistani forces instead of accepting their surrender (Ali, 1973, pp. 455–6) can hardly be taken seriously, since modern armies do not massacre their defeated adversaries, however great the provocation. (This practice is universal: the Soviet, Chinese communist, Vietnamese communist, Algerian, Cuban revolutionary armies have all adhered to it.)

a confederal Bangladesh, and also (ii) the demand for rule by an elected Bangali majority in a unitary Pakistan.[30]

The outcome

Given E.1–6 and aims A.1–6, as well as strategies S_b versus S_p, the 'equilibrium outcome' could only have been independent Bangladesh, ultimately recognized by all.[31]

The reason is that the Hobson's choice (S_p) offered by Pakistan is less general than the Hobson's choice (S_b) offered by Bangladesh. The latter 'contains' (i.e. provides explicitly for) an independent Bangladesh, made feasible by E.1–6 and aims A.1–6, the former does not. This implies that Bangladesh had considered *all possibilities*, knew her mind about all of them, and rejected the Hobson's choice offered to it by Pakistan *in toto*. But Pakistan had *not* considered all possibilities, did not know her mind about S_b (ii), so she had *not* rejected the Hobson's choice offered to her by Bangladesh *in toto*. In the result, Pakistan accepted S_b (ii) as the 'least worst' outcome, so that this became the equilibrium outcome for *both* Bangladesh and Pakistan (in the sense that it could not be improved upon).

In the foregoing exposition, reference to the parties directly or indirectly involved in the Bangladesh conflict is to 'Bangladesh', 'Pakistan', 'India', U.S.A.', etc. This might seem odd. During the Bangladesh struggle, each of these countries was split by internal political divisions; at least Pakistan, India, and the U.S.A. were. However, internal political (inter-party and inter-class) conflicts in these countries were then focused on *other* major issues. There was no effective opposition inside these countries to the aims and strategies adopted by their governments or dominant political parties *vis-à-vis* the Bangladesh struggle.[32]

[30] Other alternatives thought up by the Pakistani military regime seem to have been even worse, and not taken seriously by anyone. These were (iii) strengthening the balance of internal power in favour of a West Pakistan-dominated centre by partitioning Bangladesh and carving out a non-Bangali settlers' state in North Bengal, (iv) driving the entire Hindu population of Bangladesh to India so as reduce the Bangali electoral majority in Pakistan.

[31] The Chinese have been dragging their feet the longest. They vetoed the entry of Bangladesh into the U.N. until the Pakistani prisoners of war were repatriated (making a special demand for the repatriation of the 156 prisoners accused of war crimes by Bangladesh). They withheld full recognition until the overthrow of the government headed by Mujibur Rahman after his assassination.

[32] In *Bangladesh*, the demand for an independent Bangladesh was first made publicly by the main challenger of Mujibur Rahman's political supremacy in Bangladesh, Bhasani. He sided with India during the Bangladesh war, and turned against her afterwards, but has not gone back on his demand for an independent Bangladesh. In *Pakistan*, i.e. in Western Pakistan, through political

The Hobson's choice game-theoretic model used in this section belongs to the same ('battle of wills') class of models as the model used in Chapter 2 above to discuss the Vietnamese paradox, or the 'battle of the sexes' archetype of such models, already referred to in Chapter 2. But it differs from the former because in this case, (i) the manifestly 'weaker' side did *not* win[33] and (ii) the 'side-liners' U.S.A., U.S.S.R., and China did *not* determine the outcome. It also differs from the latter. In a battle of the sexes model, the *key* assumption is that *both* want to *stay together*, which is the *opposite* of what Bangladesh at least wanted to do in this case. (Of course, Bhutto misread the nature of the game being played, and consistently tried to make Pakistan play it as a battle of the sexes type of game, by (i) insisting on a joint centre manned by Mujibur and himself, a constitution for Pakistan drafted jointly by Mujibur and himself, (ii) insisting, after the Bangladesh war, on a constitutional 'link' between West Pakistan and 'Muslim Bengal'. Because Mujibur Rahman refused to play this game, but played another, Bhutto was outplayed at every stage.)

8.4 An interpretation in terms of ethics

In the Bangladesh struggle, Pakistan was clearly worsted by her inflexibly 'selfish' motivation. She was certainly not lacking in intelligence, cunning, or even patience.[34] The determination to retain

---

and economic convulsions which ousted Ayub Khan, installed Yahya Khan, groomed Bhutto for office in Pakistan's first parliamentary democracy, a Yahya Khan–Bhutto joint policy to prevent the emergence of Bangladesh never encountered serious opposition. In *India*, the political crisis in Bangladesh was paralleled by a political crisis in which the Congress party's central government was isolated for a while from the majority of states which had anti-Congress coalition governments, the Congress party was split, and there was a Maoist communist insurgency problem in West Bengal. But through all this, *all* parties, starting from an initial indifference to the Bangladesh struggle, were either demanding Indian military intervention (not expecting it to take place) or were strictly neutral, when the intervention actually occurred. (There was no outright political opposition, or sabotage and armed obstruction in West Bengal even from the dominant Maoist communist faction led by the late Charu Majumdar, when the Indian army marched through it on the way to Bangladesh.) In the U.S.A., in the massive political crisis generated by the anti-Vietnam war movement, there was hardly any attention paid to the Bangladesh struggle, and official policy encountered no serious opposition.

[33] because (i) the U.S.A. did not, in the end, enter the war to rescue its military ally, Pakistan, (ii) it did *not* intervene *directly* (as in Vietnam or more recently in Israel) to make good Pakistan's loss of arms before the Bangladesh war ended (though she did this partially and indirectly through Iran, France, etc.). This left the winning side in a stronger position militarily.

[34] Yahya Khan showed all these qualities in his dealings with Mujibur Rahman. He agreed to hold elections, agreed to let Mujibur Rahman contest even though he would not pledge loyalty to Pakistan, negotiated with him on the formation

a colonial hold over Bangladesh at all costs made it inevitable that she should lose her. This was undiluted selfishness, if selfishness is defined as the desire to gain at the expense of others.

It might seem that Bangladesh's policy was the polar opposite of a 'selfish' policy, i.e. that it was a policy of 'selfless sacrifice'. Mujibur Rahman risked his own life to try to protect his people from being massacred.[35] The East Pakistan Rifles and the Bengal Regiment, and most of the formations of the East Pakistan police, put up an armed resistance without any hope of success, at the first round of armed clashes at the beginning of the war. Two to three million Bangalis lost their lives, around ten million found refuge in India, but anti-Pakistani resistance did not cease. The rhetoric of liberty or death seems, for once, to have led to victory in an armed revolution such unlikely allies as experts in fighting parliamentary elections and in non-violent civil disobedience, as well as army-police mutineers and guerrilla youth and sailors and port-and-dock workers engaging in sabotage.

Doubts arise when one recalls the basic aim and strategy adopted by Bangladesh in the struggle, as identified in the previous section. The aim—to end Pakistani élitist control over Bangladesh at all costs—was by no means 'selfless', though it was not 'selfish' (like Pakistan's aim), in the sense that Bangladesh did *not* fight to metamorphose West Pakistan into a Bangali colony. (If she had, she would certainly have met with disaster, instead of victory.) Like the Soviet and Chinese communist strategy discussed in Chapter 2, Bangali strategy, too, was 'unselfish', i.e. it was a hard-headed defence of Bangali self-interest, without hurting the interest of West Pakistan by trying to invert the process of colonial exploitation. This was illustrated by the terms of the Hobson's choice successfully imposed on West Pakistan. It was also reflected in the refusal by the Bangladesh Government to allow the repatriation of the Pakistani prisoners-of-war, or to agree to drop the trial of war criminals among them, until Pakistan was forced to recognize independent Bangladesh. The refusal showed Bangladesh was not 'selfless'; the eventual consent showed she was not selfish.

---

of a new Pakistan government with Rahman as prime minister. He staged a show-down only when he could provoke Mujibur Rahman to declare independence, and when Pakistan was militarily ready to suppress the independence movement, or so he thought.

[35] Ministry of External Affairs, New Delhi (n.d.), 'Bangladesh Documents', vol. ii, pp. 614–15.

Doubts of a different kind arise when one looks at the mounting evidence in the *aftermath* of the successful emergence of Bangladesh, that the former anti-Pakistani resistance forces are engaged in the pursuit of naked, clawing, selfish interest, in sharing the spoils of victory. But this tells us nothing of their joint success against Pakistan before Bangladesh was born. It does, however, remind us that Bangladesh's freedom-fighters fought to partition Pakistani state capitalism, and *not* for socialism, as noted at the beginning of this chapter.[36]

8.5 Bangladesh: 1974, 1975

It is impossible to close this chapter without some remarks on the persistent economic and political convulsions in Bangladesh in 1974 and 1975. They reopen a debate about the nature of the struggle for Bangladesh which was never really closed, as noted at the beginning of the chapter. Was it a revolution or a counter-revolution? If either—of what kind? Or was it neither?

Of course, 'we can view the past, and achieve our understanding of the past, only through the eyes of the present' (Carr, 1961, 1973, p. 24). But a suitably 'revised' history of the struggle for Bangladesh —analysed in this chapter—is not likely to be very different.

For one thing, it is doubtful whether the achievement of an independent Bangladesh will be undone by a forcible reintegration, with U.S. backing, of a 'Muslim Bengal' into an anti-Indian Pakistan. India will act, at least as decisively as in 1970, to oppose such a course. The U.S.S.R. is likely to be even more decisive in its opposition. (Both have been provoked by the current Kissinger guide-lines for U.S. policy, viz. (i) the U.S. claims the fundamental right to 'destabilize' regimes it does not like, as in Chile in the 1970s,[37] and (ii) the U.S. must intervene *everywhere* to counter Soviet communist influence, if it is to intervene *anywhere*.[38]) Even Bhutto and the central Government of Pakistan can hardly relish the prospect,[39] though the assassination of Mujibur Rahman and the overthrow of

[36] Though, as we shall see in Chapter 9, dedication to socialism (by communist revolutionaries) is by itself not a sufficient condition of *non*-involvement in a state-capitalist spoils system.

[37] which may have been invoked to 'destabilize' Mujibur Rahman's one-party rule, and may be invoked again to 'destabilize' the central Government of India.

[38] announced by Kissinger to justify arms delivery to anti-Soviet factions in independent Angola.

[39] especially in view of difficulties with Pakhtoon and Baluchi movements for greater autonomy (quelled largely with Iranian military support), and weaker Sindhi and Punjabi demands for autonomy.

the one-party state in Bangladesh is said to have vindicated Bhutto's stand in 1970 on the secession of Bangladesh. Indeed, a firm and *final* recognition of the independence of Bangladesh by Pakistan[40] may be responsible for the U.S. Government's publicized refusal to grant political asylum to the self-proclaimed assassins of Mujibur Rahman and for the disavowal of terrorist liquidation of politicians and political mutinies in the armed forces.[41] Even the Chinese communist Government, after the three successive shifts in the power-balance in Bangladesh in August–December 1975, detonated by rival military factions,[42] made their long-delayed announcement of their 'readiness' to extend official recognition to the state of Bangladesh, which now enjoyed 'stability'. Though somewhat bizarre,[43] the announcement did mean that the Chinese Government had taken the penultimate step towards the recognition of Bangladesh.

It is also doubtful whether there will be an effective 'counter-revolution' changing the institutional *status quo* back to a licence-based West Pakistani-dominated colonial state capitalism, from a Bangali-managed state capitalism with a large (nationalized) public sector established in 1972. Though there is some sign of a governmental intention to do so, for reasons stated in note 3 of this chapter, it may be a case of wishful thinking.

On the other hand, there are hardly any signs pointing to the emergence of communist revolutionaries—of any kind—as serious contenders for political power in Bangladesh.

In this context, the ruthless Darwinian struggle for the survival of the fittest has rapidly extended from political contention around ballot boxes in rigged elections to 'voting with guns' by terrorist guerrillas and politicized military factions. Swings of the pendulum

[40] along with the Kissinger assessment that Bangladesh is an 'international basket case', i.e. a liability to the international community.

[41] The disavowal was made by a State Department official who, like the one who earlier objected to U.S. arms delivery to anti-Soviet factions in independent Angola, may be overruled. On the other hand, it may be Henry Kissinger's own policy. For, with Kissinger, as Cardinal Zambelli in Jean Anouilh's *Becket* says it is with him, 'sincerity is a form of strategy, just like any other . . . In certain very difficult negotiations, when matters are not going ahead and the usual tactics cease to work, I have been known to use it myself' (Anouilh, 1961, 1971, p. 90). The disavowal may be Kissinger's own, and it may even be sincerely meant.

[42] All of them seem to have been led by military men who fought in the liberation war on the soil of Bangladesh, including Ziaur Rahman, who was the first to declare independence in March 1971 in a radio broadcast.

[43] Since 'instability' seems to be somewhat greater after the overthrow of Mujibur Rahman than it was before. But earlier, the Chinese emphasized 'instability' in Bangladesh, while they now emphasize 'stability'.

have brought changes in the apparatus of state power: from a multi-party state dominated by one party, to a one-party state, on to a non-party state, with some prospect of a return to a multi-party state. If the prospect materializes, Bangladesh will be back to square one, with one king on the chessboard (Mujibur Rahman?) obliterated, and another (Bhutto?) checkmated.

Appendix to Chapter 8

Hobson's choice— a mathematical restatement

In this 'Hobson's choice' game the assumptions about the environment and players' aims and preferences are as stated in Chapter 8.

The *players* are numbered: 1. U.S.A.; 2. China;
                                       3. U.S.S.R.; 4. India;
                                       5. Pakistan; 6. Bangladesh.

The *outcomes* are numbered: $+1$. Confederal Bangladesh;
                                       $+2$. Independent Bangladesh;
                                       $+3$. Bangali-majority rule in unitary Pakistan

and

                                       -1. *Not* confederal Bangladesh;
                                       -2. *Not* independent Bangladesh;
                                       -3. *Not* Bangali-majority rule in unitary Pakistan.

Players 1–4 are 'side-liners', whose aims A.1–5 (see Chapter 8) leave the outcome completely open (in the sense that even the *status quo ante*, viz. West Pakistani minority rule in a unitary Pakistan, is not ruled out).

But player 5 offers player 6 what amounts to a Hobson's choice between what player 6 regards as *two* evils (which are not ordered, cardinally or ordinally), viz. (-1) and (-3).

Player 6, on the other hand, offers a Hobson's choice to player 5 between what player 5 regards as *three* equal evils, viz. between $(+1)$, $(+2)$, and $(+3)$.

The fact that each player is offered a Hobson's choice by the other is indicated by the assumptions made as regards the preferences of players 5 and 6.

The orderings of alternatives offered to each player can therefore be written down as:

$$F^5(1) = F^5(3)$$
$$F^6(-1) = F^6(-3).$$

But player 6 (Bangladesh) has nothing to choose between two 'evils' (-1) and (-3) offered to it, and rejects both.

Player 5 (Pakistan) also has nothing to choose between the equally evil alternatives $(+1)$ and $(+3)$, rejects them, but has no place for the third alternative offered to him, viz. $(+2)$. (The failure to *consider* alternative $(+2)$ may be explained by (i) the conviction that this is 'unthinkable' because Bangladesh 'would not dare', or at least India, U.S.S.R., etc. 'would not dare' to back up Bangladesh if it did dare, or (ii) a fanatical 'perish the thought' attitude towards such a possibility, or (iii) a *rational* conviction that such an outcome was against the ideology on the basis of which the ideological state of Pakistan was formed and exists, viz. a 'homeland for all Muslims of Indian origin'.)

It follows that the only possible 'equilibrium point' is $(+2)$ or Independent Bangladesh.

The characteristic feature of a 'Hobson's choice' game such as this seems to be that each player is offered a choice between *equally* evil alternatives between which he is indifferent. (It is implied, of course, that the 'evil alternatives' offered exhaust all possible outcomes.) In such a game, a determinate outcome is only possible if one player is offered one choice which he has ruled out as 'unthinkable', so that if there is a determinate outcome, it is unique.

CHAPTER 9

Intercommunist Warfare in West Bengal and Its Aftermath

9.1 Introduction

THE struggle for Bangladesh in East Bengal, discussed in the previous chapter, was for *partitioning* state capitalism in Pakistan. The struggle in West Bengal, over roughly the same period, which became to some extent cross-connected with it, had a more far-reaching aim, though this was not very coherently or consistently articulated. Its aim was to secure a foothold for a communist people's power, which could engage in a protracted revolution for the eventual *abolition* of state capitalism, and its replacement by socialism, in the entire Indian subcontinent. Moreover, for three crucial years—vital or bizarre, according to taste—there was persistent promise of fulfilment of this aim.

The statements just made, somewhat recklessly, are likely to provoke immediate protests. In the 1970s the communist upheaval in West Bengal of the 1960s seems almost to have vanished without leaving a trace, though it will be argued below that dramatic new directions in Indian politics in the 1970s are interpretable as its aftermath. Indeed, it might seem that the events in West Bengal in the 1960s are being blown up to larger-than-life proportions with an ulterior motive. This ulterior motive could be suspected to be the *apologetic* motive of a pro-communist partisan. Alternatively, it might be thought that a charade is being deliberately invented to justify the game-theoretic interpretations set out in the present chapter.

To disarm such objections, some forgotten facts must first be recalled. This is what is attempted in the next two sections. The essential paradox of intercommunist warfare as the *main* cause of failure of the communist initiative is then identified, after considering other (inadequate) explanations. A game-theoretic model interpreting aspects of West Bengal's intercommunist warfare is subsequently presented. The remaining sections are devoted to the all-India repercussions, including what is interpretable as a post-communist aftermath in Bihar in the mid-1970s, and frankly speculative remarks about what might have happened, but did not, and what could still happen.

9.2 Communist aims

The characterization of the political upheaval in West Bengal in the 1960s as communist, made in the opening paragraph of this chapter, could be objected to on the technical ground that it represented an 'anti-Congress' political initiative, inchoate in nature, rather than a communist one. But this objection is easily overruled, given the professed communist ideology of all the political parties and groups (except one, viz. the Bangla Congress[1]) which rode the political storm in West Bengal in the 1960s. Among these were two communist parties at the beginning of the period, and three at the end.[2] There were, in addition, two communist factions of Trotskyite origins, and at least three others which did not call themselves communist, but swore by a Marxian communist ideology, thought in terms of Marxian political theory, acted on Marxian inspiration, and imitated communist political practices. (Surprisingly, anarcho-syndicalism was very much in evidence in practice, as we shall note later, but was never upheld in theory.)

More serious objections to the characterization arise because of the Orwellian double-speak, and, to a lesser extent, a schizophrenic double-think, indulged in by all communist factions in West Bengal. Moreover, doctrinal hair-splitting obscured the long-term strategy of a *version* of a protracted communist revolution which was implicit in the political practice of all communist factions.

The hair-splitting is about (i) the multi-stage or one-stage nature of the Indian revolution,[3] (ii) the nature of the Indian revo-

---

[1] The Bangla Congress was a prematurely born, politically less efficient, precursor of the radical Congress party forged in the 1960s. It was politically a non-starter, and suffered a split during the revolutionary upheaval, with one half disappearing eventually into the radical Congress. The other half went through many vicissitudes. It first became an adjunct of the Communist (Marxist) party. In 1974 it disappeared into the newly formed right-of-centre Bharatiya Lok Dal. But in 1975, as the outpost of the B.L.D. in West Bengal, it veered again towards the C.P.(M.) in a civil rights movement in West Bengal, linked with the Bihar struggle dedicated to a 'total revolution', which will be discussed later.

[2] These were (1) Communist party of India, (2) Communist party of India (Marxist), and (3) Communist party (Marxist-Leninist). In what follows (1) is referred to as 'C.P.', (2) as 'C.P.(M.)', and (3) as 'C.P.(M.-L.)'.

[3] Orthodox Trotskyite and semi-Trotskyite theories have upheld the perspective of a one-stage revolution (or an 'intertwining' of stages) in Indian conditions. Multi-stage theories originally referred to the 'anti-feudal', 'anti-imperialist', and the 'anti-capitalist' or socialist stages of the revolution in India (or China). In recent years, with reference to the Indian revolution, 'anti-monopoly-capitalist',

lution after 1947 (or after the Sino-Indian border conflict, the Sino-Soviet communist schism, the emergence of 'Soviet social imperialism' or 'Maoist Chinese chauvinism', etc.),[4] (iii) the role of parliamentary politics *vis-à-vis* the revolution.[5] (Somewhat surprisingly, there is no evidence of *any* controversy about the Indian political economy as being 'state-capitalist' in nature, in the sense identified in Chapter 8 above, which will be much emphasized in later sections of the present chapter. However, some of the issues involved *have* been discussed, in substance, though not by name, in inconclusive controversies over the danger of 'economism', over attitude towards 'bureaucratic capitalism' represented by the Government-owned and/or Government-controlled public sector, etc.[6])

But there has been no dispute (at least in theory) that: (a) communist political activity must be revolutionary (i.e. its purpose must be to make revolution, rather than to restrain it, or to find excuses for not making it), and must be oriented towards a proletarian socialist (ultimately communist) revolution. (The 'socialist' stage refers to the stage which ends with the socialization of the means of production, but preserves an incentive system based on the principle 'to each according to his work, from each according to his capacity'. This is supposed to lead on to a higher 'communist' stage, where the rule is 'to each according to his needs, from each according to his capacity'.) (b) Whatever the stage, and whatever its forms, the revolutionary process should continue uninterrupted through the ebb and flow of the revolutionary struggle. (c) There must be a conscious communist leadership throughout the revolutionary process.[7] (d) Communist leadership or 'hegemony' over the revolutionary process

---

or 'people's democratic' or 'national democratic' stages have been added to the list. A redefinition of the 'anti-imperialist' stage to specify that it must also be 'anti-(Soviet)-social-imperialist' may not be far away.

[4] i.e. whether it is mainly 'anti-feudal, anti-imperialist', or 'anti-feudal, anti-imperialist and anti-social imperialist', or 'national democratic' or 'people's democratic', etc.

[5] i.e. whether it is (a) counter-revolutionary, as held by Maoist communists, or (b) partially revolutionary, at least as instruments of exposure of parliamentary politics, as held by the C.P.(M.), or (c) revolutionary, as held explicitly in 1975 by the C.P., rather explicitly in 1975.

[6] The Maoist communists of the C.P. (Marxist-Leninist) have paid more attention to these issues than either the C.P.(M.) or the C.P.

[7] Only one Marxian writer, Mohit Sen (1970, pp. 80–1), has explicitly argued that in the first, the 'national-democratic', stage of the Indian revolution (at least), there should be *no* communist insistence on the 'hegemony of the working-class' over the 'non-monopoly national bourgeoisie' or 'the intermediate strata'.

must be established step by step by seizing one after the other the instruments or levers of the structure of political power.

Of these four items of a common catechism accepted by all communist factions in West Bengal (though each thought the others pay only lip-service to them) (d) has hardly been articulated in the literature, though it formalizes the practice of all communist factions, at least since the early 1950s. Communist factions have systematically concentrated on seizing control over (i) the trade unions (which have always been organized in India since the 1930s as adjuncts of rival political parties), especially of Government administrative personnel, and workers and salaried employees in Government-owned factories, (ii) peasant associations, especially those that were *supported* by the effective managers of rural economics and politics in Bengal since the late 1930s, viz. the *jotedars* or rich peasants, (iii) any and every other organized centre of opinion or, in the language of Antonio Gramsci,[8] 'molecule' of the 'civil society' (e.g. clubs, co-operatives, school and college managing committees, theatre groups, *ad hoc* committees set up for organizing *pujas* or religious festivals, etc.).

Up to the late 1960s West Bengal communists had concentrated on seizing control over the above-mentioned types of 'molecules of civil society' which were, strictly, *outside* the superstructure of political power, and represented only its *infrastructure*. In the next few years, they turned urgent attention to seizure of the levers of the *superstructure* of political power. Those communist factions who formed the state-level ministries in this period seized control over the key portfolios (home, police, finance, land revenue, labour). What is more, they made serious attempts to consolidate their ministerial control by strengthening their hold over trade unions of Government employees at all levels (not excluding the police, jail staff, and even the officer cadres running the administration at the state level). Those communists who opposed this involvement in parliamentary politics, and later formed the Communist party (Marxist-Leninist), ideologically committed to Maoism, *also* proclaimed their intention of establishing armed people's power by organizing revolutionary bases and liberated areas. In other words, they concentrated on

---

[8] 1971, Part II, sect. 2, especially pp. 233–8. Gramsci's theory of the state and civil society has already been referred to in Ch. 5 and 8 above, and will be referred to again in Ch. 13, sect. 13.6 below. There is no evidence that the architects of communist policy in West Bengal paid any attention to Gramsci's extension of the Leninist theory of state and revolution. But Gramsci's concept referred to seems to formalize their practice in the period under consideration.

creating levers of the superstructure of revolutionary people's power.

The new departures just noted imply that in the late 1960s West Bengal's communists were working on the basis of alternative perspectives of 'protracted revolution' under communist leadership in India.

9.3 Communist successes and failures

As already stated in sect. 9.1, viewed *ex post*, after the event, the communist initiative in West Bengal in the late 1960s seems to have receded into the limbo of a dead past. But *ex ante*, in the late 1960s, things looked very different. Communism seemed to possess a magic touch. *Failure* eluded it, no matter what it did or did not do. On the other hand, *success* eluded Congress nationalism: it seemed to be able to do nothing right.

For some three or four years the more (fiercely) communism divided in West Bengal, the stronger it grew, at the expense mainly of the Congress, which has been the only political alternative to it since 1947.

The more striking indicators of communism's unbroken string of successes in this period are: (i) the uninterrupted growth of communist votes and seats in the state legislature through three elections, till the C.P.(M.) replaced the Congress as the largest single party in the state. (ii) The successful organization, *without* active picketing, of several push-button *bandhs* or work-stoppages throughout the state, at a sign from the communist-dominated government or communist trade union centres. (There was no opposition from any quarter, including the Congress, to these strike calls.) (iii) The persistence of Maoist communist (mainly 'Naxalite'[9]) insurgency (and jacquerie) for two years,[10] which defied suppression either by the C.P.(M.)'s armed volunteers, or by the state police force which was unionized and semi-politicized by it, especially when it held the home and police portfolios.

By contrast, till about 1970, as the Congress party divisions grew,[11]

[9] i.e. the dissidents of the C.P.(M.) who led an agrarian struggle in Naxalbari, North Bengal, for the distribution of land to the tillers and were expelled on the specious technical ground that they had violated party discipline. A Maoist splinter group led by an ex-terrorist, Ananta Singh, also tried to organize rural insurgency.

[10] A longer period of insurgency has never been known since 1857 in a nerve-centre of Indian economics and politics, with the exception of Bangladesh.

[11] It split into two in West Bengal when an ex-minister and ex-president of the state-level Congress Committee formed the Bangla Congress. It split into three

the weaker it became. Both its acts of political intervention and *non-intervention* in West Bengal's politics were counter-productive.

Thus when the Congress party was still the largest in the state legislature, short of a majority by only 28 in a house of 280, it remained oppressively inactive. It allowed a communist-dominated ministry to be formed, and did nothing to prop up a ministry formed by defectors from the communist-dominated coalition who claimed a dubious majority. Later, it allowed the C.P.(M.) to seize control of the home and police portfolios without protest from the Governor (an appointee of the radical Congress central Government) or from the Congress party in the state legislature, which was reduced in strength but by no means insignificant. The highlights of Congress 'non-intervention' in West Bengal occurred when no move was made either through the state legislative party, or through the Governor, or through the central Government's home ministry, when there were armed clashes involving security guards in a munitions factory near Calcutta, and a dramatic mutiny by the police.[12]

Of course, it was *not* 'non-intervention' all the way. There was one major intervention through the Congress central Government to suppress a communist agrarian movement for the redistribution of Government-held surplus land in Naxalbari in North Bengal.[13]

But at the end of it all, around 1971, almost as suddenly as it had begun, the charmed life of West Bengal communism came to an end. The roles were dramatically reversed. A divided communism was now at the mercy of a rejuvenated radical Congress which ousted the communists systematically from one segment after another of the superstructure and the infrastructure of political power in West Bengal. A descriptive outline of the dénouement is given in a later section on the anti-climax in West Bengal. In the next section several explanations of communist failure in West Bengal are considered, but found to be either untenable or inadequate. A paradox is then identified, which also supplies the basis of a reasonable explanation.

---

when the radical Congress (Requisition) separated from the conservative Congress (Organization).

[12] who clamoured for protection for themselves and their families after some policemen were killed by unidentified assailants. The mutiny ended when the Communist (Marxist) home minister, detained (*gheraoed*) in his room in the legislative assembly, threatened to send for workers to disarm them.

[13] The intervention was devious. The non-communist chief minister was instigated to ask for the central reserve police who were sent to complete the job.

9.4 Untenable or inadequate explanations

As a first step towards unravelling the mysteries of communism's sudden debâcle in West Bengal, it is necessary to sort out those explanations which must be rejected outright as untenable on logical or factual grounds.

Perhaps the most prominent among them are variations on the theme:

S.1 Enemy infiltration destroyed the movement.

This seems to be epitomized in Utpal Dutt's play *Ferari Fouj*, apparently about Bengali terrorism in the 1930s, but often interpreted as an allegorical play about communist terrorism in the late 1960s. In this play the clues point to the master-mind behind the conspiracy being located in the camp of the enemy. Specifically, there have been suggestions that Indian police agencies,[14] or the U.S. Central Intelligence Agency hired *agents provocateurs* to promote intercommunist warfare (or organize the murders of policemen in 1970 which were then blamed on the Naxalites). Now, an explanation of the West Bengal communists' revolutionary initiative *solely* in terms of 'enemy infiltration' is logically impossible.[15] It is impossible, because if the enemy controlled the revolutionaries before the revolution started, he would not make a revolution against himself. If he did not, and the revolution started in spite of him, there is no reason to suppose the enemy would be able to subvert a growing revolution from inside, but could at best defeat it from outside. (Indeed, it is not even certain that he would *want* to subvert a potentially successful mass revolution of which he would emerge as the leader.[16]) This *also* implies that an explanation of the failure *mainly* in terms of 'enemy infiltration' is equally untenable.[17] The explanation has to be in terms of something else as the main cause, even if the facts show that there *was* 'enemy infiltration', and that the enemy *did* aim at subverting the communist initiative in

---

[14] Dasgupta (1974), p. 89.

[15] Assuming, of course, that what we are discussing is *not* a terrorist conspiracy, as in Utpal Dutt's play, or even in Bengal in the 1930s, but a revolutionary ferment featured by increasingly successful parliamentary and extra-parliamentary *mass* activity, as well as by persistent rural and urban insurgency.

[16] Which is why no successful communist revolutionary leader, accused of being an enemy agent, has ever been proved to be one. It is worth recalling that Lenin was accused of being a 'German agent' on the evidence of his transit visa to return to Petrograd from Switzerland in a sealed German train.

[17] As are attempts to give similar explanations of communist failures in India in the 1920s, 1930s, or in 1948–50, some of which are reflected in reminiscences by veteran Indian communists in the 1960s.

West Bengal in the late 1960s. It is by no means self-evident that this *was* the case. The C.I.A. probably had a strong motive to keep alive centre-state tension, internal tensions in the communist-dominated ministry, as well as intercommunist warfare in West Bengal, in order stop Indian military intervention during the struggle for Bangladesh. It is hard to see what motive it had to promote president's rule and the eventual return of a Congress ministry in West Bengal, which facilitated Indian military intervention in Bangladesh, and which, as far as can be guessed, the C.I.A. emphatically did *not* want. Indian police agencies probably did have a strong motive to annihilate Naxalite terrorists when a police–Naxalite blood-feud developed in the last phase of Naxalite insurgency. But this was *after* the communist-dominated ministry had already fallen, and intercommunist warfare had declined.[18]

We turn now to the second, rather more widely believed explanation, viz.:

S.2 Parliamentary illusions killed communist revolutionary initiative.

The difficulty with this explanation is that it is imprecise and not directly testable by empirical evidence. With some tests that could be devised, the explanation seems to be untenable. Thus there is no question that the Naxalites denounced all parliamentary politics and boycotted elections, though they could not impose a *mass* boycott by voters, which they tried to enforce in the fourth general election at the end of the period under survey. Of course, all other communist factions refused to boycott elections. But those who made the best use of elections (and parliamentary politics in general), viz. the C.P.(M.), were precisely those who specialized in the exposure of the corruption and futility of parliamentary politics.[19] Moreover, none of them shrank from, or dared to oppose, massive extra-parliamentary political actions, i.e. general strikes and *bandhs* (referred to in sect. 9.3 above), or seizure of an enhanced share of the crop by share-croppers or of land, etc., *provided* they were under their own party control, or joint control of the party machines represented in the 'united front'. There is no evidence that they stopped

---

[18] i.e. after March 1970, when there was president's rule, and intercommunist group clashes involving the C.P.(M.) on one side and almost every other left party on the other (except the Naxalites) had ended abruptly after the fall of the ministry with a C.P.(M.) home minister.

[19] For a rationalization of the C.P.(M.)'s tactics as classically Leninist as set out in Lenin's 'Leftwing Communism', see Dasgupta (1974), p. 124.

or restrained such actions for fear of rocking the boat of the parliamentary political system. The only apparent exception occurred in the context of the agrarian peasant uprisings under the leadership of the Naxalites, e.g. at Naxalbari and at Gopiballavpore. The agrarian issues brought into focus by these peasant uprisings were redistribution of Government-held surplus land in Naxalbari, and an enhanced share of the crop in Gopiballavpore, along with peasant self-government. All communist factions were committed to programmes which conceded these demands. What is more, in *some* of their peasant bases the C.P.(M.) in South Bengal led similar agrarian peasant struggles, weakened landlord and *jotedar* resistance by de-licensing their firearms,[20] and decreed (by utilizing their control over the police) non-interference by the police in agrarian armed clashes. (To a lesser extent, the C.P.I. also did this, in their fewer peasant bases, hampered to some extent by their failure to ensure non-interference by the police.) On the use of methods of coercion, intimidation, and violence in politics also, all parties of the united front (except the Bangla Congress) permitted it. They also practised it under their respective party flags.[21] 'Parliamentary illusions' did not deter them. They persisted in the use of these methods, risking the downfall of two communist-dominated ministries and the dissolution of three communist-dominated legislatures. But when the Naxalites of Naxalbari wanted surplus land to be redistributed by the tillers themselves, the communist-dominated West Bengal ministry insisted that only the local committee of the united front should have the power to do so. When gun licences were issued to *jotedars'* resistance committees (formed mainly by local Gorkha League elements) on the orders of the Bangla Congress chief minister, and the Border Security Force units crushed peasants' resistance, neither the C.P.(M.) nor any other party forced a political crisis by resigning from the ministry on the issue.[22] Essentially the same story was

[20] In Naxalbari, on the contrary, the first step taken to counter the peasant movement for land redistribution was the issue of gun licences to the *jotedars* by the then chief minister (belonging to the Bangla Congress) who was also the home minister, acting on the recommendation of the home minister of the Congress central Government.

[21] However, at the climax of inter-party clashes between the C.P.(M.) on one side and the C.P., the Revolutionary Socialist party, the Forward Bloc (Marxist), and the Socialist Unity Centre on the other, on the eve of the downfall of the second communist-dominated ministry, which had a C.P.(M.) home and police minister, the C.P. wanted the C.P.(M.) to desist from armed parades, but the C.P.(M.) refused to do so.

[22] The C.P.(M.) condemned the initial police action, and secured an agreement within the united front to treat the problems of the Naxalbari uprising as

repeated over the struggle for enhanced share of the crop for tillers at Gopiballavpore during the second communist-dominated ministry which had a C.P.(M.) home minister.[23] However, in view of what has been said above, to put all this down to 'parliamentary illusions' of the C.P.(M.), etc. is only to obfuscate the issues involved. A much better explanation is available, in terms of 'competitive hegemonism' discussed below.

According to a third untenable explanation:

S.3 Underestimation of the agrarian problem, of the importance of the agrarian revolution, was the prime cause of communist failure.

This criticism seems to ignore two essential features of the economics and politics of West Bengal which were rather more pronounced there in the late 1960s than in the rest of India. These features are: (i) the high degree of dependence of the rural economy on government economic interventionist policies;[24] (ii) the existence of a network of other reciprocal linkages between the rural and urban sectors of the economy, operating through (a) a large urban free (or black) market for controlled agricultural products, and a rural free (or black) market for controlled manufactures,[25] (b) a class of income-earners who earn incomes and make investments in *both* sectors. (Given the preponderant demographic status of the population of the Calcutta–Howrah megalopolis in the West Bengal region, these reciprocal linkages de-emphasize the agrarian problem and agro-centric politics.)

A fourth explanation, which is also essentially untenable on factual evidence, could read:

S.4 The failure to create a 'revolutionary vested interest' in the

---

socio-economic, and *not* as a political challenge or as a problem of 'law and order'. But when these were violated, they did *not* resign or even threaten to resign. Given their rising popularity in West Bengal, and an unresolved infighting in the Congress central cabinet, which soon culminated in a split in the Congress, if they *had* resigned, the demands of the Naxalbari peasants would in all probability have been conceded.

[23] The suggestion that the C.P.(M.) minister in charge of the police portfolio stalled police action (Dasgupta, 1974, p. 45) is not very convincing, since on his orders the Eastern Frontier Rifles were sent to crush the uprising.

[24] In Bengal such policies date back to the 1930s when the Krishak Proja Minister curbed money-lenders and controlled acreage under raw jute to support raw jute prices, and the 1940s when the Muslim League Ministry under Suhrawardy controlled food-grain prices after the 1943 famine. The main beneficiaries probably were the *jotedars* who were in control of both these political parties.

[25] The former was more important than the latter because of the high degree of urbanization in the West Bengal region.

preservation of the communist initiative was the chief cause of failure.

In fact, however, sections belonging to almost all potentially 'revolutionary', or at least 'neutralizable' classes and social strata registered gains in terms of a favourable redistribution of income, improved bargaining strength and social and political status, and, to a lesser extent, in terms of favourable legislation. (The Congress central Government *did* use its veto powers to kill legislation to redistribute land and reform industrial and labour relations, as well as a proposal to nationalize the jute industry. But this happened only when the second communist-dominated state ministry was on its last legs, and the renovated, radical Congress was already showing signs of re-emerging as a viable electoral alternative in West Bengal.) Among the gainers were: (i) industrial workers in the old, pre-1947 industries, viz. jute, engineering, and tea plantations, as well as the new, post-1955 industries in the Durgapur–Asansol belt. (ii) Every category of middle-class salaried employees in the 'mercantile firms' of pre-1947 vintage, as well as in government enterprises and most large-scale enterprises in the private and public sectors. (iii) Urban small traders and office employees engaged in spare-time trade to increase their earnings, who gained during the first communist-dominated ministry from a sharp decline in bribe-taking by police-men and petty government officials. (iv) City slum-dwellers (including better-off sub-letting tenants) who benefited by an ordinance of the state ministry forbidding eviction by landlords.[26] (v) Share-croppers in the South Bengal districts, who gained both in struggles, already referred to, for an enhanced share of the crop, and also from restoration as cultivable land of large tracts which had been flooded with saline water and converted into fisheries by landlords.

Some reference must now be made to explanations which are *inadequate* in the sense that they refer to facts which must be taken into account in a *full* explanation of communist failure, but do not, by themselves, explain what happened.

One such explanation, often heard in non-Naxalite communist circles, is:

S.5 Adventurist Naxalite insurgency killed communist revotionary initiative.

---

[26] By a parallel ordinance *all* urban tenants, including the affluent ones, were given protection from eviction, for which all of them blessed the communist-dominated ministry!

This explanation is inadequate for several reasons. *First*, it was certainly not clear before the start of the Naxalite armed insurgency, or *ex ante*, that such insurgency *was* 'adventurist', doomed to isolation from the masses. The context was: (i) a Congress central government paralysed and essentially non-interventionist in West Bengal (as noted above), (ii) almost the whole of eastern and northern India was under the control of non-Congress ministries which included communists and were similarly paralysed, (iii) the C.P.(M.) was the dominant partner in the first communist-dominated ministry, and controlled the coercive instruments at the state level in the second communist-dominated ministry in West Bengal. *Second*, as already noted, the Naxalite insurgency in its various phases developed out of a split in the *rising* mass movement in West Bengal manifested not only in the rising communist vote, but also in strikes, *bandhs*, etc. *Third*, as also noted earlier, armed 'counter-coercion' against hostile political forces (if not against the police which they controlled) was also used by the C.P.(M.), and was not always distinguishable from manifestations of Naxalite insurgency. (So that in some sense the C.P.(M.)'s criticism of adventurist Naxalite insurgency is rather like the pot calling the kettle black.) Nevertheless, the last phase of Naxalite armed insurgency, when something like a blood-feud developed between the Naxalite insurgents on one side and the re-politicized (as an anti-communist force) West Bengal police, was pretty obviously adventurist. It could have been avoided by the intervention of other political parties to arrange for a cease-fire. This was not asked for, nor was it forthcoming. Ultimately, there was a unilateral cease-fire by the Naxalite insurgents after the 'de-recognition' of the C.P.(Marxist-Leninist) leader earlier recognized by the central committee of the Chinese Communist party. This was followed by the arrest of all top leaders of the C.P.(M.-L.) followed by splits.[27]

A second explanation which is inadequate in the sense defined above could be elaborated as follows:

S.6 West Bengal communism suffered an eclipse when small property-owners, who were potential allies, turned against it owing to (i) communist rhetoric about armed revolution which never

[27] 'De-recognition' was suggested by the silence of Peking Radio about the last phase of the Naxalite (urban) insurgency. There are reports, with many discrepancies between alternative versions emanating from police sources, about an unauthenticated criticism by the central committee of the Chinese C.P. which made the 'de-recognition' explicit.

materialized,[28] and/or (ii) communist failure to provide security of property and person (with or without police protection[29]) to small property-owners, (iii) the unpredictability about the targets chosen by the Naxalites in their 'annihilation' campaigns against 'enemies'![30]

This explanation refers to facts which cannot be ignored in any full explanation. Its chief inadequacy is that it ignores the fact that the growing successes of communism for a time, as indicated by the 'success indicators' referred to in sect. 9.3 above, suggest that the facts summarized in S.6 (i)–(iii) did *not* cause a communist eclipse until they *coincided* with *non*-property-owners' loss of confidence in communist capacity to create *new* 'production relations'[31] while making the *old* production relations unworkable. The hypothesis is supported by the evidence that communism did *not* suffer a serious setback when, during the first communist-dominated ministry, groups of defectors acting as champions of propertied interests brought about the downfall of the ministry. But it *did* suffer an eclipse when the communist champions of *non*-property-owners became involved in a major triangular split between the C.P.(M.), the Naxalite factions, and the rest.

The third 'inadequate' explanation, denied only by its target, the C.P.(M.), at one time was:

S.7 C.P.(M.) 'hegemonism' was the chief cause of communist failure.

This explanation needs, first of all, a clarification of the meaning

---

[28] There was such rhetoric not only in Naxalite slogans, posters, and journals, but also in the speeches of the C.P.(M.) peasant leader who was minister in charge of land revenue in the communist-dominated West Bengal ministries. This, and armed parades in village and town by C.P.(M.) peasant activists, and their slogan 'bury the traitors', created an atmosphere of imminent armed communist revolution.

[29] The C.P.(M.) minister in charge of home and police departments sometimes promised to entrust trade unions and public organizations instead of the police with the responsibility of maintaining public order, while the police force concentrated on prevention of crimes by professional criminals. At other times he tried to transform the police force from an instrument of coercion into an instrument of co-operation between the communist-dominated ministry and the people.

[30] It was impossible to tell against whom—'notorious' landlords, suspected police informers, C.P.(M.) cadres, educationists, doctors, shop-keepers, or statues of cultural or nationalist leaders of Bengali society—the Naxalite commando units would strike next. The uncertainty climaxed when the C.P.(M.-L.) leadership formally 'decentralized' their organization by giving full freedom to lower units to take specific decisions about the targets of their 'annihilation campaign'.

[31] This is a useful Marxian term which refers primarily to relations between men involved in the production process arising from the form of property ownership of the means of production.

of the word 'hegemonism'. It is a Marxian 'first principle' that the
hegemony of the working class, or at least its proxy, a revolutionary
(communist) group which is its ideological representative, is essential
for a successful communist revolution. Up to date, this principle has
passed the test in every successful communist revolution. But the
hegemonistic ambitions of communist factions have often exceeded
their capacities. In at least one classic case, the Hungarian Soviet
revolution of 1920, this has resulted in an unsuccessful revolution.
In another, the Cuban communist revolution in the late 1950s, a
revolutionary group whose capacities were instrumental in establishing hegemony became communist in the process. (On the other
hand, those whose capacities were below requirements, but who
claimed 'hegemonistic rights' because they had formed a communist
party, failed in this case to prevent a successful revolution.) Thus it
is possible to distinguish between communist 'hegemony', which
seems to be the *sine qua non* of any successful modern revolution,
and communist 'hegemonism' where hegemonistic claims and ambitions exceed the capacity to establish revolutionary hegemony.

If communist 'hegemonism' is defined in this way, there is little
doubt that the C.P.(M.) tried hard to make itself the instrument of
communist hegemony in a protracted revolution in West Bengal in
the late 1960s. This aim was dramatically revealed in two episodes.
The first was the negotiations for the formation of the second
communist-dominated ministry. The second was its decision to treat
the Naxalbari uprising led by its local leading cadres as a matter of
party discipline, which has already been referred to. In both episodes
the C.P.(M.) insisted on exercising its hegemonistic claims to certain
key instruments of revolutionary decision-making. In the first case
it claimed (and secured) the right to control the police force so as to
put it out of action as a coercive instrument.[32] In the second it
claimed but did *not* secure (since the Naxalites defied them) the right
to control the tempo of revolutionary struggles. But the proof of the
pudding is in the eating. In the final analysis, the C.P.(M.)'s claims
to hegemony exceeded its capacity to exercise it. It only succeeded

[32] The C.P.(M.) insisted on holding (a) the chief minister's portfolio *or* (b) the
home (and police) minister's portfolio. It gave up (a) and got (b). Later, it also
wanted sole control, in between cabinet meetings, of the home and police departments. This was the proximate cause of the downfall of the ministry. Still later,
during the attempt to form a third communist-dominated ministry, it agreed to
have a police minister nominated by the C.P., in return for the latter's consent to
a C.P.(M.) nominee as the chief minister, but nothing came of it.

in restoring the hegemony of a renovated Congress in West Bengal's politics.

All this is true. But S.7, i.e. an explanation of the failure of the communist revolutionary initiative in terms of C.P.(M.) 'hegemonism', is still *inadequate*, for the reason that most other communist factions were also engaged in 'hegemonism'. As already hinted at, or referred to explicitly in discussions of explanations S.2 and S.4–7 earlier, they too aspired to emerge as effective instruments of communist hegemony,[33] they too failed to do so, and only helped restore Congress hegemony in West Bengal politics.

If this is so, we can correct explanation S.7 to read:

S.8 Competitive hegemonism by rival communist factions was the chief cause of communist failure.

This is an explanation in terms of a paradox. It says that *dedication* to communist aims by rival communist factions was the chief cause of communist failure! (It is thus the polar opposite of explanation S.1 in terms of 'enemy infiltration' discussed above. But it is entirely compatible with (i) each communist faction distrusting every other as a possible 'enemy agent', and (ii) any facts which may be unearthed about 'enemy infiltration' into any communist faction. (i) only makes hegemonistic competition between communist factions more intense. (ii) would make no difference to the outcome.)

But it turns out, as shown in the explanation from game theory in the next section, that recognition of the paradox also provides an explanation which is logically adequate.

9.5 Communist failure explained

In this section, the paradox identified at the end of the previous section is interpreted with the help of a model from game theory.

[33] Naxalite aspirations have already been referred to. One of the newer communist factions, the Socialist Unity Centre, which gained rapidly in influence in these years, made no secret of its hegemonistic ambitions. It used the Labour portfolio which it controlled in the first communist-dominated ministry to encourage anarcho-syndicalist seizure of small factories and *gherao* or detention of its managers or owners to secure a foothold among the industrial workers. The C.P.(M.) did the same with *its* control over the Labour portfolio in the second ministry (as well as the control over the police), except that it relied more on strike-action. Only the Revolutionary Socialist party supported the C.P.(M.)'s claims to hegemony rather than its own (though its district units in North Bengal challenged the C.P.(M.) and C.P. to extend their influence). On the other hand, the C.P. sometimes concentrated on trying to check the C.P.(M.)'s hegemonism rather than to indulge in it themselves. But it also tried sometimes to make the C.P.(M.) serve as an instrument for furthering its own hegemonistic ambitions. When this failed, it tried to make the radical Congress serve as an instrument for realizing vicariously these ambitions.

The model is adapted from the archetypal 'prisoners' dilemma', though in some respects it resembles the 'pollution problem' model, which itself is an adaptation of the 'prisoners' dilemma' (both have been referred to in Chapter 2 above). The chief distinguishing features of the present model are that (i) what is purely formally the 'best outcome' is *absurd* (which is emphatically *not* the case in either of the two models just mentioned), (ii) no enforced contract is possible (this *is* possible in the other two models). The outcome— intercommunist warfare, followed by wider repercussions in West Bengal and in the rest of India—is discussed in the next section. A possible escape from the outcome is discussed, speculatively (and not very hopefully), in the concluding section.

Definitions

1. A revolution is a protracted revolution under communist leadership in which a nucleus of power is established, preserved, and extended, through a protracted period of ebb and flow of the revolution.
2. A communist faction is one which is for rather than against a revolution.
3. 'To lead' is to claim, *ex ante* (i.e. *before* the revolution is made), hegemonistic rights in the revolution.
4. 'To follow' is to surrender both hegemonistic rights claimed *ex ante* and achievement of hegemony *ex post* (i.e. as the revolution is made).
5. When a communist faction decides to 'conserve its strength', it is engrossed in political[34] or 'economist'[35] feather-bedding at the expense primarily of rival communist factions, and is addicted to 'party jingoism'[36] directed against them.

[34] A communist faction is engaged in 'political feather-bedding' when it converts instruments of the superstructure of power by constitutional methods (i.e. its control over ministries, or trade unions which politically control individual ministers), or by clandestine penetration into instruments of 'hegemonism' or of 'conservation of strength'.

[35] 'Economist feather-bedding' represents conversion of instruments of collective bargaining for economic benefit embedded in the infrastructure of power (e.g. trade unions, peasant unions, *ad hoc* committees for conducting mass movements, clubs, activist and volunteer groups, etc.) into instruments for securing collective gains for members or supporters of one's own faction at the expense of members or supporters of rival factions (or the uncommitted). In the limiting case, a trade union engaged in economist feather-bedding functions like a joint stock company whose main asset is its membership.

[36] i.e. political action on the principle 'my party right or wrong', which ultimately leads to the cult of unconditional defence of every act, if not every word of every member of one's own faction.

6. A communist 'side' represents one, or a combination of more than one, communist faction.

Environment

1. A revolution is feasible (for reasons explained in sect. 9.3).
2. There *exist* those who are opposed to communist revolution.
3. Communist preferences are unaffected by preferences of those who are opposed to communist revolution.[37]
4. There may be many (actual or potential) communist factions, but there are always two communist 'sides'.
5. The revolution is successful when there is a decisive majority (or minority) under communist hegemony for revolution, achieved *ex post*.

Communist political psychology

1. Each communist faction prefers communists to be for, rather than against, the revolution (i.e. the somewhat perverse preference by one communist faction that another rival communist faction should be against, rather than for, the revolution, is excluded).
2. Each communist faction distrusts every other (i.e. judges them by what they do, rather than by what they say, and by what they think rather than by what they do).
3. Each communist faction wants 'to lead', rather than 'to follow'.
4. If a communist faction cannot 'lead', it prefers to 'conserve its strength', rather than 'to follow', regardless of the consequences.

Outcome

Before the outcome is discussed, it should be noted that assumption 4 about the environment, and assumption 1 about communist political psychology have been introduced chiefly because they were factually true in the case under study. (Assumption 4 about the environment was true most of the time in the late 1960s in West Bengal, except for very brief, and rare, quiescent interludes. Assumption 1 about communist political psychology was true, at least if we

---

[37] This 'strong' assumption is made to drive home the point that the outcome would have been unaffected even if no communist faction were 'corrupted' by 'bourgeois' ideology or political influence. In fact, they almost certainly were, in varying degrees, or, at any rate, every communist faction was *believed*—by at least one rival faction—to be so corrupted. The remaining argument stands, even if this assumption is dropped.

take public utterances into account, and accept them as sincere.)
Both could be dropped, without loss, i.e. without affecting the outcome, or speculation about alternative outcomes in section 9.7.[38]

Ignoring for a moment constraints imposed by meanings of words
or definitions, implied by the context, there are, conceivably, six
possible outcomes, writing 1 and 2 for the two sides, viz.:

1. Both 'lead'.
2. 1 'leads', 2 'follows'.
3. 2 'leads', 1 'follows'.
4. Both 'follow'.
5. Both quit politics, or, at least, communist politics.
6. Each 'conserves his strength', regardless of the consequences.

Now, it is at once obvious that 1 is absurd, because by definition
(as well as communist ideology in general) both cannot 'lead', if one
leads the other must follow. By the same argument, 4 also is excluded:
both cannot 'follow'. Outcome 5 is ruled out by the general context:
a communist never quits politics. Thus, we are left with outcomes
2, 3, and 6 as the only *really* possible outcomes. Now, by assumption
3 about communist political psychology, 1 prefers 2 to 6, which is
preferred to 3. On the other hand, by the same assumption, 2 prefers
3 to 6, which is preferred to 2. Ignoring assumption 2 about communist political psychology, this leaves us with the 'equilibrium
point' represented by 6, from which any move which is really possible
will be Pareto-inferior (i.e. not make one better off without making
the other worse off). Assumption 2 about communist political
psychology only reinforces this outcome. By this assumption, neither
trusts the other to 'follow' its 'lead', and not stab it in the back, even
if it *seems* to 'follow'.[39] Indeed, this immediately gives us outcome
6 as the uniquely determined 'equilibrium point', independently of
assumption 3 about communist psychology.

Now, outcome 6, which is the uniquely determined 'equilibrium
point', says each faction will 'conserve its strength' regardless of
the consequences. This outcome is definitely Pareto-inoptimal (since

[38] By contrast, in a standard 'prisoners' dilemma' game model, at least one
assumption similar to these is useful in avoiding complications (see Sen, 1969,
pp. 12–15).
[39] This was operative, for example, when with the formation of the second
communist-dominated ministry in West Bengal, on the initiative of the C.P.(M.)
home minister, the arrested leaders of the C.P.(M.-L.) were released unconditionally (they had been arrested on the initiative of the chief minister of the first
communist-dominated ministry who was also the chief minister of the second).
But neither side trusted the other to 'follow', and both insisted on 'leading'.

assumption 1 about communist psychology says both prefer all communists to be for the revolution). But the outcome was also bizarre: an escalation of intercommunist tension into intercommunist warfare, which was abruptly stopped only by the restoration of Congress hegemony in West Bengal politics, albeit after its 'radicalization'. Given communist preference patterns, this could have been avoided only if assumption 2 about the environment, evidently ignored by the communist factions (until it was too late), was in fact ignorable. In short, the communists fought for the spoils of the revolution as if all opposition had been obliterated! To vary the analogy, they fought for the right to 'lead' in the revolution after first assuming that it was already victorious! However, as noted in section 9.1 above, contrary to first impressions, there is no evidence that the abortive communist protracted revolution, which *could* have started in the late 1960s in West Bengal, has vanished without leaving a trace. There *has* been an aftermath, which is discussed in the next section.

9.6 The aftermath: up to 1974

The immediate aftermath in West Bengal has been:

1. Decimation of communist cadres as much through mutual attrition (plus mutual expulsion from each other's strongly held base areas), as through counter-insurgency operations by the police and the military, co-ordinated with drives by youth and student activists of the radical Congress. (Many of the facts are recorded in Dasgupta, 1974, *passim*.)

2. Discredit of communist electioneering, rather than of parliamentary electioneering as such; this was the main feature of the first phase of the aftermath, from which the main beneficiary was the radical Congress. From roughly 1973 onwards there has been a somewhat unusual decline in the percentage of votes polled during by-elections (which have been boycotted by the C.P.(M.)). This *may* possibly be the first sign of a tendency among voters to leave the business of elections to electors who are selected and managed by those who are nominated (or tolerated) by rival radical Congress factions.

3. Perfection of the techniques of political and economist featherbedding (as defined in nn. 34 and 35 of this chapter) by radical Congress factions to consolidate state capitalism. Improvements introduced on the original communist version are: (i) encouragement of

militant trade unionism by the better-paid and better-placed technocrats for upgrading their status in the Government bureaucracy,[40]
(ii) extension of the nationalized sector[41]—aided by active backing
from the Congress central Government, which the communist-
dominated ministries did not have—to provide greater scope for
political and economist feather-bedding, (iii) *both* strike-making *and*
strike-breaking—sometimes in concert with the Government apparatus specially geared for the purpose—used as the *general* method
of mass action,[42] (iv) the signing-up of unemployed (mainly urban)
youth, first to act as storm-troopers against communist activists
(Naxalite or C.P.(M)), or as strike-makers or strike-breakers, and
later to be more permanently settled in public sector enterprises.[43]

4. Communism survived up to 1974 as the only opposition to
Congress radicalism in West Bengal, with intercommunist warfare
in suspension, each communist faction having disengaged from
active combat with others. Its survival is expressed in: (i) the
alienated cadres in prison and underground of a splintered Naxalite
communism who are completely outside the parliamentary political
system, and exercising no political rights,[44] (ii) the extra-parliamentary probing *bandhs* organized by the C.P.(M),[45] which boycotts
sessions of the West Bengal state legislature, but is very active in
the Indian Parliament, (iii) the combined parliamentary plus extra-
parliamentary political activity of the C.P. which seeks to work

[40] e.g. the power engineers' demand for better pay and parity of status with
'generalist' bureaucrats was conceded after a lightning strike and major power-
breakdown (never encouraged or permitted earlier by the communist factions,
except once, in North Bengal, by a Naxalite faction). But the junior doctors'
strike for similar demands was broken by politically mobilized strike-breakers.

[41] by nationalizing the coal mines, the Burnpur steel plant, and the network
controlled by what was the largest monopoly network in India in the 1930s,
Andrew Yule and Company.

[42] The adoption of the technique of strike-*breaking* by the Congress radicals
was easier in the initial stages, because of their weakness among the employed,
as opposed to unemployed, workers. Once they also developed a foothold among
the former, rival Congress factions have fought on *opposite* sides to make and
break strikes, e.g. in the Calcutta State Transport services in 1974. By contrast,
the rival Communist factions refrained from strike-breaking, however intense
their competitive economist feather-bedding in the late 1960s.

[43] Notably in the Durgapur steel plant, to outnumber C.P.(M.) oriented
activists. Semi-permanent employment to radical Congress activists has also been
provided under refugee relief programmes during the Bangladesh war, drought
relief programmes, and the distribution of employment in Government projects,
or licences (e.g. for operating minibuses in Calcutta).

[44] including the minimum political rights accorded to *détenus* and prisoners.
However, in 1974, for the first time, some Naxalite prisoners called off a hunger-
strike after receiving assurances from a Congress minister that their minimum
political rights would be safeguarded.

[45] Some of them were synchronized with *bandhs* called by the C.P.

out a 'uniting and struggling' relationship with both the radical Congress and the C.P.(M.) (with more emphasis on the former).[46]

In a wider context, for India as a whole, the major repercussions, at least up to the end of 1974, were:

1. The adoption by the Congress radicals of political and economist feather-bedding, first tried out in West Bengal, as standard practices throughout India. (One strong indication was a general change-over from a 'licence-quota'-based state capitalism to a state capitalism with a large 'nationalized' core.[47] Another was the adoption of some novel methods of strike-breaking,[48] and also of strike-making.)

2. The right-of-centre political parties of northern India have switched from commitment to 'law and order' to sympathy for agitational disorder, from strike-breaking to militant strike-action, from a commitment to an independent Government bureaucracy to a policy of politicizing the bureaucracy, from *laissez-faire* to toleration of state capitalism with a 'nationalized' (and unionized) core. (The important switch from general opposition to strikes and commitment to strike-breaking rather than to strike-making was symbolized by the unanimous support given by all opposition parties to the unsuccessful railway general strike of 1974 which was called off unconditionally. The change-over from *laissez-faire* to state capitalism was signalled by (i) the formal dissolution in 1974 of the Swatantra party which was formed to fight for a *laissez-faire* Utopia, and (ii) the switch by the Jana Sangh (in 1972 and 1974) from rejection of nationalization of industries to unionized penetration of nationalized industries. (Only the Bharatiya Lok Dal, an extension of the dissolved Bharatiya Kranti Dal, which absorbed politically active remnants of the Swatantra party and a splinter group of the Sanyukta Socialist party, continued to assume a partial *laissez-faire* stance. It wanted *laissez-faire*, except that it also wanted enhanced

---

[46] Congress–C.P. co-ordination committees have been formed and dissolved.

[47] The nationalized sector was extended to cover coal mines, oil refineries, and oil distribution networks, the second steel plant in the private sector, and a significant proportion of the textile factories. The profitability of the nationalized undertakings was also shown to have improved, partly by better operation, and partly by changed accounting procedures. Only the networks owned by the Indian 'monopoly houses' were not nationalized, and were allowed to expand, though they were harassed for utilizing Government loans to extend private ownership and control, or for evading taxes and their obligations as licence-holders.

[48] e.g. by witholding wage-payment to striking railway workers by amending the Payment of Wages Act, and by giving extra increment to an estimated one-third of employees who helped break the strike.

support prices for agricultural products and no tax increases on, or rise in prices of, agricultural inputs.)

3. Indian communism marked time throughout India in the immediate aftermath of the débâcle in West Bengal, except for marginal gains by the C.P. from experiments in utilizing the radical Congress (and of in-fighting within the radical Congress) for promoting its hegemonistic ambitions. This was attempted in Kerala, with a C.P.–Congress coalition ministry, and in Bihar, through parliamentary and extra-parliamentary 'antagonistic co-operation, between the C.P. and the Congress, *without* forming a coalition ministry.[49])

A delayed, *post-communist* aftermath of the West Bengal communist débâcle of the late 1960s was reflected in the initially student-led political upheavals in Gujarat and Bihar in 1974. They represent an indirect sequel to the West Bengal dénouement because they have developed where neither the Congress radicals, nor the right-of-centre political challenge to both Congress radicalism and communism, nor the communist factions were able to apply the lessons of the West Bengal events to modernize politics. The sequel was *post-communist* in the sense that (i) it represented the attempted entry of new forces—student youth, including those of rich peasant origin, *sarvodaya* politicians,[50] peasant lobbies (e.g. the *khedut samaj* in Gujarat)—into the closed ring of the established power-structure consisting of political factions in Government and opposition, (ii) it ushers in politics in which both communism and the opposition to communism are represented by forces on both sides of the barricades,[51] (iii) these political upheavals are marked by such communist or post-communist features as (a) the rise of student power, in the campus, in the streets, as in Paris and West Germany in 1968, and in America during the early anti-Vietnam draft movement later, (b) suspension of education as a prelude to a revolution in education resembling the Chinese cultural revolution or its Naxalite version in West Bengal, (c) mass coercion of legislators (successful in

---

[49] The C.P. has also experimented with 'antagonistic co-operation' without joining radical Congress ministries in Orissa and Uttar Pradesh. But there both the activity and the gains seem to be mainly parliamentary, in contrast to Bihar, where, at least till 1974, they were also extra-parliamentary.

[50] The *sarvodaya* politicians owe their inspiration to Gandhi's call for dissolution of the Congress party made just before his assassination in 1948. They have also remained outside the parliamentary political system ever since.

[51] This development may bring to an end the basic dichotomy in Indian politics between communism and the opposition to communism which emerged in the 1942 Quit India movement and became the dominant dichotomy in India after the separation of Pakistan in 1947.

Gujarat, partially successful in Bihar), reminiscent of mass coercion of defectors from the communist-dominated united front in West Bengal in the late 1960s (or of pro-Pakistan legislators in Bangladesh in the early 1970s), (d) the demand for drastic overhaul of the parliamentary political system to provide for direct mass intervention in the higher levels of the pyramidal parliamentary structure (similar demands had been made, but not pressed, by the C.P.(M.) in the late 1960s), (e) the perspective of a *protracted* total (i.e. political, social, moral) revolution which formalized the implicit, blurred perspective of the West Bengal communist political upheaval in the late 1960s, as suggested in section 9.2 above.

9.7 The 1975 show-down

The genesis of the 1975 political show-down has something to do with moves in global politics, which are better discussed in other chapters of this book. (They have already been touched upon in Chapters 6–8, and will be referred to again in Chapter 10.) But in the main it was a part of the zigzag sequel to the cross-currents in domestic politics stretching back to the type of events analysed earlier in this chapter.

In 1975 the first novel, and somewhat unexpected, development was the runaway hegemony over the 'post-communist' movement of new entrants into politics established by a consortium of all parties belonging to India's Political Establishment (including a somewhat distrustful C.P.(M.)[52]), except the radical Congress and the C.P. The consortium, showing growing cohesion, tried to concentrate on a 'short and swift' struggle to paralyse the central Government and the Indian Parliament, modelled on the visions and realities of Indian politics in the 1920s, 1930s, and 1942.

Forced into a corner, the radical Congress Government had either to abdicate, or to hit back. Hit back it did, and the immediate impact was something in the nature of a shock, though, as already stated in Chapter 7, it remains to be seen whether it was a traumatic shock. Traumatic or not, there was an element of surprise about the impact caused, originating in several distinct factors. First, the central Government, seemingly engrossed in trivialities (the implications of the failure of the railway general strike were strangely ignored by the opposition 'janata morcha' or people's front), suddenly acted

[52] reluctant, as always, to give up its claims to political hegemony over any political movement in which it participated.

decisively against its tormentors. Second, its tormentors, who really wanted to govern vicariously, 'from outside'—i.e. without the taint of corruption it heaped on holders of all political office—played into the hands of the radical Congress in central (i.e. federal) politics, by trying to monopolize the noises and clichés of politics, and the instruments of central political power, without having power. The leader[53] of the extra-parliamentary opposition 'janata virodhi morcha' (the opposition people's front) tried to function like the head of a shadow cabinet which ruled the country, claiming the prerogative of the 'first among equals'. Thus there were attempts to dictate a summary dismissal of central cabinet members charged with corruption by the opposition front, and to nominate a new prime minister. When these moves failed, there were attempts to outvote the central Government leadership within the radical Congress party's caucus in the central Indian Parliament, etc. These methods were superficially reminiscent of some successful moves by Gandhi in the 1930s, when he was not even formally a member of the Congress organization.[54] But while Gandhi never made such a move without being sure of success,[55] the leaders of the 1975 opposition front did. The result was that Gandhi never burnt his fingers; they did. Third, the working class, as well as the salaried, and sections of the non-salaried, professional middle classes were getting tired of militant struggles with no holds barred organized by all political factions without exception, for sectional gains at each other's expense. This was because—apart from the shock of the failure of the general railway strike—all sectional gains were being rapidly swallowed up by inflation, itself partly generated[56] by such competitive militancy by the organized rich and the organized poor alike. Fourth, the Government had already launched its drive against smugglers, tax-evaders, and corrupt officials before the show-down in June 1975. This tended to de-activize them politically as financiers of political corruption, since both the Government and the opposition were now committed to anti-corruption crusades, and it was more difficult

---

[53] there were two candidates who contended for leadership.

[54] against some members of provincial Congress ministries charged with corruption, and also against Subhas Bose, who defeated Gandhi's nominee to become president of the Congress, but resigned, complaining of 'non-co-operation' by Gandhi's supporters.

[55] e.g. he made no such move against the Nehru–Patel leadership's consent to the separation of India and Pakistan, to which he was opposed.

[56] Of course, domestic inflation was also caused by crop failures plus food-price support, and aggravated by 'imported' inflation.

for the financiers of corruption to gain by playing them off against each other.

The 'post-communist' challenge in Indian politics in the 1970s has ended, temporarily at any rate, in much the same way as the communist challenge in West Bengal politics in the 1960s had ended earlier. But there are some novel features in the dénouement. First, the 'post-communist' challenge, by 1975 in the iron grip of conservative Congress leaders and militant nationalist Jana Sangh cadres, survived to run the state-level administration in one of its two original bastions, i.e. in Gujarat, up to the spring of 1976.[57] Second, Hindu anti-Muslim communalism, already steadily obsolescent in Indian politics since the break-up of Pakistan in 1970, has probably become finally obsolete and irrelevant in Indian politics, with the banning of the militant Hindu Rashtriya Swayam Sevak Sangh (R.S.S.) which was modelled on the Nazi SS.[58] Third—and this is of special interest in the context of the present chapter—Indian communism has become irrelevant in any struggle for political power in India, perhaps for a generation. This is chiefly because most of its totems and weapons have been stolen by other contenders for power, who are to the right or left of centre.

However, it must be added that splintered Indian communism survives, partly because, as noted in the previous section, there are few 'total anti-communists' left in Indian politics, though almost everybody, including almost all communists, are now selective anti-communists, tolerant towards one's own 'good' communists, and intolerant towards the other's 'bad' ones. But another, at least equally durable reason for communist survival is the communist attachment to notions of 'hegemonism', which minimally means communists do not accept the hegemony of others, even when they cannot impose their hegemony on others. So the Naxalite communists survive in internal emigration in rural hide-outs, as is portrayed in in Hritwik Ghatak's film *Jukti Takka Goppa*, or in some sequences in Satyajit Ray's film *Protidwandi*. The C.P.(M.) hibernates, in inactive opposition to the radical Congress, resisting summons to commit political suicide by merging with the opposition 'janata virodhi morcha' (or with the C.P. which co-operates with the radical Congress). The C.P., which co-operates with the radical Congress, with

[57] In the extensive *panchayat* (commune) elections, held for the first time on adult franchise, there were losses and gains by both sides in December 1975.

[58] The Jana Sangh's acceptance as leaders of a former admirer of Ayub Khan's 'basic democracies', and an admiring biographer of Bhutto's, are indicators.

fewer ifs and buts, after June 1975, co-operates on the basis of 'unity and struggle'.[59]

Thus the upshot of the discussion in this chapter is depressing for those who are curious about the possibility of West Bengal's communists ultimately fulfilling their somewhat incoherent aims of the late 1960s, either by themselves, or, vicariously, through their post-communist successors in West Bengal, or elsewhere in India. It seems that the very strength of communist political psychology, viz. 'hegemonism', which, as just noted, helps them to survive, is the cause of their ill luck as contenders for power.

A strictly historical analysis of intercommunist warfare in West Bengal could have ended at this point. But political analysis permits, even enjoins, speculative predictions about alternatives. This is attempted in the next section.

9.8 An alternative outcome

Reverting to the explanation of the failure of the communist initiative in West Bengal in sect. 9.5 above, we cannot postulate a change in the assumptions about the environment to suggest an alternative to failure. If anything, the change in the environment in the 1970s—as assessed in the preceding two sections—rubs out assumption 1 about the environment made there, viz. that a 'revolution' (as stated by definition 1) is 'feasible' (for reasons given in sect. 9.3). But it may be that the assumption will become valid again, perhaps only after a generation, with Indian communism reviving as entirely new wine in new bottles. Yet the revival will hardly occur, still less be successful next time, if there are no changes in communist political psychology as represented by the assumptions made about it in sect. 9.5 above.

However, not simply *any* change in communist political psychology will radically change the outcome from failure to success. To see this, suppose for a moment that assumption 1 about communist political psychology given in sect. 9.5 is replaced by the 'perverse' assumption mentioned in parenthesis and discarded, and assumptions 3 and 4 are deleted as irrelevant.[60] Then, the purgatory in

---

[59] mutually accepted by the leadership of *both* the radical Congress and the C.P., rather than on the basis of uninhibited 'tailism' behind the radical Congress by the C.P., or with the C.P. exercising a 'vicarious hegemony' through its control over an inchoate radical Congress.

[60] Such a 'perverse' assumption would hold, for instance, if one communist faction were to decide that the best proof that a political movement is

which Indian communists found themselves in the 1970s would last as long as these assumptions hold.

By contrast, if assumptions 2–4 about communist political psychology are *substituted* by another assumption, 2a, which says:

2a. Each communist faction participates in the revolution unconditionally (regardless of what other communist factions do)—the communists can emerge out of the purgatory. They will then achieve a decisive majority (or minority) for the revolution, and the hegemony of the fittest communist faction, which are the two conditions of successful revolution (see assumption 5 about the environment).

The successful outcome just visualized can be given an interpretation in terms of ethics. Thus the assumptions 2 and 3 about communist psychology, which, as noted in sect. 9.5, accounted for communist failure, could be labelled 'selfish' motivations. Two alternative negations of such 'selfishness' are conceivable. One is for each communist faction to 'follow', i.e. surrender all claims to hegemonistic rights *ex ante*, as well as abandon all aspirations to achievement of hegemony *ex post*, or be 'selfless'. But this, as already noted, is impossible, and absurd.

On the other hand, assumption 2a just stated, which could take the place of assumptions 2–4 and mean success, implies that the communist faction is neither 'selfish' nor 'selfless', since it imposes no conditions (i.e. makes no claims), but also accepts none imposed by others (i.e. the communists do not renounce aspirations to achieve hegemony *ex post*). To distinguish it from 'selfish' and 'selfless' motivation, we may label motivation indicated by assumption 2a as 'unselfish'.

Appendix to Chapter 9

Hegemonism—
a mathematical restatement

In this 'hegemonism' game the assumptions are as stated in sect. 9.5 of Chapter 9. The two communist 'sides' are 1, 2. The possible out-

---

'revolutionary' is that it should be opposed by 'counter-revolutionary' forces which include other communist factions.

comes, listed there, are numbered 1, 2, 3, 4, 5, 6—of which, however, only 2, 3, 6 are feasible, that is, these alone are compatible with definitions and assumptions.

The pay-off functions may be written down as:

$$P^k = F^k(i), \text{ for } k = 1, 2$$
$$i = 1, 2, 3, 4, 5, 6$$

The orderings of the feasible strategies by the two communist 'sides' 1 and 2, are (for reasons explained in sect. 9.5):

$$F^1(3) \quad \angle \quad F^1(6) \quad \angle \quad F^1(2)$$
$$F^2(2) \quad \angle \quad F^2(6) \quad \angle \quad F^2(3)$$

Even ignoring assumption a.2 about 'communist political psychology', the 'equilibrium outcome' is (6) for each, since it is impossible to move from (6) to any other feasible outcome without making at least one player worse off. Formally, a.2 (i.e. mutual distrust between communists, based on the feeling that 'the other side' is 'an agent of the enemy') is therefore redundant, though in point of *fact*, as noted in Chapter 9, such distrust was very much in evidence. However, assumption a.4 about communist political psychology, viz. that each communist faction must either 'lead' or 'strengthen itself' at the expense of other communists, may be rooted in a.2. In other words, communist 'hegemonism' may be rationalized by a prior conviction that if other factions do not accept my hegemony, it is because they are hidden 'agents of the enemy'. If this interpretation is accepted, the 'communist hegemonism' game is indistinguishable from the 'pollution problem' game, adapted from the 'prisoners' dilemma'. If it is not accepted, this is a pure 'power' game, which Thomas Hobbes (1651, 1974, Ch. x, pp. 150–60) and Bertrand Russell (1938, 1946, Ch. 1, p. 10) thought was at the heart of all political activity.

CHAPTER 10

Oil, Self-reliance, and Nuclear Power

10.1 Introduction

IN this chapter the focus is on an analysis of the implications of three major developments in the Indo-West Asian region, viz. West Asian use of the oil weapon, their drive—as well as India's—towards self-reliance, and the emergence of India as a nuclear power.

The implications are first discussed separately, with a necessary digression on patterns of dominance and dependence between countries in the region and those outside it (which was referred to, but not elaborately considered, in Chapter 7). These compartmentalized analyses are based on discussions of the geo-politics of oil, the institutional economics of self-reliance of backward capitalist countries, and both the geo-politics and the institutional economics of a backward capitalist country's nuclear capability.

But each of these separate analyses (in sect. 10.2–4) leaves clues which point to the possible advantage of a juxtaposition which yields some interesting, though somewhat startling, predictions. These are then pursued—with two additional developments brought in at this stage, viz. the Israeli–Palestinian crisis and India–China contradictions. They are pursued, not so much because the predictions refer to *probable* outcomes, but because the uncertainties are such that they cannot be ruled out. Unlike the analyses in most other chapters in this book, the analyses in this chapter are improvised and informal (except for one reference to a 'battle of the sexes' type of game situation). A more rigorous and formal analysis of the five interacting problems considered in later sections has not been attempted chiefly because the uncertainties about the facts do not make it worth while.

10.2 The geo-political economy of West Asian oil

The 1973 oil price hike, and the deliberate use of the 'oil weapon' on the joint initiatives of the Arab States[1] and Iran,[2] is a most unusual

[1] which took the political decision to use the oil weapon mainly to settle accounts with Israel, and avenge previous defeats.

[2] who was uninvolved in the Arab–Israel conflict, but stepped in to use the oil weapon in waging an economic war in which she had fired, alone and less successfully, the first shot in her dispute in the 1950s with the Anglo-Iranian Oil Company. (If the Shah is to be believed, Iran also uses the oil weapon in a moral

event in the annals of 'geo-politics', which is more correctly called geo-political economy.

The event is unusual, because the 'geo-political' weapon has been used in this case (i) by resource-*rich* and manpower-*poor* countries, (ii) by semi-colonies against their imperialist overlords, and (iii) this has been accompanied by drastic nationalization measures directed against the so-called 'multinational'[3] oil corporations.

Unusual feature (i) emphasizes contrasts with Japanese geo-politics which had to do with the classic case of a resource-*poor* and man-power-*rich* country scoring phenomenal successes, even though it may be that the potent Arab–Iranian oil weapon might finally stop her in her tracks.[4] It also emphasizes contrasts with geo-politics as practised by capitalist colonial and imperialist powers in their hey-day.[5] These were manpower-*rich* countries, which were using their control over particular rich resources to secure a grip over other rich resources.[6]

Unusual feature (ii) emphasizes that the weapons of geo-politics have been used more often precisely by *imperialist* powers to *establish* semi-colonies,[7] or to hold them.[8] Attempts to use them to *prevent* aggression by imperialist powers,[9] or to weaken their hold over domi-nated countries and peoples,[10] have not been successful in the past.[11]

---

crusade to rid the world of western 'permissiveness', which is diagnosed as being the result of the oil-based over-heating of bedrooms.)

[3] The name is slightly misleading. Though the 'multinationals' are sometimes more powerful than the single countries from where their share-holders are drawn, the share-holders are mostly based in the advanced capitalist countries. Their essentially *imperialistic* nature, as the term is defined later in this chapter, is obscured when they are simply called multinationals.

[4] But, as we shall see below, this is by no means certain.

[5] in terms of either modernized labour skills, or population or both (e.g. England in the nineteenth century).

[6] e.g. Britain used her coal and iron resources to seize control over other scarce materials.

[7] e.g. the Italian conquest of Libya, which was justified on the ground that Italy needed oil, the Japanese conquest of Manchukuo, justified on the ground that Japan needed captive coal and iron ore resources.

[8] Algerian independence was resisted by France on the ground, among others, that she (and West Europe) needed Algerian oil. Belgium's hold over her Central African territories was sometimes justified on the ground that the world's largest copper and uranium deposits were to be found there.

[9] such as oil sanctions against Italy when she attacked Ethiopia in the 1930s, which was sabotaged by Anglo-French intrigue.

[10] e.g. the Iranian attempt to nationalize the Anglo-Iranian Oil Company in the 1950s. It foundered, because Iran could not find buyers of her nationalized oil, and was forced to go into partnership in a 'multinational' corporation with U.S. capital.

[11] An exception was India using her 'sterling balances' earned during World War II to loosen Britain's hold over her.

Unusual feature (iii) establishes one important link between the oil-weapon-based developments in West Asia and the developments within the framework of the 'modern Indian syndrome' which has been discussed in Chapter 7, and will be further discussed in later sections of the present chapter. There are other such links, as will be noted below.

10.3 Patterns of dominance and dependence

In presenting the 'modern Indian syndrome' in Chapter 7, changing patterns of dominance and dependence between advanced capitalist countries and India have been referred to, especially when discussing such features as 'statism' and 'parliamentarism' (but mostly the former). But a fuller discussion is needed, especially of the 'radical capitalist' drive towards 'self-reliance' (along with the 'radical capitalist' drive towards nationalization of existing industrial assets, etc.).

But, if we are to do so, we first need a terminology of the *different* patterns of dominance and dependence between advanced and backward capitalist countries. Since the terminology which is most convenient for our purpose does not coincide entirely with the terminology frequently used in standard literature, the following definitions might prove helpful.[12]

D.1 A capitalist country adopts a *colonialist* policy when it takes advantage of an uneven balance of *global* economic, political, and military power, to engage in outright plunder of goods and treasure, and create 'empty spaces' for settlement of its excess population, so as to secure an inflow of resources from colonies to the colonialist 'mother country'.

D.1a A dependent capitalist country which is a victim of capitalist colonialism is a *colony*.

D.2 A capitalist country adopts an *imperialist* policy when a colonialist alternative is restricted by a more even balance of global power (which dictates the use of more sophisticated methods of domination), but the capitalist country is in a position to take advantage of uneven balances of regional power. It can then *preserve* (rather than destroy or assimilate) pre-capitalist populations in annexed (e.g. India) or subordinated (e.g. China, Persia) territories, and change their consumption and production patterns in the interests of the imperialist country. A policy of capitalist imperialism involves

[12] They have also been used in Bose (1975), Ch. 10, sect. 1, 2, 3, 4 (pp. 161–71).

the imposition of 'free trade' (e.g. 'open door' in India under the Moghuls, and later in China) or 'common markets' (e.g. the German Zollverein, or the British 'Imperial Preference') on dependent countries. It also involves large-scale government and private investment by the imperialist country in the dependent country for 'opening up' the latter, but in no case a long-period *net* inflow of resources from the former to the latter.

D.2a A dependent capitalist country which is a victim of capitalist imperialism becomes a *semi-colony*.

D.3 A capitalist country adopts a *neo-imperialist* policy when (or where) colonialist or imperialist policies are blocked by (i) the balance of global (nuclear) super-power, (ii) the balances of regional power, involving, in particular, strongly protected national markets in backward capitalist countries, or (iii) are unattractive to the dominating country because the dependent backward capitalist country is 'resource-poor' (i.e. lacking in scarce raw materials such as oil), though it has a large market potential (e.g. India after World War II).[13] Capitalist neo-imperialism involves government-to-government foreign aid (though private undertakings may also be involved in either donor or receiving country), generally on a loan basis (whether interest-free or not), and with commodity-tying or country-tying of the gift-component of foreign aid (as with Public Law 480 U.S. food aid to India). In sharp contrast to colonialist or imperialist policies, with neo-imperialist policies there *is* a net inflow of resources on a long-term basis from the dominating to the dominated (dependent) country. Neo-imperialist foreign aid involves transfer of resources on concessional terms to (i) help exports from the neo-imperialist country to jump the protective trade barriers and penetrate the neo-colonial country, or (ii) achieve neo-imperialist foreign policy objectives (e.g. U.S. subversion of the Allende regime in Chile in the early 1970s through funds 'laundered' through third countries by the Central Intelligence Agency). It also involves, theoreti-

---

[13] In fact, India was bypassed in the scramble for sources of scarce materials such as (natural) rubber, oil, non-ferrous metals in the twentieth century. With the weakening of her strength in her monopoly control over jute fibre, and her share in the tea oligopoly, she ceased to attract foreign private investment after the 1930s on a scale large enough to make her an economically important semi-colony.

cally at least,[14] the aid-receiving country going through a period of 'over-self-reliance' or net *outflow* of resources when it is liquidating its foreign debt obligations. This may be indefinitely postponed,[15] if the net outflow required exceeds the long-term rate of growth of *per capita* income achieved, or the long-term rate of growth of *per capita* income desired,[16] so that concessional imports from the aid-giving country continue to 'jump' protective trade barriers. Alternatively, pursuit of 'over-self-reliance' may impose long-term stagnation in *per capita* incomes in the backward capitalist countries.[17] For *both* these reasons, government-to-government foreign aid from advanced to backward capitalist countries is properly classified as a 'neo-imperialist policy'.

D.3a A dependent capitalist country which is a victim of capitalist neo-imperialism is a *neo-colony*.

D.4 A dependent capitalist country adopts a policy of *radical capitalist self-reliance* when it stops receiving (imperialist) private foreign investment, or (neo-imperialist) foreign aid.

Before these definitions are used in the next two sections, a few initial comments about them may be useful.

First, the terminology of these definitions is not orthodox, and ignores certain distinctions which are of interest in other contexts, e.g. *both* India and China before 1947–50 are 'semi-colonies', though the former was under direct political control of imperialism, and the latter was under indirect political control;[18] *both* Pakistan, a recipient

---

[14] since the whole of foreign aid is never received as a gift, either *ex ante* or *ex post*, by backward capitalist countries. (War-devastated *advanced* capitalist countries have been luckier with U.S. aid.)

[15] as seems to be the case with India, which hoped to achieve 'self-reliance' in the 1980s after it had learnt to do without net U.S. aid in the 1970s. With most of the outstanding Rupee debt on Public Law 480 account written off in 1974, it might at best achieve zero net foreign aid *via-à-vis* a reluctant U.S.A. (i.e. receive U.S. aid which is entirely used up to meet U.S. debt obligations).

[16] including maintenance or intensification of the pattern of (unequal) distribution of personal incomes, which aggravates the problem of utilizing aid to end aid by stepping up the rate of growth (see Bose, 1975, Ch. 11, sect. 2, especially pp. 178–9, for a discussion).

[17] India's insistence on meeting these obligations (which are mounting) in the 1970s is one reason for stagnating growth-rates. On the other hand, Pakistan's unilaterally imposed 'moratorium' on meeting foreign aid obligations which have matured, has helped her to resume growth after the Bangladesh war.

[18] Actually, as hinted at in Chapter 8 above, direct political rule over India by British imperialism in a certain important sense began to end in the 1930s. On the other hand, this was the period when direct political control by (Japanese) imperialism was more important than at any other period of modern Chinese history.

of large-scale U.S. military aid under military pacts and alliances, and India, a recipient of large-scale U.S. economic aid in the 1960s, are 'neo-colonies'. But for our purposes the basic distinctions *between* 'semi-colonies', 'neo-colonies', and colonies as defined above are more important than these finer distinctions *within* groups of semi-colonies and neo-colonies.

Second, these are 'behaviourist' definitions, which describe patterns of dominance and dependence between advanced and backward capitalist economies, without analysing causes and motivations. But analytical models of capitalist production and accumulation which do so *have* been formalized at a somewhat technical level, and are available for consultation (see Bose, 1975, Ch. 9–11).

Third, we could say roughly that capitalist colonialism dominated on a world scale in the seventeenth and eighteenth centuries, capitalist imperialism dominated in the nineteenth century, and capitalist neo-imperialism has been dominant in the twentieth century. But in the nineteenth and twentieth centuries at least, within the over-all globally dominant imperialism or neo-imperialism, there have been important cases of colonialism, imperialism, and neo-imperialism.[19]

Fourth, a capitalist country can start as a colony, become a semi-colony, then an imperialist, and, finally, a neo-imperialist country (though only the U.S.A. has so far achieved this).[20] A country can also start as a capitalist semi-colony and end up as an imperialist and neo-imperialist country (though only Japan has achieved this). As we shall see in sect. 10.4 below, whether any West Asian oil-rich country can emulate Japan in this, is very much an open question. Prospects of resource-poor India doing so, as assessed in sect. 10.4 and 10.5 below, seem even more remote.

10.4 India's moves towards radical-capitalist self-reliance

As already indicated in n. 13 of this chapter, India ceased to claim a large share of global private foreign investment as a major repository of internationally scarce raw materials long before she secured formal political independence in 1947.[21] Moreover, India

[19] e.g. U.S. neo-imperialism in parts of Latin America in the nineteenth century, U.S.–Israeli colonialism in West Asia, and Pakistani colonialism in Bangladesh in the twentieth century.

[20] A repetition of such a cycle of development by South Africa is unlikely, partly because her strongly held oligopolistic position *vis-à-vis* gold production is likely to become less potent with the declining importance of monetary gold after the U.S.A. went off the last relic of an international gold standard in the world monetary crisis of the early 1970s.

[21] Briefly, when international commodity flows were seriously disrupted in

after 1947 had a strongly protected[22] domestic market, plus a battery
of state-capitalist controls which was rather more extensive and more
effectively manipulated as instruments of domestic 'political competition' (referred to in Chapter 7, sect. 7.3 of this book) than in most
other backward (or advanced) capitalist countries in the world. For
these various reasons, India was by no means the classic prototype
of a semi-colony in the 1950s and 1960s, though almost all successful political parties of the left, centre, and right were preoccupied with
resisting an imperialist penetration of the Indian economy through
foreign private investment.[23]

But in the 1960s India somewhat unexpectedly emerged as a classic
capitalist neo-colony of the world's leading neo-imperialist power,
the U.S.A. She resisted the form of neo-imperialist U.S. aid which
was most common in other backward capitalist countries (including
Pakistan), viz. arms aid.[24] But India was the major recipient of economic aid from advanced capitalist countries to backward capitalist
countries in this period even though *per capita* aid received by India
was far below *per capita* aid received by Pakistan.

In the late 1960s and early 1970s India's neo-colonial economy ran
into heavy weather. First, the U.S.A., her chief neo-imperialist aid-
giver (who had also become her largest trading partner by jumping
her trade barriers through concessional aid), began to cut back on
fresh aid for several reasons. Among these were: (i) the U.S.A.
realized, first during the Indo-Pakistan war of 1965 over Kashmir,

---

Afro-Asia during World War II, India regained a commanding position as a
source of food-stuffs and raw materials for allied forces in Afro-Asia. The allied
purchases were financed by accumulated sterling balances (and linked currency
inflation in India), a part of which was written off in the 1946 agreement referred
to in n.11 of this chapter, and another part was spent in the restoration of the
pre-war Indian economy (reconditioned to meet the consequences of Pakistan's
separation) during the first five year plan. (The inflation, which produced the last
major famine in India, in Bengal, in 1943, is vividly portrayed, with masterly
understatement, in Satyajit Ray's film *Ashani Sanket*.)

[22] not only by import duties, but also by a system of import quotas, foreign-
exchange controls, capital issues controls, conciliation laws governing labour
disputes, etc.

[23] Although the U.S.A. replaced Britain as the main source of foreign private
investment in India by the 1960s, aggregate foreign private investment in India
was rapidly outstripped by government-to-government economic aid. (The only
significant inflow of U.S. private investment was in the oil refineries set up after
the crisis over Iranian oil in the 1950s; see Bose, 1965, pp. 519–27; Bose (1969),
pp. 681–7, for data on foreign private investment.) But all political parties emphasized the need to control or resist *private* foreign investment rather than to resist
foreign economic aid.

[24] Her objections were relaxed to a minor extent after reverses in the border
conflict with China in the early 1960s.

and then finally during the 1971 Bangladesh war, that by her arms aid to Pakistan and economic aid to India she could not dictate an Indo-Pakistan parity in the subcontinental power-balance, (ii) India's mounting repayment obligations after ten to fifteen years of increasing U.S. aid inflow had created a 'transfer problem', whose solution could have been facilitated by the U.S. lowering her protective trade barriers. But protection of her domestic market was an American article of faith since the War of Independence, not to be easily revised,[25] (iii) the gold drain from the U.S.A. (the repository of most of the world's monetary gold after World War II) to West Germany and Japan had made it imperative for the U.S.A. to cut back on dispensable economic aid programmes, such as India's had become, (iv) with the beginnings of U.S.–Chinese and U.S.–U.S.S.R *rapprochements* in 1973 there were hopes that larger and more stable and efficiently managed markets for U.S. exports could be opened up in China and the Soviet Union on the basis of complementary U.S. imports of scarce raw materials, to compensate for a tapering-off of Indo-U.S. aid and trade relations. Second, on the Indian side, too, 'doing without foreign economic aid' became practical politics when it was realized that (i) the economic aid from the U.S.A. would taper off for reasons specified above, (ii) other advanced capitalist countries were unlikely to step into the shoes of the U.S.A. for reasons similar to reasons (ii) and (iv) specified above in case of the U.S.A.,[26] (iii) expanded trade with the U.S.S.R. and the Comecon countries[27] (and to a lesser extent with Japan[28]) could compensate for the tapering-off of Indo-U.S. aid-based trade, (iv) with the adoption of radical-capitalist nationalization programmes in India (referred to in Chapters 8 and 9 above) the stress on expansion of the Government-owned public sector in India by establishing *new* undertakings was reduced. This also meant that the Government's need for foreign economic aid to supplement budgetary resources available for ex-

[25] even though the U.S.A. advised Western European countries to throw open *their* protected markets.

[26] An additional reason was the inability of such advanced capitalist countries as the countries of Western Europe's E.E.C. and Japan to make good India's food (and fertiliser) deficits. These countries were disinclined to increase aid to India which would largely be spent in repaying debts to the U.S.A. and buying food and fertiliser from her at booming world prices.

[27] facilitated by the willingness of these countries to enter into long-term agreements for planned expansion of (self-liquidating) balance of trade with India.

[28] which was hungry for scarce raw materials like iron ore and coal, at least until there was willingness in Japan to rely wholly on China as an alternative source of supply.

pansion of the Government-owned sector was correspondingly reduced.[29]

10.5 The oil-price hike

Until the oil-price hike in 1973 the crisis of India's neo-colonial
economy had produced the following main results: (i) India began
to receive zero net aid from the U.S.A.,[30] (ii) net aid began to come
mainly from the other advanced capitalist countries and the U.S.S.R.
and other Comecon countries, (iii) India made serious attempts to
switch to a long-term strategy of 'trade not aid' as the basis for her
international economic relations by stepping up her exports, assisted
by (a) devaluation of the rupee which floated down with the devalu-
ing floating sterling, (b) changes in the direction of her foreign trade,
mainly in the direction of the U.S.S.R., which became her leading
foreign trade partner, (iv) India adopted a long-term radical-capitalist
goal of 'self-reliance',[31] defined to mean zero aid from all sources,
and a medium-term goal of zero *net* aid from *all* sources as a first
step.

But already before the impact of the oil-price hike was felt, India's
moves towards a radical-capitalist 'self-reliance' were frustrated by
three main factors. The first was an upsurge in allocation of resources
for increased consumption *today*, as against increased consumption
tomorrow (the consequence of 'competitive feather-bedding' policies
adopted by all political parties, to which reference was made in
Chapter 9). This exerted pressure for postponing progress towards
achievement of 'self-reliance', and relying on foreign economic aid
for financing excess consumption on a continuing basis. The second
factor was the inflation in advanced capitalist countries which raised
all import costs, including (a) cost of investment goods, and (b)
cost of imports from the U.S.S.R. and Comecon countries in so
far as their prices were adjusted to world-market price levels. A third
factor was the tapering-off in the rising of curve of food-production
and domestic food-procurement by the Government's public distribu-

---

[29] How far this method of expanding the Government-owned sector has
actually been used has not been estimated, but there is no doubt that *a priori*
foreign economic aid can be used for this purpose to supplement budgetary
resources, at least in the short run.

[30] i.e. U.S. aid began to be used entirely for meeting debt-servicing and repayment obligations to the U.S.A. It was announced during Henry Kissinger's
visit to India in the autumn of 1974 that such a position had in fact been reached.

[31] See Government of India, 'Draft Fifth Five Year Plan 1974–79', vol. 1,
pp. 3–4, 41.

tion system which had been achieved in the late 1960s by an integration of (a) improved agricultural technology (i.e. by use of high-yielding hybrid seeds, chemical fertilisers), (b) credit-support to agriculture through the nationalized banking system, and (c) price-support to agricultural products. Drought reduced output of food-grains directly, as well as indirectly through a fall in hydro-electric power generation which reduced the effectiveness of irrigation through tube-wells. 'Competitive feather-bedding' cut into foreign exchange available for import of chemical fertilisers, as well as the credit-support for agricultural production. Inflation in advanced capitalist countries also cut into foreign exchange available for import of chemical fertilisers and machinery for domestic production of chemical fertilisers.

The oil-price hike of 1973 made it even more difficult for India to maintain whatever progress she had made towards a radical-capitalist self-reliance, let alone to make further progress in that direction. The second and third of the 'frustrating factors' enumerated in the preceding paragraph were directly aggravated (the second by a further escalation in the rate of worldwide inflation, since the benefit India received by a rise in prices of her exports was more than offset by the sharp rise in her import bill, led by petroleum imports; the third by a further rise in petroleum-based chemical fertiliser prices). Only the first of the frustrating factors, the pressure for increases in present consumption as against future consumption, was marginally checked, since many imported or import-based 'luxury' products, especially the petroleum-based ones, were priced out of the market. (As against this, however, the domestic inflation made 'feather-bedding', which continued without let-up, more expensive.[32])

Thus with a ground-swell originating in the competitive price hikes in advanced capitalist countries and the oil-rich countries which was adverse to India's progress towards self-reliance, her bureaucracy and technocracy, rather than her politicians,[33] have been experimenting with alternative responses to the problem, viz.:

[32] e.g. the direct consumption expenditure financed by Government was pushed up with increased dearness pay and upward revision in pay scales to neutralize the rise in the cost of living. Since, in general, the principle of 'to him that hath more shall be given' was adhered to, and there was no narrowing of differentials in the process, the cost of political and trade-union feather-bedding was enormously increased. There were, however, some attempts to impose deferred pay agreements to partially offset this.

[33] There were no signs in 1974 that *any* political party had done any integrated rethinking on the kaleidoscopic effects of the inflation originating in the advanced capitalist countries and the retaliatory oil-price hike.

1. To become reconciled to a *neo-colonial future* for an indefinite period, by relying on new (oil-rich) neo-imperialist financiers.
2. To *preserve* whatever progress towards self-reliance has been achieved by cultivating large-scale expansion of Indo-U.S. trade on the basis of mutual tariff concessions (rather than the old basis of U.S. aid).
3. To *preserve* whatever progress towards self-reliance has been made by expanded trade with the U.S.S.R. and Comecon countries on mutually favourable terms and a long-term (self-liquidating) barter basis.
4. To *accelerate* progress towards attainment of self-reliance by joining the oil-rich backward capitalist countries in a global economic war to secure sharp gains in terms of commodity trade.

The outlines of *strategy 1* became quickly visible with a self-confident, oil-surplus Iran extending credits and sponsoring Indo-Iranian ventures in India for the industrial development of Iran, in return for assistance to India to meet her oil-import bills. However, the other oil-rich West Asian countries (e.g. Saudi Arabia or Libya[34]) have concentrated instead almost exclusively on using their large 'petro-dollar' surpluses to (i) buy arms (from France or the U.S.A.), (ii) to invest in advanced capitalist countries in loans to governments (e.g. to Japan) or to buy shares in private companies, and (iii) to extend economic aid, first to the Muslim-majority Islamic countries, and second to the backward economies of oil-poor Africa. Moreover, the ambitions of *all* these countries to engage in neo-imperialist adventures are subject to certain limitations to be discussed in the next section.

Strategy 2 looked like becoming a practical proposition when it received official U.S. encouragement in the autumn of 1974.[35] But the unfolding of such a strategy may be retarded by (i) revival of 'beggar-my-neighbour' protectionism in the U.S.A. in the context of developing political isolationism and a 'depression' psychology in economics in the late 1970s, (ii) the successful opening-up of either the Soviet or the Chinese markets for expanded U.S. exports on commercial terms (either directly or indirectly via expansion of tri-

[34] Oddly enough, Libya, which encouraged Pakistan's anti-Indian tirades at the 1974 Islamic summit conference, has agreed to joint Indo-Libyan projects for oil-prospecting in Libya.

[35] when Henry Kissinger, on a visit to Delhi, put main emphasis on an expansion of Indo-U.S. trade on commercial terms, including food-grains imports into India on commercial terms.

angular trade relations involving Japan). The settlement of the U.S.-held Public Law 480 rupee counterpart funds in Indian banks in 1974 on the model of the Indo-British sterling balances agreement of 1946 actually underlines the *difficulties* of dramatic expansion of Indo-U.S. trade on a non-concessional basis rather than the reverse. As in the case of the sterling balances agreement, a part of the rupee funds was written off, and another part was proposed to be released in a phased manner for financing jointly approved projects in India so as to offset an inflationary impact in India. However, *U.S. objections* to liquidation of the U.S.-held rupee funds through large-scale commodity transfers from India to the U.S.A. (made possible through (i) import on U.S. Government account for sale in the U.S. market at whatever price it would fetch, or (ii) devaluation of the rupee in terms of the dollar, or (iii) through lowered U.S. tariffs) as a possible alternative basis of settlement were probably partly responsible for producing the agreement.[36]

Strategy 3 looked promising in the context of dramatic expansion of Indo-Soviet trade, and matching expansion of Indian trade with most of the Comecon countries. But limiting factors are (i) Soviet incapacity to become the major source of India's oil imports (owing to (a) her growing domestic demand for petroleum, linked with her fertiliser needs and her expanded automobile production, (b) her commitments to oil-short Comecon countries, (c) delays in signing of Soviet–Japanese or Soviet–U.S. collaboration agreements for development of her Siberian oil resources), (ii) Soviet incapacity to substitute India's high-priced food-grains and chemical fertiliser imports from the U.S.A. (or Canada), (iii) the delays and failures of Indian planning which make long-term planning of commodity exchanges with the Soviet Union and Comecon countries difficult, (iv) the basic Soviet (and Comecon) preference for trade rather than aid with backward capitalist (or socialist) countries, which makes rescheduling of debt-servicing and repayment agreements and increases in the 'gift' element in Indo-Soviet exchange agreements difficult, and write-offs impossible.

Though there is some scope for *strategy 4* with respect to India's iron ore exports (or her coal export capacity), or potential steel exports,[37] this is inhibited by: (i) her own existing capacity for pro-

---

[36] rather than the U.S.A.'s politically motivated anxiety to correct the 'tilt against India' during the Bangladesh war, partly as a counter-weight to her overtures for a long-term *détente* with China.

[37] In 1974 Indian steel was probably the cheapest in the world.

cessing her iron ore and coal reserves for domestic use, and (ii) her basic position as a 'resource-poor' rather than a 'resource-rich' country.[38]

However, India does have a unique asset which can tilt the balance of advantage in her favour, independently of, or in co-operation with, the oil-rich backward capitalist countries of West Asia. This has to do with India's possible emergence as a nuclear economic power, or, much more problematically, as a nuclear military power in the Indo-West Asian region. With the experimental nuclear explosion at Pokhran in 1974, India has already emerged as the likely winner in the race in the region (in which Israel, Pakistan, and Iran are also entrants) to become a country with an indigenous nuclear capacity.

Ignoring some difficulties which might stand in the way,[39] India seems well set, especially with the commissioning of her breeder reactors in 1976, to become a nuclear economic power, using her nuclear capacity for increased power generation, and perhaps for much greater utilization of water resources for irrigation, for more intensive utilization of oil resources, etc. However, these benefits are unlikely to convert India from a 'resource-poor' to a 'resource-rich' country until the world energy map is drastically changed with the exhaustion of the oil reserves, especially of the West Asian countries.

On the other hand, if there is an escalation of the conflict between the U.S.A. and Israel on one side, and West Asia on the other, and Israel emerges as a nuclear military power in the region, there may possibly be a joining-together of the West Asian oil weapon, and an Indian nuclear umbrella for West Asia. This may checkmate both U.S. gun-boat diplomacy and a potential Israeli nuclear blackmail against Arab West Asia to force a compromise settlement on both the oil-price issue, and on the complex issues of the Arab–Israel conflict. How such an outcome may be forced on a reluctant India is discussed in sect. 10.7 below.

10.6 West Asia's chances of achieving self-reliance

While India was faltering in her progress from a neo-colonial to

---

[38] It is not impossible that India might achieve, more or less permanently, an intermediate position, with a balanced resource position, if she attains self-sufficiency in oil through off-shore oil supplies.

[39] India shares with the U.S.A. a commanding position in the world with her thorium reserves. But a 'nuclear revolution' in technology is unlikely to be thorium-based.

a self-reliant, radical state capitalism, as just noted, West Asian capitalist semi-colonialism was being quickly metamorphosed into a self-reliant radical state capitalism, towards a fulfilment of India's unfulfilled aspirations. This was true, not only of Iran, which had already made the first, inconclusive move in the 1950s against British-owned Anglo-Iranian oil, but also of Saudi Arabia,[40] to say nothing of Iraq, which had taken decisive steps in that direction a few years earlier.

However, there is every reason to believe that the astonishing initial successes in West Asia's use of the oil weapon in 1974 constituted only the first step in a long war.

These initial successes seem to have been the unexpected outcome of a fusion of several distinct developments, viz. (i) a political Arab–Israel war, in which the restoration of Palestinian independence quickly became the key issue, (ii) an economic war over oil, in which not only Iran, which had kept out of the Arab–Israel war, but also oil-surplus countries in Latin America were quickly involved, (iii) an international civil war within the U.S.-sponsored military alliance systems in Europe and Asia, dramatized by the head-on clash, verging on war, between the U.S.A. and Saudi Arabia, and the diplomatic war between the U.S.A. on one side and not only France, but also West Germany on the other in their response to the embargo imposed by the Arab states during the Arab–Israel war on the U.S.A. and other allies of Israel, (iv) the atrophy of the U.S.-controlled multi-national oil corporations of West Asia which failed to engineer Chilean-style subversion against the Arab governments wielding the oil weapon with Soviet and Chinese encouragement.

What made the oil-rich West Asian countries win the first battle in this war of many dimensions was that it was fought and won essentially as a 'battle of the sexes' type of game, to which reference was made in Chapter 2, sect. 2.3, in which the U.S.A. lost because it could not decide to break irrevocably with its West Asian and West European allies. In the language of the 'battle of the sexes' game, the husband and wife could not decide to spend the evening *separately*, still less seek a divorce. The wife (e.g. Saudi Arabia) threatened to commit suicide[41] if the husband (the U.S.A.) did not join her to

---

[40] which was the main base of the largest multinational oil corporation in the world, ARAMCO, and was so anti-communist that she had no diplomatic ties with the U.S.S.R. until she used the oil weapon against the U.S.A.

[41] i.e. blow up her oil wells in the event of a U.S. landing to break the oil embargo.

watch the ballet, convinced him that she was serious, and won. (Of course, other contributory factors were also at work, viz. U.S. anxiety (i) to buy a stalemate in the Arab–Israel war, particularly at a time when the U.S. pull-out from Vietnam was being finalized, (ii) to wean Egypt from a Nasserite tilt towards the U.S.S.R., towards a Sadatist tilt towards the U.S.A., and (iii) to buy time to allay panic about a catastrophic oil famine in Japan and Western Europe.)

Later, it seems to have dawned on the U.S.A. that Arab threats to blow up their oil wells in retaliation against a military strike by the U.S.A. need not be taken too seriously. The threat was unlikely to be implemented when a count-down really began, at least not by all or most of them, even if some of them were fanatical enough to do so. This is chiefly because, without their oil wealth, these states have nothing to fall back on.[42] (There is an analogy with the Egyptian misadventure when she blocked the Suez Canal in a previous Arab–Israel war, and got very little out of it for many years, except a loss of revenue.)

10.7 U.S. counter-strategies

The outcome of U.S. rethinking just noted has been U.S. experiments with three alternative counter-strategies to the 'oil weapon' wielded by West Asia (and ultimately backed by the African, South-East Asian, and Latin American oil-surplus countries), viz:

1. An international oil-consumers' cartel (including deficit oil producers like the U.S.A.) to counter the wielders of the oil weapon.
2. The use of the 'food weapon' to counter the 'oil weapon'.[43]
3. Gun-boat diplomacy in West Asia, to 're-internationalize' oil-pricing and oil supplies from the Persian Gulf region.

Now, counter-strategy 1 has not made much headway because of the extreme vulnerability of oil-poor Western Europe and Japan. This vulnerability will remain until and unless (i) North Sea off-shore oil is found to be enough to make not only Britain, but the entire Western E.E.C. countries self-sufficient in oil, (ii) Siberian gas (or Chinese oil surpluses) frees the resource-poor, energy-starved Japanese economy from its abject dependence on West Asian oil, (iii) economically competitive substitutes for high-priced petroleum products are marketed which force a scaling-down of oil prices. (Para-

---

[42] until they are industrialized.
[43] rather than a price hike in machinery exports, which is more difficult to contrive, because of the multiplicity of products.

doxically, as long as high, 'politically fixed' oil prices are *not* accepted as a fact of life, costly investment in developing substitutes which are competitive *only* with high oil prices are *not* likely to be undertaken.[44])

Counter-strategy 2 has, of course, been used in a mild form by the U.S.A.,[45] notwithstanding disclaimers on 'humanitarian' grounds. But with their small share in the aggregate world demand, and for food exports, because of their comparatively small populations, the West Asian oil-rich countries enjoy the 'importance of being unimportant' in side-stepping a potential 'food weapon' wielded by the U.S.A.[46]

Thus counter-strategy 3 remains as the most likely basis for U.S. policy to counteract the West Asian use of the oil weapon. Pointers are: (i) the U.S. threat of intervention to break the oil embargo imposed against those who were not with the Arab countries against Israel in the Arab–Israel war during which the oil weapon was used,[47] (ii) U.S. moves for expansion of the leased British Indian Ocean base at Diego Garcia island, for (a) protecting U.S. shipping in times of crises, (b) more effective U.S. intervention during crises like the Bangladesh crisis than is possible with the Mediterranean Sixth Fleet[48] or the Pacific Seventh Fleet, (c) countering the expanded Soviet naval presence, which could be further enlarged after the reopening of the Suez Canal,[49] (iii) an attempt to rejuvenate the moribund U.S.-sponsored military alliance system, including some of the West Asian oil-surplus countries (notably Iran, whose Shah plans to make it the dominant Indian Ocean sea-power).

10.8 West Asian responses

West Asian responses to the unfolding of U.S. counter-strategy 3 have included two major proposals:
1. An 'indexation' formula to maintain parity between the values of

---

[44] There is the additional complication that substitutes may remain uneconomic because of the rise in the cost of their raw material requirements as a result of the high oil prices.

[45] e.g. when cost of Public Law 480 food shipments was raised against India during the monetary crisis, and commercial food shipments became more costly because of heavy Chinese and Soviet purchases in the U.S.A. later.

[46] and buying their food in smaller food-surplus countries.

[47] The Crown Prince of Saudi Arabia was empowered to blow up oil wells in the event of a landing by the U.S.A.

[48] after the reopening of the Suez Canal with a West Asian peace.

[49] In fact, up to the spring of 1976, despite the reopening of the Suez Canal, there has been no sign of this, though temporary factors like a Soviet–Egyptian estrangement, the postponement of an over-all West Asian peace settlement, may be chiefly responsible.

oil exports from West Asia and imports from advanced capitalist countries into West Asia.

2. Proposals for a 'nuclear-free' Indian Ocean, the elimination of super-power rivalry in the Indian Ocean, the universal acceptance of the Indian Ocean as a 'zone of peace', etc.

Proposal 1 has been pressed by the Shah of Iran, but is unlikely to serve as the basis of a major compromise for several reasons. First, there are technical difficulties in maintaining an 'indexed' parity between relatively homogeneous oil products, and heterogeneous capital goods (and consumer goods) imports into West Asian countries, which pose 'index number' and bargaining problems[50] in an acute form. Second, a compromise in the oil-based economic war seems difficult in the absence of a parallel compromise in the political war over the territorial claims of Israel, the Palestinian national movement, and the oil-rich Arab states, who are involved in both wars.

Proposal 2 in the above list is also unlikely to serve as the basis for a long-term compromise because it amounts to the beginning of a process of atrophy of nuclear super-power on a global scale. As noted in Chapters 5 and 6 of this book, the balance of global super-power ensures nuclear peace, global non-domination by super-powers, and the growth of regional power off the high roads of global politics. But, as stressed in Chapter 6, sect. 6.4, the balance of global super-power does *not* rule out legitimization of revolution or counter-revolution *anywhere*. More generally, it does not rule out super-power intervention, including 'gun-boat diplomacy'[51] anywhere. Still less does it countenance the atrophy of global super-power in any region, as implied by proposal 2, which, if implemented, would make nonsense of the concept of global super-power.

However, there *is* a somewhat far-fetched, startling, and tortuous, but potentially effective reply to the U.S. counter-strategy 3, i.e. of U.S. 'gun-boat diplomacy' to force a climb-down by the West Asian wielders of the oil weapon. Moreover, the reply *could*, if implemented, in effect enforce a withdrawal of global nuclear super-power

[50] the problem is that an index number indicating the general price level of a heterogeneous collection of goods is never uniquely determined.

[51] modern-style, with high-speed, wide-ranging manoeuvrability based on nuclear propulsion, use of aircraft carriers and missile delivery systems, etc., or its variant, air-borne paratroop landings (e.g. from Israeli bases, or from Diego Garcia).

[52] China may hold back also because she may develop a sufficient oil surplus to break the OPEC's world monopoly, and may *want* to do so.

from the Indo-West Asian region. This 'reply' has already been referred to at the end of the previous section, viz. the joining-together
of the West Asian oil weapon with nuclear protection against U.S.
'gun-boat diplomacy' supplied by a nuclear *non*-super-power.

Now, India seems well placed for fulfilling this role. She is better
placed than China, perhaps because of geographical proximity, but
also because China is unlikely to back such an anti-U.S. strategy, for
fear of upsetting the nuclear super-power balance in favour of the
U.S.S.R. India is also better placed than Pakistan or Egypt, or Iran,
who are less capable of making nuclear weapons without outside
assistance. *If* India is asked to fulfil this role, and *if* she agrees to do
so, a firm basis would have been laid for a global compromise between the advanced capitalist countries and the backward capitalist
countries of West Asia and India, probably with Soviet endorsement,
to settle the oil crisis on terms which would make India a beneficiary,
rather than a victim, of the compromise.

10.9 Uncertainties

The perspectives just sketched cannot be ignored, if only because
they represent the best alternative visible to a long-term stalemate in
the oil crisis. But the uncertainties about the unfolding of such a
joint Indo-West Asian strategy can hardly be over-stressed.

First of all, up to the spring of 1976, whatever indications there
are of West Asian countries thinking in terms of such a finale to the
oil crisis are *not* serious. In any case, there are *no* indications at all of
their turning to India for a nuclear umbrella.[53]

Secondly, there are *no* reasons for not taking seriously India's persistent disclaimers of any intention of becoming a 'nuclear weapons
power,[54]—even though she can probably make a nuclear bomb more
cheaply than any other power. This is because, as she demonstrated
during the Bangladesh war, she is better off *without* nuclear weapons,
in asserting herself as a regional power in the Indian subcontinent.

But there may be a dramatic kaleidoscopic change in the scenario
with two developments which cannot be ruled out.

[53] As already stated, Egypt's occasional claim that she can develop a nuclear
capability to match Israel's is not to be taken very seriously, because she is unlikely to get aid from either the U.S.A., the U.S.S.R., China, or France—and has
not approached India. Nor is Iran likely to develop as a nuclear weapons power,
or seek a nuclear umbrella from India, though she is interested in India's help in
developing nuclear power plants.

[54] Only the Jana Sangh, alone among the Indian political parties, has been
wanting India to make atom bombs, at first to fight China, and more recently to
negotiate with China from a position of strength.

First, the West Asian countries might be forced to opt for a combined oil weapon plus nuclear bomb strategy, if Israeli intransigence in the interconnected territorial dispute with Arab West Asia begins to be backed by evidence of Israeli nuclear weapons power brandished against the Arab countries.[55] With storm signals hoisted pointed towards unilateral nuclear strikes against Arab West Asia, India—which is better off as a *non*-nuclear regional military power—for good reasons[56]—might be tempted to reconsider her decision not to be a nuclear military power. (The cost of an Indian nuclear weapons system would be less than that of any other country—with the possible exception of China. 'Hired' out to the imperilled Arab oil-rich countries, the *quid pro quo* payment received out of the proceeds of their oil revenues could help India write off some of her own losses from the oil-price hike, or from the diversion of her domestic resources to the manufacture of nuclear weapons.) In this way, (i) the oil crisis, (ii) the Israeli–Palestinian crisis, and (iii) India's nuclear capability may get cross-connected—on Israeli–U.S. initiative.

Second, a parallel development, coinciding in time with the developments just noted, might force India to develop a nuclear weapons capacity. China might (i) secure formal and final recognition as being a nuclear non-super-power which is exempted from restrictions (a) on non-nuclear powers under the nuclear non-proliferation treaty, and also (b) on the super-powers under the SALT agreements. China has practically secured this recognition from the U.S.A. and its treaty partners (not excluding Japan). There is tacit recognition from the U.S.S.R. also (since she does not make this an issue). With a partial 'change of colour' in Soviet politics which favours Communist China in this matter,[57] India would be deprived of a Soviet

[55] A threat of a U.S. strike against both Israel—on the brink of going 'nuclear' —and selected West Asian countries, justified as a 'peace-keeping' mission, could also detonate the chain-reaction. On the other hand, in April 1976 there were reports in the U.S. Press that Israel had 13 atom bombs of 20-kiloton yield, with a delivery system ready for use since October 1973. The news may have been 'leaked' to justify a controversial step-up in U.S. arms delivery to an abrasively anti-Soviet Sadat regime in Egypt, to which there have been strong objections in Israel and the U.S.A. If true, this might set off another kind of chain-reaction, with a pro-U.S. Egypt demanding—and receiving—an American nuclear umbrella against Israel, or even an American-sponsored nuclear-weapons proliferation in the West Asian countries.

[56] i.e. India could rely on a Soviet super-power nuclear checkmate on U.S. or Chinese nuclear blackmail of India, as during the Bangladesh war.

[57] Such a 'change of colour' is likely to preserve Soviet–Chinese communist ideological schism, but make the U.S.S.R. 'non-aligned' in the Sino-Indian contradictions.

nuclear super-power checkmate on nuclear blackmail by either the
U.S.A. or the privileged nuclear *non*-super-power, China. Added
moves by Communist China could be: Chinese communist intermediate range ballistic missiles with nuclear war-heads being fired
across India, and China re-tilting the Indian subcontinental power
balance against India by backing Pakistan in reopening the Kashmir
question by force of arms, or establishing military co-operation with
Bangladesh on the pattern of her military co-operation with Pakistan.
For these reasons, if India decides to change her policy and become
a regional nuclear military power, it would be natural for her to
recover some of the economic costs by 'hiring' out her services to the
Arab countries in the shape of a nuclear umbrella. In that case,
cross-connections would be established between (i) the oil crisis, (ii)
the Israeli–Palestinian crisis, (iii) India's nuclear capability, and (iv)
a sharpening of an endemic Sino-Indian political crisis.

Pursuing these uncertain, somewhat Orwellian perspectives to
the bitter end, it is easy to see that there would be three definite
outcomes:

1. The oil crisis may be resolved by an international compromise,
   with India as a beneficiary, rather than as a victim. *But* the compromise may not benefit the 'resource-poor' backward capitalist
   countries other than India, but make them the victims (as all
   resource-poor backward capitalist countries have been in the first
   phase of the oil crisis).
2. The Israeli–Palestinian crisis may be defused, on the basis of recognition of Israeli as well as Palestinian statehood and their
   mutual co-existence. *But* this would establish a long-term stalemate, basically on the pattern of the Pakistan–India–Bangladesh
   stalemate since 1971, but somewhat more unstable.
3. A nuclear super-power withdrawal from the Indo-West Asian
   region may be achieved (which even the communist victories in
   the Indo-China region has not). *But* a balance of *regional* nuclear
   power would take its place. Like the 'global balance of nuclear
   super-power'—analysed in Chapter 6—this would permit local
   revolutions and counter-revolutions which would, judging by
   growing trends in the mid-1970s (e.g. in Israel, Lebanon, Syria,
   or Bangladesh), use terrorism as the main weapon.

[58] as, on indications available up to the end of 1975, she *might*, if she holds
down her luxury consumption of oil. Of course, there is no possibility of India
ever becoming an 'oil-rich' country.

10.10 Ethical assessment

The three outcomes just considered show how difficult it is to classify political strategies in terms of ethics, which has served us well in earlier chapters. In particular, it reminds us that a strategy may be linked, initially, with an 'unselfish' motivation, but end up by being 'selfish' (according to the definitions of these terms used earlier).

Thus if India does achieve self-sufficiency in oil,[58] and the limited 'change of colour' in Soviet politics, referred to in n. 57 of this chapter, does not materialize, India would be acting 'selfishly' in becoming a nuclear military power and providing a nuclear umbrella to the West Asian oil-rich countries. Her only motivation will be to sell her nuclear umbrella dear to the wielders of the oil weapon, who, as we have noted, might still reach a compromise with the advanced capitalist countries which would be at the cost of the resource-poor backward capitalist countries. On the other hand, if she does not achieve self-sufficiency in oil, her hiring out a nuclear umbrella to the West Asian oil-rich countries might look like an 'unselfish' strategy. But if the compromise on oil hurts the resource-poor backward capitalist countries, and India's failure to achieve self-sufficiency in oil is due to her failure or refusal to cut down on consumption of oil as a luxury consumer good, it would look more like a 'selfish' strategy. Of course, if China develops as a uniquely privileged nuclear power, and uses it to dominate the Indian subcontinent, as visualized in the previous section, India would be compelled to become a nuclear weapons power, unless she is reconciled to a strategy of 'selfless' submission to Chinese dominance in the Indian subcontinent (and, on the assumptions we have made, in the wider Indian Ocean region). Her strategy would then qualify as an 'unselfish' strategy, especially because it would establish on a permanent basis 'non-dominance' over the Indian subcontinent and the Indian Ocean region by *both* the regional nuclear *non*-super powers, viz. China and India, as noted in outcome 3 in the previous section.

On the other hand, as far as the non-Palestinian Arab countries are concerned, the joining-together of their oil weapon with an Indian nuclear umbrella would illustrate a strategy which started out by being 'unselfish' (against the advanced capitalist countries' exploitation of Arab oil wealth) but which may end up by being 'selfish', directed mainly against the oil-poor backward countries other than India. Only from the point of view of the Palestinian

Arabs will it qualify unambiguously as an 'unselfish' strategy. For, as noted in outcome 2 in the previous section, it would secure recognition of a Palestinian state, which is as rational as recognition of the State of Israel.

PART III

Science, Ethics, and Politics

In Parts I and II of this book some of the paradoxes of modern politics have been resolved by using analytical methods whose novelty lies in their resemblance to the methods used in modern game theory, or the theory of collective choice, or in modern mathematical economics. Some of the exercises undertaken represent 'experimental' use of these theories, in which the observed environment and the observed outcomes are data, and the motivations which make them self-consistent are identified. Others represent 'operational' theorizing, where the precise changes in the assumptions about motivations (or about the environment) which could change the observed outcomes are discussed. Thus the exercises of previous chapters promise to supply analytical tools which can be used to explain rationally, *post factum*, what has happened, as well as (hopefully) to *predict* future political events.

The techniques of reasoning adopted in these exercises invariably take into account the interaction between the environment and the motivation of the actors who operate within the environment. These are to some extent classifiable, as we have seen, in the language of ethics, of which politics originally formed a branch, as it did in Indian dharmashastra and arthashastra literature, in Chinese Taoist and Confucian literature, or in Aristotle, or Machiavelli, or Hobbes.

There is also, as seems to emerge from the findings of earlier chapters, a sufficient similarity between the basic *logic* of these various exercises to suggest, tentatively, the possibility of a *unified science* of political events, or, more narrowly—for that is the preoccupation of the present work—of revolution and counter-revolution in the modern world, which resolves several paradoxes which are hard to explain.

Thus there is some reason to expect that what has been said so far in this book might be generalized to answer some important questions which have been repeatedly asked, and variously answered, since the beginnings of systematic investigations into political processes, to the present day. In these concluding chapters of the book, we try to find out how far this expectation is justified.

CHAPTER 11
Can there be a Science of Political Behaviour?

11.1 Introduction

THE question inscribed as the title to the present chapter hardly seems to have been asked, either before or after politics became separate from ethics (of which it was, and is, a branch[1]), until very recently.

Defining 'science' very broadly as a systematic inquiry whose goal is knowledge, and 'practical science' as one whose goal is 'practical knowledge'—i.e. knowledge of what to do rather than knowledge of what is the case[2]—there is no doubt that Plato, Aristotle, Kautalaya, Machiavelli, Hobbes, Mandeville, Rousseau, Marx, Lenin, and Mao Tse-tung, all belong to a long and impressive list of writers who thought that a science of politics was *possible*, even though many of them disagreed with other attempts to construct such a science. Thus the somewhat neglected writer Bernard Mandeville,[3] whose contributions to economics have received more attention than his contributions to politics, clearly distinguishes between three possible systems of political science, viz. (i) pagan or Christian stoicism or 'rigorism',[4] (ii) Christian 'benevolism' of some of his contemporaries,[5] which is also found in Rousseau's *The Social Contract*, just as Rousseau's views about 'social man' in his earlier *Discourse on Inequality* are closer to 'rigorist' conceptions,[6] (iii) his own, based on the notion of 'private vices, publick benefits'. Though the weapons used in controversies about political *science* have sometimes been as lethal as those used in political *practice*, the *possibility* of political science has hardly ever been questioned in the past.

However, in recent years there has been a kaleidoscopic change in the intellectual approach to political problems, reflecting seemingly

[1] See Nowell-Smith (1954, 1969), p. 15.   [2] Ibid, p. 11.
[3] 1714, 1970. The Introduction by Phillip Harth to the 1970 English translation gives the interpretation used here.
[4] based on the notion that the passions were anti-social and should be tamed by precept to establish social order.
[5] based on the notion that man was rational and his feelings were benevolent or sociable.
[6] See Rousseau (1763, 1968, 1972), Introduction by Maurice Cranston, for the interpretation used here.

insoluble crises in political reality, as well as in political thought. This change has articulated two charges explicitly, and an additional one made implicitly, which deserve serious attention.

The first charge, made very forcefully, is about the *non*-existence of a 'system of non-trivial hypotheses on behaviour, or on the factors that give rise to it, supported by evidence, with some demonstrable bearing on matters of human concern' (Chomsky, 1970, 1973, p. 12; 1968, 1972, pp. viii–ix).

The second explicit charge, already referred to in the General Introduction to this book, is the charge that all extant 'political science' is spurious as science, and that it imitates the surface features of the sciences to purvey political *apologetics* of one kind or another, with a vested interest in, and a well-endowed capacity to lay claims to, infallibility (Chomsky, 1970, 1973, pp. 12, 104–50; 1969, 1971, pp. 23–105; 1968, 1972, p. xi).

Now, the first of these condemnations will almost certainly be regarded as an overstatement, except, perhaps, in the specific, narrow context in which it was made, viz. B. F. Skinner's attempts to construct a behaviourist political science based on the hypothesis of 'human malleability'.[7] There is much provocation for making the second charge. But, as already stated in the General Introduction, this is also an overstatement, though hardly a *gross* one.

But in the present chapter we are not much interested in these two charges which have been explicitly made. What *is* of interest to us here is the *implied* challenge that there *cannot* be a science of political behaviour. It must be admitted at once that there is *no* explicit claim to this effect. On the contrary, there is even a (somewhat hesitant) claim that a 'libertarian' social theory 'that will be grounded in a science of human capacities, needs and behaviour . . .' (Chomsky, 1970, 1973, p. 12) may some day become available (ibid., pp. 185–6). However, it is definitely implied that such a 'human science' does *not* resemble the physical sciences, but 'scientific morality', about which more will be said in Chapter 13. Meanwhile, we try to make an inven-

[7] It is worth noting that Mao Tse-tung is reported to have used this idea to say (in January 1958) that 'Those who are poor have nothing to call their own. Those who are blank are like a sheet of white paper. To be poor is fine because it makes you inclined to be a revolutionary. With blank paper many things can be done. You can write on it or draw designs. Blank paper is best for writing on' (Schram, 1974, p. 92). Actually, the idea goes back at least to Hobbes, who wrote ' . . . the Common-peoples minds, unless they be tainted with dependence on the Potent, or scribbled over with the opinions of their Doctors, are like clean paper, fit to receive whatsoever by Publique Authority shall be imprinted in them' (Hobbes, 1651, 1974, p. 379).

tory, in the next section, of the most interesting arguments as to why it is impossible to have a political science which resembles the physical sciences. Objections to these arguments are presented in sect. 11.3.

11.2 The impossibility of political science?

It is extraordinarily difficult to pin down the many reasons which people have in mind when they argue that there can be no science of politics. Nor can we, in this book, go into certain profound questions posed about the possibility of political science which come up when we take into account the work of Pavlov,[8] Freud,[9] and Camus.[10] (None of them denied the possibility of political science.)

What should, and is, attempted in this section is to make an inventory of some of the arguments about the impossibility of political science on which some light is thrown by the subject-matter of the preceding chapters of this book.

An initial point to be borne in mind is the obvious one that in all these arguments 'science' is implicitly more narrowly defined than the 'broad' definition referred to at the beginning of this chapter, which we have been using so far. According to this broad definition, the distinction between what is sometimes called 'philosophy' (as distinct from 'science') and science proper is obliterated, and *both* represent scientific disciplines. With such a broad definition of 'science', none of the arguments listed below would arise. But if 'science' is more narrowly defined to refer only to a discipline which resembles the physical sciences and employs mathematical techniques of analysis, the arguments listed below do arise, and are worth discussing.

S.1 There can be no science of politics because any science must

---

[8] The reference is to the work of the Russian scientist Ivan Petrovich Pavlov, whose work on 'conditioned reflexes' raises questions about the possibility and desirability of 'conditioned reflexes' as an aid to the science of political action.

[9] The reference is to the work of Sigmund Freud who proposed as long ago as in 1932 the development of sociology as 'applied psychology' to supplement Marxism and convert Marxism into a 'genuine social science' (Freud, 1933 [1932], 1973, p. 216). His 'dissection of the personality' (ibid., Lecture 31) into an interaction between the somewhat imprecise categories of the id, the ego, and the super-ego, which overlap and together interact with 'reality', formalizes obvious aspects of political processes of the past fifty years. They are compatible with the simpler analytical framework in terms of assumptions about the environment and about motivations used in this book.

[10] The reference is to Albert Camus's seminal contributions to political philosophy, viz. *The Myth of Sisyphus* (1942, 1975), and *The Rebel* (1951, 1974), which also refute nihilistic attitudes to the possibility of political science (as we have defined it) but from a viewpoint different from ours.

have a unifying, universal, or fundamental principle or law, on which its theorems are based.

S.2 The inclusion of value-judgements or normative propositions about what 'ought' to be, among the initial assumptions incorporated in most hypotheses about political action, makes political theory 'unscientific'.

S.3 There can be no political science because political analysis *cannot* be mathematized.

S.4 A science of political behaviour is a chimera because political behaviour *cannot* be analysed by methods used in analysing the behaviour of animals or the functioning of machines (including electronic brains) or other inanimate objects.

S.5 Political events are unique and non-repeatable, events governed by the 'laws' of the physical sciences (or of mathematics) are not. This makes it impossible for us to have a political science.

Now, it is at once obvious that in the last analysis these various objections to the notion that there *can* be a science of politics (which to some extent repeat the same ideas) are based on the notion that any science must (i) exclude value-judgements in its assumptions (i.e. consist only of facts or 'is'-propositions) and (ii) employ the deductive methods of reasoning used in mathematics and the physical sciences. But, as argued in the next section, (i) seems arbitrary, and (ii) is at least partly based on a misunderstanding of the nature of these methods.

11.3 Discussion

Objection S.1 to the notion of a science of politics demands a 'unifying' principle in politics, or principles like the laws of thermodynamics or the 'maximizing postulate' which is used in large parts of economic theory. *Comment*: This objection is unconvincing for at least two reasons. First, it is *not* quite true that modern postclassical physics or modern economic theory *do* consist of theorems tied together by some 'unifying principle', though it would be aesthetically satisfying if they were. A 'unified field theory' in physics does not seem to be available. In economic theory at least one definite class of problems relating to oligopoly *cannot* be analysed satisfactorily as simple maximizing problems, and are better analysed by the techniques of modern mathematical game theory. Second, as we have seen in Parts I and II, alternative models of modern game theory, or the 'impossibility theorems' of the modern theory of collective choice, or economic models of dominance and dependence, can be used to solve a wide range of problems of political analysis. In short, both the physical sciences (and economic science) and political science *can* do without, indeed for the present at least, *must* do without, 'unifying' principles without ceasing to be scientific in a meaningful sense of the term.

Objection S.2. is a caveat against *all* value-judgements or 'ought'-propositions in the premises admitted in a scientific analysis of processes. *Comment*: This objection seems to be based on two ideas, neither of which seems justifiable. The first is the idea that a science, *ex definitione*, must be like the physical sciences which are based *entirely* on 'is'-propositions. This seems to be mere superstition, since there is no reason why, just because physics does without 'ought'-propositions, political science should also do the same. (Actually, although no laws of physics have 'ought'-propositions among their premises, the discovery of new laws (more general than older ones) seems to depend on the conviction among physicists that it *ought* to be possible to do so. But of course it is still true that physics does without 'ought'-propositions since the discovery of new physical laws belongs not to physics as a science, but to another branch of knowledge which has *not* yet been elevated to the level of a science, according to *any* definition of science.) The second idea on which objection S.2 might be based seems to arise from a misreading of what is sometimes referred to as 'Hume's Law', viz. the impossibility of deducing an 'ought'-proposition from a series of 'is'-propositions (Nowell-Smith, 1954, 1969, p. 36). But Hume did *not* prove that an 'ought'-proposition can *only* be deduced from other 'ought'-propositions, that is to say, without reference *at all* to facts or 'is'-propositions (Hare, 1961, 1964, pp. 29, 44). Nor is it the case that 'is'-propositions can only be deduced from other 'is'-propositions. In several exercises presented earlier in this book, which analyse political processes, a blend of 'ought'-propositions and 'is'-propositions has been accepted as premises to deduce 'ought'-propositions or 'is'-propositions as conclusions.

Objection S.3 asserts that political processes cannot be scientifically analysed because political analysis cannot be mathematized. *Comment*: The assertion is partly based on the role of the 'human factor' in politics, which is separately discussed with reference to objection S.4. It is partly also based on the notion that (i) scientific analysis requires the use of mathematical methods, (ii) if mathematical methods are to be used, the problems analysed must be amenable to quantification, exact measurement, and formalization as functional relations, and (iii) the objectives of political action are *not* so amenable (e.g. even if maximization of national or international welfare were adopted as the classical utilitarian objective, it is impossible to measure amounts of welfare as unambiguously as we measure heat or energy). Now, (i) is unexceptionable, in so far as scientific analysis involves rigorous reasoning, and mathematical methods represent and express in symbolic language such rigorous reasoning. But (ii) is by no means essential, at least not exact measurement, nor formalization as functional relations, unless 'functional relations' are very broadly interpreted to refer to any statement of the 'if . . . then' form. Many scientific problems are cast in the 'either . . . or' form, without reference to magnitudes, and are formalized without algebra, by using the language of set theory or game theory. Consequently, although (iii) is true in most cases, it does not matter. The game theory models presented or referred to in Chapter 2–5, 8–9 of this book cannot be dismissed as being 'unscientific' simply because they violate (ii) (which the models used in Chapter 6 do not).

Objection S.4 is based on some unsophisticated and sophisticated ideas about the distinguishing importance of the 'human factor' in political events, as opposed to events in the inanimate physical universe, or in the animal kingdom, which are taken as self-evident, but do not seem to be so. *Comment*: To some extent this objection is based on humanistic claims to man's innate superiority to animals ('beasts') and inanimate objects. Thus Rousseau developed original and highly sophisticated theories about politics by asserting in his *Discourse on Inequality* that man was distinguished from beasts by his capacity for 'sympathy' when he lived in innocence in a 'state of nature'[11] (See Mervyn Williams, 1971, pp. 213–25, for extracts from Rousseau). Also, according to Mandeville, 'Moralists and Philosophers of all Ages' thought (wrongly, according to him) that man was superior to beasts in possessing the faculty of reason,[12] which made it possible to educate them out of their innate selfishness (which they shared with beasts) (Mandeville, 1970, pp. 81–92). As regards man's superiority to inanimate objects, there is the well-known assertion that

[11] which provoked Voltaire's ironic comment that he longed to walk on all fours after reading it (Russell, 1946, 1962, p. 663).
[12] Rousseau also believed that man ' . . . is the sole animal endowed with reason' (Rousseau's *Discourse on Inequality* quoted in Chomsky, 1970, 1973, p. 170).

man's social behaviour does not proceed according to laws akin to the laws of physics because in physics one did not have to assume that 'a rock's wish to fall is a factor in its "behaviour" ' (Chomsky, 1970, 1973, p. 108). In the presence of modern high-powered computers, also, man feels superior because computers cannot detect mistakes in calculation without specific instructions about the nature of the mistake to be detected being 'fed into' them by human brains. But it is doubtful whether the accumulation of zoological (and anthropological) knowledge since the days of Mandeville and Rousseau would uphold *either* Rousseau's distinctions *or* Mandeville's denial of those distinctions. There is no forceful verdict upholding either view. This is only partly because there is evidence that man, both in a state of uncorrupted innocence, and through the cycle of 'corrupted' civilization, shares more or less identical propensities and faculties, as is forcefully brought out in James Ivory's film *The Savages*.[13] There is also evidence that social attitudes or the capacity of 'reasoning' in the animal kingdom are to some extent as shown in Aesop's *Fables*, or the story of Androcles and the Lion,[14] or in Leonardo da Vinci's *Fables* (where some animals are slightly superior to most men in ethics and intelligence). As far as computers are concerned, it can hardly be denied that by constructing them, and watching them perform, man's self-knowledge has been considerably enriched (and, what is more important, disseminated more widely among men).

However, whether we agree with Rousseau's distinctions between man on the one hand, and beasts and machines on the other (see extracts from Rousseau's *Discourse on Inequality* in Williams, 1971, pp. 214–18), or with Chomsky's distinctions between men and machines, our attitude to objection S.4 has to be decided independently of these considerations. For, somewhat paradoxically, Rousseau, who did *not* worship the natural sciences, and has been identified as the originator of modern romanticism and the politicial philosophy of modern 'pseudo-democratic dictatorships' (Russell, 1946, 1962, pp. 660, 674), nevertheless developed a theory of injustice and concepts

[13] Just as Ingmar Bergman's film *Silence* might perhaps serve as an exquisite dramatization of a Rousseauian thesis about the corruptions of civilization.

[14] Cf. the modern story of a Greek, Major Pnevmatikos, who was tortured by the overthrown Greek military junta, as told by him during the trial of his persecutors. 'Wolfdogs', beaten up to make them mad with fury, were unleashed on him, but ' . . . as men often become beasts, animals can also be human . . . as I braced myself for the attack, they licked my hands' (Pnevmatikos, *Statesman*, Delhi, 19 Nov. 1975).

of the 'general will', of 'social contract', which turn out to be amenable to game-theoretic interpretations which make them comparable
to a sophisticated modern theory of justice (Sen, 1970, p. 136; Rawls
1972, 1973, pp. viii, 130–6).

The point which is really at issue is whether, when the human will,
preferences, and motivations are not ignorable—as they are not in
politics—events can still be rationally interpreted by methods which
are essentially similar to those employed in the physical sciences.
Now, if the relevance of the political problems analysed in earlier
chapters of this book is not denied, and incorrigible faults are not
found in them, then an affirmative answer should be returned. For it
is shown in these chapters how uniform, as well as conflicting, preferences can produce definite outcomes in political processes. Moreover, they demonstrate how a problem unknown in the 'non-human'
sciences can arise and still have a solution which can be identified by
the use of rigorously scientific methods of the modern theory of
games, and of collective choice. This is the problem that the outcome
is often the opposite of what was intended by all parties to a conflict.

Objection S.5 refers to the 'uniqueness' of each political event (in
contrast to the repeatable nature of physical events) as the reason for
the impossibility of political science, and is an objection which deserves more serious attention than the others discussed so far.[15]
Comment: This is a well-known argument which has been put forward in the controversies about 'historicism' (Popper, 1957, p. 109),
but is completely relevant in the context of the present discussion. It
is easily rejected on the ground that in physics too 'no two physical
experiments can be performed under exactly similar circumstances
(the last time you boiled water, the solar system was not where it is
now) . . . (so that) in a certain very strict sense all history is . . . completely unique . . . (but) while the whole course of history may not be
repeated, some of the relationships are' (Sen, 1959, pp. 106–7). Thus
neither the physical sciences nor the science of politics are 'impossible'
because of the 'uniqueness' problem.

There is, however, a special kind of problem in politics and history,
which does not arise in physics, is not a major problem in economics,
and resembles the so-called 'uniqueness' problem just discussed. This
is the peculiar problem that attempts to repeat in the nineteenth and
twentieth centuries, in the sense of *imitating* without innovation, the

[15] especially now that it has received the lucidly argued support of Regis
Debray (1970, 1975, pp. 87–92).

successful political revolutions of the seventeenth and eighteenth centuries have in most cases (perhaps invariably) produced a *farce*. Marx pioneered with this generalization of what seems to be some kind of a 'law' of modern revolutions, in writing about the French revolution of 1848–51, which repeated, but only as a farce, the French revolution of 1793–5, in his *The Eighteenth Brumaire of Louis Bonaparte* (Marx and Engels, 1950, pp. 225–7). Long treated as no more than a piece of rhetoric, it deserves serious attention as the discovery of a law about revolutions, in the light of the consistent failure of every major attempt to imitate *each* of the successful communist revolutions of the twentieth century, to which reference was made in Chapter 4 of this book. To recognize this is not, of course, to accept the Popperian *obiter dictum*. For, whatever dispute there may be as to whether there ever was a successful 'bourgeois' revolution after the French revolution of 1793–5, there is no doubt that in the twentieth century we have lived through several successful communist revolutions. Moreover, as incidentally noted in some earlier chapters of this book with reference to particular revolutions (e.g. the Chinese or the Vietnamese), each one of them was based on a novel but communist design of revolution. Thus it would seem that modern communist revolutions *are* repeatable, but only with innovations: there *is* a science of communist revolution in use in the twentieth century, which is innovative rather than imitative. The innovations of the Chinese and Cuban communist revolutions have been noted in some detail in earlier chapters. The lack of successful innovation has been noted in discussing the abortive communist revolution in West Bengal. As regards the Vietnamese communist revolution, apart from the innovations already noted in Chapter 2, there was the highly unorthodox, and, as it turned out, highly successful tactic of countering an incipient counter-revolution in 1944 and 1945, which was spear-headed by British and Chinese Kuomintang troops, by the Communist party's proclamation of *voluntary dissolution*, to (i) facilitate 'actual withdrawal into the underground', but also (ii) to consolidate the people's power established after an anti-Japanese uprising by (a) holding general elections, and (b) setting up a new 'front' organization, the All-Vietnam Union, to further extend the anti-Japanese Viet Minh Front for the Independence of Vietnam which organized the anti-Japanese uprising.[16]

---

[16] See Ho Chi Minh's report at the Second Congress of the Vietnam Workers' Party, Feb. 1951, where the decision is stoutly defended as 'a good measure' (see

In general, not only have all successful communist revolutions been innovative, but one could even advance the hypothesis that several modern communist revolutions have been successful precisely because they were associated with some epoch-making innovation in methods of political (or military) warfare and organization. Thus Lenin's interlinked theories of the monolithic party and the state (dictatorship of the proletariat) were responsible for the decisive successes and later consolidation of the Bolshevik revolution. Indeed, these key innovations probably outweighed whatever defects or 'deformities' may have been associated with the ruthless, single-minded, and, to an extent 'selfish' pursuit of power by the Bolsheviks. Similarly, the Maoist innovations—identified in Chapter 4 earlier—may explain why the Chinese communist revolution has been so successful, in spite of a ruthlessly 'selfish' hunger for power, which is regarded as a supreme virtue. Of course, the 'selfishness' of power-hungry communist revolutionaries is always 'less selfish' than the selfishness of power-hungry counter-revolutionaries. The 'selfish' pursuit of power by *successful* communist revolutionaries has always been linked with the 'unselfish' aim of a redistribution of power in favour of those who have no power, at home and abroad. This the counter-revolutionaries have seldom done. (Which is perhaps why they have been less successful. However, even with them, the hypothesis seems to hold that the more successful modern counter-revolutionaries (e.g. the German Nazis or Spanish Falangists) have been more successful than others (e.g. the U.S. forces in Vietnam) chiefly because they were more successful as innovators.)[17] But there have been situations, as we have seen in this book, where the decisive 'innovation' required is precisely the need to avoid *any* 'selfishness' in the pursuit of power, and to work out a strategy of 'unselfishness'. It has been argued in Chapter 4 that the Vietnamese revolutionaries succeeded against the U.S. imperialists chiefly because they did this.

Ho Chi Minh, *Selected Writings and Speeches*, Communist Party Publication, Delhi, 1975, p. 11). History seems to have vindicated the tactic in this case. However, there is no mention of this episode in the anonymously written *History of the Vietnam Workers' Party* (1970).

[17] The 'storm-trooper' and the *Blitzkrieg* techniques probably were innovations which helped the Nazis to be more successful than other modern counter-revolutionaries. On the other hand, their methods of refined torture (including the gas chambers) were probably the cause of their undoing, as also their undiluted selfishness in the cause of the Führer and the fatherland. The U.S.-led counter-revolution in Vietnam came to nothing because the U.S. was debarred, by the balance of nuclear super-power, from dropping atom or hydrogen bombs. All alternative innovations in techniques of warfare proved counter-productive.

On the other hand, it has been argued in Chapter 9 that the West Bengal communists failed, chiefly because they failed to accomplish the innovation of switching from a 'selfish' to an 'unselfish' pursuit of power.

11.4 A unified science of revolution and counter-revolution?

The upshot of the discussion in the previous section is that there *can* be a science of political behaviour. If this is correct, it follows, as a necessary logical corollary, that such a science must 'contain' a unified science of revolution and counter-revolution in the sense of common analytical frameworks to explain both types of events. For political behaviour which such a science explains must include not only 'evolutionary' political events, but also revolutions and counter-revolutions, which sometimes occur. A science of political behaviour which is helpless when revolutions or counter-revolutions occur is not much of a science, considering the trend of increasing frequency of such events in the modern world. Fortunately, as we have tried to show in earlier chapters, a common framework of analysis can often explain both a successful revolution and a successful counter-revolution, and pin-point the more decisive causes of success or failure. Partisan (and passionate) contraposition of motives of the combatants does *not* make it impossible to use a common analytical framework to analyse the actions of revolutionaries and counter-revolutionaries, as is implied in the denial of the existence of a unified science of revolution and counter-revolution. But, as we have seen in earlier chapters, in some cases, even a red-hot conflict of motives by opposing partisans alone does not decide the outcome (see Chapters 2 and 9); in other cases, such a conflict of motives is inadequate to explain the actual outcome (Chapter 8).

CHAPTER 12

Is Political Science Deterministic?

12.1 Science and determinism

THE list of objections to the notion of the possibility of political science considered in the previous chapter is by no means exhaustive. In particular, it omits all reference to the question of 'determinism' and science, which is raised in some objections. It is obvious, perhaps, that if 'practical science' is defined as broadly as in sect. 11.1 of the previous chapter, it does not have to be 'deterministic' in *any* sense of the word. However, if we use a 'narrower' definition of science when upholding the scientific analyses of political processes, as we do in Chapter 11, it might seem that political science *must* be deterministic by definition. But in fact much depends upon the sense in which the word 'determinism' is used. There are several distinct senses in which the word *is* used. In the present chapter we discuss three of these. The conclusion reached is that scientific political analyses may be deterministic in *none* of these senses, though they could also be deterministic in *some* of them. Special attention is paid to the question as to how far Marxian anarchist, and modern 'Utopian communist' theories about politics can be said to be 'deterministic' in some sense.

12.2 Non-unique and non-existent outcomes

Sometimes, political analysis leaves the outcome 'undetermined' in the sense (i) that it suggests more than one outcome is possible, i.e. that there is no outcome which is uniquely determined, or (ii) that all possible outcomes are indicated (with reference to a possible indicator of outcomes). Actually, political analysis may even produce 'impossibility' results or suggest that a solution is non-existent.

Thus the analysis of the Vietnamese paradox in Chapter 2 shows that the data given by the environment and the preferences of the 'front-liners' (i.e. the Americans and the Vietnamese revolutionaries) suggest *two* possible outcomes ('partial defeat' or 'partial victory'). This is a case of predictions which are not uniquely determined. On the other hand, taking the various models of Chapters 8 and 9 together, we have analytical models which predict all possible outcomes, viz. a *non*-breakdown of capitalism, a capitalist breakdown, and also (fitted into the 'syndrome' of Chapter 7) of consolidation of state capitalism (with an extension of the Government-owned public sector). But some of these models, like the models of Chapters 2 and 6, also 'prove' the non-existence of certain outcomes (e.g. capitalist breakdown in West Bengal, or a global nuclear war, or a total victory for either side in the Vietnam war). In Chapter 3 a standard 'impossibility theorem' of the modern theory of collective choice is interpreted to explain the phenomenon of communist 'personality cults' (as well as to discuss 'escape routes' from the impossibility result).

Now, none of the political analyses just cited are 'deterministic' in the sense that they do not give uniquely determined outcomes. (The only exception is the 'impossibility theorem'. But this is an odd example of 'determinism' since it determines 'uniquely' what is impossible.) But it is hard to dub them 'unscientific' for this reason. They belong to science, whether 'broadly' or 'narrowly' defined, because (i) they 'narrow down' the range of possibilities (e.g. in the Vietnamese models, they ruled out outright 'total' victory or 'total' defeat), or (ii) they verify that all outcomes *are* possible (this may *not* be self-evident), or (iii) they impel us to experiment with alternative testable hypotheses to narrow down the range of outcomes (if possible to achieve a unique outcome) (the models of Chapter 9 help by achieving (ii) and (iii)). (There is an analogy with algebra, which certainly belongs to 'science', however defined. Simultaneous equations systems which have non-unique solutions or no solutions are worth knowing because they help us to identify the conditions of uniqueness and existence, and non-unique solutions are still worth having in many cases.)

12.3 Necessary and sufficient conditions

Political analyses may be 'deterministic' in varying degrees, according to another sense in which the word 'deterministic' can be used.

Thus a model constructed to analyse a political process may give (i) the necessary but not the sufficient conditions, (ii) the sufficient but not the necessary conditions, (iii) neither the necessary nor the sufficient conditions, (iv) both the necessary and the sufficient conditions for solutions to exist, whether they are unique or non-unique. Thus one may hypothesize (for what it is worth) that *if* the U.S.S.R. and China were the *only* nuclear powers, the necessary conditions for American non-intervention (and *a fortiori*, of an outright 'total victory' by revolutionary Vietnam) would have existed, but *not* the sufficient conditions (for Soviet–Chinese antagonism might still have permitted American intervention). However, on the assumption of a non-nuclear America, Soviet, and Chinese nuclear power plus Soviet–Chinese communist unity, there would have been both the necessary and sufficient conditions for an outright 'total victory' (as defined in Chapter 3). On the other hand, in the context of the U.S.A., U.S.S.R., and China all being nuclear powers, and Soviet–Chinese communist disunity, neither the necessary nor the sufficient conditions for an outright 'total victory' existed, for reasons discussed in Chapter 2, but with additional assumptions about Soviet–Chinese aims being specified, *both* the necessary *and* sufficient conditions for a 'partial victory' were found to exist. In the analysis of the *raison d'être* of communist personality cults in Chapter 3, alternative 'sufficient' but not necessary conditions for the cult to exist were discussed.

Now, a political analyst who is also an activist[1] will probably have no use for (i) or (iii), may risk action on knowledge of (ii), but try to make sure of (iv) if he can. (It may, however, be necessary to go through tragedies or frustrations of (i) and (iii)—as the communist revolutionaries of West Bengal are assessed to have gone through in Chapter 9—to discover 'in action' (ii) or (iv).) All four types of models are 'deterministic' in varying degrees (or from different viewpoints), unless 'determinism' is *defined* to *require* (iv). In that case, (iv) alone is deterministic, though (i)–(iii) can hardly be dismissed as 'unscientific' or useless.

12.4 Multiple-factor or single-factor 'rationalizations'[2]

The question of determinism in political processes comes up in another way in relation to the possibilities of giving a rational interpretation of political processes by reference to many factors or a single factor in each case. Multiple-factor rationalizations of political events have attracted such writers as Machiavelli and Marx.[3] But

[1] See a precise definition, based on Marx's eleventh thesis on Feuerbach in Popper (1957), p. 8. This reads: 'The philosophers have only *interpreted* the world in various ways; the point however is to change it' (Marx and Engels, 1949, vol. 2, p. 367).

[2] For an explanation, and a warning, about the *sense* in which the term is used in this chapter here and later, see Glossary of Terms.

[3] On the other hand, Hobbes pioneered with a rigorous single-factor rationalization.

there have been difficulties experienced in delineating the contours of such models, as well as in establishing 'determinism' in such systems. This has led, repeatedly, to the search for *ultimate* determinants in multiple-factor models, or to single-factor alternatives. The present section is devoted to a discussion of the problems of 'multiple-factor' models and how they can be solved. Some attention is also paid in the next two sections to some 'single-factor' or 'single primary factor' alternatives in Marxian and neo-Marxian modern Utopian theories of revolution.

An early espousal of a 'multiple-factor' rationalization of political processes is to be found in Machiavelli, who wrote in 1514: 'I believe that it is probably true that fortune is the arbiter of half the things we do, leaving the other half or so to be controlled by ourselves' (c. 1514, 1972, sect. xxv, p. 130). It is also found in Marx's most ambitious attempt to test his 'materialistic' hypothesis of political action by (albeit impressionistic) empirical data, viz. his *The Eighteenth Brumaire of Louis Bonaparte* written in 1850 (Marx and Engels, 1950, pp. 221–311). Marx opens this tract with the remark 'Men make their own history, but they do not make it just as they please; they do not make it under circumstances chosen by themselves, but under circumstances directly encountered, given and transmitted from the past' (ibid., p. 225). Machiavelli did not try to elaborate[4] or to prove his assertion except to use the metaphor of the flood havoc of a violent river which can be partly tamed by building dykes and digging canals, as an analogy. But Marx did elaborate his hypothesis with some care, and claimed, triumphantly, in the 1869 Preface to the second edition,[5] that his predictions had been fulfilled.[6] Marx's elaboration consisted in the specification that 'the circumstances directly encountered, given and transmitted from the past' consisted of (i) 'the tradition of all dead generations [which] weighs like a nightmare on the brain of the living ... [as] a beginner of a new language always translates it back into his mother tongue ... [and] can produce freely in it only when he finds his way in it without recalling the old and forgets his native tongue in the use of the new' (ibid., p. 225), (ii) obsolete property relations (e.g. feudal property relations) from the shackles of which nascent property relations (e.g. the bourgeois property relations) must be 'unchained' (ibid., pp. 225–6), (iii) nascent 'productive power' (e.g. 'industrial productive power')

---

[4] except to replace God by 'fortune' as the non-human force.
[5] two years after the publication of *Capital*, vol. 1.   [6] Ibid., p. 222.

which must similarly be 'unchained' (ibid., p. 226), and (iv) the nature of the (political) 'class struggle' (ibid., p. 222).

However, the standard Marxian 'multiple-factor' rationalization of political processes (of slow evolution, as well as rapid revolution or counter-revolution) ran into two problems, viz. (i) an imprecise specification of its ingredients or 'factors', and (ii) a special problem of 'indeterminacy', which arises from a misunderstanding based on the inadequacy of analytical tools available until the twentieth century.

Problem (i), of imprecise specifications, refers to such problems as (a) that of law and morals, which are classified as components of the Marxian 'superstructure', also appear as components of 'production relations' which belong to the Marxian economic base that 'determines' the superstructure, (b) of the class struggle, which is both a part of the political life of society and an element of the 'economic foundation' which determines the superstructure, (c) of the word 'ideology', which is used to refer both to 'mystification' of socio-political reality in the interests of particular classes (or of a number of distinct classes, dominant or otherwise in a particular epoch), and to 'de-mystified' comprehension of such reality (again in the interests of particular classes or groups of classes, etc. (see Lange, 1963, pp. 327–32, especially n. 63 on pp. 328–9; Ollman, 1971, pp. 6–9, as examples of an extensive literature on the subject which goes back to *The German Ideology* (1845) by Marx and Engels, and to the Preface to *The Critique of Political Economy* (1859) by Marx).

There has been some discussion whether such 'sloppy conceptualization' is intrinsic in Marx's theory, and whether it is justified in any theory of political economy or not (see Ollman, 1971, Ch. 1, pp. 3–71; also Bose, 1975, Ch. 1, pp. 24, 33–4). No persuasive case seems to have been made out in defence of such imprecision. In any event, standard schemata of interaction between the 'environment' and the aims or preferences of parties to political conflicts have been used in this book to solve several problems. These schemata are irreducibly multi-factor because they incorporate the 'environment' (which consists of 'material' data, but may include preferences of those whose preferences are unchanged by the course of the conflict) and the preferences of the 'parties' to the conflict (whether they are 'front-liners' or 'side-liners'). They are also extremely versatile, and are capable of taking into account implicitly, or focusing explicitly on, all those factors—e.g. 'productive forces' including technology, production relations (including property relations), 'ideology' (however defined), the 'class struggle', etc.—which are specified in unrefined or refined Marxian schemata of the political process (an example of a highly refined Marxian schema is discussed in the next section). (As we saw in Chapters 9 and 10, the schemata used in this book are even capable of taking into account paradoxes which are encountered when men, acting with more or less uniform conditional preferences, produce unintended results, or 'the tail wags the dog' to win a battle (as those who fought for Bangladesh did, when they involved forces much more powerful than themselves, i.e. India and the U.S.S.R., to get the better of their Pakistani enemies). The inclusion of these conditional preferences which generate paradoxical outcomes fills a gap in the Marxian schemata which are sometimes unusable otherwise as rationalizations of events such as the conclusion of the American–Vietnamese war.)

Problem (i) of the Marxian schemata, viz. the imprecise specification of the multiple 'factors', has been closely related to problem (ii), viz. a special problem of 'indeterminacy' in the multiple-factor rationalizations. Reduced to its essentials, problem (ii) is identifiable as the problem of the *existence* of solutions, or of definite outcomes, when there is more than one factor or 'unknown' variable involved. Is the fallacy of 'circular reasoning' *necessarily* involved in such cases? There is evidence that, apart from their 'anti-idealist' (or anti-Hegelian) predilections,[7] Marx and Engels never shook off the uncomfortable feeling that this might be the case. Marx stressed that 'legal relations' and 'political forms' 'originate in the material conditions of life . . .' (Marx, 1859, 1970, p. 20) or that '. . . consciousness must be explained from the contradictions of material life' (ibid. p. 21). Engels stressed that 'the development of productive forces' is always the 'primary stimulus' or the 'stimulus in the last resort' in changes in the 'social formation' (or social system) (Marx and Engels, 1949, vol. 2, pp. 443–4, 457–9; see also Lange, 1963, p. 37). This uncomfortable feeling evidently arose from the fact that until the early twentieth century theorems about 'characteristic roots' or 'eigen values' in the theory of matrices had not been published by mathematicians,[8] and until the 1930s the existence of solutions in

---

[7] e.g. Marx (1859, 1970), p. 20, and a similar criticism of Victor Hugo's account of the French 1848 revolution (Marx, 1950, p. 221). But Marx also had anti-mechanical-materialist predilections against Feuerbach's materialism and Proudhon's 'objectivism' (for evidence of the latter see Marx, 1950, p. 222).

[8] until 1907 by Perron and 1908 and 1912 by Frobenius (Newman, 1962. pp. 65–6).

systems of inequalities had not been demonstrated in von Neumann's theory of games. Engels was quite clear in his mind that multiple-factor Marxian rationalizations were akin to systems of *simultaneous equations* and unlike 'simple equations of the first degree' (Engels, 1890, in Marx and Engels, 1949, vol. 2, p. 443). They seemed to have worked on the hypothesis that simultaneous equations systems could always be solved provided they contained only *one independent variable*. But we know now that this is neither a sufficient nor a necessary condition for a solution to exist. The existence of solutions can be proved even with more than one independent variable to be determined, in simultaneous equations systems which contain both independent and dependent variables.

Thus the fear that only first-order simple equation systems may have solutions, or that it is safer to work with simultaneous-determination systems of equations or inequalities with only one variable, is quite obsolete, though some modern critics of the Marxian schemata do not seem to be aware of it (e.g. Popper, 1957, pp. 13–15). We may conclude that it is not *necessary* to have only one independent 'ultimate factor' in a multiple-factor rationalization of political processes (though it is possible also to find solutions when there is one). But, of course, there *are* simultaneous equations systems with no solutions, so that there is an analogy with simultaneous-determination rationalizations with multiple factors which may have no definite outcomes. However, this only rules out a unified theory of all political processes, which, as argued in Chapter 11, sect. 11.2 and 11.3, is not necessary, though Marxists have looked long and hard for it, without success. (The disintegration of communist ideological orthodoxy, whose nature has been studied in Chapters 3 and 4, and whose consequences have been analysed in others, is a firm reminder that the quest for a unified political theory which can rationalize all political events is probably futile. If the analyses presented in the earlier chapters of this book are acceptable, they would also serve as reminders that the quest is otiose.) The conclusion just reached is reinforced when we note that several major attempts to construct single-factor or single 'ultimate'-factor rationalizations of political processes, especially of revolutions and counter-revolutions, have not been successful. Some of them are discussed in the following sections.

12.5 The question of technological determinism

One of the 'over-simplified' versions of the Marxian multiple-factor schemata of the political process is that in which technology (as a component of the factor 'productive forces') serves as the single 'ultimate factor', and is usually referred to as Marxian 'economic determinism'. This interpretation of Marxian political theory as 'fundamentalist' starts by citing a passage in Marx's publication 'The Poverty of Philosophy' of 1846–7 (a polemic against the semi-socialist P. J. Proudhon): 'The hand mill gives you society with the feudal lord; the steam mill society with the industrial capitalist' (Marx, n.d., Ch. ii, sect. 1: Second Observation, p. 122).

There is some textual evidence from Marxian writings to allow us to dismiss this 'economic determinist' interpretation of the Marxian theory as a 'caricature' of the theory (Ollman, 1971, pp. 6–11).

On the other hand, there is at least one well-known attempt by Oskar Lange to formalize such an interpretation by buttressing it with an argument from the literature of modern social anthropology (Lange, 1963, pp. 33–6). To some extent, Lange goes along with a 'multiple-factor' version of the Marxian rationalization schemata when he formulates the 'first and second basic laws of sociology', viz. (i) 'the law of the necessary conformity between production relations and the character of the productive forces', and (ii) 'the law of the necessary conformity between the superstructure and the economic base' (ibid., pp. 23, 30). These two 'laws' could very well fit into a multiple-factor version of the Marxian schemata, since in defining the terms 'production relations', 'productive forces', etc. Lange does *not* insist on the components of each category being completely independent of each other (ibid., pp. 8–12, 15–27, may be consulted to verify this). But Lange explicitly *discards* such an interpretation and *upholds* an interpretation from 'technological determinism' when he insists on the *one-way dependence* of the 'superstructure' and the 'economic base' (on which the superstructure depends), on 'productive forces' which are subject to 'the law of progressive development of productive forces' (see ibid., the 'schema of social structure and development' on p. 33, and explanation on pp. 32–9). Moreover, Lange upholds this rationalization by asserting that (i) 'social relations and the whole of social consciousness . . . [are] weighed down by conservatism . . . which can only be overcome by external stimuli . . .', (ii) on the other hand, 'in the social process of labour, man transforms his natural environment and creates a new one which consists of the products of his labour . . .' (According to Lange (1963, pp. 34–5), 'the social process of labour' represents the 'one field of human activity in which habit and routine can never prevail for long since new external stimuli are constantly appearing, forcing men to alter their behaviour'.)

The Langesque version of a neo-Marxian theory of 'technological' or 'economic' determinism in politics is neat and logically complete (unlike, for instance, Joseph Stalin's version of 'historical material-ism' on similar lines,[9] which simply *asserted*, without any supporting argument, that 'productive forces' represented the most dynamic element in the interaction between the economic base and the superstructure).

But when it is subjected to empirical testing, two crucial objections are encountered. First, although we hardly have as yet a theory (or even a persuasive hypothesis suitable for empirical testing) of techno-logical change, it is hard to endorse Lange's version of such a theory because it obviously denies the function of (i) the level of science, (ii) the laws of the country, (iii) the policies of the regime, (iv) consumer demand, etc. which self-evidently enter into the making of techno-logical change (see Ollman, 1971, pp. 7–8 for this criticism).

Second, historically the emergence of feudal societies can (perhaps) be correlated with the use of 'hand-mills', and the emergence of capitalist societies (starting with England) can certainly be correlated with the use of the 'steam-mill'. But the transition from capitalism to socialism in several countries over the past sixty years has certainly not been 'caused' by the coming into general use of any of the major technological innovations over this period, e.g. use of electrical or petroleum-based energy, mass production methods, automation, computerized processes, etc. None of these technological innovations seems to have rendered capitalist production relations 'obsolete'.[10] Moreover, as noted in assumption E.1 in Chapter 9, sect. 9.4 in the context of the discussion of a 'capitalist breakdown' model, the success of several socialist revolutions in the twentieth century in the less-developed capitalist countries shows that there is no 'techno-logical barrier' to the establishment of socialism anywhere in the modern world. In short, whatever might have been the case in the

---

[9] Stalin, 'Dialectical and Historical Materialism' (1940).

[10] though Lenin seemed to have been convinced that 'the dictatorship of the proletariat + electrification = communism' and thought that electrification would establish the 'material foundation' of socialist economic planning in the Russian Soviet Republic.

epoch of the transition from feudalism in the first capitalist countries, it does not seem possible to explain the transition from capitalism to socialism so far mainly from technology which seems to have played a 'neutral' role.

There is a third possible objection which has to do with the difficulties involved in spelling out analytically (and empirically) the chain of causation by which technological change is supposed to promote the supersession of old production relations. These relate to the Marxian notion that there is an increase in the average size of the productive unit under capitalism which undermines capitalist relations and promotes socialist relations because it (i) engineers a continuous rise in the 'average organic composition of capital' which causes the long-run average profit rate to decline, and this slows down the rate of capital accumulation, which is the *raison d'être* of capitalism, and (ii) promotes continually increased 'concentration and centralization' of capital, which accounts for the emergence of 'state monopoly capitalism', which represents the fully matured 'material basis' for socialism. Reason (i) seems to be invalid because a long-run rise in the 'organic composition of capital' cannot be established, either logically or empirically.[11] Reason (ii) is invalid because (a) increased concentration and centralization seem to have resulted in oligopolistic structures in modern capitalist (or socialist) economies, and (b) the existence of 'equilibrium solutions' with oligopolistic structures *can* be proved with the help of modern game theory (see Samuelson, 1973, pp. 503–5). In view of (b), the growth of oligopoly does *not* imply the 'breakdown' of the 'material basis' of capitalism and the establishment of the 'material basis' of socialism, through the operation of some 'technological law' with a political significance. (But it *does* imply, of course, that both oligopolistic capitalism and oligopolistic socialism are economically manageable.)

Until these objections are satisfactorily answered, neo-Marxian 'economic' or 'technological' determinism cannot be preferred to multiple-factor rationalizations of political processes discussed in the previous section.[12]

12.6 Leninism, anarchism, Utopianism, and determinism

The 'single-ultimate-factor' rationalization of political processes

[11] See Bose (1975), Ch. 7, pp. 136–40; Bose, 1974, in Gupta, 1974, pp. 1–14, for a discussion.
[12] It is an additional advantage of these multiple-factor analyses that they can also handle Freudian 'factors' (see n. 9 in Ch. 11).

just considered has a close (and more powerful) rival in an adaptation and extension of the Marxian theory of the state, which has always been the main point at issue between the more orthodox Marxists and the anarchists belonging to different trends (and ages).

In the pre-Leninist version of the Marxian theory of the state, the state was one of the components of the 'superstructure' in the basic schema of the political processes in all societies which were divided into classes. Especially after the suppression of the Paris Commune in 1871, the seizure of state power and the establishment of a communist dictatorship of the proletariat were stressed as the essential prerequisites of a successful socialist revolution. But the seizure of state power was still regarded as only one of several 'subjective' and 'objective' factors in the standard Marxian schema, in which, as already noted in the previous section, the 'maturity' of the 'productive forces' (especially of technology) was considered the 'primary' factor.

Lenin pioneered with what ultimately amounted to an *alternative* Marxian theory of political processes in which communist seizure of state power to establish a 'proletarian dictatorship' became the 'primary' factor in a successful socialist revolution. He did this when he justified the establishment of a proletarian dictatorship for the establishment of socialism in Russia in 1918, *even though* he agreed that the 'productive forces' were 'not ripe' for the establishment of socialism in Russia at the time.[13] (Lenin's theory of the monolithic revolutionary workers' party as the embryonic instrument of the proletarian dicatorship, developed in his 'What is to be done?' and other writings between 1900 and 1904, fitted neatly into this version of the Marxian theory.)

Now, this Leninist version of a 'single primary factor' Marxian rationalization of the political process, with refinements introduced by Stalin, Mao Tse-tung, Castro, etc., has provided the guide-lines of successful socialist revolutions in the twentieth century. (Among the refinements introduced are alternative versions of the cult of the party and the communist personality cult, discussed in Chapters 3 and 4 of this book.) More generally, this Leninist theory of the seizure of state power by revolutionary means, or a semi-revolutionary use of state power, has partially inspired, or partially rationalized, the unconscious practice of the organizers of military or semimilitary *coups d'état* in Asia (e.g. Iraq, Syria, Burma), Africa (e.g. Egypt, Ethiopia), southern Europe (e.g. Portugal and Greece), or

[13] See Lenin, 'Our Revolution' (1923), in Lenin (1947), pp. 836–9.

their parliamentary equivalents (e.g. in India, Bangladesh, residual (West) Pakistan, Sri Lanka (Ceylon)), who have introduced semi-revolutionary[14] *radical-capitalist* measures in large parts of the world. (It even formalizes the radical-capitalist practice of 'constitutional' radical-capitalist despots like the Shah of Iran, the kings of Nepal and Saudi Arabia.)

Of course, in a few notable instances, political action which was or could be formalized by this Leninist doctrine of seizure of state power as the 'primary factor' in political processes has been abortive, or had short-lived success (e.g. in the Hungarian Soviet revolution in the 1920s, or during the Spanish civil war in the 1930s, or during the Chilean revolution and counter-revolution in 1970–3). To explain such setbacks along with the successes of the Leninist doctrine, Antonio Gramsci developed his post-Leninist 'activist' philosophy of praxis or of political initiative as a 'primary factor', which has been referred to in previous chapters. This more general theory stressed the importance of political initiative to seize control over the segments of 'civil society', or of the 'infrastructure' of the state, as well as the state itself, since the importance of the infrastructure and the state itself may vary from country to country. The Gramsci generalization of the Leninist doctrine is summed up in the passage: 'In Russia, the State was everything, civil society was primordial and gelatinous; in the West there was a proper relation between State and civil society, and when the State trembled a sturdy structure of civil society was at once revealed. The State was only an outer ditch, behind which there stood a powerful system of fortresses and earth-works: more or less numerous from one State to the next . . .' (Gramsci, 1930s, 1971, p. 238). This extension of the Leninist doctrine has hardly been tested as yet in practice, except obliquely in Communist China in recent years when attempts have been made to 'rejuvenate' the political revolution (which originally succeeded on the basis of a Maoist variant of Leninist 'statist' strategy, rather than a Gramsci strategy) by 'cultural' or 'ideological' revolutions. (Its as yet inconclusive results are discussed in Chapter 4 of this book.) But at least in one case, viz. West Bengal in the late 1960s, a *partial* attempt (made mostly unconsciously) to adopt a Gramsci-type strategy[15] failed to initiate a successful 'protracted' communist revolution,

---

[14] The word is used in the sense defined in the Glossary.
[15] The attempt was *partial* because, while every attempt was made to seize instruments of state power and to consolidate the hold on elements of the poli-

as discussed in Chapter 9 of this book. This matter will be discussed further in the concluding chapter of this book.

The revival in recent years of anarchist criticism of the Leninist 'statist' strategy (which could logically extend to its generalization by Gramsci) focuses less on its failures[16] than on its impressive successes as 'practical political theory'. The criticism is based on two main planks: (i) increased public information about the *modus operandi* of the state in both advanced and backward capitalist and socialist countries which makes the classical anarchist dictum that the state is the source of all human ills[17] an appealing one to more and more people, (ii) the apparent self-contradiction (or at least an unfilled gap) in any Marxian political theory (especially in its Leninist version) which on the one hand insists on a 'statist' strategy, and on the other *prophesies*, rather than *predicts*,[18] the eventual 'withering-away of the state' with the abolition of classes in the 'higher stage' of a communist society.[19] Thus the very successes of Lenin-type political theories have invited censure, and intensified the search for alternatives, including anarchist ones.

Now, for a long time it was generally denied that anarchism belongs to any kind of political science. Thus Bertrand Russell referred to the classical anarchism of Mikhail Bakunin as an 'extreme form of subjectivism . . . a form of madness' (Russell, 1946, 1962, p. 481).[20] Joseph Schumpeter, writing his *History of Economic Analysis* (which included, of necessity, references to related developments in political theory), was quite sure that Bakunin has 'no place in the history of analysis as he himself would have been the first to admit' (Schumpeter, 1955, p. 458). But, with a curiosity excited by revulsion against some aspects of the successes of Lenin-type political theories, there have been challenging claims by modern writers that (i) there *is* such a thing as 'scientific anarchism',[21] and (ii) like Marxian theory, the anarchist theory can incorporate several distinct theoretical trends, including one which synthesizes ideas common to the

---

tical infrastructure, very little was done to promote a 'cultural' or 'ideological' revolution.

[16] Much stress is laid, however, on communist failure to avert the fascist counter-revolution in Spain in the 1930s originating in their refusal to allow the anarchists to do so (see Chomsky, 1969, 1971, pp. 65–103).

[17] See Maximoff (ed.) (1974), Ch. 14, pp. 136–45.

[18] since there has been very little discussion of the 'dialectics' of the process (see Bose, 1975, Ch. 14, sect. 6, for a discussion of some aspects of the problem).

[19] See Maximoff (ed.) (1974), pp. 287–8, for Bakunin's criticism on this point.

[20] Curiously, anarchists thought well of Russell (1968, 1969, p. 303).

[21] See sub-title to Maximoff, op. cit.

early Marx and the early Bakunin,[22] which could aptly be called anarcho-Marxism. In any case, in the present context it seems possible to regard classical anarchism, to which we turn immediately, as a 'science' as broadly defined in the previous chapter, and more specifically as a science in the sense in which Platonic moral and political philosophy can be identified as a science. (The rudimentary ideas of a modern 'libertarian socialist' adaptation of classical anarchism, suggested by Noam Chomsky, are best discussed separately at the end of this chapter, after a modern 'scientific' Utopianism represented by Herbert Marcuse's writings has first been considered.)

In a modern systematization by Gregori Petrovich Maximoff, the scientific logic of classical anarchism can be identified as being based on the propositions (i) '[anarchist] materialism denies free will and ends in the establishment of liberty' (Maximoff (ed.) (1974), p. 64), (ii) man 'is wholly the product of the environment that nourished and raised him—an inevitable, involuntary, and consequently irresponsible product' (ibid., p. 153), (iii) the state is the source of the corruption of man's environment (ibid., pp. 141, 211), of all violence, cruelty, crime, robbery, imposture, hypocrisy, etc., (iv) not conquest, but the destruction of state power is the task to which the revolutionary must dedicate himself (ibid., pp. 225, 345-6).

The essentially negative conclusion, (iv) above, was the common starting-point of several alternative recipes for revolutionary political action by anarchists. Of these, the best known are: (i) the 'revolutionary catechism', which is supposed to have been jointly authored by the anarchist Bakunin and the nihilist S. G. Nechaev, and which declared (a) the 'dedicated revolutionary' 'knows only one science: the science of destruction . . .' (article 3) of 'this foul society' (article 117), (b) his supreme aim is 'to concentrate the people into a single force wholly destructive and wholly invincible' (article 26); (ii) the anarcho-syndicalist 'free associations of free producers' which would serve as a 'school of anarchism' within capitalist society (Chomsky, 1970, 1973, pp. 158-9); (iii) the instrumentality of the 'general strike . . . [which] can . . . lead to a great cataclysm, which will regenerate society' (Maximoff (ed.), 1974, pp. 383-4). More explicitly, 'strikes . . . create, organise, and form a workers' army, which is bound for a new world' (ibid., pp. 384-5).

Now, it is evident that on the plane of logic, like the Lenin-type theories considered earlier, anarchist theories belong to the class of

[22] See Chomsky (1970, 1973), p. 165.

single-primary-factor rationalizations of political processes, in which *destruction* of state power determines the revolutionary outcome.[23] Indeed, on the plane of pure logic, it is superior to the Lenin-type theories in so far as it is free from the apparent 'self-contradiction' in these theories, which visualize a *consolidation* of (proletarian) state power leading to its opposite: the 'withering-away' of the state. Difficulties arise when this destructive, *negative* single primary factor is sought to be complemented by a *positive* counterpart which all anarchist trends seem to search for, e.g. 'free associations of free producers' or the use of the strike weapon, even within the capitalist society in the 'preparatory period'. Neither in theory nor in practice have these positive counterparts of the destructive recipe of classical anarchism ever worked well. Of course, there is at least one *communist* testimony of the period which *admires* the socialization of industry and the organization of a 'peasant war' by the Spanish anarchists in the civil war of the 1930s, and indicates that the anarchists were not wholly to be blamed for the surrender to fascism[24] (see *John Cornford —A Memoir*, Sloan (ed.), 1938, p. 200). Indeed there are quite a few strong similarities between the intercommunist warfare in West Bengal in the late 1960s (in which, as noted in Chapter 9, anarchist tendencies were strongly represented) and the anarchist-communist warfare in the Spanish Republic in the 1930s. But the fact remains that the major anarchist initiative in the twentieth century—in Spain in the 1930s—ended in failure, while several Lenin-type communist initiatives have succeeded. So, while the insights of classical anarchism and anarcho-syndicalism draw attention to problems which can no longer be ignored by modern communism, they do not as yet compete very strongly as viable alternatives to the Lenin-type political theories discussed above.

At this point it is appropriate to consider what could be called modern scientific Utopian socialism (or, more precisely, commun-

[23] We overlook, as not being relevant in the immediate context, the radical anarchist criticism which refers to Bakunin insisting on the absolute subordination of the individual to a central committee of action in the statutes of the *Fraternité internationale* (1864–7) authored by him (see Read, 1971, 1974, in Foreword to Camus, 1951, 1974, p. 8). However, since in Leninist theory the 'monolithic party' *is* the state in embryo—as the dictatorship of the proletariat—there *is* a parallel between Bakunin's ideas in this phase and the Marx–Lenin theory of the party and the state. (The all-powerful Bakuninist 'committee' is not very different from the Leninist party which becomes the instrument of the proletarian dictatorship.)

[24] Orthodox communist interpretations *have* tended to blame the anarchists for the surrender.

ism),[25] articulated for many years in the writings of the moral philosopher Herbert Marcuse. This shares with various Marxian theories such features as: (i) a preoccupation with the Marxian concept of 'alienation' of man in all societies divided into classes, which is made the basis of a 'unified theory' of alienated 'one-dimensional man' living in both modern capitalist and communist societies,[26] (ii) a detailed critique of the phenomenon of 'consumerism' which is regarded as the curse of both advanced capitalist and advanced communist societies, (iii) the exploitation and manipulation of the alienated man's preference for increased leisure by the élite in both advanced capitalist and communist societies. (For discussion of (ii) and (iii) see Marcuse, 1964, 1972, Ch. 1–4.) It must be stressed that (i)–(iii) are *not* to be found in the more orthodox Marxian theories, but at least (i) and (ii), if not as yet (iii), have been discussed by Marxian economists in recent years. Modern scientific Utopianism also elaborates the 'anti-State' critique of modern capitalism along anarchist lines by equating the 'welfare state' with the 'warfare state' (Marcuse, 1964, 1972, pp. 29–56).

However, this modern scientific Utopianism demarcates itself from *all* Marxian and anarchist trends by its forthright attempt to rehabilitate socialist Utopianism with the arguments (i) 'what is denounced as "utopian" is no longer what has "no place" and cannot have any place in the historical universe, but rather that which is blocked from coming about by the power of the established societies' (Marcuse, 1969, 1973, p. 13), (ii) 'the opposition is . . . sucked into the very world which it opposes . . .' (ibid., p. 69), (iii) 'utopian possibilities are inherent in the technical and technological forces of advanced capitalism and socialism. . . . But . . . neither their rational use nor . . . their collective control by the "immediate producers" [the workers] would by itself eliminate domination and exploitation' (ibid., pp. 13–14). In general, Marcuse rejects what lies at the root of all Marxian hypotheses and most (if not all) anarchist hypotheses when he declares: ' . . . the facts and the alternatives are there like fragments which do not connect . . . Dialectical theory is not refuted,

[25] since in this theory any valid distinction between the 'lower stage' of communism or socialism and the 'higher stage' of full communism is *denied*.
[26] See Marcuse (1958, 1971), pp. 162, 171, 192, 194, on 'alienation'. Marcuse *asserts*, rather than *proves*, that such alienation is necessary in both a capitalist and a Soviet-type communist society. (For some reason, he is silent about the Chinese-type communist society, where, too, a type of alienation may exist.) Why he may be wrong is discussed in Bose (1975), Ch. 14, sect. 6.

but it cannot offer the remedy. It cannot be positive . . .' (Marcuse, 1964, 1972, p. 197).

Thus, in the end, this modern scientific Utopianism reaches a conclusion which is made to look like a single-factor rationalization of revolution, but actually incorporates a hypothesis about the *impossibility* of a successful revolution to end exploitation and alienation in modern advanced capitalist or socialist societies. A feeble suggestion that 'total rebellion' (Marcuse, 1969, 1973, pp. 82–93), initiated by 'the substratum of the outcasts and outsiders, the exploited and persecuted of other races and other colours, the unemployed and the unemployable . . . who exist outside the democratic process' (Marcuse, 1964, 1972, pp. 199–200) may succeed, is unconvincing, above all, because it exhibits an inconsistency in Marcuse's *a priori* argument. For if, as is asserted in the argument, ' "the people", previously the ferment of social change, have "moved up" to become ferment of social cohesion' (ibid., p. 199), by what process will the outnumbered 'outsiders' activize the consistently corrupted and corruptible 'people' in a successful 'total rebellion'? The rationale of a successful Great Refusal is *not* spelt out. What we *do* have is a well-argued case, based on important insights, for the beatitude, rather like that of the early Christians in the Roman catacombs,[27] arising from a Great Despair, which only helped to usher in the hierarchic rule of the Roman Catholic Church, which lasted for centuries.[28] We conclude that Marcuse's insights clarify and enrich our knowledge of the components of Gramsci's 'civil society', of some of the 'fortresses' and 'earthworks' lying behind the 'outer ditch' of the state, which had not been taken into account in the original Gramsci thesis. It also argues against the possibility, visualized by Gramsci, of revolutionary forces seizing control over all these hidden components of the 'civil society'. Whether the Gramsci thesis can survive these cogent objections and permit an escape from Marcuse's Great Despair, will be considered in the concluding chapter of this book, where

[27] or Buddhist *bhikshus* in their monasteries, who became members of the lama hierarchy which ruled Tibet, or (in modern futurist political fiction) the anarchist protesters who withdrew from society and the earth's surface, to live in underground tunnels as in Jack London's *The Iron Heel*.

[28] This is to be contrasted with Camus's prescription in *The Rebel* or *The Myth of Sisyphus*, which sanctifies and justifies an eternal revolt, based on reason, plus restraint, rather than resignation. Camus's prescription is more likely to make life bearable for active revolutionaries, since no revolutionary career is likely to be based on a permanent euphoria. On the other hand, of course, it might make some intellectuals live a schizophrenic life, in which private revolt is continuously reconciled to public conformity.

some of the conclusions of Chapters 2, 4–5, and 9 will be generalized.

In sharp contrast to Marcuse's counsel of despair, we have the linguist Noam Chomsky's attempt to reconstruct classical anarchism (and anarcho-syndicalism) by eliminating an ambiguity or inconsistency in the classical anarchist argument. Chomsky is fully committed to the 'anti-State' preconception which he claims is the dividing line between Marxian and anarchist theories (Chomsky, 1970, 1973, p. 155), but which need *not* be (ibid., pp. 165–6), since Marx also shared the ideal of the highest possible measure of individual freedom with the anarchists. In other words, he thinks a frank recognition and elimination of the inconsistency in Marxian theory on the question of 'statism' could establish bridges between Marxism and anarchist 'libertarian socialism'. But, as noted above, there is a parallel internal difficulty in anarchist theories, connected with the problem of reconciling the commonly held 'anti-statist' *negative* aim, with suitable *positive* counterparts. Chomsky *implicitly* (for this point does not seem to have been stated explicitly anywhere by him) removes an ambiguity or inconsistency in the original anarchist argument, to solve this problem on the plane of logic. The inconsistency lies in Bakunin saying at one and the same time that (i) 'man is wholly a product of his environment' (Maximoff (ed.), 1974, p. 153), and that (ii) ' . . . to make men moral it is necessary to make their social environment moral . . .' by assuring justice or 'the complete liberty of everyone in the most perfect equality for all', for 'inequality of conditions and rights, and the resulting lack of liberty for all, is the great collective iniquity begetting all individual iniquities' (ibid., p. 154). The inconsistency shows up also in Bakunin's insistence that (iii) it is 'the unanimous opinion of the authorities of modern physiological science' that there is no such thing as the innate moral attributes with which man is born (ibid., pp. 150–4), but *also* that (iv) there is a 'moral law' which 'emanates from the very nature of human society, the root basis of which is to be sought not in God but in animality' (ibid., p. 156). Chomsky eliminates the inconsistency by denying propositions (i) and (iii), which complement each other, and by affirming that there *are* 'innate moral attributes' which are inborn in men (Chomsky, 1970, 1973, pp. 148, 184–6). This brings him very close to asserting that there *is* such a thing as 'scientific morality', which has been dismissed as a 'chimerical idea' (Nowell-Smith, 1954, 1969, p. 18).

If the existence of a 'scientific morality' which governs man's conduct could be proved, and its principles as applied to social and political life could be identified, we would have at our disposal a 'single-factor' rationalization of political processes which could compete with the successful, but morally not wholly satisfying Lenin-type rationalizations. But, so far, the Chomsky hypothesis is tied to observed reality by a very slender thread. The hypothesis is anchored to Chomsky's work in linguistics in which he has (i) shown that a 'behaviourist' model of 'stimulus-and-response' cannot account for all the facts of language behaviour (though he has *not* been able to show that it cannot explain *any* of them) (Lyons, 1970, 1972, p. 110), (ii) deduced from (i) that there might be a 'universal grammar' which underlies all languages, and which imposes limits on the theory of 'transformational grammar' in modern linguistics (ibid., pp. 96–108), (iii) deduced from (ii) that there are some characteristics of 'human nature' common to all members of the species, which justify the concept of an 'autonomous man' and a humanistic science of social behaviour based on it (ibid., pp. 9–15).

If the account of the essential steps in the derivation of Chomsky's 'libertarian socialist' thesis of political action given in the previous paragraph is a fair one, two conclusions follow immediately. First, the Chomskyan 'anti-behaviourist' hypotheses in linguistics seem to explain important aspects of language behaviour, though it is not clear whether they can serve as the basis of a 'unified' theory of linguistics to explain *all* language behaviour.[29] Second, it is by no means certain that even if his linguistics are acceptable, a Chomskyan political science—based on the 'scientific morality' of human nature, which explains rationally many important aspects of man's political behaviour—can be found. The chain of causation is too long, with too many gaps in it, to be acceptable *a priori*, on purely logical grounds. Empirical testing, attempted by Chomsky in his numerous publications, cited, and partially discussed, in this and other chapters of this book, does not as yet seem to have produced convincing results. Until such results are forthcoming, the analytical methods employed in the present work deserve attention. In the next chapter an attempt is made to generalize some of the results of earlier chapters of this book, bearing in mind the issues raised in the chapters of Part III.

[29] For the contrary verdict, that 'not only does his [i.e. Chomsky's] theory of language acquisition have very little plausibility, but, more significantly, has virtually no empirical evidence in support of it, either', see Derwing (1973), p. 21, Ch. 4, 6, *passim*.

CHAPTER 13

Morality, Realism, and Reason
in Politics

13.1 Introduction

THE main conclusions reached so far in the chapters of Part III of this book are:

S.1 Scientific methods resembling those used in the physical sciences *can* be used in analysing political processes, even though (i) no unified principle on the basis of which *all* political processes can be analysed seems to be available, and (ii) political revolutions (and probably also counter-revolutions) do not seem to be exactly repeatable, but repeatable only with innovations. In particular, scientific methods can be used to resolve paradoxes represented by outcomes which differ from, or are opposite to, those intended, which are not encountered in the physical sciences. (This implies that the application of scientific methods to political problems has not only solved many of these problems, but also enriched the pure sciences (Chapter 11).)

S.2 The application of scientific methods to the analysis of political processes yields results which are deterministic in some sense, though not in others (Chapter 12).

S.3 The more successful models of political analysis seem to be models formalizing a simultaneous determination of outcomes involving (i) several independent factors (variables), or (ii) single primary (or ultimate) factors (variables). Questions which remain open and undecided are:

S.4 Can a single-primary-factor rationalization[1] of political processes be found which is more general than the Leninist 'statist' rationalization or its extension to incorporate control and manipulation of components of the 'civil society' as suggested by Gramsci?

S.5 How far can the conditions of successful political action identified in analytical models be interpreted in terms of 'self-guaranteeing moral principles'?

S.6 What weights are to be attached to morality, realism, and

[1] See Glossary for the sense in which the term is used in this chapter.

reason as factors determining successful political action?

It is evident that these three 'undecided' questions are interrelated, and so are the likely answers. But it is convenient to segregate them for purposes of discussion, as is done in the rest of this chapter.

13.2 Motivations and successful political action

It has been claimed in the previous chapter, in sect. 12.6, that of all the single-primary-factor rationalizations of political processes, the Leninist versions of the Marxian theory seem to have been the most successful in historical practice. Gramsci's extended version of this theory seems to explain, at least in part, the failures of some political actions which could be formalized as unsuccessful attempts to apply the pure Leninist 'statist' theory. However, Marcuse draws pointed attention to some developments in modern societies (both capitalist and socialist) which seem to pose insuperable objections to Gramsci's generalization of the Leninist theory, or at least to suggest that the generalization is inadequately specified. By contrast, anarchist theories, and the skeletal ideas of their modern 'libertarian socialist' extension by Chomsky, do not as yet seem to compete very well with the Lenin-type theories as instruments for handling and shaping political realities and possibilities.

The purpose of the present section is to explore how far there are common features in the analytical models used in the chapters in Parts I and II of this book, which can supply an alternative 'single-primary-factor' rationalization of political processes which is more general than Gramsci's.

We note, first of all, that in the many 'multiple-factor' game-theory models used earlier, 'unselfish', 'selfish', or 'selfless' political action determines several paradoxical outcomes, or suggests 'escape routes' from such paradoxical outcomes. Thus in Chapter 2 on the Vietnamese paradox, 'unselfish' motivation rationalizes the paradox of the 'partial victory' won by the weaker side. By changing the assumptions about political motivation, it is hypothesized that 'selfish' action would have produced a 'partial defeat', while 'selfless' action of various types would have produced at best a 'partial victory' and at worst a 'total defeat' (see Chapter 2, sect. 2.5). In Chapter 4 on Chinese communist ideology (sect. 4.4), there is a reference to game-theory models which prove that 'selfishness' paradoxically *prevents* a 'communist breakdown' or 'change of colour' of a communist society, and 'selflessness' is *not* required to guarantee *non*-breakdown.

Reference is made in Chapter 5 (sect. 5.3) and elaborated in Chapter 9 on intercommunist warfare in West Bengal and its aftermath that *both* 'selfish' and 'selfless' political action ensures the *non*-breakdown of capitalism, while it is hypothesized that 'unselfish' political action would ensure capitalist breakdown. In Chapter 8 on Bangladesh paradoxes, it is argued that 'unselfish' political action was responsible for the liberation of Bangladesh. It is argued in Chapter 6 on the balance of global super-power that, somewhat ironically, a commitment to 'enlightened self-interest' by the global super-powers assures a global nuclear peace and global *non*-domination by nuclear super-powers (in the sense in which the term 'global non-domination' is defined there). Though the implications are not considered in the chapter, in this particular case, the 'objective environment' (i.e. the nature of nuclear super-power) dictates global nuclear peace, but 'selfish' motivations make it an antagonistic peace, with attempts at regional domination. ('Selfless' motivation would also give global nuclear peace, though it would also ensure global domination by the *non*-selfless nuclear super-power.) But in Chapter 10 on oil, self-reliance, and nuclear power, there is a prediction that joint political action by West Asian wielders of the oil weapon and a nuclear India might materialize, though this is unlikely. If it does materialize, whether India's action or the action of the West Asian oil-rich countries is 'selfish' or 'unselfish' depends on the exact circumstances in which the joint strategy takes shape, as suggested in the concluding sections of the chapter.

The foregoing summary of the findings of earlier chapters also makes it clear that no *single* moral or ethical principle or motivation can serve as the 'single primary factor' in a rationalization of political processes which is more general than Gramsci's. In particular, it turns out that 'altruism', generally interpreted to mean what in our terminology would amount to 'selfless' motivation—which is often expected to provide an escape from self-defeating 'selfish' motivation—in many cases does nothing of the kind. Instead, it produces an outcome which coincides with the outcome of 'selfish' motivation.

Of course, the results of earlier chapters do indicate that 'unselfish' motivation does, in many cases, resolve the paradoxes resulting from 'selfish' motivation, and also produces outcomes which are generally more palatable, according to our value-judgements. But this by no means makes the moral principle of 'unselfish' political action qualify as the desirable 'single-primary-factor' rationalization of political processes, which is more general than Gramsci's. As noted at the end of Chapter 11, 'selfish' political motivations also seem to explain many political events quite rationally. It is hard to tell which 'moral principle' is of greater generality. Besides, there are certain political objectives, e.g. the objective of doing without personality cults in communist societies, which, according to the analysis of Chapter 3 (sect. 3.7), may be achieved—if at all—by changes in the structure of political institutions, i.e. along the route indicated by Gramsci.

13.3 Moral principles and political action

We now turn to S.5, viz. How far can the conditions of successful political action identified in the analytical models used earlier be interpreted in terms of a *set* of 'self-guaranteeing moral principles' (rather than a *single* moral principle)?

The main difficulty about identifying the conditions of successful political action in terms of 'self-guaranteeing moral principles' is that 'selfish', 'selfless', or 'unselfish' political motivations, though usefully described in ethical language, cannot be made entirely operational in ethical terms. As we have seen in all cases analysed in earlier chapters, knowledge of the facts of the case is essential. Moreover, unlike 'selfish' political motivation, which is very much in evidence, and is well understood, and has been regarded as the main basis of successful political action since Hobbes, or 'selfless' political action, with which we are also familiar (at least in a country like India, as noted in Chapter 7), 'unselfish' political action, as we have defined it, can work only if new moral standards are set (which repudiate prevailing, traditional *mores*).[2]

Moreover, there is the peculiar problem, discussed in detail in Chapter 10, that intended 'unselfish' political action may easily slide into 'selfless' or 'selfish' political action and defeat its object. And this is probably connected with a deeper and more general difficulty, discussed in the modern literature on ethics, that 'Self-guaranteeing moral principles are impossible . . . A man can . . . question the morality of his own principles and try to change them; but he cannot do so while applying them . . . Moral values, like other values, are sometimes discovered accidentally. But one thing . . . [a man] cannot

---

[2] Marx tried to set such new moral standards in the preamble and the 'provisional rules' of the The Working Men's International Association or the First International, especially when he asked the trade unions 'to convince the world at large that their efforts, far from being narrow and selfish, aim at the emancipation of the downtrodden millions' (Marx, 1974, p. 92).

do is to *try* to alter his conception of the Good Life . . .' (Nowell-Smith, 1954, 1969, pp. 313–14).

The terrible dilemmas which beset those who try to follow, strictly, the 'path of virtue', however defined, and the futility of relying on 'self-guaranteeing moral principles', are well brought out in Claude Autantlara's film *L'Auberge rouge* (1950). The story is set at a lonely inn in France in 1833 where the inn-keeper and his family have just murdered a tramp with a monkey, as their normal method of making a living is by murdering and robbing travellers. The monkey escapes, and eventually leads the police back to the scene of the murder. In the meantime, a monk, walking on foot, and a coach-load of stranded travellers converge on the inn. The inn-keeper gets ready to murder the travellers (after drugging them with a sleeping potion). The inn-keeper's wife confesses the family's crimes to the monk, but wants the monk to solemnize her daughter's wedding with the handsome young novitiate who has accompanied the monk, but he falls in love with the inn-keeper's daughter. The priest checks his selfish urges, he does not escape when he could, he foregoes his meal which he needs and wants, so that he can avoid swallowing the potion and contrive to keep awake all night so as to delay the murders. Without breaking his vow of secrecy as regards confessions made to a priest, he manages to delay the marriage ceremony till dawn, when the police arrive, and makes a gesture which enables the police to recover the corpse of the murdered tramp. The priest then solemnizes the marriage, as the inn-keeper and his wife are put in chains by the police and led away. He sees off the travellers, who had narrowly escaped being murdered and are on their way to Paris, and is proud of having the culprits brought to book without straying from the path of virtue by breaking his vow. But the travellers are killed in an accident, because the inn-keeper's servant had sabotaged a bridge which their coach has to cross. The accident underscores the moral: by being virtuously self-less, the monk could have the criminals punished, but he could not save their intended victims from death.

13.4 Morality, realism, and reason in politics

Roughly speaking, three main approaches—which overlap to some extent—have been adopted by those who have tried to develop a science of political processes. One is a 'moral approach', from Plato onwards, including the approach we have been discussing in the last two sections. Another is the 'realistic' approach, e.g. the one adopted by Aristotle, but more definitely by Machiavelli, who not only prescribed a reliance on the facts (rather than on value-judgements), but above all a suspicious and ruthless attitude towards opponents and supporters (in which, as we have noted, Kautalaya somewhat outdid him). This approach emphasizes that one should be 'realistic' about man's rather sordid propensities in politics, i.e. one should be what is called 'amoral' in politics. The third approach is to hope for, and try hard to establish, the 'rule of reason' in politics, like Thomas More. It is the approach of the French Enlightenment where 'reason' was supposed to work through 'moral' rather than 'amoral' attitudes in men. This approach is reflected in what Brutus tried to do in his speech after the assassination of Caesar in Shakespeare's *Julius Caesar*, in contrast to the more effective 'Machiavellian' speech by Mark Antony.

For reasons touched upon at various places in earlier chapters of this book, and recalled and elaborated in earlier sections of this chapter, neither 'morality' (i.e. some ethical principle) nor 'realism' (which partly overlaps with 'morality', and partly attends, amorally, to the 'facts'), can serve as the main basis for the interpretation of political actions. Nor can reason, or rationality (interpreted to mean a reliance on logical deduction from a few first principles about rules of conduct), divorced from 'realism' and—at least where 'unselfish' political action averts paradoxical outcomes—from 'morality', serve as the sole basis for the interpretation of successful political action.

The 'rule of reason' is required in the special sense that it makes us recognize the limits of moralistic or realistic politics. It is also required to help us to identify the new moral standards which may sometimes have to be set, or new methods of 'realistic' politics which may sometimes have to be invented to achieve political success. In this sense, reason is the most important basis of successful political action.

References

Ahmed, Feroz (1973). 'Exploitation in South Asia', in Gough and Sharma (eds.) (1973), pp. 174–95.

Albee, Edward (1962, 1967). *Who's Afraid of Virginia Woolf?*, Penguin, Harmondsworth.

Ali, Tariq (1970). *Pakistan*, Jonathan Cape, London.

——(1973). 'Exploitation in South Asia', in Gough and Sharma (eds.) (1973), pp. 449–65.

Anonymous (1970). *History of the Vietnam Workers' Party*, Foreign Languages Publishing House, Hanoi.

Anouilh, Jean (1961, 1971). *Becket*, Penguin, Harmondsworth.

Arendt, Hannah (1963, 1973). *On Revolution*, Penguin, Harmondsworth.

——(1969, 1972). *Crises of the Republic*, Penguin, Harmondsworth.

Arrow, Kenneth J. (1951, 1963, 1970). *Social Choice and Individual Values*, 2nd edn., Yale University Press, London.

Bagchi, Amiya Kumar (1972). *Private Investment in India 1900–39*, Cambridge University Press, Cambridge.

Bakunin, Mikhail (1953, 1964). *The Political Philosophy of Bakunin (Selections)*, ed. G. P. Maximoff, The Free Press of Glencoe, Collier-Macmillan, London.

Bhattacharya, Sabyasachi (1974). 'Positivism in 19th. Century Bengal: Diffusion of European Intellectual Influence in India', in R. S. Sharma (ed.) (1974), pp. 337–55.

Black, Duncan (1948, 1969). 'On the rationale of group decision making' (*Journal of Political Economy*, 1948, pp. 23–34), reprinted in K. J. Arrow and T. Scitovsky (eds.), *Readings in Welfare Economics*, 1969, Allen and Unwin, London.

Bose, Arun (1947). 'The Indian Bourgeoisie in War and Post-War Economic Crisis', *Communist*, vol. 1, No. 4, Oct. 1947, pp. 165–75.

——(1965). 'Foreign Capital', in V. B. Singh (ed.), *Economic History of India 1857–1956*, Allied Publishers, New Delhi.

——(1974). 'Economic Factors in the Transition from Capitalism to Socialism', in N. L. Gupta (ed.), *Transition from Capitalism to Socialism and other essays* (1974), Kalamakar Prakashan, New Delhi.

——(1975). *Marxian and Post-Marxian Political Economy: An Introduction*, Penguin, Harmondsworth.

Camus, Albert (1942, 1975). *The Myth of Sisyphus*, Penguin, Harmondsworth.

——(1944, 1965). *Caligula*, reprinted in Albert Camus, *The Collected Plays of Albert Camus*, Hamilton, London, 1965.

——(1951, 1974). *The Rebel*, Penguin, Harmondsworth.

——(1961). *Resistance, Rebellion and Death*, London.

Carr, E. H. (1961, 1973). *What is History?*, Penguin, Harmondsworth.

C.C., C.P.S.U.(B.) (1940). *History of the Communist Party of the Soviet Union* (*Bolsheviks*), Foreign Languages Publishing House, Moscow.

Chandra, Satish (1959, 1972). *Parties and Politics at the Mughal Court 1707–40*, People's Publishing House, New Delhi.

Chattopadhyay, Manju (1973). 'Pabna Peasant Uprising of 1873', *Indian Left Review*, vol. 2, No. 3, May 1973, pp. 59–64.

Ch'en, Jerome (1971). *Mao Papers*, Oxford University Press, New Delhi.

Chomsky, Noam (1968, 1972). *Language and Mind*, Harcourt Brace and Jovanovich, New York.

——(1969, 1971). *American Power and the New Mandarins*, Penguin, Harmondsworth.

——(1970, 1973). *For Reasons of State*, Fontana, London.

——(1973). *Backroom Boys*, Fontana, London.

Cohn-Bendit, Daniel (1968, 1969). *Obsolete Communism . . .*, Penguin, Harmondsworth.

Communist party of China (1956). *8th National Congress of the Communist Party of China*, vol. 1, Foreign Languages Press, Peking.

——(1956a). *8th National Congress of the Communist Party of China*, vol. 2, Foreign Languages Press, Peking.

Cooper, David (1968, 1971). *The Dialectics of Liberation*, Penguin, Harmondsworth.

Cranston, Maurice (1968). *Introduction to J.-J. Rousseau*, in J.-J. Rousseau (1792, 1968, 1972), pp. 9–43.

Dasgupta, Biplab (1974). *The Naxalite Movement*, Allied Publishers, New Delhi.

Debray, Charles (1967, 1968). *Revolution in the Revolution?*, Penguin, Harmondsworth.

——(1970, 1975). *Prison Writings*, Penguin, Harmondsworth.

Derwing, Bruce L. (1973). *Transformational Grammar as a Theory of Language Acquisition*, Cambridge University Press, Cambridge.

Engels, Friedrich (1894, 1947). *Herr Eugen Dühring's Revolution in Science* [*Anti-Dühring*], Foreign Languages Publishing House, Moscow.

Fanon, Frantz (1961, 1973). *The Wretched of the Earth*, Penguin, Harmondsworth.

Freud, Sigmund (1933 [1932], 1973). *New Introductory Lectures on Psychoanalysis*, Penguin, Harmondsworth.

Giap, Vo Nguyen (1970, 1971). *The Military Art of People's War*, ed. Russell Stetler, Monthly Review Press, New York.

Glunin, Vladimir, Grigoreyev, Alexander, Kukushin, Kim, and Yuryev, Mikhail

(1973). 'International Communist Movement and Communist Party of China', *Indian Left Review*, vol. 2, No. 6, Aug. 1973, pp. 52–68.

Gopal, Surendra (1974). 'Merchants in West India in the Sixteenth and Seventeenth Centuries', in R. S. Sharma (ed.) (1974), pp. 235–47.

Gough Kathleen (1973). 'Imperialism and Revolutionary Potential in South Asia', in Gough and Sharma (eds.) (1973), pp. 3–42.

Gough, Kathleen and Sharma, H. P. (eds.) (1973). *Imperialism and Revolution in South Asia*, Monthly Review Press, New York.

Government of India (1946). 'Recent Social and Economic Trends in India'.

——(1947). 'Statistics Relating to the War Effort'.

——(1952). 'First Five Year Plan'.

——(1959). 'Report on India's Food Crisis and Steps to meet it'.

——(Aug. 1970). 'Estimates of National Product (Revised Series) 1960–61 to 1968–69, issued by the Central Statistical Organisation.

——(1972–3). 'Economic Survey'.

——(1973–4). 'Economic Survey'.

Gramsci, Antonio (1930s, 1971). *Selections from the Prison Notebooks*, Lawrence and Wishart, London.

Guevara, Che (1961). *Cuba—Exception or Vanguard?*, in Che Guevara (1969, 1972), *Venceremos! The Speeches and Writings of Che Guevara*, Penguin, Harmondsworth, pp. 196–206.

——(1968, 1970). *Reminiscences of the Cuban Revolutionary War*, Penguin, Harmondsworth.

Habib, Irfan (1974). 'The Social Distribution of Landed Property in pre-British India', in R. S. Sharma (ed.) (1974), pp. 264–316.

Hare, R. M. (1961, 1964). *The Language of Morals*, Oxford University Press, London.

Harsanyi, J. C. (1955). 'Cardinal Welfare, Individualistic Ethics and Interpersonal Comparisons of Utility', *Journal of Political Economy*, Aug. 1955, pp. 309–21.

Heimann, Eduard (1956). *History of Economic Doctrines*, Oxford University Press, London.

Ho Chi Minh (1975). *Selected Writings and Speeches*, Communist Party Publication, Delhi.

Hobbes, Thomas (1651, 1974). *Leviathan* (ed. C. B. Macpherson), Penguin, Harmondsworth.

Hu Chiao-mu (1951). *Thirty Years of the Communist Party of China*, Foreign Languages Press, Peking.

Inada, K. (1964). 'On the Economic Welfare Function', *Econometrica*, Oct. 1964, pp. 525–30.

Kissinger, Henry (1960). *The Necessity of Choice*, Chatto & Windus, London.

Kosambi, D. D. (1956). *An Introduction to the Study of Indian History*, Popular Book Depot, Bombay.

Kumar, Krishan (ed.) (1971). *Revolution* (World University Readings in Politics and Society), Weidenfeld & Nicolson, London.

Lacouture, Jean (1967, 1969). *Ho Chi Minh*, Penguin, Harmondsworth.

Lampedusa, Guiseppe di (1958, 1974). *The Leopard*, Fontana/Collins, London.

Lange, Oskar (1963). *Political Economy*, vol. 1, Pergamon, London.

Lenin, V. I. (1936, 1946). *Selected Works*, 12-vol. edn., vol. 3, Lawrence and Wishart, London.

——*Marx—Engels—Marxism*, Foreign Languages Publishing House, Moscow.

——(1961). *Collected Works*, vol. 38, Foreign Languages Publishing House, Moscow.

——(1964). *Collected Works*, vol. 21, Progress Publishers, Moscow.

Li Li-san (1956). 'Report of the 8th Congress of the Chinese Communist Party' in *Communist Party of China* (1956), vol. 2, pp. 258–58.

Lifton, Robert Jay (1968, 1970). *Revolutionary Immortality, Mao Tse-tung and the Chinese Cultural Revolution*, Penguin, Harmondsworth.

Lin Piao (ed.) (1966, 1967). *Quotations from Chairman Mao Tse-tung*, Current Book Depot, Kanpur.

Liu Shao-chi (1939, 1951). *How to be a Good Communist*, Foreign Languages Press, Peking.

——(1941). *On Inner-Party Struggle*, Foreign Languages Press, Peking.

——(1943). 'Liquidate the Menshevist Ideology within the Party', reprinted as Appendix in Liu Shao-chi (1941), pp. 73–90.

——(1950, 1951). *On the Party*, Foreign Languages Press, Peking.

——(1956). 'The Political Report of the Central Committee of the Communist Party of China to the Eighth National Congress of the Party', in *Communist Party of China* (1956), pp. 13–113.

Lu Ting-yi, (1951). 'The World Significance of the Chinese Revolution', in *The Communist Party Leader of the Chinese Revolution*, Foreign Languages Press, Peking (1951), pp. 11–19.

Luce, D. and Raiffa, H. (1957). *Games and Decisions*, John Wiley, New York.

Lyons, John (1970, 1972). *Chomsky*, Fontana, Collins, London.

Machiavelli, Niccolo (*c.* 1514, 1972). *The Prince*, Penguin, Harmondsworth.

——(*c.* 1514, 1970). *The Discourses*, Penguin, Harmondsworth.

Macpherson, C. B. (1968). 'Introduction' in Hobbes (1651, 1974), pp. 9–63.

Mandeville, Bernard (1714, 1970). (ed. Phillip Harth), Penguin, Harmondsworth.

Mao Tse-tung (1940, 1954). 'On New Democracy', reprinted in *Selected Works of Mao Tse-tung*, vol. 3 (1954), People's Publishing House, Bombay.

——(1945, 1956). 'On the danger of the Hurley Policy', reprinted in *Selected Works of Mao Tse-tung*, vol. 4 (1956), People's Publishing House, Bombay.

——(1954). *Selected Works of Mao Tse-tung*, vol. 1 (1954), People's Publishing House, Bombay.

——(1954a). *Selected Works of Mao Tse-tung*, vol. 2 (1954), People's Publishing House, Bombay.

——(1954b). *Selected Works of Mao Tse-tung*, vol. 3 (1954), People's Publishing House, Bombay.

——(1956). *Selected Works of Mao Tse-tung*, vol. 4, People's Publishing House, Bombay.

Marcuse, Herbert (1958, 1971). *Soviet Marxism*, Penguin, Harmondsworth.

——(1964, 1972). *One-Dimensional Man*, Abacus, Sphere Books, London.

——(1968). 'Liberation from the Affluent Society', in Cooper (ed.) (1968, 1971), pp. 175–92.

——(1969, 1973). *An Essay on Liberation*, Penguin, Harmondsworth.

Marx, Karl (1844, 1961). *The Economic and Philosophical Manuscripts of 1844*, Foreign Languages Publishing House, Moscow.

——(1853). 'The British Rule in India', reprinted in K. Marx and F. Engels (n.d.), *The First Indian War of Independence 1857–1859*, Foreign Languages Publishing House, Moscow.

——(1853a). 'The Future Results of British Rule in India', reprinted in K. Marx and F. Engels (n.d.), *The First Indian War of Independence 1857–1859*, Foreign Languages Publishing House, Moscow.

——(1859, 1970). *The Critique of Political Economy*, Progress Publishers, Moscow.

——(1867, 1958). *Capital*, vol. 1, Foreign Languages Publishing House, Moscow.

——(1875). 'Critique of the Gotha Programme', reprinted in K. Marx and F. Engels (1949).

——(1894, 1959). *Capital*, vol. 3, Foreign Languages Publishing House, Moscow.

——(1974). *The First International and After*, Penguin, Harmondsworth.

——(n.d.). 'The Poverty of Philosophy', Foreign Languages Publishing House, Moscow.

Marx, Karl and Engels, Friedrich (1949). *Selected Works in Two Volumes*, vol. 2, Foreign Languages Publishing House, Moscow.

——(1950). *Selected Works in Two Volumes*, vol. 1, Foreign Languages Publishing House, Moscow.

Maximoff, Gregori Petrovich (ed.) (1974). *The Political Philosophy of Bakunin*, The Free Press of Glencoe, Collier, Macmillan, London.

Mende, Tibor (1958). *Conversations with Nehru*, Wilco Publishing House, Bombay.

Ministry of External Affairs, Government of India (n.d.). 'Bangladesh Documents'.

——(n.d.). 'Bangladesh Documents', vol. 2.

Mukherjee, Ramkrishna (1973). 'The Social Background of Bangladesh', in K. Gough and H. P. Sharma (eds.) (1973), pp. 399–418.

Mukherjee, S. N. (1974). 'The Social Implications of the Political Thought of Raja Rammohun Roy', in R. S. Sharma (ed.) (1974), pp. 356–89.

Needham, Joseph (1961). *Science and Civilisation in China*, vol. 1, Cambridge University Press, Cambridge.

——(1962). *Science and Civilisation in China*, vol. 2, Cambridge University Press, Cambridge.

Neumann, J. von and Morgenstern, O. (1944, 1947). *Theory of Games and Economic Behaviour*, Princeton University Press, Princeton.

Newman, Peter (1962). 'Production of Commodities by Means of Commodities', *Schweizerische Zeitschrift für Volkswirtschaft und Statistik*, vol. 98, No. 1, pp. 58–75.

Nietzsche, Friedrich (n.d.). *Thus Spake Zarathustra*, trans. Thomas Common, Modern Library, New York.

Nove, Alec and Nuti, Domenico (eds.) (1972). *Socialist Economics*, Penguin, Harmondsworth.

Nowell-Smith, P. H. (1954, 1969). *Ethics*, Penguin, Harmondsworth.

Ollman, Bertell (1971). *Alienation*, Cambridge University Press, Cambridge.

Pattanaik, Prasanta K. (1971). *Voting and Collective Choice*, Cambridge University Press, Cambridge.

Pizzorno, Alessandro (ed.) (1971). *Political Sociology*, Penguin, Harmondsworth.

Poddar, Arabinda (1970). *Renaissance in Bengal: Quests and Confrontations 1800–60*, Indian Institute of Advanced Study, Simla.

Popper, Karl (1957). *The Poverty of Historicism*, Routledge & Kegan Paul, London.

Rapoport, Anatol (1968, 1974). Introduction in *Clausewitz on War* (ed. Rapoport), Penguin, Harmondsworth, pp. 11–80.

Rawls, John (1972, 1973). *A Theory of Justice*, Oxford University Press, London.

Ray, Prithwis Chandra (ed.) (n.d.). *The Boycott Celebration in Calcutta* (August 7, 1909), Calcutta.

Ricardo, David (ed. P. Sraffa) (1951). *The Works and Correspondence of David Ricardo*, vol. 1, Cambridge University Press, Cambridge.

Robbins, Lionel (1953). *The Theory of Economic Policy in English Classical Political Economy*, Macmillan, London.

Robinson, Joan (1967). *An Essay on Marxian Economics*, Macmillan, London.

——(1969). *The Cultural Revolution in China*, Penguin, Harmondsworth.

Robinson, Joan and Eatwell, John (1974). *An Introduction to Modern Economics*, Tata McGraw-Hill, New Delhi.

Roll, Erich (1950). *History of Economic Thought*, Faber & Faber, London.

Rousseau, Jean-Jacques (1762, 1972). *The Social Contract*, Penguin, Harmondsworth.

——(1763, 1963, 1972). *A Discourse on the Origin of Inequality* (extracts), in Mervyn Williams (1971), pp. 213–25.

Ruben, Walter (1974). 'Outline of the Structure of Ancient Indian Society', in R. S. Sharma (ed.) (1974), pp. 85–94.

Russell, Bertrand (1938, 1946). *Power*, Allen & Unwin, London.

——(1946, 1962). *History of Western Philosophy*, Allen & Unwin, London.

——(1968, 1969). *The Autobiography of Bertrand Russell, The Middle Years 1914–44*, Bantam, London.

——(1969,1970). *The Autobiography of Bertrand Russell, The Final Years 1944–69*, Bantam, London.

Samuelson, Paul (1957). 'Wages and Interest: a modern dissection of Marxian economic models', *American Economic Review*, vol. 47, pp. 884–92.

——(1960). 'Wages and Interest: a modern dissection of Marxian economic models: reply', *American Economic Review*, Sept. 1960, pp. 373–407.

——(1973). *Economics*, 9th edn., McGraw-Hill Kogakusha, New Delhi.

Sarkar, Jadunath (n.d.). *Aurangzib* (3rd edn.), vol. iii, M. C. Sarkar & Sons, Calcutta.

Schram, Stuart (1966). *Mao Tse-tung*, Penguin, Harmondsworth.

——(1974). *Mao Tse-tung Unrehearsed*, Penguin, Harmondsworth.

Schumpeter, Joseph (1955). *History of Economic Analysis*, Allen and Unwin, London.

Sen, Amartya (1959). 'Determinism and historical predictions', in *Enquiry*, 2 (Sept. 1959), pp. 99–115.

——(1961). 'On Optimising the rate of saving', *Economic Journal*, Sept. 1961, pp. 479–96.

——(1967). 'Isolation, Assurance and the Social Rate of Discount', *Quarterly Journal of Economics*, Feb. 1957, pp. 112–24.

——(1969). 'A Game-theoretic analysis of theories of collectivism in allocation', in T. Majumdar (ed.), *Growth and Choice*, Oxford University Press, Bombay.

——(1969a). 'Quasi-Transivity, Rational Choice and Collective Decisions', *Review of Economic Studies*, vol. 36.

——(1970). *Collective Choice and Social Welfare*, Holden-Day, London.

——(1973, 1974). *On Economic Inequality*, Oxford University Press, Delhi.

Sen, K. M. (1961, 1967). *Hinduism*, Penguin, Harmondsworth.

Sen, Mohit (1970). *The Indian Revolution*, People's Publishing House, New Delhi.

Sharma, R. S. (ed.) (1965). *Indian Feudalism: c. 300–1200*, University of Calcutta, Calcutta.

——(1974). *Indian Society: Historical Probings*, People's Publishing House, New Delhi.

Sheehan, Neil (1971). *The Pentagon Papers*, Bantam, London.

Shubik, Martin (ed.) (1964). *Game Theory and Related Approaches to Social Behaviour*, John Wiley, London.

——(1967). 'The Uses of Game Theory', in James Charlesworth (ed.), *Contemporary Political Analysis* (1967), The Free Press, New York, Collier/ Macmillan, London, pp. 239–72.

Sihanouk, Norodom and Burchett, Wilfred (1973). *My War with the C.I.A.*, Penguin, Harmondsworth.

Sloan, Pat (ed.) (1938). *John Cornford—A Memoir*, Jonathan Cape, London.

Snow, Edgar (1937). *Red Star Over China*, Victor Gollancz, London.

——(1971, 1972). *China's Long Revolution*, Penguin, Harmondsworth.

Spengler, Joseph (1971). *Indian Economic Thought*, Duke University Press, Durham, N.C.

Spengler, Oswald (1926, 1954). *The Decline of the West*, Allen and Unwin, London.

Sraffa, Piero (1960). *Production of Commodities by Means of Commodities*, Cambridge University Press, Cambridge.

Stalin, Joseph (1924). *Foundations of Leninism.* reprinted in J. Stalin, *Problems of Leninism* (1947), Foreign Languages Publishing House, Moscow.

——(1926). *Problems of Leninism*, reprinted in J. Stalin, *Problems of Leninism* (1947), Foreign Languages Publishing House, Moscow.

Suyin, Han (1967, 1973). *China in the Year 2001*, Penguin, Harmondsworth.

Tagore, Rabindranath (Bengali Calendar, 1368). *Rabindra Rachanabali*, vol. 10 (in Bengali), Paschim Banga Sarkar, Calcutta.

Thapar, Romila (1974). 'Social History in Ancient India with special reference to élite groups', in R. S. Sharma (ed.) (1974), pp. 95–123.

Tikhonov, O. (1974). 'The Experience of the Cuban Revolution', *Indian Left Review*, vol. 3, No. 2, Apr. 1974, pp. 61–71.

Tocqueville, Alexis de (1856). *On the State of Society in France Before the Revolution of 1789*, trans. Henry Reeve, extracts in K. Kumar (ed.) (1971). pp. 113–15, and in Pizzorno (ed.) (1971), pp. 23–6.

Ulbricht, Walter (1968). *On questions of socialist constitution in the GDR*, Verlag Zeit Im Bild, Dresden.

Viner, Jacob (1944). 'International Relations Between State-controlled National Economies' (*American Economic Review*, 1944) reprinted in *Readings in the Theory of International Trade* (1950, 1953), American Economic Association, Allen and Unwin, London.

Warder, A. K. (1974). 'Feudalism and Mahayana Buddhism', in R. S. Sharma (ed.) (1974), pp. 156–74.

Weizacker, Christian von (1973). 'Modern Capital Theory and the concept of exploitation,' *Kyklos*, vol. 26, No. 2.

Wheelwright, E. L. and McFarlane, Bruce (1970, 1973). *The Chinese Road to Socialism*, Penguin, Harmondsworth.

Williams, Mervyn (1971). *Revolutions*, Penguin, Harmondsworth.

Wilson, Andrew (1968, 1970). *War Gaming*, Penguin, Harmondsworth.

Wholstetter, A. (1964). 'Sin and Games in America,' in Martin Shubik (ed.) (1964), pp. 209–25.

Zhdanov, A. A. (1950). *On Literature, Music and Philosophy*, Lawrence and Wishart, London, pp. 15–18.

Index

Terrorism, revolutionary, 137
Thapar, 130, 258
Thoreau, 126
Thorium reserves, 203
Tibet, 80, 87, 98, 111, 112, 154, 242
Tibetan Buddhist religion, 16
Tikhonov, 25, 258
Tilt towards Pakistan in U.S. policy, 153
Tilt against India in U.S. policy, 202
Timor, 31, 113
Tit-for-tat attitude towards the enemy, 63
Tito, 18, 34
Tocqueville, 15, 258
Tolstoy, 29, 121
Tolstoy–Russell ethics, 29
Tolstoyan ethics, 29
Tolstoyan self-criticism, 52
Total rebellion, 242, 243
Total revolution, 138, 164, 185
Trade not aid as the basis of a strategy of development, 199
Trade unions, 166, 167, 178
Transfer problem, 198
Transformational grammar, 244
Trotsky, 37, 47, 59
Trotskyite factions, 164
Trotskyite theories, 164
Turkey, 66
Two-Chinas concept, 98

Ulbricht, 95, 258
Unanimous decisions, 52, 53
Unchanging societies, Marx's hypothesis of, vii, 118
Unified field theory, search for, 218
Unified science of politics, of revolution, and counter-revolution, search for, 218, 225, 232, 245
Uniqueness of historical events, theory of, 13, 222, 223
Uniting and struggling relationship, 183
Unity and struggle, tactic of, 188
United front, 170, 171, 185
United front policy, 64, 65, 71
Universal grammar, 244
Unselfish motivation, 29, 30, 93, 158, 189, 211, 246, 247, 248
Untouchability, 17
Urban guerrilla struggle, 71
Urban insurgency, 174
Urdu, 131
U.S.A., 12, 14, 17, 18, 19, 25, 26, 29, 30, 32, 33, 95, 97, 101, 102, 103, 105, 107, 109, 110, 112, 151, 152, 153, 154, 155, 156, 157, 161, 169, 194, 195, 196, 197, 198, 199, 201, 202, 203, 204, 205, 206–10, 228

U.S. food aid, 194
U.S. Seventh Fleet, 151, 206
U.S. Sixth Fleet, 206
U.S.–Vietnam War, 32, 33
U.S.S.R., 11, 33, 73, 97, 101, 102, 103, 104, 105, 106, 107, 109, 110, 112, 155, 159, 161, 198, 199, 201, 204, 205, 208, 209, 227, 228, 231
Uttar Pradesh, 184

Value judgements and hypotheses about political action, 56, 218, 219
Varnas, 127
Vicarious hegemony, 177, 186, 188
Vietnam, vi, 4, 12, 13, 14, 20, 21, 22, 23, 24, 25, 26, 27, 29, 30, 31, 32, 67, 80, 85, 97, 223, 228
Vietnam Workers' Party, 223, 224
Vietnam–America War, 14, 17, 19, 21, 22, 23, 28, 31
Vietnam War, 4, 13, 14, 18
Vietnam–Soviet–Chinese negotiations, 21
Vietnamese communist ideology, 11, 223, 224
Vietnamese communist innovations, 20, 21, 29, 223, 224
Vietnamese communist revolution, 223
Vietnamese paradox, vi, 14, 226, 227, 228
Vietnamese revolution, 21, 59, 223
Vinci, Leonardo da, 221
Viner, 85, 258
Violence in politics, 20
Violence in politics, Gandhian attitude to, 20
Vo Nguyen Giap, 13, 14, 252
Voltaire, 220
Voting system, 9, 56, 124, 125

Wang Ming, 39
War, Leninist doctrine of, 61, 62
War, Mao on war and revolution, 62
War, Marxian theory of, 61
War Communism, 52
War criminals, 158
War games, 4, 5, 32, 33
Warder, 128, 258
Warfare state, 241
Warsaw, 106
Washington, 106
Watergate, 30, 31
Weak Pareto principle, 50
Wealth, 'white', 'black' and 'spotted', 129
Webb, 46
Wei Hai, 4
Weiszacker, von, 83, 258
Welfare state, 241